Mix together the apple cider and brown sugar in a medium saucepan over medium heat, stirring frequently until the brown sugar completely dissolves. Remove from heat and stir in vinegar, paprika, cayenne, salt and pepper. Cover and refrigerate if not using right away.

— From "BBQ Makes Everything Better," by Aaron Chronister and Jason Day

PER SERVING (2 tablespoons): **calories:** 10 (11% from fat); **protein:** 0.1 gram; **total fat:** 0.1 gram; **saturated fat:** 0; **cholesterol:** 0; **sodium:** 113 mg; **carbohydrate:** 2.9 grams; **dietary fiber:** 0.3 gram

Add the parsley, ... per flakes to the bowl with ... until well-combined. Cover and refrigerate

PER SERVING (2 tables... **protein:** 0.3 gram; to... grams; **cholesterol** grams; **dietary fi...**

Simple Kansas City-style Sauce

Makes about 2 cups

This thick, classic sauce is great for glazing ribs and chicken, but has a mild flavor to not overpower meat.

1 cup ketch...
1/2 cup firm... brown
1/4 cup tab...
2 t...

Heat the olive oil in a large sauté pan over medium heat until hot. Add the sausage and cook until browned, 2 minutes per side. Transfer to a plate and set aside.
Add the onion, celery and green pepper to the pan and sauté over medium heat until the

2 tablespoons olive oil
1 pound andouille sausage (fully cooked variety)
2 cups finely chopped onion
2 cups celery, chopped
1 medium green bell pepper, chopped
2 tablespoons finely chopped garlic
2 tablespoons low-sodium, salt-free or homemade Cajun seasoning blend (see note)
1/2 cup dry white wine
2 1/4 cups chicken broth
2 cups crushed or diced tomatoes in purée
3 ounces (1/2 of a 6-ounce can) tomato paste
2 bay leaves
1 pound shrimp, peeled and deveined
2 cups cooked long-grain white rice
4 green onions, chopped
• Tabasco sauce, optional

Note: Most Cajun season... copious amounts of salt, so... low-sodium or sodium-free v... your own and then salt the jam... To make the spice blend, combi... garlic powder, 2 1/2 teaspoons papri... spoon black pepper, 1 teaspoon oni... 3/4 teaspoon cayenne pepper (or to tas... teaspoons dried oregano leaves and 1 1/2 spoons dried thyme leaves.

Alsatian Choucroute Garni

Makes 8 servings

The national dish of the Alsace region of France, choucroute garni usually features five to six different cuts of pork and sausages, all served on a bed of sauerkraut. This streamlined recipe includes a delicious combination of bacon, pork ribs and smoked kielbasa. The sauerkraut's flavor is lightened somewhat with fresh cabbage, so even those tepid on the idea of sauerkraut will like this hearty dish. Serve with boiled red potatoes tossed in butter and chives.

This recipe was developed using a 6.5-quart slow-cooker, but you can scale the ingredients down for a smaller appliance.

1 cup dry white wine, preferably pinot gris
1/2 cup chicken broth
2 pounds fresh-pack (not canned) sauerkraut, rinsed well and drained (sold refrigerated near the hot dogs)
2 medium Granny Smith apples, cored and cut into 6 pieces each
1 pound smoked (fully cooked) kielbasa, left whole
• Coarse-grain mustard, for serving

In a large sauté pan, cook the bacon over medium heat until the fat has rendered and the edges are crisp and brown, 5 minutes. Remove bacon with a slotted spoon and set aside, leaving fat in pan. Cut the pork ribs into sections 2 ribs wide, season with the salt, pepper and paprika. Brown the ribs meaty side down in batches in the bacon pan over medium-high heat; transfer to a plate and set aside.
Add the onions and carrots to the pan, and cook over medium-high heat until the onion begins to brown, 4 minutes. Add the garlic, caraway seeds, juniper berries if using, bay leaf and half of the cabbage and cook, tossing with tongs until the cabbage has wilted, 5 minutes. Add the wine and bring to a simmer, scraping up browned bits.
Transfer the sautéed cabbage... cabbage an...

4 ounces slab bacon, cut into 1/2-inch squares
3 pounds baby-back pork ribs
1 1/2 teaspoon salt
3/4 teaspoon freshly ground black pepper
1 1/2 teaspoon hot smoked paprika (pimentón de la Vera)
2 cups thinly sliced onions
1 large carrots, peeled and cut into 2-inch pieces
6 tablespoon chopped garlic
2 teaspoons caraway seeds
1 1/2 dried juniper berries (optional)
bay leaf
small head savoy or green cabbage (about 8 ounces), core removed sliced

... in a small ...
Add the parsley, ...
per flakes to the bowl with ...
until well-combined.
Cover and refrigerate

from the Cajun "holy..." etables — onions, cel... — plus andouille sausage... just a touch of chile heat. b... cooked andouille, such as th... sion available at Sheridan... that you must cook the rice sepa... adding it to the jambalaya.
This recipe was developed using... slow-cooker, but you can scale the ing... down for a smaller appliance.

ft...
ton...
stir to...
mixtu...
hours.
Fifteen...
sausage fro...
1-inch thick s...
slow-cooker. G...
into the slow-coo...
shrimp are pink an...
10 minutes. Transfer...
bowl, sprinkle with gr...
with Tabasco on the sid...

Former Foo... erts-Dominguez crea... camping trip. She says she on... idea of how she wanted the recipe to ta... out, and so packed along just about every ingredient she could think of that might work in a fresh salsa, including Walla Walla onions, roasted and peeled Anaheim chiles, garlic, tomatoes, pine nuts, olives and olive oil. The results turned out to be a master-piece, and Roberts-Dominguez said her fe... low campers devoured the bowlful in less than 10 minutes.

4 large or 7 medium Anaheim ch... roasted and peeled (see note)
1 large sweet onion, diced (or... chopped green onions)
2 2 1/2-ounce cans sliced oliv... drained
5 Roma (plum) tomatoes, d... to 2 cups diced cucumber
1/2 cup extra-virgin olive o...
1/4 cup white wine vinegar

GLUTEN FREEDOM

Quick,

BY LAURA BYRNE
SPECIAL TO THE O...

Switching to a gl... can initially pose a... even the craftiest... ing gluten-free r... bit of home co... food on the ru... the question... be more diffi... children wh... number of... who don't... miliar, Eli... "How to... 150 Rec... (Lake I... be the... you...

A... ch... ac...
This rec... slow-cooker... down for a sm...

4 dried New
3 cups boiling
1 tablespoon ve
1 1/2 cups chopped
2 teaspoons dried preferably Mexican
1 1/2 teaspoons cumin se
5 whole cloves
1 bay leaf
1 1/2 tablespoon finely cho
1 cup pepitas (shelled p toasted (see note)
1/4 cup sesame o...

The Oregonian
COOKBOOK

The Oregonian
COOKBOOK
Best Recipes from FOODDAY

Edited by

KATHERINE MILLER

Concept by GREG MOWERY

ISBN
978-0-9713555-5-2 Hardbound
978-0-9713555-6-9 Softbound
978-0-9713555-7-6 E-book

Library of Congress Cataloging-in-Publication Data available.

Illustration and permission credits appear in the back of the book.
Photographs are copyrighted per the photo credits on pages 384-385.

Published by:
The Oregonian
1320 SW Broadway
Portland, Oregon 97201

Developed and produced by Carpe Diem Books®

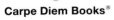

Carpe Diem Books®
Publisher: Ross Eberman
www.carpediembooks.com

Concept and editorial collaborator: Gregory Mowery
Project director: Richard L. Owsiany
Design: *the*BookDesigners
Copyeditor: Tricia Brown
Proofreader: Michelle Blair
Indexer: Cher Paul

Manufactured in China
Second printing 2012

10 9 8 7 6 5 4 3 2

To Mark, Curt, and Sarah.
With you at my table, every day is a feast.

CONTENTS

FOREWORD

When I returned to Oregon to open Wildwood Restaurant in 1994, the restaurant scene had not drastically changed since my great-grandparents opened their restaurant, Dan and Louis Oyster Bar, in 1907. Built on a foundation of local and seasonal food, oysters were harvested from their Yaquina Bay oyster farm, bay shrimp and Dungeness crab from the waters of the Pacific Ocean, and Willamette Valley strawberries topped the ice-cream sundaes.

In 1994, Portland was just beginning to emerge as a metropolitan area with a growing reputation for its restaurants, chefs, and abundant agricultural and wild food sources. It was a time of change and transition—one that combined the ethos of days past with a new conversation about Pacific Northwest cuisine: how committed cooks could partner with local producers to create compellingly delicious food from the source.

At the heart of this partnership are Oregon's ranchers, fisheries, foragers, farmers, and dairies, who are focused on the quality of the food and the integrity of the ingredients. Those closest to their harvest speak of weather, climate, animal diet, soil for the plant, or cycle of the moon as points of determining the essence of flavor. This understanding of the land is a seasonal reminder of why the producers work so hard to preserve its precious bounty and continue as stewards and guardians of what cannot be replaced or replicated.

Chefs, and their interpretation of these quality ingredients, have helped drive the enormous growth of Oregon's culinary reputation over the past two decades. You can see some of their inspired creations starting on page 317. But while a recipe can provide a framework from which to build a dish and combine flavors, the ingredient selection remains the decisive point, one that can both inspire the chef as well as determine the outcome of a dish.

The land, food producers, and chefs have all contributed to make the Pacific Northwest a culinary destination. But it is in the enjoyment of the eating and how we embrace its place in our lives that truly transcends and defines this bountiful place we call Oregon. For thirty years, the writers and contributors of Foodday have given readers a window into the skills and minds of our great cooks—whether they work in a restaurant or a home kitchen. In turn, these cooks have greatly enriched our lives.

The Oregonian Cookbook celebrates this connection with our community. With its vast variety of recipes, it is a contemporary glimpse into how these talented cooks interpret ingredients. The infusion of influences from around the world is now a common part of their repertoire, and it demonstrates that there are multitudes of ways to create Northwest cuisine. It also serves as a bookmark for our culture of food, and a reflection on how it remains built on the foundation of what generations of Oregonians have embraced.

I hope you embrace and celebrate how fortunate we are to continue on this path of exploration as we enjoy the fruits of so many who came before and anticipate the contributions that we have yet to see.

—**Cory Schreiber**
Founding chef, Wildwood;
culinary artist-in-residence,
The International Culinary School
at The Art Institute of Portland

INTRODUCTION

When we set out to do a cookbook commemorating the thirty-year anniversary of Foodday, we thought that it would be *The Oregonian*'s first.

So imagine our surprise when research turned up a modest title published in 1910: *The Oregonian Good Housekeeping Everyday Cook Book*. It is plain and sensible, with a chapter called "Invalid Cookery" and recipes for things such as Stuffed Beef Heart; Good Mincemeat Without Intoxicants; and Jelly Prune Ring.

Which just goes to show that, as with almost everything in life, tastes change.

This certainly applies to Foodday. For years, *The Oregonian* and *The Oregon Journal*, Portland's afternoon paper, had separate food sections. They also had departments staffed with home economists devoted to helping readers with every kind of domestic concern—from tips on party games to laundry stains. *The Oregonian*'s service was called "Hostess House"; the *Journal*'s, "Mary Cullen's Cottage."

In the early 1980s, the two newspapers merged, and two food sections were combined as Foodday, with Ginger Johnston as its editor.

In the early days, Foodday often had twenty-four pages a week, and was staffed with three writers, a copy editor, four home economists, an assistant editor, and a clerk. These days we're a much leaner department, but we still have a front-row seat on the amazing changes in the food scene in Portland, throughout Oregon, and beyond.

From the start of this project, we knew that culling 354 recipes from the thousands that the paper has published over the past three decades would be a big job. But the archives quickly revealed that even as recently as a decade ago, we cooked much differently. Food was less spicy, and smoked paprika and quinoa were nowhere to be seen. Dried herbs were the norm.

Vegan fare was something very fringe. And words like "locavore" and "100-mile diet" were unheard of.

Over the past decade many more of us have discovered the simple joy of shopping at farmers markets, which has led to their astonishing growth. The Oregon Farmers' Markets Association lists more than one hundred markets, about half of which are in the Portland metro area. A growing number are open year-round. Sales at the city's flagship market, Portland Farmers Market, have climbed year over year even in the middle of a recession.

Then there are Portland's famed food carts, offering an amazing tapestry of both the traditional and the new, including Bosnian pitas, Korean tacos, hand-smoked pastrami, and vegan barbecue.

Still, even before all these changes, Oregonians ate very well, thank-you-very-much. And for this book we wanted to honor the rich variety of dishes that span all three decades, as well as the diversity of our readers.

This, then, is not a book of the moment, but one of many moments, all of them delicious. It's also a book of many voices. In the end we hope each recipe stands on its own merits, no matter how old or new. We welcome you to our table and this celebration of Oregon, with its amazing homegrown ingredients and its incredible cooks.

—Katherine Miller
Foodday editor

APPETIZERS

HAM, GRUYÈRE, AND DIJON PALMIERS

MAKES 48 HORS D'OEUVRES

These hors d'oeuvres from former Fooddday editor Martha Holmberg are flaky, chewy, and impossibly good with a chilled glass of riesling. The palmier (PAHL-me-yay) is a classic shape in French pastry that's easy to form and shows off fillings beautifully. Get the ham sliced very thinly at the deli counter. If the ham falls apart a bit, that's OK; you can piece it together as you assemble the palmiers.

> 1 sheet frozen puff pastry, thawed
>   (about 9 ounces)
> 2 tablespoons Dijon mustard
> 1 cup shredded aged gruyère cheese
>   (3 ounces)
> ¼ cup freshly grated parmesan cheese
>   (½ ounce)
> 4 ounces very thinly sliced good-quality
>   baked ham, such as Black Forest

Position the sheet of pastry on a lightly floured counter so that a short side is closest to you. Roll the pastry into a 10-by-14-inch rectangle. Trim the edges, if necessary, to make the rectangle neat.

Using the back of a spoon or an offset spatula, spread the mustard over the pastry. Distribute the gruyère and parmesan evenly over the surface. Arrange the ham in a single even layer, tearing or cutting pieces to fit. Lay a piece of parchment paper or wax paper on top and gently compress the layers with the rolling pin. Peel off the paper without disturbing the ham.

Cut the rectangle in half widthwise to make two 10-by-7-inch bands. With your fingers, gently roll one long edge of one of the bands into the center and then roll the opposite edge in so the two rolls meet in the middle and resemble a double scroll. Press lightly so the rolls stick together (spread a few drops of water

PUFF THE MAGIC PASTRY

Frozen puff pastry can be a terrific time-saver. For best results, however, the pastry should be thawed slowly in the refrigerator. If you leave it out on the counter, the outside tends to get too warm before the inside has fully thawed, which can make the pastry difficult to handle.

Pepperidge Farm: In the freezer case of almost every grocery store (in a 17-ounce box, two sheets per box), and it's very easy to roll and shape. The downside is that it is not made with butter—only vegetable shortening—so while the flaky-factor is brilliant, the flavor is fairly flat. There's a trade-off between ease of use and full flavor (it's vegan, however, which can be a plus).

DuFour Pastry Kitchens: Available at Whole Foods, Zupan's Markets, and other specialty stores in 1-pound packages (one large sheet). DuFour is more expensive than other brands, but it's made with all butter, and it's luxurious and delicious. Easy to use, but it does get soft quickly if your kitchen is warm.

Grand Central Baking Co.: This bakery, founded and based in Seattle, offers its own frozen puff pastry in 1-pound, 12-ounce rolls. All-butter and beautiful, it's a nice option if you can swing by one of the bakery's several Northwest locations to pick it up (grandcentralbakery.com).

where the two rolls meet to help them stick, if you need to). Repeat with the second band. Wrap the rolls in plastic and chill until they firm up, at least an hour in the refrigerator or 30 minutes in the freezer.

When you're ready to bake, heat the oven to 425 degrees and line two baking sheets with parchment paper or a silicone baking mat. With a very sharp knife, slice each roll into 24 pieces, arrange them on a sheet at least 1 inch apart, and bake until the pastry is nicely browned and flaky (break one apart to be sure it's not still doughy in the center), and the cheese is melty but not burned, 10 to 12 minutes. If your oven doesn't heat evenly, swap the pans' positions halfway through cooking. Transfer the palmiers to a cooling rack. Serve just slightly warm or within the hour, if possible.

Make ahead: You can assemble the rolls to the point just before slicing and freeze them for up to one month. To refresh any leftovers, reheat them in a 350-degree oven for 5 to 7 minutes.

— From *Puff: 50 Flaky, Crunchy, Delicious, Appetizers, Entrees, and Desserts Made With Puff Pastry,* by Martha Holmberg (Clarkson Potter)

COCONUT-CURRY MACADAMIA NUTS

MAKES 5 CUPS

This recipe became a staff favorite after we ran it in a story about what to nibble while watching the Oscars. While macadamia nuts are expensive, you're likely to have the remaining ingredients on hand, and one recipe feeds a slew of guests. Note that buying macadamia nuts in bulk can often be less costly than buying them packaged.

1½ teaspoons ground ginger
1½ teaspoons ground cumin
1½ tablespoons curry powder
½ teaspoon cayenne pepper
¼ cup firmly packed dark brown sugar
¾ teaspoon kosher salt
2 egg whites
5 cups macadamia nuts (about 1¼ pounds)
1 cup coconut flakes (sweetened or unsweetened)

Preheat oven to 300 degrees. In a small bowl, combine the ginger, cumin, curry powder, cayenne, brown sugar, and salt; set aside.

In a medium bowl, beat the egg whites with a small whisk until frothy. Whisk in the reserved spice mixture. Stir in the nuts and the coconut flakes.

Spread the mixture in a single layer onto two lightly greased baking sheets. Bake, stirring the nuts and rotating the pans halfway through cooking, until the nuts are dry, 20 to 25 minutes.

Transfer to parchment paper to cool.

Make ahead: The nuts may be kept in an airtight container at room temperature for 1 week.

— From *Martha Stewart's Hors d'Oeuvres Handbook* (Clarkson Potter)

BLUE CHEESE AND JAM SAVORIES

MAKES ABOUT 3 DOZEN

These savory little cookies topped with fig jam are easy but very elegant. And the surprising combination of tart and tangy with sweet is a real treat—like a great cheese plate all wrapped into one crunchy little morsel. A good-quality fig jam is crucial here; if you can't find it, substitute another lightly sweetened jam, such as quince, apricot, or pear jam.

> 1 cup all-purpose flour
> ½ cup butter, room temperature (1 stick)
> 4 ounces blue cheese, crumbled
> Freshly ground black pepper
> About 3 tablespoons fig jam (see note)

Preheat oven to 350 degrees. Line a baking sheet with parchment paper.

In the bowl of a food processor, place the flour, butter, blue cheese, and a few grinds of pepper. Process until the dough just comes together and starts to form a ball.

Dump the dough onto a lightly floured surface and knead a few times to pull the dough together. Roll out to ⅛ inch thick with a floured rolling pin. Cut rounds out of the dough with a floured 1-inch cutter and transfer the rounds to the baking sheet.

Using the back of a round ½-teaspoon measure or your knuckle, make an indentation in the top of each dough round. Spoon about ¼ teaspoon of fig jam into each indentation, using your finger to push the preserves as best as possible into the indentations.

Bake the savories for 10 to 14 minutes, until the preserves are bubbling and the pastry is light golden on the bottom.

Let savories cool on the baking sheet for at least 10 minutes, then remove to a wire rack to cool.

Note: Fig jam is sometimes shelved with the gourmet jams and jellies.

Make ahead: You can make these a day ahead and keep them in two layers separated by wax paper in an airtight container.

> — From Perre Coleman Magness, therunawayspoon.com
> (via Food52)

5

APRICOT COINS

Cheese expert Laura Werlin pairs tangy goat cheese and apricots with sweet candied walnuts for an original and easy-to-make hors d'oeuvre. The versatile candied nuts go beautifully with other cheeses besides fresh goat cheese, including blue cheese or gruyère.

CANDIED WALNUTS:

¼ cup powdered sugar
⅛ teaspoon cayenne pepper
⅛ teaspoon salt
40 walnut halves (about 1 heaping cup or 4 ounces; don't use pieces)

APRICOT COINS:

4 ounces fresh goat cheese
2 teaspoons milk, plus more if needed
40 dried apricots (about 6 ounces), preferably Turkish
2 teaspoons honey
1 tablespoon finely chopped fresh thyme leaves (or 1½ teaspoons dried thyme)
40 Candied Walnuts

To make walnuts: Preheat oven to 350 degrees.

In a medium sized bowl, mix together the sugar, cayenne, and salt.

Bring a small saucepan of water to boil. Add the walnuts and blanch them for 3 minutes. Drain well and then immediately roll the walnuts in the sugar mixture until thoroughly coated. The sugar will melt slightly. Transfer the walnuts to a baking sheet or pan lined with parchment paper, or a silicone baking mat, and bake, stirring occasionally, until nuts are a deep golden brown, about 10 minutes. Watch carefully because the sugar can burn easily. Let cool completely before serving or assembling the hors d'oeuvres.

To make Apricot Coins: In the bowl of a stand mixer, place the cheese and milk (or use a medium-sized bowl and a wooden spoon). Using the paddle attachment, whip the cheese (or stir it vigorously) for at least 5 minutes, or until it is very smooth and creamy. If the cheese is still crumbly, add more milk ½ teaspoon at a time.

Spread about ⅛ teaspoon of cheese on each apricot. (If using California apricots, put the goat cheese on the shiny side.) Drizzle a little honey over the cheese and top with a light sprinkling of thyme. Place a walnut half on top, arrange the apricots on a platter and serve.

— From *The All American Cheese and Wine Book*, by Laura Werlin (Stewart, Tabori & Chang)

FREEZE NUTS TO ENSURE FRESHNESS

Nuts are not inexpensive, and they will eventually turn rancid when stored at room temperature. So to avoid waste, wrap them well and freeze. Many recipes call for toasting nuts, which heightens their nutty flavor. But it won't save rancid nuts. So always taste before using; and if the nuts have an off flavor, throw them away.

PAN-SEARED GREEN BEANS WITH SPICY REMOULADE

MAKES 4 TO 6 APPETIZER SERVINGS

We were hooked at first bite on these smoky, peppery tender-crisp beans, mottled black from their dance in a red-hot skillet. They're also quick to make and as close to guilt-free as you can get, especially if you use reduced-fat mayonnaise in the spicy remoulade. Leftovers don't keep well, so give yourself license to gobble them up in one sitting—preferably within ten minutes of cooking.

A cast-iron skillet and good kitchen ventilation are vital to recipe's success. Alternately, you can cook these on the grill—where the smoke stays outside—by getting the skillet smoking hot indoors before setting it over high heat on the grill. The only way to mess these up is to not burn them enough. After making this recipe, the skillet will be a mess, but it's nothing a little scrubbing and a vegetable-oil rubdown won't fix.

SPICY REMOULADE:

½ cup mayonnaise

⅛ teaspoon cayenne pepper

2 teaspoons Dijon mustard

1 teaspoon capers, rinsed, drained and finely chopped

½ clove garlic, minced

1 teaspoon minced fresh parsley

2 teaspoons freshly squeezed lemon juice

BEANS:

1 pound fresh green beans, trimmed

1 tablespoon Dijon mustard

¼ teaspoon cayenne pepper

½ teaspoon paprika

1 teaspoon ground cumin

1 teaspoon chili powder

1 clove garlic, minced

½ teaspoon salt

USE A LITTLE TLC WITH CAST IRON

Every cook should own a cast-iron skillet. They're indestructible, they conduct heat well, and with proper seasoning and care, they are almost non-stick.

But cast iron is porous, and it rusts easily if exposed to air and water. So the object of seasoning is to protect the metal by coating it with oil. To season it:

Apply a thin layer of shortening or vegetable oil over the entire surface, inside and out, including the lid. Don't use butter or any other fat with a low smoke point. Next, put the pan, upside down, in a preheated 350-degree oven for one hour. (Place some foil on the bottom of the oven to catch any drips.) You don't want an excess of oil sitting in your pot because any oil not absorbed will turn rancid and ruin the taste of your food.

After seasoning, wipe out any excess oil and it's ready to use. Remember that harsh detergents—especially those made for the dishwasher—will strip off the seasoning. It's best to clean your pan with just hot water and a nylon brush.

If your skillet develops serious baked-on food, here's a great tip: Place it on the bottom of the oven when you run the cleaning cycle. The crud will magically disintegrate, and after rinsing and re-seasoning the skillet, it will be good as new. Note: We don't recommend this trick for other types of cookware.

Also, don't store food in the pot unless you like the taste of metal—cast iron isn't nonreactive. Besides, the acids in the food can break down the seasoning if left in contact for too long.

To make remoulade: Mix mayonnaise, cayenne, mustard, capers, garlic, parsley, and lemon juice until combined. Cover and refrigerate until serving time. Makes ⅔ cup.

To make beans: In a large bowl combine green beans, mustard, cayenne, paprika, cumin, chili powder, garlic, and salt; toss to coat beans.

Heat a large skillet (preferably cast iron) over high heat until smoking. Add the beans, being careful not to crowd the pan too much (cook in two batches, if necessary). Cook beans, without disturbing, until charred patches appear, about 5 minutes. Toss beans and cook 3 to 5 minutes more. Transfer to a bowl or plate and serve immediately with remoulade.

— From Sara Bir

ZUCCHINI FRITTERS

MAKES ABOUT 25 FRITTERS

These fritters get crisp around the edges while the centers puff up like little soufflés. And you'll polish one off in two bites. You can make them ahead (see note below), but they're never quite as good as when they're eaten straight from the pan.

> 1½ pounds zucchini, shredded (about 3 cups)
> 1 medium onion, shredded
> 2 medium carrots, shredded
> 1 clove garlic, minced
> ½ green bell pepper, shredded
> 2 tablespoons chopped fresh parsley
> 4 eggs
> ¾ teaspoon salt, or to taste
> Freshly ground black pepper
> ½ cup all-purpose flour
> ⅓ cup grated parmesan cheese
> 1 teaspoon baking powder
> Vegetable oil

In a large bowl, combine zucchini, onion, carrots, garlic, bell pepper, and chopped parsley; set aside.

In medium bowl, beat eggs, salt, and pepper. Add flour to the mixture and beat as you would for pancake batter (mixture will be a little thicker than pancake batter). Add cheese and baking powder and beat well; set aside.

Pour oil, ½ inch deep, into a skillet and heat until oil is hot enough to deep-fry (about 300 to 325 degrees).

When oil is almost ready, pour batter over vegetables and gently combine. Using a slotted spoon, lift out about 1 to 1½ tablespoons vegetable batter, shape and press into a small disk, then carefully turn out into the hot fat. (As batter sits, it will get more watery—don't worry, it's easy to press much of the excess liquid out through the slotted spoon).

Continue making and frying fritters, adding no more than six fritters at a time to the pan. Fry until golden brown, turning once.

Remove fritters to paper towels to drain. Very lightly salt one side and sprinkle with freshly ground pepper. Repeat until batter is gone.

Make ahead: These fritters can be made the night before, then reheated in a 325-degree oven until they're warm. Or freeze in a single layer, then carefully enclose in a plastic bag. Reheat frozen fritters in an ovenproof container in a 350-degree oven for about 12 minutes. Do not reheat in a microwave.

— From Chris Christensen

MUSHROOM PÂTÉ

MAKES 3 CUPS

Who says pâté has to be made with meat? Cremini mushrooms have their own meatiness, and when combined with cream cheese, butter, green chiles, and seasonings, they make a spread that's every bit as savory and satisfying.

1¼ pounds fresh cremini mushrooms, chopped
½ cup diced onion
1½ tablespoons chopped garlic
½ teaspoon salt
½ teaspoon crushed red pepper flakes
½ cup unsalted butter (1 stick)
2 (3-ounce) packages cream cheese
¼ cup canned mild diced green chiles
Sliced French bread or crackers

In the bowl of a food processor, combine the mushrooms, onion, garlic, salt, and red pepper flakes. Pulse to finely mince the mushrooms.

Melt butter in a large, heavy saucepan. Transfer the mushroom mixture to the saucepan and sauté on low heat until all the liquid that the mushrooms release has been cooked off, about 15 to 20 minutes.

Combine the mushroom mixture with the cream cheese and green chiles; blend well. Place in a 1-quart bowl and refrigerate until chilled, preferably overnight.

Serve the chilled pâté with bread or crackers.

— From Abdel Omar, former owner Brasserie Montmartre and current owner of Bistro 153, Beaverton

SMOKED OYSTER SPREAD

MAKES 1 CUP

For anyone who loves smoked seafood, this spread is addictive. It gets a double hit of savory flavor from the smoky oysters and the soy sauce. And it's even better when made ahead; just be sure to allow it to come to room temperature before serving.

1 (3-ounce) package cream cheese, softened
¼ cup mayonnaise
1 clove garlic, minced
2 teaspoons soy sauce
1 tablespoon minced fresh parsley
1 (3.75-ounce) can smoked oysters, drained and chopped
Water crackers

Blend cream cheese with mayonnaise, garlic, soy sauce, and parsley. Gently stir in chopped oysters. Serve at room temperature with crackers.

— Adapted from *Mystic Seaport's Seafood Secrets Cookbook*, edited by Ainslie Turner (Mystic Seaport Museum)

HALL STREET HOT DUNGENESS CRAB APPETIZER

MAKES ABOUT 4 APPETIZER SERVINGS

Foodd“day requested this dish from Hall Street Grill in 1990. Today it's still on the restaurant's menu, which just shows how good a simple recipe can be.

⅔ cup mayonnaise
1 (4-ounce) jar marinated artichoke hearts, drained and chopped
1 (6-ounce) can Dungeness crabmeat, drained
¼ cup grated parmesan cheese
¼ cup diced onion
Warm baguette slices

Combine mayonnaise, artichoke hearts, crabmeat, parmesan cheese, and onion, and refrigerate until ready to serve.

Bake in an ovenproof dish at 300 degrees for 10 to 12 minutes. Serve immediately with warm baguette.

— From Hall Street Grill, Beaverton

CLAM DIP WITH BACON AND CHIVES

MAKES 2 CUPS

In some circles, clam dip may be retro fare, but we think this recipe would be welcome at almost any party. The tiny bit of bacon and Worcestershire sauce give the dip that savory "umami" taste that's so addictive.

3 (6½-ounce) cans minced clams
8 ounces cream cheese, at room temperature
½ teaspoon Worcestershire sauce
2 tablespoons minced fresh chives (divided)
1 strip bacon, fried crisp and minced (divided)
½ teaspoon grated lemon zest
Freshly ground black pepper
Potato chips or crackers, for serving

Drain the minced clams and reserve the clams and clam juice separately.

Pour the clam juice into a small saucepan and bring to a boil over medium-high heat. Reduce heat to medium and gently boil the juice until it is reduced to ¼ cup, about 20 minutes. Set aside to cool.

Place the cream cheese in the bowl of a food processor, add the cooled clam juice concentrate, and process until smooth. If the cream cheese is too thick for dipping, add a teaspoon or two of water to thin. Add the clams, Worcestershire sauce, 1½ teaspoons chives, 1 tablespoon bacon, and the lemon zest, and process to combine. Season with black pepper.

To serve, bring to room temperature. Sprinkle with remaining chives and bacon. Serve with chips or crackers.

Make ahead: You can make the dip up to one day ahead, cover it tightly with plastic wrap and refrigerate. Save the remaining chives and bacon for garnish, and add just before serving.

— From Linda Faus

CLASSIC HUMMUS

MAKES 2½ CUPS

Everyone should have a good hummus recipe. This one is a bit lighter and smoother than most versions, because the oil is added to the food processor in a thin stream to create an emulsion. For a classic presentation, spread the hummus on a plate and make concentric circles in the dip with the back of a spoon, then drizzle with good-quality olive oil.

2 cups cooked or canned garbanzo beans
(from two 15½-ounce cans, drained; freeze
leftover beans)
3 to 4 cloves garlic, minced
¼ cup fresh lemon juice
¼ cup water
¼ cup tahini (sesame seed paste)
½ teaspoon ground cumin
½ teaspoon smoked paprika (pimentón
de la Vera)
Pinch cayenne pepper
¼ cup olive oil
Salt to taste
Chopped fresh parsley (for garnish)
Lemon wedges (for serving)

In the bowl of a food processor add the garbanzo beans, garlic, lemon juice, and water. Pulse a few times, then scrape down the sides of the bowl and continue processing until puréed, about 1 minute. If the mixture is very thick, thin it with a tablespoon or so of water.

Add the tahini, cumin, paprika, and cayenne; pulse until well-combined. With the processor running, add the oil in a slow, steady stream. Season to taste with salt, sprinkle with chopped parsley, and serve with lemon wedges.

— From Ken Hoyt

SMOKY PIMIENTO CHEESE

MAKES 2 CUPS

Pimiento cheese is a Southern classic. But this version achieves a much more complex favor by combining three types of cheese and seasoning the mixture with smoked paprika and pickled peppadew peppers. Serve it in celery sticks, or on cherry tomatoes or crackers.

4 ounces smoked gouda cheese, shredded (we
used Willamette Valley Cheese Co.
brand from New Seasons)
4 ounces gouda parrano cheese, shredded (we
used UnieKaas brand from New Seasons)
¼ cup grated parmesan cheese
½ cup mayonnaise
¼ cup finely chopped peppadew peppers
(see note)
½ teaspoon smoked paprika (pimentón
de la Vera)
¼ teaspoon freshly ground black pepper

In a medium bowl, toss together the three cheeses. In a small bowl, whisk together the mayonnaise, peppadew peppers, smoked paprika and black pepper. Stir the mayonnaise mixture into the cheeses until well-moistened.

Note: Pickled peppadew peppers are sweet yet slightly spicy. Find them in jars with other pickled foods, refrigerated near gourmet cheeses, or in bulk at an olive bar.

Make ahead: Spread keeps in the refrigerator for up to 2 weeks.

— From Linda Faus

HOT SEVEN-LAYER DIP

MAKES 8 SERVINGS

Trust us: This isn't your ordinary bean dip. Foodday contributor Ivy Manning riffs on the usual rendition by using chorizo, smoky chipotle chiles and lime juice. Note that she recommends uncooked chorizo sausage links. Soft Mexican chorizo (the kind that comes in plastic-wrapped cylinders) has a mushy texture and loads of fat. If you can find only Mexican chorizo, be sure to drain the cooked meat in a fine sieve or it will make the dip greasy.

To make this dish vegetarian, omit the chorizo. To make it vegan, substitute soy cheese and dairy-free sour cream.

2 (15-ounce) cans black beans, rinsed
    and drained
⅔ cup chopped fresh cilantro (divided)
3 medium cloves garlic, finely chopped
1½ tablespoons chopped chipotle chiles
    in adobo sauce
¼ cup plus 1 tablespoon freshly squeezed
    lime juice (divided)
1 teaspoon ground cumin
Salt and freshly ground black pepper
8 ounces chorizo sausage links,
    casings removed
1½ cups shredded asadero or Monterey
    jack cheese (6 ounces)
¼ cup plus 2 tablespoons finely chopped
    white onion (divided)
1 tablespoon finely chopped jalapeño chile
2 ripe avocados, skins and pits discarded
8 whole canned tomatoes, chopped (about

1 cup)
2 tablespoons Secret Aardvark hot sauce,
    or other hot sauce
½ cup light sour cream
5 scallions, finely chopped

Preheat oven to 350 degrees. Spray an 8-inch square baking dish with nonstick cooking spray. In the bowl of a food processor, place the beans, ⅓ cup cilantro, garlic, chipotle chiles, ¼ cup lime juice, and the cumin; pulse until nearly smooth, stopping to scrape down the sides of the bowl once or twice. Season the bean mixture with salt and pepper to taste; transfer to the baking dish.

In a small sauté pan over medium heat, cook the chorizo, breaking it up with a spatula into small chunks, until the meat is cooked through and browned. Drain off the fat from the pan, and sprinkle the chorizo and the cheese over the bean mixture.

Bake the dip until the cheese has melted and the dip is bubbly around the edges, about 30 minutes. While baking, prepare the other layers. With a mortar and pestle or in a small bowl, mash 2 tablespoons of the onion, jalapeño, and ½ teaspoon salt until the mixture is reduced to a fine, wet paste. Add the avocado and the remaining tablespoon of lime juice, and mash until the mixture is smooth with a few chunks. Set aside.

In a small bowl, combine the tomatoes, remaining ⅓ cup cilantro, remaining ¼ cup onion, and the hot sauce. Season the salsa with salt and pepper to taste; set aside.

When the dip is bubbling hot, remove it from the oven, and let it stand for 10 minutes. Top the bean mixture with the avocado mixture, tomato mixture, and dabs of sour cream. Sprinkle with scallions and serve immediately.

Make ahead: After the chorizo and the cheese have been sprinkled over the bean mixture, the dip can be covered and refrigerated for up to three days before baking.

— From Ivy Manning

BRIE WITH ROASTED GARLIC AND KALAMATA OLIVES

MAKES 10 TO 12 SERVINGS

Baked brie has been around forever, but this version raises the bar with mild roasted garlic and piquant kalamata olives. Caterer Nancy Taylor removes the cheese rind, because the cheese melts more easily and doesn't end up with white flecks in the mixture. However, this step is optional.

    1 pound brie cheese, well-chilled
    2 whole heads roasted garlic (see note)
    ½ cup pitted kalamata olives, chopped
    ¼ cup chopped fresh parsley
    Sliced French bread or crackers

Scrape the outer white rind off the brie. Cut the brie in half horizontally and place with cut sides up in a heatproof serving dish. Top with the roasted garlic that has been squeezed out of their skins. Top with olives.

Bake in a preheated 350-degree oven, uncovered, until the cheese starts to melt and gets soft enough to spread, about 15 to 20 minutes. Sprinkle with parsley and serve with sliced French bread or crackers.

Note: To roast garlic, separate cloves from the head. Place unpeeled cloves in a baking dish with 1 tablespoon of olive oil per garlic head. Bake in a preheated 400-degree oven, uncovered, about 25 to 30 minutes, or until the cloves are richly browned and soft. Remove from oven and cool. At this point, the skins are crisp and can be easily removed.

Make ahead: Roasted garlic can be prepared several days ahead and stored in refrigerator.

— From Nancy Taylor, Fabulous Food catering, Portland

PEPPER-CURED SMOKED SALMON WITH SAUCE VERTE

MAKES 6 TO 8 SERVINGS

An herb-flecked "sauce verte" turns smoked salmon into a sophisticated starter. This has long been a popular dish at The Stonehedge Gardens, a romantic restaurant on six secluded acres in the Hood River Valley.

SALMON:

1½ to 2 pounds salmon fillet, cut into
    4-ounce portions
2 cups water
2 cups white wine
½ cup firmly packed brown sugar
½ cup salt
1 teaspoon dried thyme
1 teaspoon garlic salt
¼ cup freshly cracked black peppercorns

SAUCE VERTE:

1 cup mayonnaise
¼ cup honey
1¼ teaspoons minced fresh chives
2¼ teaspoons dried tarragon
3¾ teaspoons prepared mustard
1 tablespoon finely minced fresh cilantro
1 cup finely minced fresh parsley

To make salmon: Lay the salmon in a single layer in a shallow pan. In a large bowl combine the water, wine, brown sugar, salt, thyme, and garlic salt; pour mixture over the salmon fillets to cover. Cover and refrigerate for 6 to 8 hours.

Rinse the salmon and pat dry. Dredge in the cracked peppercorns, and lay on a smoker rack. Let dry in the refrigerator for 12 to 15 hours. Smoke in an electric smoker for 2 hours (more or less, depending on the brand of smoker). Salmon should feel semisoft to the touch.

To make sauce: Stir together the mayonnaise, honey, chives, tarragon, mustard, cilantro, and parsley. Serve chilled for dipping the smoked salmon.

— From The Stonehedge Gardens, Hood River

TUNA POACHED IN OLIVE OIL WITH OLIVE TAPENADE AND GARLIC AIOLI

MAKES 8 APPETIZER SERVINGS

This appetizer would be equally good served with a salad as a light lunch or dinner. All three components can be made from one to two weeks ahead. The poached fish also makes wonderful tuna salad, served alone or as a stuffing for peppers.

TUNA:

1 pound fresh yellowfin tuna
Extra-virgin olive oil to cover (2½ to 3 cups)

TAPENADE:

1 cup pitted niçoise olives
1 tablespoon chopped roasted red bell pepper, bottled or fresh
½ teaspoon crushed red pepper flakes
3 cloves garlic
1 tablespoon extra-virgin olive oil, if needed

AIOLI:

2 egg yolks (see note)
8 cloves garlic
2 tablespoons fresh lemon juice
1 to 1½ cups extra-virgin olive oil
Salt and freshly ground black pepper
Flatbread, crackers or toasted pita bread
Sea salt, for serving

To make tuna: Cut the tuna into 1- to 2-inch pieces. Pour enough olive oil into a medium saucepan to cover the tuna. (You can add the tuna to help measure depth of oil, but you'll need to remove it before heating the oil.) Heat the olive oil over low heat until a thermometer reaches 170 degrees. Add the tuna to the oil; adjust heat to hold the temperature at 170 degrees. Cook until the tuna is still rare in the center, about 6 to 7 minutes. Remove from the heat and let the tuna stand in the hot oil until the oil is cool. Cover and refrigerate in the oil until ready to use.

To make tapenade: Combine the olives, roasted pepper, pepper flakes, and garlic in the bowl of a food processor. Process until the mixture is a paste. Add 1 tablespoon olive oil, if necessary. Transfer tapenade to a covered bowl; store in the refrigerator until ready to use.

To make aioli: Combine the egg yolks, garlic, and lemon juice in the bowl of a food processor. With the motor running, very slowly drizzle in the olive oil until the mixture resembles mayonnaise. Season to taste with salt and pepper. Refrigerate, covered, until ready to use.

To serve, arrange pieces of flatbread or crackers on a platter; spread each with garlic aioli and olive tapenade. Flake the tuna into large pieces and arrange over the tapenade. Sprinkle with sea salt, if desired.

Note: This recipe uses uncooked eggs, which carry the risk of salmonella. Use pasteurized eggs, or else avoid serving this dish to people in a high-risk group for contracting food poisoning, including the elderly, the very young, the chronically ill, pregnant women, or others with a weakened immune system.

Make ahead: Covered by the olive oil that it's poached in, the tuna can be refrigerated for 1 to 2 weeks. Tapenade can be made and refrigerated up to 2 weeks ahead. Aioli can made and refrigerated for 1 to 2 weeks.

— From Adam Berger, co-founder,
Tabla Mediterranean Bistro

BAGUETTE SLICES WITH SHRIMP, AVOCADO, AND GOAT CHEESE

MAKES 3 CUPS

Local author Janie Hibler complements the sweetness of bay shrimp with the bright flavors of lemon and cilantro in this easy and versatile dish. Once you've enjoyed the shrimp mixture as an appetizer, try it in a sandwich or as a salad served on lettuce.

1 pound bay shrimp (tiny cooked shrimp; approximately 2 cups)
1 avocado, pitted, peeled, and diced (¾ to 1 cup)
¼ cup chopped red onion
¼ cup fresh cilantro leaves
2 ounces mild, crumbled goat cheese
1 tablespoon lemon juice

2 tablespoons mild olive oil
¼ teaspoon salt
Scant ¼ teaspoon freshly ground black pepper
Thinly sliced baguette or tortilla chips

In a medium bowl add the shrimp, avocado, onion, cilantro leaves and goat cheese.

In a small bowl, whisk together the lemon juice, olive oil, salt and pepper; pour over the shrimp mixture. Toss and serve surrounded by baguette slices or tortilla chips.

— From *Dungeness Crabs & Blackberry Cobblers*, by Janie Hibler (WestWinds Press)

CHINESE POT STICKERS

MAKES 30 TO 35 POT STICKERS, FOR 6 TO 8 DIM SUM SERVINGS

If you've never made pot stickers, you'll be surprised how easy it is. A pot-sticker press is very inexpensive but not essential. After you've pleated a few by hand, you'll quickly become adept and may even find it an enjoyable Zen exercise.

1 (10-ounce) package frozen chopped spinach, thawed
1 pound ground pork
½ cup minced scallions
3 tablespoons minced fresh cilantro
2 tablespoons soy sauce
2 tablespoons dry sherry
1 tablespoon peeled and grated fresh ginger
2 teaspoons dark sesame oil
4 large cloves garlic, minced or pressed (4 to 5 teaspoons)

1 package round pot-sticker wrappers (at least 35, 3 to 3½ inches in diameter, see note)
1 egg white, lightly beaten
½ cup vegetable or peanut oil (divided)
2 cups chicken broth (divided)

SESAME-SOY DIPPING SAUCE:
½ cup soy sauce
2 tablespoons Chinese black vinegar (or 1 tablespoon distilled white vinegar and 1 tablespoon Worcestershire sauce)
1 tablespoon minced garlic (3 cloves)
1 teaspoon peeled and minced fresh ginger
1 teaspoon dark sesame oil
Hot chile oil (see note)

Firmly squeeze all the moisture from the spinach, then combine with pork, scallions, cilantro, soy sauce, sherry, ginger, sesame oil, and garlic; mix filling well.

To assemble using pot-sticker press, lay a pot-sticker wrapper on the press. Spoon 2 teaspoons of filling into the center of the wrapper. Brush the edges of the wrapper with egg white. Firmly press together the two halves of the press; gently remove the folded, crimped dumpling.

Alternatively, if no press is available, use your hands to bring edges of pot sticker wrapper up over filling and press together. Crimp edges with a wide-tined fork or pleat with your fingers.

Lay the dumplings on a flat surface, crimped edges up, to form a flat bottom. Repeat with remaining filling and wrappers.

To cook the pot stickers, heat 2 tablespoons vegetable oil in a 12-inch heavy skillet over medium-high heat. Add as many pot stickers as you can get in the pan without crowding; cook until golden brown on the bottom.

Add ½ cup broth and cover the pan immediately. (Be careful. A major amount of splattering and sizzling occurs as soon as the broth comes in contact with the oil.) Reduce the heat to medium-low; cook the dumplings until most of the liquid has been absorbed and the pot stickers are nicely plumped and a deep golden brown on the bottom.

Remove from the heat and keep them warm in a 200-degree oven while you use the remaining oil and broth to cook the remaining pot stickers in the same manner.

To making dipping sauce: In a small container, combine soy sauce, vinegar, garlic, ginger, and sesame oil. Makes about ⅔ cup.

To serve, provide guests with individual small dishes containing hot chile oil and the Sesame-Soy Dipping Sauce.

Note: Hot chile oil is readily available in the Asian foods section of most supermarkets. But you can make your own by sautéing 2 teaspoons of crushed red pepper flakes in ½ cup of peanut oil for 3 minutes. Remove from heat and let stand until cool. If desired, stir in 1 tablespoon prepared chile-garlic sauce, also available in the Asian foods section. Store in refrigerator.

Make ahead: Assembled (uncooked) pot stickers may be placed on a baking sheet, covered lightly, and frozen. When frozen, pack in airtight packaging and freeze up to 6 months. When ready to serve, just proceed with the recipe; no thawing is necessary.

—From Jan Roberts-Dominguez

STEAMED BUNS WITH BARBECUED PORK (CHAR SIU HUM BAO)

MAKES 20 BUNS, FOR 6 TO 8 DIM SUM SERVINGS

Traditional hum bao is made by marinating and barbecuing pork loin and making a homemade dough. But this recipe expedites the buns by using frozen dinner roll dough and ready-to-eat Chinese barbecued pork. The buns are steamed in a two-level bamboo steamer, available at kitchenware stores and Asian markets; the bamboo absorbs some of the steam, allowing the buns to cook to fluffy perfection without being doused in condensation. If you don't have a steamer, then immediately before serving you can bake the buns on a parchment paper-lined baking sheet in a 350-degree oven until golden brown and cooked through, 20 to 25 minutes.

20 frozen dough balls (we used Rhodes
    Bake-N-Serv white dinner rolls)
2 tablespoons hoisin sauce
4 teaspoons soy sauce
4 teaspoons shao hsing (Chinese rice wine)
    or dry sherry
1½ teaspoons cornstarch
¼ cup chicken broth or water
1½ cups finely chopped Chinese barbecued
pork (char siu; 7 ounces)

Four hours before making the buns, spray a baking sheet with nonstick cooking spray; place the balls of dough at least 2 inches apart on the baking sheet. Spray one side of a piece of plastic wrap with nonstick cooking spray and place it loosely over the baking sheet with the ungreased side facing up. Allow the rolls to defrost and rise until doubled in size, about 4 hours. (Alternately, place the frozen rolls on the prepared baking sheet, cover with the greased plastic wrap, and refrigerate overnight. Proceed as directed when ready to fill.)

In a small saucepan combine the hoisin sauce, soy sauce, and rice wine. Place the cornstarch in a small measuring cup and gradually whisk in the chicken broth; add to saucepan. Bring mixture to a simmer over medium heat and cook until bubbly and thick, 2 minutes. Chop the barbecued pork and combine with hoisin mixture.

Cut 20 (3-inch) squares of parchment paper. Spray the rack of the bamboo steamer with nonstick cooking spray. Take one roll and flatten, forcing out any large gas bubbles. Make a slight indentation in the center and fill with 1 tablespoon of the pork filling. Create a small purse by bringing the edges of the roll up and over the filling and pinching them together at the top of the bun. Place seam side down on a square of parchment paper and put in the bamboo steamer, leaving at least 1 inch of space between each roll. Repeat with remaining rolls and filling. Let stand at room temperature for 15 minutes if dough was defrosted at room temperature, 30 minutes if defrosted overnight in the refrigerator.

Place the top of the steamer over the rack and place over boiling water in a wok, making sure that the bottom of the steamer is not resting in the water. Steam buns for 20 to 25 minutes, until they are fluffy and a skewer inserted into the dough comes out clean. Remove steamer from wok and transfer the buns to a serving platter.

Make ahead: The pork and sauce can be combined and refrigerated up to 3 days ahead. The buns can be steamed up to 24 hours in advance. Cool completely ▶

and wrap buns individually in plastic wrap. To reheat, remove plastic wrap and place on a serving plate; cover with a moist white paper towel and microwave until heated through, about 2 minutes.

— From Ivy Manning

SPICY MINCED CHICKEN AND WATER CHESTNUT LETTUCE WRAPS

MAKES 6 TO 8 DIM SUM OR APPETIZER SERVINGS

Foodday contributor Ivy Manning says the wonderful texture of the filling for this recipe depends on hand-chopping the chicken, which gives you a better texture than ground chicken. Partially freezing the meat makes chopping easier.

> About 1½ pounds boneless, skinless chicken thighs, partially frozen
> 2 tablespoons vegetable oil
> 1 tablespoon minced garlic
> 1 tablespoon peeled and minced fresh ginger
> 2 scallions, sliced, green and white parts divided
> 1 tablespoon plus 1 teaspoon soy sauce
> 1 teaspoon unseasoned rice vinegar
> 2 tablespoons sweet chili sauce (see note), plus more for serving
> ½ cup finely chopped water chestnuts
> 2 teaspoons chili oil (see note)
> ¼ cup chopped fresh cilantro
> 1 head Boston or bibb lettuce

Finely chop the chicken thighs until they are a little coarser than ground beef. Heat the oil in a skillet or wok over medium-high heat until it shimmers. Add the garlic, ginger and white part of the scallions and stir-fry until fragrant, 20 seconds. Add the chicken and stir-fry until chicken is opaque and cooked through, about 8 minutes.

Reduce heat to medium; add green part of the scallions, soy sauce, rice vinegar, sweet chili sauce, water chestnuts, and chili oil; stir-fry for 1 minute. Pour the chicken mixture into a serving bowl and fold in the cilantro.

Separate the leaves from the head of lettuce and wash them thoroughly. Spin-dry leaves in a salad spinner or pat dry with paper towels. Tear the largest leaves in half lengthwise. Pile leaves on platter and serve alongside the chicken filling with a small bowl of sweet chili sauce on the side. Allow guests to fill their own lettuce leaves with the chicken, drizzle them with chili sauce, and eat them taco-style.

Note: Sweet chili sauce is a translucent sauce with minced chiles. You can find it at grocery stores and (for much less) at Asian markets. We recommend the Mae Ploy and Caravelle brands.

Note: Chili oil is vegetable oil that is steeped with red chiles and varies from mildly spicy to atomic. We love S&B La-Yu brand, which comes in a tiny 1.1-ounce bottle.

Make ahead: The chicken filling can be prepared and stir-fried up to 3 days in advance. Once cool, cover tightly with plastic wrap and refrigerate. Reheat in microwave.

— From Ivy Manning

MOROCCAN CHICKEN DRUMETTES

MAKES 20 APPETIZER SERVINGS

With salty olives, sweet dates, honey, and Moroccan spices, these drumettes are unlike any chicken wings you've ever had. After the chicken has baked in the chunky marinade, you can serve any leftovers on top of couscous. And if you don't care for spicy food, cut way back on the crushed red pepper flakes.

1½ cups pimiento-stuffed green olives
1 cup dates
1 bunch fresh cilantro
2 tablespoons ground cinnamon
2 tablespoons crushed red pepper flakes,
    or to taste
2 tablespoons turmeric
2 tablespoons kosher salt
2 tablespoons freshly ground black pepper
¼ cup ground cumin
¼ cup paprika
¼ cup sesame seeds
1 cup lemon juice
1½ cups honey
5 pounds chicken wing drumettes
Lime wedges, for garnish

Roughly chop the olives, dates, and cilantro (reserve a few sprigs for garnish). In a large zip-top plastic bag or a large bowl, combine the chopped olives, dates, and cilantro with the cinnamon, red pepper flakes, turmeric, salt, black pepper, cumin, paprika, sesame seeds, lemon juice, and honey. Mix well and add chicken wings, turning to coat well. Refrigerate for at least 5 hours or overnight, stirring or turning occasionally.

Preheat oven to 350 degrees.

Divide the contents of the bag between two large baking pans so the chicken wings are a single layer deep. Bake for 45 to 50 minutes or until done, rotating the pans halfway through the baking time. Garnish with cilantro sprigs and lime wedges and serve hot.

— From Elephants Delicatessen

TO STEM OR NOT TO STEM

Plucking the leaves from a few sprigs of fresh herbs isn't difficult. But what if a recipe calls for ½ cup or more? Chances are you'll only run into a measurement this large with parsley or cilantro. With cilantro, the flavorful stems are tender enough to chop or mince and include in a dish. The lower part of parsley stems, however, can be tough and should be separated from the leaves. But rather than plucking them individually, you can lay a bunch on a cutting board, hold the stems with one hand, and use a fork with your other hand to rake the leaves off the stems. Or, simply hold a bunch by the lower stems and chop the whole lot off at the base of the lowest leaves. Don't worry about the top of the stems, which will be tender enough to include.

SALADS

ORANGE SALAD WITH SMOKED PAPRIKA VINAIGRETTE, ICED ONIONS, AND CILANTRO

MAKES 6 SERVINGS

Sweet-tangy oranges and smoked paprika are sublime together. If you're not a cilantro fan, basil or parsley would work fine here.

SALAD:

⅛ of a small red onion, sliced as thinly as possible

3 juicy oranges

2 tablespoons roughly chopped fresh cilantro

VINAIGRETTE:

3 tablespoons fresh-squeezed orange juice

1 tablespoon sherry vinegar

½ teaspoon granulated sugar

¼ teaspoon kosher salt

¾ teaspoon smoked paprika (pimentón de la Vera)

¼ cup vegetable oil

To make salad: Soak the onion slices in a small bowl of water with some ice cubes for at least 30 minutes and as long as 2 hours. Meanwhile, prepare vinaigrette as directed below, then proceed with preparation of oranges: Cut off both ends of an orange, then stand it on a flat end and slice away the peel, including all of the white pith. Turn orange on its side and cut crosswise into ¼-inch slices; repeat with remaining oranges.

Add orange slices to the bowl of vinaigrette and gently toss to coat. Arrange the orange slices on a serving plate, overlapping them slightly. Pour any extra vinaigrette and juices from the bowl into a small pitcher for serving on the side. Drain the onions and pat thoroughly dry with paper towels. Scatter onion over the oranges, then sprinkle with the cilantro.

To make vinaigrette: In a bowl that's big enough to hold the orange slices, whisk together the orange juice, sherry vinegar, sugar, salt, and paprika until the sugar and salt are dissolved. Whisk in the oil a few drops at a time until dressing is creamy and emulsified. Taste and adjust seasoning as needed.

Make ahead: You can prepare the salad as much as 4 hours ahead and refrigerate it. But it's best when not served ice cold, so take it out of the refrigerator at least 20 minutes before serving.

— From Martha Holmberg

TAKE THE BITE OUT OF ONIONS

To mellow the sharp flavor of fresh onions, soak them—sliced or diced—for 15 to 30 minutes in ice water and a splash of vinegar. Then drain well and add to your recipe.

PATTY'S KILLER NOODLE SALAD

MAKES 8 TO 10 SERVINGS

After winning a Foodday contest for potluck recipes, Patty McNally's Noodle Salad went on to became one of our most frequently requested recipes. She says it goes great with grilled chicken and Japanese beer.

12 to 15 ounces dried chuka soba noodles (two 6-ounce packages or three 5-ounce packages; these are also labeled chow mein noodles)
1½ teaspoons dark sesame oil
⅓ cup rice vinegar or distilled white vinegar
Juice and grated zest of 1 fresh lime
½ cup soy sauce
2 teaspoons crushed red pepper flakes or 2 teaspoons garlic chili sauce
2 tablespoons granulated sugar
2 cloves garlic, minced
1 cup shredded carrots (about 2 medium)
¾ cup coarsely chopped dry-roasted peanuts
½ cup chopped fresh cilantro

In a large pot, bring 3 quarts water to a boil; add noodles and boil as package directs, about 2 minutes. Drain, rinse with cold water and let cool in colander.

Meanwhile, in a large bowl, combine oil, vinegar, lime juice and zest, soy sauce, red pepper flakes or chili sauce, sugar, and garlic. Mix until sugar is dissolved. Add carrots, peanuts and cilantro, and toss with dressing.

Cut through noodles to make manageable lengths. Toss noodles into bowl with other ingredients and chill salad for at least an hour to let flavors mingle.

Toss just before serving. If it seems a little dry, add a little more soy sauce and vinegar. Serve cold or at room temperature.

— From Patty McNally

> ## GREEN SHOOT INDICATES OLD AGE
>
> Frequently you'll find a little green shoot inside a clove of garlic. It's a sign of old age, and the green shoot can give food a bitter flavor. But it doesn't mean you have to discard the whole clove. Just slice the clove lengthwise, nip the green shoot off and mince or chop the rest of the clove as usual.

MOROCCAN ORZO SALAD

MAKES 16 TO 20 SERVINGS

There are pasta salads, and there's Ron Paul's Orzo Salad, simply one of the best recipes ever. There's a fair amount of slicing and dicing to do, but the result—an intoxicating combination of pasta, dried fruit, nuts, citrus, cilantro, and warming spices—is well worth the effort. This recipe also feeds a crowd, and leftovers keep well in the refrigerator.

SALAD:
1 red bell pepper, cut into small dice
1 yellow bell pepper, cut into small dice
½ red onion, minced

1 cup or 16 to 18 dates, chopped
¾ cup or 16 dried apricots, chopped
½ cup dried currants
¼ cup chopped pistachios
¼ to ½ bunch chopped cilantro (according
    to personal preference)
Grated zest of 1 orange
Grated zest of 1 lemon
4 to 6 cups cooked orzo (⅓ cup raw orzo
    yields 1 cup cooked)

DRESSING:
Juice of 1 lemon (¼ cup)
Juice of 1 orange (⅓ cup)
1 teaspoon ground cumin
½ teaspoon ground cardamom
½ teaspoon ground cinnamon
1 tablespoon honey
½ teaspoon turmeric
1 teaspoon fresh ginger juice (squeeze juice
    from 1 tablespoon grated ginger)

Salt to taste, about 1 teaspoon
½ cup extra-virgin olive oil

To make salad: In a large bowl, mix together the peppers, onion, dates, apricots, currants, pistachios, cilantro, zests, and cooked orzo.

To make dressing: In a blender, place lemon and orange juice, cumin, cardamom, cinnamon, honey, turmeric, ginger juice, and salt. Blend. Then stir in olive oil. Pour over salad and mix well. Chill. Serve at room temperature or chilled.

Make ahead: Can be made and refrigerated up to a day ahead.

— From Ron Paul Catering & Charcuterie

WATERMELON, CUCUMBER, AND TOMATO SALAD

MAKES 6 TO 8 SERVINGS

While this may sound like an odd combination of fruit and vegetables, it's both refreshing and colorful. Cut the watermelon in half crosswise and scoop out one half to use as a serving bowl.

2 tablespoons granulated sugar
2 tablespoons white wine vinegar
¼ cup slivered red onion
Pinch salt
Pinch crushed red pepper flakes
2 tablespoons extra-virgin olive oil
2 cups diced (¾-inch) seeded watermelon
2 ripe firm, meaty tomatoes, cut into
    16 thin wedges
1 seedless cucumber, peeled and halved

lengthwise and cut crosswise into
    ½-inch pieces
¼ cup slivered fresh basil leaves
Freshly ground black pepper

In a small saucepan, place sugar, vinegar, onion, salt, and red pepper flakes; stir over medium heat until sugar dissolves. Remove from heat, add oil, and set aside to cool.

In a large bowl, place watermelon, tomatoes, cucumber, and basil. Pour dressing over mixture and mix gently. Add salt and pepper to taste.

Serve in scooped-out watermelon half, if desired.

—From the Foodday Test Kitchen

CRAN-APPLE SPINACH SALAD WITH SPICED PECANS

MAKES 10 SERVINGS

This recipe is a delicious riff on a Waldorf salad. It's also ideal for entertaining because it needs to be made ahead, with a little last-minute assembly.

SALAD:

½ cup cranberry juice concentrate, undiluted
⅓ cup olive oil
3 tablespoons raspberry balsamic vinegar or a mixture of half raspberry vinegar and half balsamic vinegar
⅛ teaspoon salt
4 cups chopped, unpeeled tart red apples, such as Gala or Braeburn
1 cup dried cranberries
8 cups torn fresh spinach leaves
1 cup thinly sliced celery, cut diagonally

SPICED PECANS:

⅓ cup honey
1 tablespoon water
½ teaspoon ground cinnamon
¼ teaspoon ground ginger
⅛ teaspoon salt
2 cups pecan halves
1 tablespoon granulated sugar

To make salad: In a small bowl, whisk together cranberry juice concentrate, olive oil, vinegar, and salt.

Place apples and cranberries in 2-quart shallow glass dish. Pour cranberry juice mixture over apple mixture. Refrigerate, covered, at least 3 hours, stirring occasionally.

To make pecans: Preheat oven to 325 degrees.

In a medium bowl, combine honey, water, cinnamon, ginger, and salt. Stir in pecans until coated with honey mixture.

Using slotted spoon, place pecans in single layer on a baking sheet lined with parchment paper. Sprinkle with sugar. Bake 16 to 18 minutes, turning halfway through baking time. Cool slightly on baking sheet. Remove and cool completely. Makes 2 cups.

To serve, toss spinach and celery in a large shallow bowl or platter. Top with cranberry-apple mixture. Sprinkle with pecans. (You may not want to add all of the nuts to the salad; if not, save the rest for munching.)

Make ahead: Nuts can be made and stored in a tightly covered container at room temperature up to 3 days in advance. The cranberry-apple mixture can be made and refrigerated, covered, up to 1 day in advance; stir occasionally. If the mixture has been refrigerated several hours, allow to stand at room temperature about 15 minutes for olive oil to liquefy; stir before using.

BUTTER LETTUCE SALAD WITH VINAIGRETTE ROYALE

MAKES 4 SERVINGS

This salad, with its French-inspired dressing of egg, Dijon mustard, champagne vinegar, fresh chives and tarragon, has been on Café Castagna's menu for years. It's a simple dish, so for best quality use the most tender leaves of butter lettuce you can find.

VINAIGRETTE:

1 egg yolk (see note)
2 teaspoons Dijon mustard
⅓ cup olive oil
¼ cup peanut oil
4 teaspoons champagne vinegar
Salt and freshly ground black pepper

SALAD:

2 heads butter lettuce (about 1 pound;
    use the tender, pale yellow leaves)
4 teaspoons chopped fresh chives
4 teaspoons chopped fresh tarragon
Salt

To make vinaigrette: Whisk egg yolk with mustard. Gradually add oils, whisking to emulsify. Add champagne vinegar and thin with a little water. Season with salt and pepper.

To make salad: Toss lettuce with vinaigrette to taste, chives and tarragon. Sprinkle lightly with salt. Reserve remaining vinaigrette for another use.

Note: This recipe uses uncooked egg, which carries the risk of a salmonella infection. Use a pasteurized egg, or else avoid serving this dish to people in a high-risk group for contracting food poisoning, including the elderly, the very young, the chronically ill, pregnant women, or others with a weakened immune system.

— From Café Castagna

PAPARAZZI CHOPPED SALAD

MAKES 4 SERVINGS

There's nothing particularly fancy or unusual about this salad, but when made with the best ingredients you can find, you simply can't get enough of it. Chef Joe Rapport served this salad at the now defunct Paparazzi East.

DRESSING:

1 cup olive oil
3 tablespoons red wine vinegar
3 tablespoons balsamic vinegar
½ teaspoon salt
¼ to ½ teaspoon freshly ground black pepper
3 to 4 cloves finely minced garlic

SALAD:

1 head romaine lettuce
1 cup diced tomato (¼-inch dice)
1 cup cucumber, peeled, seeded, and diced
    into ¼-inch cubes
½ cup kalamata olives, pitted and chopped
½ cup crumbled gorgonzola cheese

¼ cup freshly grated parmesan cheese (preferably Parmigiano-Reggiano)

Thinly sliced red onion to garnish

To make dressing: In a jar with a tight-fitting lid, combine the olive oil, both vinegars, salt, pepper, and garlic. Shake jar well. Dressing will separate and needs to be shaken just before use.

To make salad: Thinly slice the romaine and then chop into small pieces. Toss romaine with the tomato, cucumber, olives, and cheeses. Add ½ cup of the dressing and toss to mix well. Garnish with red onion slices.

Variations: One cup finely diced cooked chicken breast or salami may be added for a more substantial salad. Substitute feta cheese for the gorgonzola. Or add other cooked vegetables such as green beans or summer squash.

— From Joe Rapport

HEARTS OF ROMAINE SALAD WITH GRILLED PARMESAN CROUTONS AND GRILLED LEMON

MAKES 4 SERVINGS

Since it's on just about every restaurant menu in town, it's easy to get bored with Caesar salad. This from-scratch interpretation will remind you why it's a classic, with its elixirlike dressing full of bold anchovy, garlic, and lemon juice. And here's the smoky twist: the croutons are made from artisan bread that's grilled and dabbed with a citrusy butter, then tossed with the salad along with bits of grilled lemon.

DRESSING:

1 heaping tablespoon freshly grated Parmigiano-Reggiano

1 teaspoon packed grated lemon zest

1 teaspoon Dijon mustard

2 to 3 medium anchovy fillets

1 to 2 medium cloves garlic

¼ teaspoon kosher salt

⅛ teaspoon freshly ground black pepper

2 tablespoons fresh lemon juice

6 tablespoons extra-virgin olive oil

CROUTONS:

¼ cup butter, room temperature

1 medium clove garlic, finely minced or grated

⅛ teaspoon kosher salt

½ teaspoon grated lemon zest

½ cup grated Parmigiano-Reggiano

3 large, 1-inch-thick slices artisan bread

1 tablespoon extra-virgin olive oil

SALAD:

1 lemon (optional)

1 tablespoon extra-virgin olive oil

Kosher salt

1 large heart of romaine lettuce, cut into 1-inch ribbons

¼ cup roughly chopped fresh Italian (flat-leaf) parsley

To make dressing: In a food processor add the cheese, lemon zest, mustard, anchovies, garlic, salt, pepper, and lemon juice; process until well-blended. With the motor running, slowly pour in the olive oil, and process until creamy and blended. Taste and adjust the seasonings; set aside.

To make croutons: Heat a gas or charcoal grill to medium (see note). Stir together the butter, garlic, salt, lemon zest, and cheese; set aside. Brush one side of the bread with olive oil. Grill oiled side until nicely browned, about 2 minutes. Flip, top the grilled side with the butter-cheese mixture, spreading evenly, close the lid, and grill until the bottom is browned also and the cheese is melted and bubbly, another 2 to 3 minutes. Transfer to a cutting board (do not turn off grill). When cool enough to handle, cut into cubes.

To make salad and grilled lemon: Slice the lemon into ⅛-inch slices and flick out any seeds with the tip of a knife. Brush with olive oil and season generously with salt. Wrap in a sheet of heavy-duty foil, sealing edges so the oil doesn't leak out. Place the packet on grill over medium heat until lemon slices are soft and browned, about 15 minutes. Transfer to a cutting board and chop into small pieces.

Toss the romaine with the dressing, then toss in the croutons, the parsley, and the chopped grilled lemons, if using. Serve immediately.

Note: To check grill temperature, count the seconds you can hold your hand, palm side down, 2 to 3 inches above the rack, until it feels uncomfortable: 4 seconds for medium.

— From Martha Holmberg

VIETNAMESE COLESLAW WITH SHREDDED CHICKEN AND PEANUTS

MAKES 6 SERVINGS

This main-dish salad has that unbeatable combination of sweet, salty, and tangy flavors. The only unusual ingredient is Vietnamese coriander; if you don't want to make a special trip to an Asian market, just add extra mint and/or cilantro. And if you're in a hurry, you can make this using leftover cooked chicken.

CHICKEN:

10 cups water
1 pound boneless, skinless chicken breast
    halves, trimmed of any fat

DRESSING:

3 tablespoons fresh lime juice (2 limes)
2 tablespoons plus 1 teaspoon fish sauce
1 tablespoon rice vinegar
1 tablespoon vegetable oil
1 tablespoon firmly packed palm sugar or
    light brown sugar
2 small cloves garlic, minced
2 teaspoons minced Thai or serrano chiles

COLESLAW:

½ cup thinly sliced onion (cut in half, then
    sliced into half-moons)
2 tablespoons sesame seeds
4½ cups shredded green cabbage
½ cup shredded carrot
⅓ cup fresh mint
⅓ cup fresh cilantro
⅓ cup Vietnamese coriander (rau rom), or
    additional mint or cilantro
Freshly ground black pepper
1 tablespoon unsalted dry-roasted peanuts,
    crushed in a mortar or finely chopped

To make chicken: In a 4- to 5-quart saucepan, bring the water to boil over high heat. Add the chicken and bring to a simmer. Cook for 5 minutes, then reduce heat to maintain a gentle simmer (the liquid should bubble just enough to break the surface); cook for 10 minutes.

Remove the pan from the heat and let the chicken stand, uncovered, in the liquid until cool enough to handle, or up to 1 hour. (At this point, the chicken will be very nearly cooked through and will finish the last bit of cooking in the hot liquid. It will also keep moist until ready to serve.)

Transfer the cooled chicken to a cutting board and shred it with your fingers, or cut into slices.

To make dressing: In a small mixing bowl, combine lime juice, fish sauce, vinegar, oil, sugar, garlic, and chiles. Stir until the sugar is dissolved and the dressing is well-blended.

To make coleslaw: Mix the sliced onion into the dressing to marinate and soften a bit.

Meanwhile, put the sesame seeds in a small skillet and toast over medium-low heat, stirring often, until light golden brown, about 3 minutes. Transfer to a small bowl and set aside.

Combine the shredded chicken, cabbage, carrots, mint, cilantro, and Vietnamese coriander in a large serving bowl. Remove the sliced onion from the dressing and add it to the bowl. Season with black pepper; add the peanuts and toasted sesame seeds.

Toss the coleslaw with the dressing until well-coated. Serve immediately.

— From *From Bangkok to Bali in 30 Minutes*, by Theresa Volpe Laursen and Byron Laursen (Harvard Common Press)

WARM CABBAGE AND GOAT CHEESE SALAD

MAKES 4 SERVINGS

Laura Werlin, author of *The New American Cheese*, has been a source for many Foodday stories. She describes eating this salad for the first time:

"I felt like a kid in a candy store, picking out the lush pieces of goat cheese here, the crunchy nuts there, the salty pancetta neutralized by the sweet balsamic, and the strings of cabbage that I could sort of twist around my fork. Being a salad fanatic anyway, I knew that the salad would soar to the top of my 'favorites' list. And there it remains."

½ medium red cabbage (about 1½ pounds)
½ cup pecan halves, toasted (see note)
3½ ounces Humboldt Fog or other fresh goat cheese, cut or pinched into small pieces (depending on the softness of the cheese)
½ cup coarsely chopped pancetta or 4 to 6 slices bacon, coarsely chopped
¼ cup olive oil
¼ cup balsamic vinegar
Salt and freshly ground black pepper

Slice the cabbage ¼ inch thick. Cut each slice in quarters and then separate the layers of cabbage. You'll end up with individual strands of cabbage about 1½ to 2 inches long. In a large bowl, toss the cabbage with the pecans and cheese.

In medium sauté pan, cook the pancetta over medium-high heat until crispy and dark brown. Drain on a paper towel and set aside. Discard the pancetta fat, but do not wash the pan. Return the pan to the stove and, over medium heat, add the olive oil. Heat the oil until it's very warm, but not hot or smoking. Turn off the heat, and add the vinegar. Mix well and immediately pour over the cabbage mixture.

Add the pancetta, and salt and pepper to taste. Toss and serve.

Note: To toast nuts, spread on baking sheet and bake in 350-degree oven for 5 to 8 minutes or until they start to brown.

— From *The New American Cheese*, by Laura Werlin (Stewart, Tabori and Chang)

LACINATO KALE SALAD WITH DRIED CRANBERRIES, CASHEWS, APPLE, AND CURRIED DRESSING

MAKES 6 TO 8 SERVINGS

The dark green, spear-shaped leaves of lacinato kale (aka cavalo nero, dinosaur, or Tuscan kale) are tender enough to eat raw, especially when they are marinated briefly in this easy curried dressing. Be sure to wash the leaves well and dry them in a salad spinner, or pat dry with paper towels, before slicing them.

SALAD:

1 bunch lacinato kale (10 ounces)
¼ small head red cabbage, finely
    shredded (2 cups)
1 cup roasted cashews
½ cup dried cranberries
½ Braeburn apple, unpeeled, cored,
    and cut into ½-inch dice

DRESSING:

½ Braeburn apple, peeled, cored, and chopped
1½ tablespoons apple cider vinegar
2 teaspoons honey
1 small clove garlic

1 teaspoon curry powder
Salt
¼ cup extra-virgin olive oil
Freshly ground black pepper

To make salad: Tear the kale leaves away from their tough center rib. Discard the ribs and slice the kale leaves into ½-inch-thick ribbons. Toss the kale, cabbage, cashews, cranberries, and apple together in a large serving bowl.

To make dressing: In a blender, combine the apple, vinegar, honey, garlic, curry powder, and ¼ teaspoon salt; blend until smooth. With the blender running and the lid slightly ajar, add the oil in a slow, steady stream.

Pour the dressing over the kale mixture and, with clean hands, "massage" the dressing into the salad leaves. Allow the mixture to marinate for 30 minutes before serving to allow kale leaves to wilt and turn tender. Season to taste with salt and pepper.

Make ahead: The salad components can be pre-pared up to 4 hours in advance. The dressing can be made up to two days in advance. Keep the salad greens and dressing refrigerated in separate containers; toss 30 minutes before you are ready to serve.

— From Ivy Manning

GREEN BEAN SALAD WITH RED ONION AND APRICOT VINAIGRETTE

MAKES 4 SERVINGS

Our taste testers raved about this salad. The key is the dressing: Its sweet, tart flavor and beau-tiful colors make this dish a standout. If fresh beans are not available, use high-quality frozen whole green beans and just defrost them rather than cooking them further.

RED ONION AND APRICOT VINAIGRETTE:

1 cup olive oil (divided)
½ medium red onion, diced
½ cup champagne vinegar
6 tablespoons diced dried apricots
¼ cup granulated sugar
Salt and freshly ground black pepper

SALAD:

1 pound fresh green beans
½ cup Red Onion and Apricot Vinaigrette
8 tablespoons crumbled gorgonzola cheese
    (4 ounces)
4 tablespoons chopped toasted almonds
    (see note)

To make vinaigrette: In a medium saucepan over medium heat, heat 1 tablespoon olive oil and sauté the red onion until translucent, about 3 to 4 minutes. Add the vinegar, apricots, and sugar, and bring just to a boil. Remove from the heat and cool.

Whisk in the remaining olive oil and salt and pepper to taste. Taste the dressing. If it's too sharp, add a little more sugar; if too sweet, add a little more vinegar. Makes 2 cups.

To make salad: Trim the stem ends from the green beans. Drop the beans into boiling salted water and when the water returns to the boil, time for 2 minutes. Drain and plunge the beans into ice water to chill and set the color. Drain and pat dry and chill.

When ready to serve, toss the chilled beans with ½ cup vinaigrette and divide among 4 salad plates. (Reserve remaining vinaigrette for another use.) Sprinkle with gorgonzola and almonds and serve.

Note: To toast nuts, spread on baking sheet and bake in 350-degree oven for 5 to 8 minutes, or until they start to brown.

Make ahead: Beans may be blanched, covered and refrigerated up to a day ahead before tossing with the vinaigrette. Vinaigrette can also be made ahead, and leftovers will keep for 2 to 3 weeks.

— From Caffe Mingo

FRESH ROMANO BEAN SALAD WITH BASIL DRESSING

MAKES 6 SERVINGS

Unlike many dressings, this one contains no vinegar or lemon juice, so that the beans keep their fresh green color. But thanks to some shallots and fresh herbs, there's plenty of flavor. If you're having guests, serve the beans in the center of a platter and surround them with overlapping slices of ripe red tomatoes, drizzled with some of the extra dressing.

BASIL DRESSING:
2 medium shallots
1 teaspoon Dijon mustard
1½ teaspoons salt
2 teaspoons granulated sugar
½ teaspoon freshly ground white pepper
2 tablespoons water
¾ cup vegetable oil or mild olive oil
20 fresh basil leaves

SALAD:
Salt
1½ pounds fresh romano beans or thin green beans, trimmed and cut into bite-size pieces
Ice water

To make dressing: With food processor running, drop shallots onto spinning blade to mince. Add mustard, salt, sugar, pepper, and water and process to blend.

With processor running, slowly drizzle in oil. Add basil and process to mince finely. Makes about 1 cup.

To make salad: Bring large pan of water to vigorous boil. Stir in 1 tablespoon salt. Add beans and cook 6 to 7 minutes only. Lift out with slotted spoon and place in big bowl of ice water. When beans are thoroughly cooled, spread them out on clean dish towel to dry.

When ready to serve, toss beans well with ½ cup dressing in a large mixing bowl. Taste and add more dressing or salt as needed. Serve immediately.

Make ahead: Dressing can be made up to a day ahead. When beans have been blanched, cooled, and dried, they can be placed in a zip-top plastic bag along with a dry paper towel. Squeeze out air, seal, and refrigerate until ready to use.

— Adapted from Shirley Corriher

PANZANELLA DI FRATELLI

MAKES 4 SERVINGS

Panzanella is a very simple recipe and depends on the very-best-quality tomatoes. If you don't have homegrown tomatoes in your garden, then go to a local farmers market or roadside stand. Do not attempt this recipe with poor-quality tomatoes.

2 cups cubed (¾-inch) fresh artisan bread
¼ cup fresh artisan breadcrumbs
1 cucumber, peeled, seeded, and cubed
1 red onion, julienned
2 homegrown tomatoes, cut into wedges
3 red bell peppers, roasted, seeded, and julienned (see note)
2 tablespoons drained and mashed capers
5 anchovy fillets, mashed into a paste
1 tablespoon minced garlic
⅓ cup red wine vinegar
Kosher salt and freshly cracked black pepper
1 cup extra-virgin olive oil
6 cups mixed salad greens
¼ cup freshly grated parmesan cheese
½ cup small fresh basil leaves

Preheat oven to 300 degrees.

Arrange the bread cubes in a single layer on a baking sheet. Place the breadcrumbs on another baking sheet. Bake until each is crisp and toasted (bread cubes may take as long as 30 to 45 minutes). Toss the breadcrumbs once or twice while baking. When crisp, remove from the oven to cool.

Meanwhile, in a mixing bowl, combine the cucumber, red onion, tomatoes, red peppers, and capers.

In a small bowl, combine the mashed anchovies, garlic, red wine vinegar, and salt and pepper to taste. Whisk in the olive oil.

Pour the dressing over the vegetables in the mixing bowl. Toss gently to coat and refrigerate for about 3 hours. Bring to room temperature before finishing the salad.

When ready to serve, drain the excess dressing from the vegetable mixture. Add the mixed greens, parmesan cheese, basil, toasted bread cubes, and toasted breadcrumbs. Toss gently and taste for seasoning. Adjust seasoning with salt and pepper. Arrange on one large plate or on 4 smaller plates and serve.

Note: To roast peppers, place on broiler pan, and broil about 5 to 6 inches from the heat source, turning often, until skin is charred on all sides. Place in a bag or covered bowl for about 15 minutes. Scrape or peel skin off.

— From Fratelli Ristorante

KEEP YOUR TOMATOES OUT OF THE COLD

Refrigeration turns tomatoes mealy and flavorless. So store them stem side up at room temperature—not in a sunny windowsill—and use them within a few days. Cherry tomatoes are the exception and seem to do fine with refrigeration. All tomatoes should be refrigerated after they've been cut or cooked.

ROASTED RED PEPPER AND MOZZARELLA SALAD

MAKES 10 SERVINGS

Annie Cuggino, executive chef at Veritable Quandary, says this is a great side dish with grilled Italian sausage. If you make the salad ahead, you may prefer to toss the cubes (or slices) of mozzarella cheese at the last minute, since they discolor in the balsamic vinegar, making them less attractive.

1 cup dry white wine

2 tablespoons golden raisins

3 pounds red bell peppers or a combination of yellow and red (about 6 large; see note)

½ to 1 pound fresh mozzarella cheese, drained

1 large or 2 small bunches fresh basil leaves, torn into pieces

2 cloves garlic, minced

Pinch of crushed red pepper flakes, or more to taste

3 tablespoons extra-virgin olive oil

3 tablespoons balsamic vinegar

Kosher salt and freshly ground black pepper

In a small saucepan, bring wine to a simmer, add golden raisins, remove from heat, and let set until raisins plump, at least 15 minutes.

Meanwhile, char bell peppers over a gas flame or under a broiler. Place peppers in a bag or covered bowl for about 15 minutes. Scrape or peel skin off. Seed peppers and cut into 1-inch squares, reserving any liquid that accumulates.

Cut mozzarella into 1-inch cubes. Toss together peppers, raisins and white wine, mozzarella, basil, garlic, and red pepper flakes.

Whisk together oil, vinegar, and any accumulated liquid from charred peppers, and drizzle over salad. Season with salt and pepper and serve at room temperature.

Note: You can use three 13- or 14-ounce jars of roasted peppers, drained on paper towels to remove excess juice.

— From executive chef Annie Cuggino,
Veritable Quandary

GET FRESH WITH MOZZARELLA

Most stores now carry fresh mozzarella as well as the regular variety that's typically shredded for pizza. Fresh mozzarella has a much softer texture and a more delicate flavor. It comes in a couple sizes—including little balls called bocconcini—and is often packed in whey or water. Fresh mozzarella is very perishable and should be used within a day or two of purchase. While it does very nicely on pizza, regular mozzarella is not a very good substitute for fresh.

CUMIN-SPICED CARROT SALAD

MAKES 4 SERVINGS

This Moroccan-flavored dish is a perfectly balanced combination of pungent cumin, sweet carrots and honey, tangy vinegar and hot chiles. Fooddαy contributor Matthew Card says the salad benefits from being allowed to rest before serving, which mellows the flavor and makes it convenient for entertaining.

- 1 medium clove garlic, grated or minced very fine
- 1 large jalapeño chile, seeded and minced fine
- 3 tablespoons white wine vinegar
- 2 teaspoons very mild honey (or 1 teaspoon each honey and sugar if honey has a strong flavor)
- ½ teaspoon ground cumin
- 3 tablespoons extra-virgin olive oil or vegetable oil
- Salt
- Cayenne pepper
- 1¼ to 1½ pounds carrots, peeled, trimmed and shredded
- 1 cup chopped fresh cilantro or Italian (flat-leaf) parsley

In large mixing bowl, whisk together garlic, jalapeño, vinegar, honey, and cumin; let sit for 15 minutes to macerate. Whisk in oil until dressing is emulsified; adjust seasoning to taste with salt and cayenne (the dressing should be assertive and tart). Stir in carrots and herb, adjust salt to taste and serve.

Make ahead: Salad can be made from 1 hour up to 1 day ahead, which will mellow the flavors a bit.

— From Matthew Card

TAMING THE TASTE OF RAW GARLIC

If you dislike biting into pieces of raw garlic, grate the cloves on a Microplane-style grater instead of chopping or mincing them. The grater ensures tiny, uniform bits and avoids larger, harsh-tasting pieces.

MOROCCAN SWEET POTATO SALAD

MAKES 6 SERVINGS

In the Moroccan kitchen, a delicious marinade known as charmoula often flavors fish and vegetable dishes. With a bit of olive oil mixed in, the charmoula becomes a vinaigrette that's delicious on sweet potatoes—as well as on grilled fish or chicken.

Be sure to keep a close eye on the potatoes as they cook, because a few extra minutes in the oven can leave their texture softer than you want for a salad.

- 4 medium sweet potatoes (about 2½ pounds total; see note), peeled and cut into 1-inch cubes
- ⅓ cup plus 2 tablespoons olive oil (divided)
- ¾ teaspoon salt (divided)
- 2 cloves garlic, minced
- 1 teaspoon ground cumin
- 1 teaspoon paprika
- ⅛ teaspoon cayenne pepper
- 3 tablespoons lemon juice
- ⅓ cup chopped fresh parsley

▶

⅓ cup chopped fresh cilantro
⅓ cup sliced almonds, lightly toasted
(see note)

Preheat oven to 425 degrees. Toss the sweet potatoes with 2 tablespoons olive oil and ¼ teaspoon salt. Put the sweet potatoes on a baking sheet or in a roasting pan and cook, stirring once, until tender, about 15 minutes. Keep warm in a large bowl.

Meanwhile, in a small bowl, make the charmoula by combining the garlic, cumin, paprika, cayenne, lemon juice and the remaining ½ teaspoon salt. Whisk in the remaining ⅓ cup olive oil and then add the parsley and cilantro.

Gently combine the roasted sweet potatoes with the charmoula and the toasted almonds. Serve at room temperature.

Note: There are several varieties of sweet potatoes, but for this recipe you should use the red-skinned, orange-fleshed potatoes that are usually labeled "yams."

Note: To toast nuts, spread on baking sheet and bake in 350-degree oven for 5 to 8 minutes, or until they start to brown.

Make ahead: Salad can be made and refrigerated up to one day ahead. Bring to room temperature before serving.

— From Laura B. Russell

> ## YAMS: MISTAKEN IDENTITY
> There are several varieties of sweet potatoes, but for this recipe we recommend the dark-skinned, orange-fleshed potatoes that are usually labeled "yams." Despite the fact that true yams aren't common in the U.S., stores still persist in calling dark-skinned sweet potatoes, such as garnets and jewels varieties, yams.

BLACK BEAN SALAD WITH MANGO, CITRUS, AND CRUNCHY JICAMA

MAKES 4 TO 6 SERVINGS

Former Foodday editor Martha Holmberg punches up her black bean salad with oranges and limes as well as chipotle chiles, which are dried and smoked jalapeños. For this recipe you'll want chipotles canned in adobo sauce, available in the Mexican foods section of most supermarkets. You can freeze the extra in a plastic container for up to a year.

DRESSING:
1 teaspoon finely grated orange zest
¼ cup fresh orange juice
1 teaspoon finely grated lime zest
¼ cup fresh lime juice
2 teaspoons granulated sugar
1 teaspoon seeded and finely minced canned chipotle chile in adobo sauce
1 teaspoon minced garlic
½ teaspoon kosher salt
¼ teaspoon freshly ground black pepper

SALAD:
2 (15-ounce) cans black beans
1 ripe mango, cut into ¼-inch dice (to yield about 1⅓ cups)

1 cup ¼-inch diced jicama (about half of a
   2-pound jicama)
2 tablespoons minced red onion
¼ cup finely sliced fresh basil
3 tablespoons extra-virgin olive oil

To make dressing: In a medium bowl, add the orange zest and juice, the lime zest and juice, the sugar, chipotle, garlic, salt, and pepper; whisk together until the sugar has dissolved; set aside.

To make salad: In a medium saucepan, heat the beans in their liquid until warm, but not boiling.

Drain and rinse gently in warm water and drain again well.

Add the warm beans to the dressing and fold together, using a rubber spatula to gently fold so the beans are well-coated but not smashed. Let the beans sit for a few minutes and then toss a few more times. It may seem like too much liquid at first, but the beans will gradually absorb it all.

Gently fold in the mango, jicama, onion, basil, and olive oil; serve.

—From Martha Holmberg

ROASTED BEET SALAD WITH TOASTED PECANS AND GOAT CHEESE

MAKES 4 SERVINGS

Sweet, earthy beets and tangy goat cheese were made for each other. And oven-roasting the beets gives them a silken texture and a more concentrated flavor than beets that have been boiled.

1 bunch (4 medium) beets with tops (one
   color or a mix)
5 tablespoons extra-virgin olive oil
3 tablespoons sherry vinegar or mild fruit
   vinegar
½ teaspoon finely minced garlic
½ teaspoon kosher salt
Freshly ground black pepper
4 cups packed mixed baby salad greens
¼ cup finely slivered sweet yellow onion
½ cup broken pecans, walnuts or other nuts,
   toasted (see note)
3 ounces very cold goat cheese, crumbled
   onto a plate and refrigerated until ready
   to serve

Preheat oven to 400 degrees.

Cut green tops from beets, leaving about ½ inch of stem attached. Set tops aside to braise and serve as a side dish at another meal, if desired.

Wash beets and dry. Wrap each tightly in a square of foil, and roast until tender when pierced with a skewer, about 1 hour or more, depending on size of beets. Cool, unwrap foil, and rub off skin. Trim stems and ends, and cut into ½-inch wedges. Set aside in a small bowl. Strain any juices left in foil over beet wedges.

In a large bowl, whisk together the olive oil, vinegar, garlic, salt, and pepper to taste until blended. Add 1 tablespoon of dressing to beets in small bowl and toss to coat. Add salad greens and onion to large bowl; toss to coat with dressing.

Divide greens among 4 salad plates. Top with beets and drizzle with any reserved juices; add toasted nuts and goat cheese, dividing evenly. Or serve in a large salad bowl, beginning with greens and topping with beets, reserved juices, nuts, and goat cheese.

▶

Note: To toast nuts, spread on baking sheet and bake in 350-degree oven for 5 to 8 minutes or until they start to brown. This can be done while oven is still hot from roasting beets.

— From Marie Simmons

WILD RICE SALAD WITH DRIED CHERRIES AND HAZELNUTS

MAKES 6 SERVINGS

It doesn't get much more local than wild rice, cherries and hazelnuts. Peter Leigh Gallin, Applewood Restaurant's executive chef and owner, created this colorful salad and likes to pair it with grilled salmon or roasted pork loin.

2 tablespoons vegetable oil
¼ cup apple cider vinegar
¼ cup firmly packed brown sugar
2 teaspoons ground cinnamon
Pinch ground cloves
Pinch ground cardamom
Salt and freshly ground black pepper
2 cups cooked and cooled white rice, preferably basmati or jasmine (⅔ cup uncooked)
2 cups cooked and cooled wild rice (⅔ cup uncooked; see note)
½ cup dried Bing cherries
½ cup toasted, coarsely chopped hazelnuts (see note)
2 tablespoons minced fresh chives

In a medium bowl, whisk together the oil, vinegar, sugar, cinnamon, cloves, cardamom, and salt and pepper to taste.

In a large bowl, mix the cooked white and wild rice with the cherries and hazelnuts. Just before serving, toss with dressing and chives. Season to taste with salt and pepper.

Note: To cook the wild rice, cook ⅔ cup rice in 2⅔ cups simmering water, covered, for 35 to 40 minutes. The rice is done when two-thirds of the grains have "exploded." Uncover, fluff with a fork and simmer an additional 5 minutes. Drain off any excess liquid.

Note: To toast hazelnuts, spread the shelled nuts in a shallow pan and roast in a 350-degree oven for 8 to 10 minutes or until the skins crack. Rub warm nuts with a rough cloth or between your hands to remove as much skin as possible.

Make ahead: The dressing can be made up and refrigerated up to several days ahead. The salad can be made without the hazelnuts and refrigerated up to a day ahead; bring to room temperature, then toss with dressing and nuts just before serving.

— From Peter Leigh Gallin, executive chef/owner,
Applewood Restaurant and Bar, Vancouver, Washington

Toast hazelnuts until skins crack and nuts are brown, then rub the warm nuts in a rough towel or between your palms until most of the skin is gone.

TUNA SALAD WITH MANGO CHUTNEY

MAKES 4 MAIN COURSE SERVINGS OR 6 TO 8 SANDWICHES

This unlikely sounding combination of ingredients works—quite well in fact. The key is to drain the tuna and rinse it several times before adding the other ingredients. Major Grey's mango chutney is widely available, but you can substitute another brand.

5 (5-ounce) cans light tuna in spring
   water, drained
¼ cup mayonnaise
¾ cup Major Grey's mango chutney
2 tablespoons curry powder
2 tablespoons sliced almonds plus extra for
   garnish, toasted (see note)
Lettuce leaves
Tomato wedges
Shredded Monterey jack cheese, to garnish
Shredded cheddar cheese, to garnish

Place the drained tuna in a strainer and rinse several times, until the water runs clear. Drain well, pressing as much water out of the tuna as possible. In a medium bowl, combine the tuna, mayonnaise, chutney, curry powder, and toasted almonds. Stir well.

Line four plates with lettuce leaves and divide the tuna salad among the plates. Garnish each plate with tomato wedges, shredded Monterey jack and cheddar cheeses, and toasted almonds.

Note: To toast nuts, spread on baking sheet; bake in 350-degree oven for 5 to 8 minutes or until they start to brown.

— From Geoff Hyde, former owner of Pot Belly Deli

SOUPS

3

GUBANC'S CHICKEN TORTILLA SOUP

MAKES 20 CUPS

Although the ingredient list for this soup is long, it's not difficult to make, and the results are well worth it. For a shortcut, follow the note at the end of the recipe on substituting canned broth for the homemade chicken stock. The recipe makes enough soup for a party, so we suggest you throw one.

CHICKEN STOCK:

2 onions, sliced

2 carrots, sliced

2 stalks celery, sliced

½ head garlic, cut crosswise and broken into cloves

1 jalapeño chile, cut into pieces

1 (4-pound) chicken, cut into 10 pieces

1 teaspoon black peppercorns

½ teaspoon dried oregano

1 bay leaf

2 sprigs fresh parsley (optional)

8 cups cold water

SEASONING MIX:

4 teaspoons kosher salt

2½ teaspoons dried oregano

1 teaspoon onion powder

1 teaspoon garlic powder

½ teaspoon ground black pepper

½ teaspoon ground cumin

¼ teaspoon paprika

¼ teaspoon chili powder

SOUP:

3 tablespoons butter or olive oil

2 cups chopped onion (divided)

3 tablespoons minced garlic (divided)

2 cups sliced carrots (3 medium carrots)

1 (28-ounce) can diced tomatoes in juice

8 cups Chicken Stock (see note)

2 cups diced green bell peppers

(2 medium peppers)

2 cups sliced zucchini (2 small zucchini)

1 cup sliced ripe olives

1 (4-ounce) can mild green chiles

1 fresh jalapeño chile, seeded and minced

2 cups frozen corn

1 (15-ounce) can tomato sauce

Reserved chicken meat

¼ cup fresh lime juice (2 to 3 limes)

8 ounces shredded Monterey jack cheese (2 cups)

1 bunch fresh cilantro, leaves and tender stems chopped

1 (15-ounce) bag tortilla chips

To make stock: Preheat oven to 400 degrees.

Line a baking pan with foil and spray with non-sick cooking spray. Place onions, carrots, celery, garlic, and jalapeño on pan. Place chicken pieces on top of the vegetables and roast for 1 hour, tossing occasionally.

Remove from oven, and place chicken and vegetables in a stockpot with peppercorns, oregano, bay leaf, parsley, and water. Bring to a boil, reduce heat, and simmer for 30 minutes.

Remove chicken from stock. When chicken is cool enough to handle, remove meat from skin and bones, and chop meat. Refrigerate meat until ready to use. Return bones and skin to stockpot; simmer for another 1½ hours.

Strain chicken stock and refrigerate in a shallow pan to cool. When stock has cooled, skim and discard fat.

To make seasoning mix: In a small bowl, combine the salt, oregano, onion powder, garlic powder, black pepper, cumin, paprika, and chili powder. Stir to mix well.

To make soup: In a stockpot, heat the butter or oil over medium heat. Add the onions, the seasoning mix, and garlic. Sauté for 5 to 8 minutes, or until onions are translucent. Add the carrots, diced tomatoes and their juice, and the chicken stock. Bring to a boil, reduce heat, and simmer until the carrots are almost tender, about 5 minutes.

Add the green pepper, zucchini, olives, green chiles, jalapeño, corn, and tomato sauce. Bring to a simmer and simmer until the zucchini is tender-crisp, being careful not to overcook vegetables. Add the reserved chicken and lime juice. Season to taste with the remaining garlic and any additional seasonings desired. Garnish each serving with shredded cheese, cilantro, and tortilla chips.

Note: You can use canned chicken broth in place of homemade stock. Be sure to eliminate the salt and cook about 1 pound of boneless skinless chicken breast in the broth for about 20 minutes. Use this chicken in the recipe.

Make ahead: Stock will keep in the refrigerator for up to 3 days. Freeze for longer storage.

— From Gubanc's Pub, Lake Oswego

WEST AFRICAN CHICKEN-PEANUT SOUP

MAKES 6 SERVINGS

Several of Portland's McMenamins taverns serve this spicy, warming soup, which made Foodday's "Best of" list in 2000.

1 cup diced cooked chicken
⅔ cup diced onion
1½ teaspoons minced garlic
2 tablespoons dark sesame oil
1½ teaspoons curry powder
½ teaspoon salt
½ teaspoon freshly ground black pepper
½ teaspoon crushed red pepper flakes
3 cups chicken broth
¼ cup tomato paste
1 cup chopped stewed tomatoes, drained
3 tablespoons chunky peanut butter

In a large pot, sauté the chicken, onion and garlic in the sesame oil until the onion is tender, about 10 minutes. Add the curry powder, salt, pepper, and red pepper flakes; sauté 1 minute more.

Add the chicken broth, tomato paste, stewed tomatoes, and peanut butter, stirring until well-combined. Heat until very hot, but not boiling. Serve immediately.

— From the Blue Moon Tavern and Grill

BASICS ON BROTH AND STOCK

Strictly speaking, stock is made with bones, and broth is not. The gelatin in the bones helps give stock, and your food, more body and richness. If a Foodday recipe involves making a homemade stock, we refer to it as stock. Otherwise, we just call for broth, although commercial stock is now becoming more widely available. Whether you buy broth or stock, it's important that it smell and taste good. If it doesn't, it won't do your food any favors. Also, since many brands of regular broth can be loaded with salt, it's a good idea to choose a reduced-sodium option and season your dish with salt to taste.

THAI GINGER-CHICKEN SOUP

MAKES 16 SERVINGS

This recipe ran with our story on making large-batch meals to freeze. There's no pre-cooking required before freezing, which makes it especially easy. Wait and buy the fresh garnishes when you're ready to thaw the soup and heat.

3 (14-ounce) cans unsweetened
    coconut milk
3 (14-ounce) cans unsweetened
    lite coconut milk
8 cups low-sodium chicken broth (2 quarts)
4 pounds boneless, skinless chicken thighs,
    either cooked or uncooked, sliced into
    ½-inch chunks
1 (4-inch) knob fresh ginger, peeled
    and grated
¼ cup plus 2 tablespoons fish sauce
1 cup fresh lime juice (5 to 6 limes)
¼ cup grated lime zest (4 to 5 limes)
½ cup thinly sliced scallions, including
    some tender green tops
¼ cup chopped fresh cilantro
2 cups thinly sliced sugar snap peas
2 (10-ounce) bags frozen corn kernels
Garnishes: 2 cups sliced fresh mushrooms,
    Thai red curry paste to taste, lime wedges,
    chopped fresh cilantro

To assemble: In a large pot, combine coconut milks, broth, chicken, ginger, fish sauce, lime juice, lime zest, scallions, cilantro, sugar snap peas, and corn. Divide mixture among four 1-gallon zip-top freezer bags. Label with contents and reheating instructions, and freeze.

To serve: Heat the soup in a pot over medium heat. Simmer until chicken is cooked through and flavors have melded. Stir in fresh sliced mushrooms. At the table, add curry paste to taste (start with ¼ teaspoon or less per serving) and garnish with lime wedges and cilantro.

— From Linda Faus

NOT ALL COCONUT MILK IS THE SAME

Few of us have the time to crack, peel, and grate a fresh coconut, so hurray for store-bought coconut products. Just be sure you're using the right one:

Coconut milk: The unsweetened liquid made from the flesh of a coconut. If the can you open has a layer of thickened cream at the top, just stir it into the milk. (Some producers of canned milk, worried that consumers may be put off by this separation, add thickening agents to keep the milk "homogenized.")

Lite coconut milk: Contains 60 to 70 percent fewer calories than regular coconut milk. It can be used as a substitute in most recipes, but be warned that it's thinner and less rich than regular.

Cream of coconut: A thick, intensely sweet mixture of coconut paste, water, and sugar used in drinks such as piña coladas and in some desserts. Find it at most supermarkets in the aisle with the bar supplies and mixers.

Coconut cream: The thick, fat-rich part of coconut milk that rises to the top of coconut milk, something that occurs naturally and is not a sign of poor quality. You can also buy coconut cream in Asian markets.

UHT (Ultra High Temperature) coconut cream: Shelf-stable coconut cream sold in aseptic boxes. Sold in Asian markets.

CHICKEN, MUSHROOM, AND WILD RICE SOUP

MAKES ABOUT 10 CUPS

Former Foodday home economist Sharon Maasdam developed this recipe specifically for make-ahead meals that you can freeze. Note that the milk and sherry aren't added to the soup until just before serving time.

½ cup uncooked wild rice
2 tablespoons butter
1 medium onion, chopped
½ cup diced celery
1 pound fresh mushrooms, thinly sliced (5 cups)
7 cups chicken broth (divided)
½ teaspoon freshly ground black pepper
¾ teaspoon curry powder
¾ teaspoon dry mustard
¾ teaspoon paprika
¾ teaspoon dried chervil or ½ teaspoon dried sage
2 cups diced cooked chicken breast
½ cup all-purpose flour
2 cups milk
3 tablespoons dry sherry
Salt

Cook wild rice according to package directions, about 45 to 55 minutes.

Melt butter in large skillet over medium heat. Add onion and celery, and sauté about 5 minutes. Add mushrooms and cook until liquid is gone, about 10 minutes.

Place 6 cups chicken broth in a 3-quart saucepan and heat to simmering; add vegetable mixture, pepper, curry powder, dry mustard, paprika, chervil, and chicken.

Mix remaining 1 cup chicken broth with the flour and whisk until lumps disappear. Add to soup and stir until soup thickens slightly. Either freeze now as directed below, or to serve, add milk, sherry, and salt to taste.

Make ahead: After flour mixture has been added and the soup thickened, remove from heat, cool slightly, and place in freezer containers. Refrigerate until thoroughly chilled. Freeze for 2 to 3 months. When ready to serve, defrost in refrigerator, heat and add milk, sherry, and salt, if desired.

— From Sharon Maasdam

MUSHROOMS NEED MINIMAL CLEANING

Mushrooms arrive in markets quite clean, since they're grown in sterilized peat instead of dirt. So the best way to clean them is to wipe them with a damp cloth, or rinse quickly in cool water and pat dry with paper towels. Don't soak them, because they're like a sponge and absorb liquid quickly. To clean under the caps, or the folded edges of chanterelles, use a soft-bristled toothbrush and water. Cut off the bottom of the stem if it's dirty or dried out.

MAMA LEONE'S CHICKEN SOUP

MAKES 15 CUPS

New Yorkers who miss the homey Italian restaurant Mama Leone's will love this soup, which Elephants Delicatessen says was inspired by a version served at that late and lamented restaurant. It goes together quickly and is perfect for a chilly weeknight meal.

8 ounces boneless, skinless chicken
   breast halves
Kosher salt and freshly ground black pepper
2 tablespoons vegetable oil
3 tablespoons butter
1 medium onion, diced
3 stalks celery, diced
1 tablespoon minced garlic
½ teaspoon dried tarragon
½ teaspoon dried oregano
2 teaspoons sweet Hungarian paprika
½ cup plus 2 tablespoons all-purpose flour
8 cups chicken broth
1 (14½-ounce) can diced tomatoes in juice
¾ cup whipping cream
2 cups thinly sliced fresh spinach

Preheat oven to 375 degrees.

Season chicken with salt and black pepper to taste and place on a baking sheet. Bake for 15 to 20 minutes. Remove from oven and cool. When cool enough to handle, dice the meat and set aside until needed.

While the chicken is baking, heat the oil in a stockpot over medium heat. Add the butter and melt. Sauté the onions and celery until the onions are translucent, about 6 to 7 minutes. Add the garlic, tarragon, oregano, paprika, 2 teaspoons salt, and ½ teaspoon pepper. Cook, stirring, for 3 or 4 minutes. Add the flour and stir until well-combined.

Slowly whisk in the chicken broth and bring to a boil. Add the tomatoes and cream. Reduced heat and simmer for 20 minutes. Add the reserved chicken and simmer 10 minutes more. Just before serving, stir in the spinach.

— From Scott Weaver, co-owner and executive chef,
   Elephants Delicatessen

SANTA FE CHICKEN AND WHITE BEAN SOUP

MAKES 10 TO 12 LARGE SERVINGS

Over the years this has been one of Foodday's most requested recipes. If you have leftover cooked chicken meat on hand, feel free to substitute it for the fresh chicken and add during the final cooking time; cook just until heated through.

2½ cups Great Northern beans, soaked in
   water to cover overnight
11 cups reduced-sodium chicken broth
   (divided)

1 tablespoon dried oregano
1 tablespoon dried parsley
4 to 5 teaspoons salt
4 teaspoons ground cumin
2 teaspoons garlic powder
1½ teaspoons onion powder
1 teaspoon paprika
½ teaspoon chili powder
⅛ teaspoon freshly ground white pepper
⅛ teaspoon freshly ground black pepper

Pinch cayenne pepper, or to taste
Pinch crushed red pepper flakes, or to taste
6 tablespoons butter
3 tablespoons olive oil
4 cups chopped onions
2 cups chopped green bell pepper
1 cup chopped celery
1½ tablespoons minced garlic (divided)
2 to 3 tablespoons all-purpose flour
1 pound boneless, skinless chicken breast
    halves, cut into ¾-inch pieces
1 (7-ounce) can diced mild green chiles
Garnishes: shredded havarti cheese, salsa,
    sour cream, and chopped fresh cilantro

Drain the soaked beans. Combine in a large pot with 8 cups chicken broth. Bring to a boil; cover and simmer 1½ to 2 hours or until tender.

In a small bowl, combine oregano, parsley, 4 teaspoons salt, cumin, garlic powder, onion powder, paprika, chili powder, white and black peppers, cayenne, and red pepper flakes; set aside.

In a stockpot, heat butter and olive oil; add onions, bell pepper, celery, ½ tablespoon garlic (1½ teaspoons), and a third of the reserved seasoning mix. Sauté over medium heat about 5 minutes. Add another ½ tablespoon garlic and another third of the seasoning mix; continue sautéing until celery is tender. Add remaining ½ tablespoon garlic, remaining seasoning mix, and 2 to 3 tablespoons flour; cook 5 to 7 minutes longer. Whisk in remaining 3 cups chicken broth, cooking until thickened.

Add cooked beans and their broth, chicken, and green chiles; heat until chicken is just cooked, about 5 to 6 minutes. Serve hot in bowls garnished with havarti cheese, salsa, sour cream, and cilantro.

— From Gubanc's Pub, Lake Oswego

A DIFFERENT KIND OF BURN

Freezer burn—those whitish patches on frozen food—is caused by dry air in the freezer circulating over exposed surfaces on the food. The food isn't unsafe to eat, but it has lost flavor and texture quality. To prevent freezer burn, remove as much air as possible from the package and ensure an airtight seal.

PEELING GARLIC

Separate cloves and press each firmly with flat side of knife until the cloves crack and skin breaks. Peel off the skin and then mince or crush in a garlic press.

SEA HAG CLAM CHOWDER

MAKES 6 TO 8 SERVINGS

This is a classic clam chowder, thick and creamy. The recipe uses lots of pots and pans, but it's worth the cleanup time.

¾ cup butter (1½ sticks), plus additional
    for garnish
1 cup all-purpose flour
3 (6-ounce) cans chopped clams
4 (8-ounce) bottles clam juice
¾ ounce clam base, about 1 tablespoon
    (optional; see note)
¼ teaspoon dried basil
¼ teaspoon dried thyme
8 ounces chopped bacon
¾ cup chopped celery
¾ cup chopped onion
3 cups peeled, diced (½-inch) potatoes
4 cups milk or half-and-half
Chopped fresh parsley for garnish

In a small saucepan, melt ¾ cup butter over medium heat. Stir in flour to make a roux. Continue to cook for 20 minutes, stirring occasionally.

In the meantime, drain clams, reserving juice. In a stockpot or Dutch oven, combine reserved juice and clam juice. Stir in clam base, if using, and basil and thyme. Bring to a boil.

In a separate skillet, cook bacon until limp and slightly brown on the edges. Drain off excess fat. Add celery and onion. Continue to cook for 5 minutes or until tender-crisp.

Cook potatoes in lightly salted water just until tender. Drain.

Stir roux into boiling clam juice, using a wire whisk to blend thoroughly. Stir in clams, bacon mixture, and potatoes. Bring mixture back to a boil, then reduce heat.

Stir in milk or half-and-half. Do not let soup boil. Top each serving with a pat of butter and chopped fresh parsley.

Note: Find clam base at stores that carry a wide selection of gourmet foods. Two brands are Better Than Bouillon, and Minor's.

— From Gracie's Sea Hag Restaurant & Lounge, Depoe Bay

NANA'S CIOPPINO

MAKES 6 SERVINGS

This cioppino tastes like you slaved all day, but the preparation is simple and it comes together quickly. Best of all, it tastes terrific. Feel free to swap in whatever seafood looks best or is most affordable.

¼ cup vegetable oil
2 cups chopped onion
2 cloves garlic, chopped

½ cup chopped celery
½ cup chopped green bell pepper
1 (28-ounce) can whole tomatoes
2 (8-ounce) cans tomato sauce
1 cup dry red or white wine
1½ cups bottled clam juice or water
    (12 ounces)
1 bay leaf
1 teaspoon dried basil

1 teaspoon dried oregano

1 teaspoon dried thyme

¼ teaspoon granulated sugar

2 teaspoons salt (less if using clam juice)

½ teaspoon freshly ground black pepper

Tabasco or other hot sauce

1½ pounds firm white fish (such as halibut, cod, or snapper)

10 ounces bay scallops

1 pound shrimp, peeled and deveined

1 (10-ounce) can clams (or substitute a couple of shell-on clams per person)

1 cooked Dungeness crab, cleaned, broken into pieces and shells cracked, but left on

In a stockpot over medium heat, add oil and sauté onion, garlic, celery, and green pepper until tender. Add tomatoes, tomato sauce, wine, clam juice, bay leaf, basil, oregano, thyme, sugar, salt, pepper, and Tabasco to taste. Break up tomatoes and heat to boiling. Reduce heat and simmer, uncovered, for 30 minutes.

Cut up fish fillets. (If you use frozen fish, do not fully thaw; this will ease cutting.) Bring tomato mixture to a boil; add fish, scallops, shrimp, clams, and crab; cook just until fish is opaque, about 10 to 15 minutes. Do not overcook, or seafood will be tough.

— From a beloved nana, Millie Wigginton

DUNGENESS CRAB IN A MANGO-COCONUT-RED CURRY BROTH

MAKES 6 SERVINGS

Local Ocean Seafoods, on Newport's historic bayfront, is one of the most popular restaurants on Oregon's coast. This spicy curry from Local Ocean chefs won the professional division of the Great Newport Seafood Cook-Off in 2009.

Vegetable oil

½ package thin rice-stick noodles (about 7 ounces)

4 cups water

1½ tablespoons granulated sugar

2 tablespoons clam base or chicken bouillon paste (such as Better Than Bouillon brand), or 4 chicken bouillon cubes

¼ cup seasoned rice vinegar

¼ cup lime juice

2 tablespoons lemon juice

1 tablespoon Thai red curry paste

1 (1-inch) knob fresh ginger, peeled and thinly sliced

1 stalk lemon grass, peeled and cut into ½-inch pieces

1 teaspoon fish sauce

2 (14- to 19-ounce) cans coconut milk

8 ounces peeled and diced fresh ripe mangoes

8 ounces cooked Dungeness crabmeat, picked over for any shell bits

½ bunch fresh basil, stemmed and cut in chiffonade (thin strips)

½ bunch scallions, trimmed and sliced on the bias

Line a large bowl with paper towels and set aside. Add 2 inches of oil to a saucepan. If you have a candy thermometer, place it into the oil and heat to 400 degrees. Break up the rice-stick noodles. If you do not have a candy thermometer, you can test to see if the oil is done with a few of the noodles; they should immediately sizzle.

Drop noodles into the hot oil, and as soon as they puff up, pull them out with tongs or a slotted spoon, and place into prepared bowl.

▶

In a stockpot or large saucepan whisk together the 4 cups water with the sugar and clam base. Once fully incorporated, whisk in the rice vinegar, lime juice, lemon juice, curry paste, ginger, lemon grass, and fish sauce. If you prefer a spicier flavor, add more curry paste. Bring mixture to a boil, then reduce heat to a simmer. Add the coconut milk; when it returns to a simmer, use a slotted spoon to remove the lemon grass and ginger. Simmer for 20 minutes.

In a serving bowl, place the mangoes and rice-stick noodles. Ladle soup over the top and garnish with crab, basil, and scallions.

— From executive chef Charlie Branford and sous chef Enrique Sanchez Rodriguez, Local Ocean Seafoods

FRESH GINGER IS AN EASY KEEPER

Fresh ginger, unpeeled, will keep for a week or two wrapped in a paper towel or brown bag. For longer storage, peel and place in a jar of dry sherry or Chinese cooking wine (shao hsing). The wine takes on some ginger flavor and can be used in stir-fries or other Asian dishes. Or, place in a freezer bag and freeze; when ready to use, peel the skin, and grate or slice it frozen. Return remainder to the freezer, where it will maintain its flavor for a month or two.

TELETHA'S CRAB, SHRIMP, AND ANDOUILLE SAUSAGE GUMBO

MAKES 10 SERVINGS

Teletha Benjamin grew up in Lafayette, Louisiana, and knows her gumbo. When we featured her in a Fooday story she told us that the key to a deeply flavored gumbo is the roux, the fat-and-flour mixture that thickens and flavors the stew. You need to cook it until it's a deep brown, so don't be tempted to rush this step. Teletha serves her gumbo in shallow soup bowls over jasmine rice, accompanied by French bread, a salad, and wine.

1¼ cups vegetable oil (divided)
1½ cups all-purpose flour
4 pounds chicken parts, skin removed on all
    pieces except wings and drumsticks
Seasoned salt
1 pound andouille sausages; split lengthwise
    and cut into 1-inch pieces

1 medium onion, chopped
3 stalks celery, chopped
3 large cloves garlic, chopped
1 cup chopped green bell pepper
1 cup chopped red bell pepper
½ cup chopped fresh parsley, plus more
    for garnish
1 bunch scallions (white and green parts),
    chopped
6 cups reduced-sodium chicken broth
6 cups water
Salt and freshly ground black pepper
Garlic salt with parsley (see note)
½ teaspoon cayenne pepper, or more to taste
1 pound large shrimp, peeled and deveined
1 large cooked Dungeness crab, cleaned,
    broken into pieces and shells cracked,
    but left on
Gumbo filé powder, to taste (see note)
Hot cooked jasmine rice

51

In a medium cast-iron skillet, heat ¾ cup oil over medium heat. Whisk in the flour to form a paste (roux). Cook over medium-low to medium heat, stirring constantly, for 15 to 20 minutes. Do not leave roux unattended while it's cooking or it could burn. When the roux is the color of refried beans (medium brown) and smells like toasted wheat, remove from heat and set aside to cool.

With a heavy chef's knife or cleaver, cut the chicken into smaller pieces: Cut each breast half into quarters, the thighs in half, separate the wings at the joint, and leave drumsticks whole. Season the chicken with seasoned salt and set aside.

In a large cast-iron skillet, heat ¼ cup vegetable oil over medium-high heat. Add the sausage and brown on all sides. Remove and set aside.

Reheat the skillet, adding a little more oil if necessary. Add the seasoned chicken pieces to the hot skillet and brown, turning several times. Remove and set aside.

In a stockpot heat the remaining ¼ cup oil over medium-high heat. Sauté the onion and celery until just tender, about 2 minutes. Add the garlic and peppers, and sauté another 3 to 4 minutes. Stir in the chopped parsley and scallions. Add the reserved cooked sausage and chicken pieces.

Add the chicken broth and the 6 cups water. Slowly add the roux by spoonfuls to the broth mixture, whisking to incorporate into the broth. Season to taste with more Season-All, salt, black pepper, and garlic salt with parsley. Add cayenne pepper. Bring to a boil, reduce heat and simmer gently, uncovered, for about 30 minutes.

Add the shrimp and simmer for another 3 to 4 minutes. Stir in the crab pieces and continue to cook until the crab is heated through. Taste and adjust seasoning. Divide rice among serving bowls, spoon gumbo over rice, and sprinkle with file powder. Garnish with additional parsley.

Note: Find McCormick's garlic salt with parsley (California-style Garlic Salt) in the spice aisle of most supermarkets.

Note: Filé powder, which is finely ground sassafras root, flavors and slightly thickens gumbo. It's available at markets that carry a wide selection of gourmet foods.

— From Teletha Benjamin

TOMATO-ORANGE SOUP

MAKES 4 SERVINGS

This has been an enormously popular soup with readers, and it's blissfully simple. It uses pantry staples, so you can whip it up almost anytime.

½ cup unsalted butter (1 stick)
½ medium onion, diced
2 (14½-ounce) cans unsalted diced tomatoes
   (see note)
1 teaspoon kosher salt
½ teaspoon freshly ground black pepper
¼ teaspoon baking soda
½ teaspoon dried thyme
1 cup fresh orange juice
½ cup whipping cream

In a saucepan, melt butter; add onion and sauté until translucent. Add tomatoes, salt, pepper, baking soda, and thyme. Bring to a boil, reduce heat and simmer uncovered about 15 minutes, or until slightly thickened.

Purée tomato mixture in a food processor or blender; strain through a sieve or food mill. Return to saucepan and stir in orange juice and cream. Bring to a simmer and adjust seasonings if necessary. Serve hot.

Note: If unsalted diced tomatoes are not available, substitute regular canned diced tomatoes and omit or reduce salt, depending on your taste.

— From Elephants Delicatessen

VERY FRESH CREAM OF TOMATO SOUP

MAKES 8 SERVINGS

If you've ever been overwhelmed by home-grown tomatoes, you definitely need this recipe. Freeze the base in bags prior to adding the cream and egg yolks, and enjoy summer-fresh cooking all winter. The frozen base also makes an excellent tomato sauce.

12 very ripe tomatoes, peeled and chopped (see note)
1 cup water or broth
1 cup sliced celery
½ onion, sliced
¼ cup minced fresh parsley
3 tablespoons cornstarch
3 tablespoons butter, melted
2 tablespoons firmly packed brown sugar
2 teaspoons salt
Freshly ground black pepper
2 cups half-and-half
1 egg yolk, beaten

In a large saucepan, combine tomatoes, 1 cup water or broth, celery, onion, and parsley. Bring to a boil and simmer for 30 minutes. Purée in a food processor or blender; strain.

Mix together cornstarch and melted butter. Stir into soup to thicken over medium heat. Add brown sugar, the salt, and pepper to taste.

Stir the half-and-half and egg yolk into the hot soup, heat until steaming, and serve.

Note: To peel tomatoes, plunge into boiling water for 30 seconds to 1 minute. Remove immediately and plunge into cold water. Skins should slip off easily.

Make ahead: After adding the brown sugar, salt, and pepper, transfer to zip-top freezer bags or plastic containers and freeze for up to 6 months.

— From *Too Many Tomatoes, Squash, Beans, and Other Good Things*, by Lois M. Burrows and Laura G. Myers (Harper and Row)

GAZPACHO

MAKES 4 CUPS

Chef Jeff Nizlek says the secrets to making this soup are to use the freshest vegetables you can find and to strain it through a very fine-mesh sieve. This is easier if you strain the soup through a medium-mesh sieve first and then strain a second time using a very fine sieve. Be sure to start the soup a day ahead, because it needs to sit in the refrigerator overnight.

1 pound ripe tomatoes, peeled, seeded,
    and chopped (2 large; see note)
2 cups peeled and chopped cucumber
1½ cups peeled and chopped carrots
1½ cups chopped fennel bulb
1 large red bell pepper, seeded and chopped
2 large cloves garlic
1 teaspoon Tabasco or other hot sauce
    (or to taste)
4 ounces dry bread, processed into crumbs
    (for about 2 cups)
¼ cup sherry vinegar
Kosher salt and freshly ground black pepper
1 cup extra-virgin olive oil

In the bowl of a food processor, add the tomatoes, cucumber, carrots, fennel, red bell pepper, garlic, Tabasco sauce, and breadcrumbs; purée until smooth. Pour into a medium bowl and refrigerate overnight.

The next day, return the vegetable purée to the food processor. With the processor running, add the vinegar, salt, and pepper (we used 2 teaspoons kosher salt and ½ teaspoon pepper). Slowly drizzle in the olive oil. Taste and adjust salt and pepper, if necessary.

Strain the soup first through a medium-mesh sieve, then strain again through a fine-mesh sieve, pressing with the back of a wooden spoon to extract all of the liquid. Discard the vegetables. Refrigerate until ready to serve. Serve cold in bowls or cups.

Note: To peel tomatoes, plunge into boiling water for 30 seconds to 1 minute. Remove immediately and plunge into cold water. Skins should slip off easily.

— From Jeff Nizlek, chef/owner, the Silver Grille, Silverton

HUNGARIAN MUSHROOM SOUP

MAKES 8 CUPS

Over the years Foodday received countless requests for this soup, from the now defunct Three Lions Bakery. Former owner Michael Silva says the secret is using real Hungarian paprika. If you substitute ordinary paprika your soup won't be as flavorful.

6 tablespoons butter
1½ cups chopped onion
4 teaspoons Hungarian sweet paprika
4 teaspoons dried dill weed
2 teaspoons salt
1 teaspoon freshly ground black pepper
⅔ cup all-purpose flour
1⅔ cups milk
2⅔ cups water

4 cups sliced mushrooms
2 tablespoons soy sauce
2 tablespoons lemon juice
½ cup sour cream
3 tablespoons minced fresh parsley

In a large saucepan, melt butter. Add the onion, paprika, dill weed, salt, and pepper, and sauté until the onion is tender. Whisk in the flour and then the milk and the water. Add the mushrooms and bring almost to a boil. Reduce heat and simmer about 30 minutes, stirring occasionally. Remove from heat and stir in soy sauce, lemon juice, sour cream, and parsley. Serve immediately.

— From Three Lions Bakery

MATZO BALLS IN A LATE SUMMER CORN-PARSLEY BROTH

Chicken is usually essential for matzo ball soup. But Jenn Louis of Lincoln restaurant dispenses with it entirely and simmers a vegetarian broth out of corncobs and parsley for a broth with rich yellow color and late-summer sweetness.

MATZO BALLS:

¼ cup olive oil

4 eggs

1 cup matzo meal

2 teaspoons salt

¼ cup water

CORN BROTH:

10 corncobs, kernels cut off and reserved
    for another use, and cobs broken in half

2 yellow onions, thinly sliced

4 bay leaves

2 sprigs fresh thyme

½ bunch Italian (flat-leaf) parsley

Parsley sprigs or fennel fronds, for serving

To make matzo balls: In a large bowl, combine oil, eggs, matzo meal, salt and water; chill for 30 minutes.

When mixture is chilled, bring a pot of well-salted water to a boil. Scoop out heaping tablespoons and form balls using an ice cream scoop, or oiled or wet hands, and form into balls and drop gently in the water. Lower the heat until it's just high enough to maintain a simmer, and cover, leaving the lid slightly ajar. Simmer for 30 minutes, then turn off the heat, cover, and let sit another 30 minutes.

To make broth: In a stockpot, combine corncobs, onions, bay leaves, thyme sprigs, and parsley. Add water to cover, about 3 quarts. Bring to a boil, then reduce the heat until it's just high enough to maintain a gentle simmer. Simmer, uncovered, until the broth is richly flavored, about 45 minutes. Strain, and season with salt to taste.

To serve, place a couple of matzo balls in a bowl, and ladle in some broth. Garnish with chopped fennel frond or parsley.

— From Jenn Louis, Lincoln restaurant

CELERY ROOT AND APPLE SOUP WITH PARSNIP CRISPS

MAKES 4 APPETIZER SERVINGS

This silky puréed soup has an uncomplicated flavor, lovely ivory color and belly-warming heartiness. And if you haven't tried celery root—aka celeriac—this is a great place to start. The parsnip crisps are easy to make and add a wonderful crunchy contrast to the soup, but homemade croutons or minced fresh chives would be a nice garnish, too.

SOUP:

3 tablespoons butter
1 cup finely chopped onion
1 medium leek, white part only, thinly
    sliced (1¼ cups)
1 large celery root (aka celeriac; 1½ pounds)
1 medium Granny Smith apple, peeled,
    cored, and chopped (8 ounces)
4 cups vegetable or chicken broth
Salt
1 bay leaf
6 whole black peppercorns
1 (3-inch) sprig fresh thyme
½ cup heavy whipping cream
Ground nutmeg
Freshly ground black pepper

PARSNIP CRISPS:

1 large parsnip, peeled
2 teaspoons vegetable oil
Salt

To make soup: In a 3-quart saucepan or stockpot, melt butter over medium heat. Add the onion and leek, and gently sauté until the onion is translucent, 5 minutes. Remove from heat and set aside.

Trim the stalks and gnarly roots off of the celery root and discard. With a sharp paring knife, cut away the skin, plus any dirty crevices on the root end. Cut the celery root into ½-inch pieces.

Add the celery root, apple, broth, and 1 teaspoon salt to the saucepan. Put the bay leaf, peppercorns, and thyme sprig in a small square of cheesecloth and tie with kitchen string; add to the pot. Bring to a boil, cover, and reduce heat to maintain a simmer. Cook until a piece of the celery root is tender when smashed against the side of the pan with a spoon, about 25 minutes.

Take the saucepan off of the stove, uncover, and allow the soup to cool for 15 minutes. Purée the soup with an immersion blender, or use a regular blender and purée in four batches, leaving the lid slightly ajar to allow steam to escape. (Be careful when puréeing hot soup: it will spatter a bit, so have a kitchen towel handy.)

Return the soup to medium heat and stir in the cream. Add nutmeg, salt and pepper to taste, and serve in warm bowls.

To make parsnip crisps: Preheat the oven to 450 degrees. Line a baking sheet with parchment paper sprayed with nonstick cooking spray. Make long, thin strips of parsnip using a vegetable peeler. In a medium bowl toss the strips with vegetable oil and salt. Lay the strips on the baking sheet without any of them touching. Bake in the oven, watching closely, until the strips are golden brown and crisp, 6 to 7 minutes. Remove parsnip strips from cookie sheet and set on a paper-towel-lined plate. The strips will become crisper as they cool. Serve alongside Celery Root and Apple Soup.

Make ahead: Soup can be prepared up to 2 days in advance and refrigerated. Purée in blender to emulsify before reheating.

— From Ivy Manning

GOLDBERG'S SWEET AND SOUR BORSCHT

MAKES 4 TO 6 SERVINGS

For many years Goldberg's kosher bakery and deli was a place people from back East came for a good bagel. Although Goldberg's is no longer in business, many Fooday readers fondly recall the borscht served there.

2 tablespoons butter
¾ cup chopped onion
6 cups beef broth or stock
1½ cups peeled, chopped potato (2 medium)
¾ cup chopped, cooked beef
½ cup peeled, chopped carrot (1 medium)
¼ cup ketchup
1 cup granulated sugar
½ cup white vinegar
Salt and freshly ground black pepper
7 cups chopped cabbage

In a large stockpot, melt butter over medium heat. Add onion and sauté until softened. Stir in broth, potato, beef, carrot, ketchup, sugar, and vinegar. Add salt and pepper to taste. Bring soup to a rolling boil. Add cabbage and continue to boil until cabbage is soft, stirring occasionally, approximately 20 minutes.

— From Goldberg's Bakery & Deli

LENTIL SOUP

MAKES 12 SERVINGS

We love lentils because they don't require soaking and are packed with fiber and protein, and contain virtually no fat. Al-Amir's soup combines them with plenty of vegetables and gives them a delicate seasoning of cinnamon, allspice, and lemon.

1 pound dried brown lentils, rinsed and
　　drained (2½ cups)
3 quarts water (12 cups)
2 medium carrots, peeled and chopped
2 small zucchini, chopped
½ medium cauliflower, chopped
1 tablespoon salt
½ teaspoon freshly ground black pepper
1 teaspoon ground cinnamon
1 teaspoon ground allspice
Juice of 1 lemon, or to taste
Lemon wedges, to garnish

In a stockpot or Dutch oven, bring the lentils and water to a boil. Add the carrots, zucchini, and cauliflower; reduce heat and simmer until the lentils are tender, about 1 hour. Stir in the salt, pepper, cinnamon, allspice, and lemon juice. Simmer about 15 minutes more. Taste and adjust seasonings if necessary. Serve with lemon wedges to garnish.

— From Al-Amir Lebanese Restaurant

ITALIAN PASTA AND BEAN SOUP (PASTA E FAGIOLI)

MAKES 4 SERVINGS (5 TO 6 CUPS)

A great way to give soups added depth and savoriness is to add a rind from a wedge of Parmigiano-Reggiano, a trick Fooday contributor Ivy Manning uses here. She also likes using pieces of no-boil lasagna noodles for the pasta because they cook quickly right in the soup.

1 tablespoon extra-virgin olive oil
1 cup finely chopped onion
1 large carrot, peeled and finely chopped
2 ribs celery, finely chopped
1 large clove garlic, chopped
1 teaspoon Italian seasoning blend
⅛ to ¼ teaspoon crushed red pepper flakes
2 cups chopped tomatoes in purée (such as Pomì brand)
1 (15-ounce) can cannellini beans, rinsed and drained
3 cups vegetable, chicken or beef broth
1 (3-inch-long) rind from Parmigiano-Reggiano cheese
2 sheets no-boil lasagna noodles, broken into 1-inch pieces
Salt and freshly ground black pepper

In a stockpot or Dutch oven, heat the oil over medium heat. When the oil is hot, add the onion, carrot, and celery; sauté slowly until the onion is softened, about 8 minutes. Add the garlic, Italian seasoning, and red pepper flakes; sauté until fragrant, 45 seconds.

Add the tomatoes, beans, broth, and cheese rind; bring to a simmer. Reduce heat to maintain a gentle simmer, cover and cook, stirring occasionally, until the vegetables are tender, about 20 minutes.

Use a potato masher to mash about half of the beans in the pot to create a slightly creamy consistency. Add the broken lasagna noodles and cook, covered, until the pasta is tender, about 10 minutes.

Remove the cheese rind from soup. Season with salt and pepper to taste.

— From Ivy Manning

SPANISH BEAN SOUP (POTAJE DE GARBANZOS)

MAKES 12 SERVINGS

This is a vegetarian version of a dish that originated around 1910 at the Columbia Restaurant in Tampa, Florida. Much of the soup's beguiling flavor comes from smoked paprika. As the potatoes cook, they fall apart and give the soup a thick, hearty texture.

2 tablespoons olive oil
4 medium onions, chopped (about 2 pounds)
5 cloves garlic, minced
4 (14½-ounce) cans garbanzo beans, rinsed
    and drained
1 bay leaf
2 small russet potatoes (about 1 pound),
    peeled and quartered
3 cups vegetable broth
3 cups water
1 tablespoon smoked paprika (pimentón
    de la Vera)
Salt and freshly ground black pepper
Chopped fresh Italian (flat-leaf) parsley
    to garnish

In a stockpot, heat the olive oil over medium heat. Add the onions, and sauté until tender and lightly browned, about 20 minutes. Add the garlic; sauté for another minute.

To the pot add the beans, bay leaf, potatoes, broth, and water. Bring to a boil over high heat; reduce heat and simmer about 30 to 40 minutes or until the potatoes are very tender.

Stir in the paprika, and season to taste with salt and pepper. Using a potato masher or the back of a spoon, mash a portion of the beans and potatoes until the soup is thick and chunky. Add additional water if soup is too thick. Garnish with chopped fresh parsley.

— From Sara Bir

VEGETABLES AND LEGUMES

4

SAVORY STUFFED TOMATOES

MAKES 6 SERVINGS

These tomatoes are summer on a plate, and are inspired by a recipe from the Los Angeles Times. We love the way they bake up soft and juicy, the anchovies and balsamic vinegar adding depth and savoriness to the warm cheese, fresh herbs and toasted crumbs. They're the perfect side dish for simple grilled steaks or chops. Because this recipe is so simple, it relies on top-quality tomatoes, preferably from the farmers market or your own garden. Pallid supermarket tomatoes just won't do it justice.

6 medium garden-fresh tomatoes
Kosher salt and freshly ground black pepper
1½ teaspoons balsamic vinegar
Crushed red pepper flakes
6 anchovy fillets, cut in half (about 2 ounces)
8 ounces marinated bocconcini or plain fresh mozzarella
¾ cup fresh breadcrumbs (do not use the store-bought variety)
2 cloves garlic, minced
2 tablespoons chopped fresh oregano, basil, thyme or parsley, or a combination
Extra-virgin olive oil

Thinly slice the top off the tomato. Use a spoon to scoop out the pulp and seeds, but leave the sides and bottom intact.

Lightly sprinkle the inside of each tomato with kosher salt and turn upside down on a plate to drain for 30 minutes. This will help keep the tomatoes from baking up too watery.

Preheat oven to 350 degrees. Shake out any remaining liquid in the tomatoes and place in a shallow baking dish. Lightly season the inside of each tomato with salt and pepper. Add to each ¼ teaspoon balsamic vinegar, and a pinch of crushed red pepper flakes. Cross two halves of anchovy fillets in the bottom of each tomato. If using bocconcini, put one ball in each tomato. If using fresh mozzarella, cut cheese into six chunks and place one in each tomato. Bake tomatoes for 20 minutes, or until tender but not collapsed.

Meanwhile, in a small bowl, stir together the breadcrumbs, garlic, and fresh herb. Remove tomatoes from oven and turn setting to broil. Spoon breadcrumb mixture over top of each tomato. Drizzle with olive oil and broil until breadcrumbs are lightly browned.

TIAN OF BASIL

MAKES 4 SERVINGS

This is a fabulous way to use bumper crops of basil, tomatoes, and zucchini. It's quick to assemble, and you can be loose with the amounts of ingredients. Leftovers reheat nicely in a microwave oven.

2 medium-small zucchini, thinly sliced
4 cups stemmed and loosely packed fresh basil, coarsely chopped
3 to 4 ripe tomatoes, thinly sliced
¾ cup (or less) shredded kasseri cheese
¾ cup (or less) shredded Monterey jack or pepper jack cheese
¼ cup (or less) fruity extra-virgin olive oil
Salt and freshly ground black pepper

Preheat oven to 350 degrees. Oil a shallow (about 2 inches deep) ovenproof serving dish. Place the zucchini slices over the bottom and press chopped basil leaves firmly over the zucchini (the basil will cook down the way spinach does).

Arrange the tomato slices over the basil. Then scatter the cheese evenly over the tomatoes, drizzle with olive oil, and bake about 35 minutes, until hot through and cheeses are melted.

— From Maryanne Caruthers

SAUTÉED EGGPLANT (MELANZANA SALTATA)

MAKES 6 SERVINGS

Many eggplant recipes can be tedious, what with salting and rinsing the flesh, breading, frying, etc. This divine Italian dish requires none of that. Just peel the eggplant, cube, and sauté with a few other ingredients. If you want to add a pinch of crushed red pepper flakes, be our guest.

¼ cup olive oil
½ cup finely chopped onion
1 medium green pepper, seeded and finely chopped (½ cup)
1 large or 2 medium eggplants (1½ pounds), ends trimmed, peeled, and cut into 1-inch cubes
4 canned Italian plum tomatoes, well-drained, halved, seeded, and coarsely chopped
2 tablespoons minced fresh basil or 2 teaspoons dried basil
1 teaspoon salt
½ teaspoon freshly ground black pepper
2 tablespoons minced fresh Italian (flat-leaf) parsley
½ cup freshly grated parmesan cheese

In a 12-inch skillet, heat olive oil over medium heat until haze forms. Add onion and bell pepper; sauté, stirring constantly, until soft but not browned, about 3 minutes. Add eggplants and sauté just until tender when tested with a fork, 5 to 8 minutes.

Stir in tomatoes, basil, salt, and pepper. Continue to cook, stirring constantly, until well-incorporated, about 2 minutes. Remove from heat; stir in parsley and parmesan cheese. Transfer to a platter and serve immediately.

— Adapted from *Italian Family Cooking Like Mama Used to Make*, by Anne Casale (Ballantine Books)

ROASTED CAULIFLOWER

MAKES 6 SERVINGS

When you roast cauliflower in the oven, a little bit of magic happens. The vegetable reduces by almost half as the water evaporates, which concentrates and caramelizes the sugars, leading a crunchy exterior.

1 medium head cauliflower
3 tablespoons olive oil
1 tablespoon Dijon mustard
1 teaspoon curry powder
1 teaspoon ground cumin
1 teaspoon herbes de Provence
Salt and freshly ground black pepper
1 whole lemon, cut into 6 wedges

Preheat oven to 400 degrees.

Cut cauliflower into medium, golf ball-sized florets, discarding tough, woody base of the stem and leaves. Cut softer parts of stem into bite-sized chunks.

In a large bowl, add olive oil, mustard, curry powder, cumin, herbes de Provence, and salt and pepper to taste; whisk until dressing is well-incorporated and smooth. Add cauliflower pieces to bowl; toss until evenly coated.

Spread cauliflower in an even layer on a baking sheet, and roast until florets are tender and golden brown, 20 to 25 minutes.

Serve with lemon wedges for garnish.

— From Grant Butler

SPINACH WITH SESAME DRESSING (HORENSO GOMA)

MAKES 4 SERVINGS

This is a traditional dish served at restaurants throughout Japan and often in Japanese restaurants in the U.S., too. It's delicious, and with only five ingredients, it's simple to make.

1 pound fresh spinach, washed well
   and stemmed
3 tablespoons sesame seeds
3 tablespoons soy sauce
2 tablespoons mirin (sweetened rice wine)
1 teaspoon granulated sugar (optional)

Bring a large pot of water to a rolling boil and add spinach. Boil 1 to 3 minutes until the spinach barely wilts. Immediately drain spinach in colander and run cold water over it.

Toast sesame seeds in a heavy skillet over medium-high heat until they are lightly browned. While still warm, grind seeds lightly in mortar and pestle or an electric blender. Add soy sauce and grind again briefly. Add mirin and sugar, and mix well.

Squeeze excess water from cooked spinach; chop coarsely. Toss in a medium bowl with soy sauce-sesame dressing until lightly coated. Serve chilled or at room temperature in small bowls.

— From Amy Martinez Starke

RUTH'S CHRIS CREAMED SPINACH

MAKES 4 SERVINGS

This recipe was created by Ruth Fertel, who as a single mother in 1965 mortgaged her house to purchase Chris Steak House in New Orleans and renamed it Ruth's Chris. Representing that steakhouse's Southern heritage, the recipe begins with the classic first step of Creole cuisine: "First, you make a roux."

> 5 tablespoons butter
> 3 tablespoons all-purpose flour
> ⅔ cup half-and-half (divided)
> ½ teaspoon salt
> ½ teaspoon freshly ground white pepper
> 1 pound fresh baby spinach leaves, chopped

Make a roux by melting the butter in a large saucepan over medium heat and stirring in the flour. Continue to cook the roux until it turns tan, stirring occasionally, about 5 minutes. Check the roux frequently, since its color on the bottom will be darker than on the surface.

Remove from the heat, and stir in ⅓ cup of the half-and-half, the salt, and white pepper.

Add the spinach to the pan and stir. Return the pan to the heat and stir occasionally, until spinach is fully wilted and warmed through.

Add the remaining ⅓ cup half-and-half, and stir until creamy throughout, and no clumps of roux mixture remain. Serve immediately, or keep warm over low heat until ready to serve.

— From Ruth's Chris Steak House

CREAMY BRUSSELS SPROUTS GRATIN

MAKES 6 SERVINGS

Roasting Brussels sprouts and then adding cream brings out their sweet, mellow side. This gratin can convert even the most confirmed Brussels-sprouts critic into a devotee.

> 2 pounds Brussels sprouts, stem ends trimmed and outer leaves removed; sprouts cut in half through the stem end
> 2 tablespoons unsalted butter, melted
> Kosher salt and freshly ground black pepper
> 1 cup coarse fresh breadcrumbs
> 6 slices bacon, fried until crisp, drained and crumbled; drippings reserved (divided)
> ¼ cup finely shredded aged gruyère
> 1¼ cups whipping cream

Preheat oven to 425 degrees. Put the Brussels sprouts in a shallow baking dish that will hold them in a snug single layer (10-inch round or slightly larger oval is good). Toss them with the melted butter, ¾ teaspoon salt and several grinds of pepper. Spread them evenly in the dish and roast, tossing once or twice, until browned in spots and tender-crisp when pierced with a knife, 15 to 20 minutes.

While the sprouts roast, combine the breadcrumbs with 1 tablespoon bacon drippings and ⅛ teaspoon salt in a small bowl. Mix in the gruyère; set aside.

When the Brussels sprouts are ready, sprinkle them with the crumbled bacon.

Pour the cream over the Brussels sprouts and continue baking until the cream has thickened to a saucy consistency and coats the sprouts, 5 to 7 minutes. Remove the pan from the oven. Set the oven to broil and position a rack to 6 inches below the broiler. Sprinkle the breadcrumb mixture evenly over the Brussels sprouts. Broil the gratin until the crust is deep golden brown, about 3 to 6 minutes. Watch closely so the topping does not burn.

Make ahead: The day before serving, sprouts can be made as far as sprinkling with the bacon and then refrigerated separately from the topping. The next day, pour cream over sprouts and proceed as directed above.

— Adapted from Eva Katz

GRILLED GREEN BEANS WITH WARM GORGONZOLA VINAIGRETTE

MAKES 6 SERVINGS

This dish has been a long-time favorite of many Fooddday staffers. Grilling green beans gives them a slightly nutty flavor, but if you'd rather not light the grill, just sauté the beans and add the sauce to the same pan.

1 pound fresh green beans
3 teaspoons olive oil (divided)
¼ cup balsamic vinegar
¼ cup crumbled gorgonzola cheese
1 tablespoon firmly packed brown sugar
¾ teaspoon chopped garlic
¾ teaspoon chopped shallots
½ teaspoon chopped fresh thyme, or
⁣ ¼ teaspoon dried
½ teaspoon chopped fresh basil, or
⁣ ¼ teaspoon dried
Salt and freshly ground black pepper

In a medium saucepan, bring about 6 cups of lightly salted water to a boil. Add the beans and blanch by boiling them for 4 minutes. Drain the beans in a colander and immediately immerse them in ice water to stop them from cooking; drain.

In a small saucepan, combine 1½ teaspoons olive oil, vinegar, gorgonzola, brown sugar, garlic, shallots, thyme, and basil. Warm over medium heat until the ingredients start to combine, about 7 minutes.

Toss the green beans in the remaining 1½ teaspoons olive oil and season lightly with salt and pepper. Quickly grill the beans on a hot charcoal or gas grill, about 30 seconds on each side. Toss the beans in the warm vinaigrette and serve immediately.

— From chef Allen Kovalencik, The Company of the
Cauldron, Nantucket Island, Massachusetts

ASPARAGUS WITH MUSTARD-DILL SAUCE

MAKES 4 SERVINGS

Although this recipe came from a California farm, the Northwest grows wonderful asparagus. You don't have to peel the stalks, but be sure to snap the woody ends off where they naturally break.

1 cup yogurt
¼ cup Dijon mustard
¼ cup mayonnaise
1 tablespoons fresh dill weed or 1 teaspoon dry dill weed, crumbled
1 teaspoon dried thyme, crumbled
1 pound asparagus, trimmed and peeled

In a small bowl, combine yogurt, mustard, mayonnaise, dill weed, and thyme. Refrigerate for at least 30 minutes to allow flavors to meld.

When ready to serve, cook asparagus in boiling water until just barely tender, but still crisp, about 3 minutes. (If using purple asparagus, add a tablespoon of lemon juice to the water to help retain the color.) Immediately plunge asparagus into cold water to stop the cooking process and set the color. Place on a large oval or rectangular platter, and spoon some of the sauce over the stalks; pass the remaining sauce at the table.

— From Victoria Island Farms, Stockton, California

THIN ISN'T ALWAYS BETTER

It's a common misconception that thin asparagus is more tender than thick. In fact, younger plants produce larger shoots, which means thicker spears may be more tender than thin. No matter whether they're fat or thin, look for firm spears with tips that have tight, overlapping scales. Avoid those with seedy, tasseled tips or shriveled stems, both signs of age.

BRAISED RED CABBAGE WITH PEARS

MAKES 8 TO 12 SERVINGS

There's nothing like the tang of sweet and sour cabbage to offset the flavor of pork dishes. If you make this a day ahead and let it mellow, it will only be that much better.

½ cup firmly packed light brown sugar
7 tablespoons apple cider vinegar
½ teaspoon dried thyme
1 bay leaf
¾ teaspoon salt
¼ teaspoon freshly ground black pepper
4 pounds red cabbage, cored and finely shredded
3 large Bosc pears, peeled, cored and cut into ½-inch pieces
½ cup raisins

In a large saucepan, combine the brown sugar, vinegar, thyme, bay leaf, salt, and pepper. Bring to a boil over medium-high heat, stirring to dissolve the sugar. In thirds, stir the cabbage into the saucepan, covering the saucepan and letting each batch wilt before adding the next. Stir in the pears and raisins.

Reduce the heat to medium-low and simmer, covered, until the cabbage is very tender, 50 to 60 minutes.

Transfer to a warmed serving dish and serve immediately.

Make ahead: The cabbage can be prepared up to 2 days ahead, covered, and refrigerated. Reheat slowly before serving.

— From *An Edible Christmas*, by Irena Chalmers (William Morrow)

ROASTED PARSNIPS WITH BALSAMIC VINEGAR AND ROSEMARY

MAKES 4 TO 6 SERVINGS

Parsnips become chewy and a bit crunchy when roasted, almost like oven fries. The balsamic vinegar glazes the roasted parsnips and keeps them from tasting overly sweet. These are especially good with meat or poultry.

> 2 pounds parsnips, peeled (4 large)
> 2 tablespoons extra-virgin olive oil
> Salt and freshly ground black pepper
> 2 tablespoons balsamic vinegar
> 2 teaspoons minced fresh rosemary leaves

Preheat oven to 425 degrees.

Cut the larger ends of parsnips lengthwise into quarters; if there are any woody cores, cut those away. Cut all parsnips into 1½-inch chunks and toss with oil on a large, rimmed baking sheet. Sprinkle with salt and pepper to taste. Roast, turning once, until golden brown, about 40 minutes.

Combine the vinegar and rosemary in a small bowl. Drizzle the mixture over the roasted parsnips on the baking sheet; toss to coat. Continue to roast just until the parsnips are glazed, about 3 minutes. Adjust the seasoning to taste and serve immediately.

— From *Vegetables Every Day*, by Jack Bishop (William Morrow)

CUMIN CARROTS

MAKES 6 SERVINGS

These lightly seasoned carrots in a very thin, creamy sauce are a hit even with people who aren't crazy about cooked carrots. And we love how easy they are to make.

> 4 medium carrots, peeled and thinly sliced
>   on the bias
> ¾ cup water
> 1 teaspoon granulated sugar
> ¼ teaspoon ground cumin, or to taste
> ¼ cup whipping cream
> ¼ teaspoon prepared horseradish (optional)
> Salt and freshly ground black pepper
> Chopped fresh cilantro, to garnish (optional)

In a skillet, combine carrots, the water and sugar; cover and simmer until most of the water is evaporated and carrots are tender-crisp. Add cumin, cream, horseradish, and salt and pepper to taste; simmer just until carrots are coated. Garnish with cilantro, if desired, and serve.

— From Joanne Leech and John Nelson, co-owners and chefs, The Sanctuary Restaurant, Chinook, Washington

ROASTED FENNEL AND PEARS WITH PARMIGIANO-REGGIANO AND TARRAGON

MAKES 4 SERVINGS

The combination of fennel and pears may not be something you can immediately relate to, but trust us, it's delicious. It makes a fabulous partner for roast pork or ham, or even as a topping for a hearty vegetarian pasta.

    2 pounds fennel (about 2 large), trimmed,
        quartered, cored, and cut in ½-inch pieces
    2 Bartlett pears, halved, cored, and cut in
        ½-inch pieces
    4 tablespoons extra-virgin olive oil (divided)
    1 teaspoon chopped fresh thyme
    Kosher salt and freshly ground black pepper
    2 tablespoons chopped fresh tarragon
    1½ tablespoons balsamic vinegar
    16 shaved strips of Parmigiano-Reggiano
        cheese

Preheat oven to 425 degrees.

In a large bowl, toss the fennel, pears, 2 tablespoons oil and the thyme. Sprinkle generously with salt and pepper, about ½ teaspoon of each.

Transfer to an 11-by-13-inch pan and roast, flipping fennel and pears every 10 minutes or so, until they are tender and browned in places, about 30 minutes.

Transfer to a serving platter and toss with the tarragon, vinegar and the remaining 2 tablespoons oil. Top with the Parmigiano-Reggiano and serve immediately.

— From Tony Rosenfeld

NOT ALL PARMESAN IS THE SAME

You'll notice that some recipes in this book call for parmesan cheese and others call for Parmigiano-Reggiano. Generally, we have left the choice up the recipe developer. Parmigiano-Reggiano, which is imported from Italy, has a nuttier, richer flavor than other parmesan, and in dishes where the cheese is a prominent flavoring or when it's used to finish a dish—such as in risotto or shaved over bruschetta—using the import will make a difference. In lasagna, where the cheese is layered with many other ingredients, the choice isn't nearly as critical.

STEWED ZUCCHINI WITH CORIANDER, CILANTRO, AND POMEGRANATE MOLASSES

MAKES 6 SERVINGS

This Middle Eastern-inspired dish is similar to a ratatouille, but with a brighter play of flavors and a meltingly soft texture from the long braise. The thick slices of zucchini are simmered in a tomato sauce touched with coriander, fresh cilantro, and a dollop of sour-sweet pomegranate molasses. Sprinkle this dish lightly with feta and pair with a simple vermicelli-rice pilaf.

3 tablespoons olive oil

1 onion, finely chopped

4 cloves garlic, minced

1½ teaspoons ground coriander

½ teaspoon freshly ground white pepper

½ teaspoon ground cinnamon

½ teaspoon ground allspice

2 pounds zucchini, cut into ¾-inch rounds

1 bunch fresh cilantro, coarsely chopped
    (divided)

1 (28-ounce) can whole tomatoes

½ cup water

½ teaspoon salt

½ teaspoon granulated sugar

1 tablespoon pomegranate molasses
    (available at Middle Eastern grocery
    stores, or substitute the juice of half a
    lemon and add an additional ½ teaspoon
    sugar)

4 ounces feta cheese, crumbled (optional)

In a large pot, heat the olive oil over medium heat. Sauté onion until translucent, 5 minutes. Add the garlic and sauté another 2 minutes. Add the coriander, white pepper, cinnamon, and allspice; stir for a moment to toast the spices.

Add the zucchini and half the cilantro; stir to coat with the toasted spices. Add the tomatoes, water, salt, sugar, and pomegranate molasses. Raise the heat to bring it to a boil, then lower the heat to maintain a simmer. Cover and simmer gently for 1½ hours (you can cook it for less time, but the full cooking time turns the zucchini meltingly soft and infuses it with the flavors from the sauce). Stir occasionally and adjust seasonings to taste. Top with feta, if desired, and remaining cilantro, and serve.

— From Deena Prichep

IRISH MASH

MAKES ABOUT 6 SERVINGS

In Ireland, there are many kinds of "mash." For this version, Foodday contributor Joan Harvey says the proportions don't have to be exact; one beautiful, small, blushing rutabaga more or less won't detract from the deliciousness.

1 pound rutabagas

8 ounces celery root (celeriac)

1 small, yellow onion, chopped

Chicken broth or stock, preferably
    without salt

1 tablespoon or more butter

Salt and freshly ground black pepper

Peel the rutabagas and celery root; cut into 1-inch dice. To a large saucepan, add the diced vegetables, the onion, and enough chicken broth to cover and simmer until rutabaga pieces are tender (celery root will soften earlier), about 30 minutes. Drain off excess broth, but reserve. Mash vegetables with a potato masher, adding reserved broth if necessary, to achieve a consistency similar to mashed potatoes. The mixture should have a little texture, but you can also use an electric mixer if you prefer a smoother consistency. Add butter, salt, and pepper to taste.

— From Joan Harvey

BUTTERNUT SQUASH AND YUKON GOLD GRATIN WITH GRUYÈRE CHEESE

MAKES 8 SERVINGS

Caramelized onions, sweet butternut squash, and nutty gruyère make this a divinely rich and savory entree or side dish. Don't be tempted to substitute ordinary Swiss cheese for the gruyère.

2 tablespoons unsalted butter

4 cups thinly sliced onions (about 1 pound)

1¼ pounds butternut squash, peeled, seeded and cut into ¼-inch slices

1¼ pounds Yukon Gold potatoes, peeled and cut into ¼-inch slices

1 cup half-and-half

1 teaspoon salt

½ teaspoon freshly ground black pepper

2 cups fresh breadcrumbs made from sourdough bread

8 ounces shredded gruyère cheese (about 2 cups, packed)

1½ tablespoons chopped fresh sage

Butter a 9-by-13-inch baking dish. In a large, heavy skillet, melt butter over medium-high heat. Add onions and sauté until onions are deeply caramelized, about 20 to 30 minutes.

Meanwhile, preheat oven to 350 degrees.

Lay alternating layers of squash and potatoes in prepared baking dish. Layer onions on top. Mix half-and-half, salt and pepper, and pour over onions. Cover tightly with foil and bake 90 minutes.

Increase oven temperature to 400 degrees. In a medium bowl, mix breadcrumbs, cheese, and sage. Sprinkle over gratin. Bake uncovered until top is golden brown and crisp, about 30 minutes.

— From David Martin, former executive chef, In Good Taste Cooking School

MAKE-AHEAD MASHED POTATOES

MAKES 12 SERVINGS

At Thanksgiving, we need all the help we can get. That's why this recipe is so brilliant. It can be made up to a week in advance and reheated either in the oven or in a slow-cooker.

5 pounds russet or Yukon Gold potatoes

6 ounces reduced-fat cream cheese, at room temperature

1 cup light sour cream

2 teaspoons onion powder

1 teaspoon salt

½ teaspoon freshly ground black pepper

2 egg whites, slightly beaten, or 1 whole egg

1 tablespoon butter

Cook potatoes whole or quartered, unpeeled or peeled, in a large pot of boiling water until tender, about 20 to 30 minutes if whole, 15 to 20 minutes if quartered. Stick paring knife gently into center of potatoes to see if they're tender. Drain thoroughly; mash or send through ricer or food mill until there are no lumps.

Add cream cheese, sour cream, onion powder, salt, pepper, and egg whites; blend well.

▶

Spray a 9-by-13-inch casserole with nonstick cooking spray. Add potato mixture and dot with butter. Cool slightly, cover and refrigerate up to 7 days.

To serve, remove from refrigerator 30 minutes before baking, and preheat oven to 350 degrees. Bake, covered, 40 minutes or until steaming hot in center.

To use a slow-cooker, take potatoes out of refrigerator about 3½ hours before you plan to serve them; place in slow-cooker. Dot with butter, cover, and cook on low heat for 3 hours, stirring once or twice. Or, if cooker is very slow to heat, start on high; as potatoes heat up, reduce to low.

— Adapted from Jeanne Jones' "Cook it Light" column, King Features Syndicate

POTATOES PREFER TO HIDE IN THE DARK

Potatoes, like tomatoes, shouldn't be refrigerated. Chilling them causes their starches to turn to sugar and makes them taste sweet. It also causes them to darken when cooked. Instead, store them in a dark, cool, well-ventilated place. Exposure to sun or artificial light causes the formation of chlorophyll, indicated by a green tinge. Chlorophyll, in itself, is tasteless and harmless. The concern with green potatoes is solanine, a potentially toxic alkaloid that develops as a result of the chlorophyll. The concentration of solanine is greatest in or directly beneath the skin. Deeply peeling the green area from the potato will remove the solanine.

NEW POTATOES WITH PEAS AND CORIANDER

MAKES 4 SERVINGS

This vegetable dish from India is like a spicy potato salad, and it's just as tasty served cold, hot, or at room temperature—like a spicy potato salad. It's a snap to make, but it delivers complex flavors you find in more complicated Indian dishes.

6 to 8 small new potatoes
¼ cup peanut or vegetable oil
1 teaspoon ground cumin
2 teaspoons minced fresh turmeric or ½ teaspoon dried ground turmeric (see note)
1½ tablespoons peeled and minced fresh ginger
2 small fresh or dried red chiles, coarsely chopped
1 cup chopped fresh cilantro
1¼ teaspoons salt, or to taste
1 teaspoon garam masala
1 tablespoon ground coriander

¼ cup fresh lemon juice (1 large lemon)
6 tablespoons water
½ cup fresh or frozen peas

Wash and dice the potatoes with the skin on. Put them in water to cover until ready to use.

Heat the oil in a skillet. Drain the potatoes and add to the skillet with the ground cumin. Cook, stirring, for 2 minutes; then add the turmeric, ginger, and chiles. Cook, stirring, another 3 minutes.

Add the cilantro, salt, garam masala, ground coriander, lemon juice, and water. Lower the heat, cover, and simmer for 15 minutes, checking from time to time to make sure there's still liquid; add a little water, if necessary. Add the peas just before serving. Remove the cover, turn up the heat and cook, stirring, until most of the liquid is gone.

Note: Fresh turmeric is $7 to $9 per pound and is available at Portland-area food co-ops, Asian, and Indian grocery stores and New Seasons markets. Fresh turmeric stains fingers, clothing, and kitchen surfaces. Use cutting boards, pots, and pans that are stain-resistant, and wear rubber gloves.

— From *Ginger East to West*, by Bruce Cost (Running Press)

SMOKY BEER-STEWED BEANS (BORRACHOS)

MAKES 4 TO 6 SERVINGS

This recipe, from contributor Matthew Card's "Good Food for Less" column, makes a thrifty but totally satisfying meal. Choose a light-flavored lager or ale; hoppy beers will make the dish taste bitter and unbalanced. Serve over rice, or with flour or corn tortillas. Store-bought salsa may be substituted for the garnishes.

4 slices bacon, finely chopped
2 tablespoons extra-virgin olive oil
1 medium onion, minced
1 teaspoon cumin seeds
Salt
6 cloves garlic, minced
1 to 2 canned chipotle chiles in adobo sauce, or to taste
2 teaspoons firmly packed brown sugar
1 pound dried pinto beans, sorted well, soaked overnight, drained, and rinsed
5 cups water, chicken broth or combination of both
1 fresh pig's foot (not smoked ham hock; optional; see note)
1 bay leaf
1 (12-ounce) bottle lager beer or ale (light-flavored, not hoppy)

GARNISHES:
2 ripe tomatoes, seeded and chopped
¼ cup chopped fresh cilantro leaves
3 scallions, sliced thin on bias
1 lime, cut into wedges
Sour cream

In a large saucepan set over medium heat, cook bacon and olive oil until bacon is partially rendered and just beginning to brown, about 5 minutes. Add onion, cumin seeds, and large pinch salt and cook, stirring occasionally, until onions are beginning to brown and turn sticky, 8 to 12 minutes. Add garlic, chipotle chile(s), and brown sugar; cook 1 minute longer. Stir in beans, 5 cups water/broth, pig's foot, if using, and bay leaf; bring to simmer, reduce heat to medium-low, and cook until just tender and water has largely evaporated, 1 to 2 hours. Remove pig's foot if using; shred the meat and return it to pot. Add salt to taste and the beer; increase heat to medium and cook until thickened to desired consistency, 15 to 30 minutes.

Serve topped with tomato, cilantro, and scallions and accompanied by lime wedges and sour cream.

Note: A pig's foot adds flavor, and the high gelatin content lends a lush mouth feel. Buy a few at an Asian or Latino market to freeze and keep on hand.

— From Matthew Card

CHORIZO AND GARBANZO BEANS

MAKES 4 SERVINGS

Fast, versatile, and luxurious tasting, chorizo is a great tool in the thrifty cook's toolbox when used sparingly, in this case just 3 ounces. Serve this zesty sauce-stew on a bed of creamy polenta, or tossed with hot pasta, or even as a topping for slabs of grilled bread.

3 ounces Spanish-style smoked chorizo (not the raw Mexican variety)
2 tablespoons extra-virgin olive oil (divided)
1 medium onion, thinly sliced through root end
1 (15-ounce) can garbanzo beans, rinsed and drained
1 (15-ounce) can diced fire-roasted tomatoes with green chiles
1 teaspoon paprika
6½ cups water (divided)
1 ear corn
1 cup yellow polenta
¾ teaspoon salt, plus more to taste
⅓ cup grated parmesan cheese
¼ teaspoon freshly ground black pepper
⅓ cup chopped fresh Italian (flat-leaf) parsley

Remove the papery casing from the chorizo and discard. Cut the chorizo into ¼-inch-thick slices. In a large sauté pan, heat 1 tablespoon oil over medium heat. When the oil is hot, add the chorizo and onion; sauté until the onion is softened, 5 minutes. Add the garbanzo beans, tomatoes, paprika, and ½ cup water. Bring to a simmer, cover, and cook over medium-low heat, stirring occasionally, until the flavors have melded, 25 to 30 minutes. The mixture will be the consistency of thick stew. Add a bit more water when the dish is finished, if desired.

While the sauce cooks, make the polenta. Shuck the corn, and hold the ear upright on a cutting board. With a sharp knife, cut the kernels away from the cob, discard cob, and set aside the kernels. In a medium saucepan, bring remaining 6 cups of water to a boil. Add the salt and gradually whisk in the polenta. Reduce heat to low and simmer, stirring frequently, until the polenta grains are softened, 25 to 30 minutes. The last 10 minutes of cooking, add the corn. Immediately before serving, add the remaining tablespoon of olive oil and the cheese; stir to combine. Season to taste with salt.

Stir the pepper and parsley into the chorizo mixture, and season with salt to taste. To serve, place a generous helping of the polenta in 4 bowls. Ladle the chorizo mixture over the polenta and serve.

— From Ivy Manning

FRED'S HONEY-BAKED BEANS

MAKES 10 SERVINGS

This has been a hugely popular recipe with Food-day staff and readers, partly because it's so forgiving and adaptable, as you can see from the variations that follow the basic recipe. If mixing up multiple batches, cut back on honey so they're not overly sweet, and on liquid. Older beans can take longer to cook, so be sure to monitor the liquid level and don't let them dry out.

> 1 pound dried pinto beans, soaked at least 8 hours in at least 6 cups water
> 1 pound meaty bacon, sliced and cut into bite-size pieces
> 1 cup diced onion
> 2 cloves garlic, minced
> 1 cup honey
> 1 teaspoon dry mustard
> 2 tablespoons ground ginger
> 1 teaspoon salt
> ½ teaspoon freshly ground black pepper

Drain soaked beans and place in a large saucepan. Cover with 2½ quarts fresh water, bring to a boil, reduce heat to a simmer, and cook until the beans are tender, about 45 minutes. Drain the beans, reserving the cooking liquid.

Preheat oven to 300 degrees.

Put the beans in a 5½-quart casserole or Dutch oven with a lid; toss with the bacon, onion, and garlic. Measure 2 cups of the reserved cooking liquid and stir in the honey, mustard, ground ginger, salt, and pepper. Pour the liquid over the beans, cover with lid, and bake for 3 hours. Remove lid and bake 30 minutes longer, or until most of the liquid is absorbed and the beans are a rich mahogany brown.

Add a ham hock: Add a meaty ham hock or two with the beans when you're simmering them, then cut ham off bones to add to beans in Dutch oven. Cut back on bacon, if desired, reserving half a dozen whole strips for the top of the dish before baking. Bake as directed above.

Use two kinds of ginger: Use 1 tablespoon dry ginger and 1 tablespoon minced fresh ginger. Bake as directed above.

Make it in a slow-cooker: Use only half the liquid called for. Cook on high for 1 hour, then on low for 10 to 12 hours. A double batch almost (but not quite) fits in a 6-quart slow-cooker.

— Adapted from *Dungeness Crabs & Blackberry Cobblers,* by Janie Hibler (WestWinds Press)

TIPS FOR COOKING BEANS

- For those who have trouble digesting beans, researchers say you can minimize tummy trouble by soaking the dry beans in abundant water and changing it several times during soaking (over at least eight hours).
- If you haven't made time for several hours of soaking, use the quick-soak method: put the beans in a large saucepan with water to cover by 3 inches. Boil for 2 to 3 minutes, cover, remove from heat, and let stand 1 hour; drain and use as directed in your recipe.
- If beans are more than a year old, you can soak them overnight and cook them all day and they likely still won't get soft. Unfortunately, there's no way to tell when beans get old. So when purchasing beans, write the date on the package.

CRISPY BLACK BEAN CAKES WITH CARIBBEAN FLAVORS

MAKES 4 SERVINGS

Serve these filling cakes with fried plantains or a big green salad topped with mango slices and a simple lime vinaigrette. Guacamole and salsa are nice accompaniments, too.

- 5 tablespoons olive oil (divided)
- 1 cup finely chopped onion
- ½ cup finely chopped red bell pepper
- 1 teaspoon peeled and minced fresh ginger
- 1 large clove garlic, finely minced
- ¾ teaspoon ground allspice
- ½ teaspoon ground mace
- ½ teaspoon salt
- ¾ cup uncooked long-grain rice
- 1 cup coconut milk
- ½ cup water
- 3 slices day-old, whole-wheat sandwich bread
- 1 (15-ounce) can black beans, rinsed and drained
- 1 to 2 tablespoons habanero hot sauce
- 2 scallions, finely chopped
- 1 egg, beaten

In a large skillet, heat 1 tablespoon olive oil over medium-high heat. Add the onion, bell pepper, ginger, and garlic. Sauté until the onion is translucent, about 8 minutes. Add the allspice, mace, salt, and rice; sauté for 1 minute. Add the coconut milk and ½ cup water, and bring to a simmer. Reduce heat to low, cover, and cook until rice is tender, about 20 minutes. Meanwhile, tear the bread into 2-inch pieces and place in a food processor. Pulse until bread is reduced to fine crumbs and pour into a large mixing bowl.

Combine the rice mixture and beans in food processor, and pulse until the mixture is coarse; do not purée.

Add bean-rice mixture to the breadcrumbs in the mixing bowl. Add hot sauce and scallions. Taste, adding more hot sauce and salt and pepper to taste. Stir in the egg and refrigerate mixture for 20 minutes.

Use an ice cream scoop or ½-cup measure to divide the mixture into 8 portions. Pat each portion into a 3-inch patty. Heat remaining 4 tablespoons of oil in a large skillet over medium-high heat. Add the cakes and fry until crisp on one side, about 4 minutes. Using 2 spatulas, carefully flip the cakes over, and fry on the second side until crisp and brown, 4 minutes more. Serve warm.

— From Ivy Manning

MEGADARRA WITH HARISSA

MAKES 4 SERVINGS

Megadarra, or mujadara, is a dish that appears throughout the Middle East in many guises, but it's really nothing more than lentils and rice topped with caramelized onions. Simple, yes, but there's something about the combination of flavors and textures that makes this dish unbeatable. And with such simple ingredients, it costs pennies a serving.

Feel free to omit the harissa and serve with your favorite hot sauce. Commercial harissa can be purchased in Portland at Pastaworks or Barbur World Foods, but it is a very different product.

1 bay leaf
3 large cloves garlic
8 cups of water (divided)
Kosher salt
1 cup French lentils (also labeled lentils du Puy), rinsed
1 cup uncooked long-grain brown rice, rinsed and drained
¼ cup unsalted butter
2 large onions, thinly sliced (about 4 cups)
Freshly ground black pepper
1 cup full-fat or low-fat plain yogurt
Harissa (see accompanying recipe)

In medium saucepan, combine bay leaf, garlic, and 6 cups water; season liberally with salt. Bring to boil over medium heat, add lentils and simmer until lentils are just tender, 25 to 30 minutes. Drain and discard bay leaf; mash garlic into lentils and transfer to mixing bowl.

In medium saucepan, combine rice, remaining 2 cups water, and a large pinch salt. Bring to boil over medium-high heat, cover, and reduce to low. Cook 1 hour, until the rice is very soft, then transfer to bowl with lentils and toss to combine. Season to taste with salt and pepper.

While rice cooks, melt butter in large skillet or saucepan over medium-high heat. Add onions and cook, stirring frequently, until very well browned and dramatically reduced in volume, about 12 to 20 minutes. (Add a splash or two of water, if necessary, to prevent sticking or burning.) Season with salt and pepper.

Adjust oven rack to middle position and preheat to 400 degrees. Spread lentil and rice mixture into 9-by-13-inch baking dish or other casserole, and cover with an even layer of onion mixture. Wrap tightly with foil and bake for 30 minutes. Allow to cool for 5 minutes, then serve accompanied by yogurt, harissa (see accompanying recipe), or hot sauce, and salt.

— From Matthew Card

HARISSA

MAKES 1 CUP

Be sure to use vegetable oil; olive oil will taste bitter if puréed in the processor for the extent of time it takes to purée the tomatoes and chiles.

1 teaspoon cumin seeds
1 teaspoon caraway seeds
3 cloves garlic, halved
3 dried New Mexico chiles
12 sun-dried tomato halves (about ½ cup)
6 tablespoons vegetable oil
1 teaspoon white vinegar
Salt
Cayenne pepper

In very small skillet combine cumin and caraway seeds and garlic and cook over medium-low heat until very fragrant and garlic begins to color, about 5 minutes. Transfer the garlic to a food processor. Grind the toasted cumin and caraway seeds with a mortar and pestle or electric spice grinder; add to the food processor.

Return skillet to heat and add chiles. Toast until lightly browned and very aromatic, 2 to 5 minutes. Transfer to a bowl; add sun-dried tomatoes, cover with boiling water, and cover with plastic wrap. Allow to sit until chiles are quite soft, about 20 minutes. Drain through fine-mesh strainer, reserving the soaking liquid.

Transfer chiles and tomatoes to the food processor, add oil and vinegar, and process until very smooth and uniformly blended, 3 to 5 minutes, scraping down sides of work bowl as necessary. Adjust seasoning with salt and cayenne to taste. If the harissa is too stiff, add 1 or 2 tablespoons of the reserved soaking liquid. Transfer to bowl and refrigerate until needed.

Make ahead: Harissa can be made, covered and refrigerated for at least 1 week.

— From Matthew Card

PASTA AND NOODLES

5

BUCATINI ALL'AMATRICIANA

MAKES 6 SERVINGS

For this Roman pasta sauce, it's important to find meaty pancetta; fatty pancetta will make the sauce greasy. At the deli counter, ask to have it sliced into ¼-inch slices. If you can't find bucatini, a long, tubelike pasta, just substitute spaghetti.

2 tablespoons unsalted butter

1 tablespoon olive oil

6 ounces pancetta, cut into ¼-inch cubes

1 medium onion, minced

Salt

½ teaspoon crushed red pepper flakes, plus additional for serving

1 (28-ounce) can diced tomatoes, partially drained

1 pound bucatini pasta

1 cup grated pecorino Romano cheese, plus additional for serving

In large saucepan, heat butter and oil over medium heat; once butter has melted, add pancetta. Cook, stirring frequently, until browned and crispy, 5 to 7 minutes. With slotted spoon, transfer pancetta to small bowl.

Add onion, a large pinch salt and red pepper flakes and, stirring frequently (scraping any browned bits off bottom of pan), cook until onions are soft and lightly browned, 5 to 7 minutes. Add tomatoes and remaining liquid and cook, stirring occasionally, until slightly thickened and flavors have blended, about 10 minutes. Adjust seasoning with salt and pepper flakes.

While sauce simmers, prepare pasta according to package directions. Drain pasta, reserving ½ cup pasta water. Toss pasta, reserved pancetta, sauce, and cheese, adjusting consistency with reserved pasta water if necessary. Serve immediately, accompanied by grated cheese and additional pepper flakes.

— From Matthew Card

PASTA WATER WORKS MAGIC

An important trick to use when cooking pasta is to always pull out a cup of the water you used to boil the pasta. This water is rich in starch and is often used to pull the sauce ingredients together and adjust the consistency. Add it back a little at a time as needed, tossing the hot pasta with the sauce over and over until it's, well, saucy enough. You'll be shocked at the difference it can make.

ORECCHIETTE DI OCCI

MAKES ABOUT 18 CUPS SAUCE

Toasted fennel and balsamic vinegar give this sauce a sweet depth of flavor. The recipe makes a ton of sauce, so you can freeze it and have plenty on hand. Chef Brian Quinn told Fooday he sneaks a little bacon fat in with the oil when sautéing the vegetables.

SAUCE:

½ cup olive oil or vegetable oil (a little bit of bacon fat doesn't hurt)
8 cups diced onion
2 cups diced celery
1 cup diced carrots
3 tablespoons fennel seeds
2 tablespoons dried oregano
4 tablespoons dried basil
1 tablespoon dried thyme
¼ cup minced garlic
1½ cups red wine (merlot or other fruit-forward, voluptuous red)
¾ cup balsamic vinegar
16 cups canned tomatoes with juice (five 28-ounce cans)
Kosher salt

In an 8-quart pot, heat the oil over medium heat. Add the onion, celery, and carrots and sauté, stirring occasionally, until the onions are beginning to color.

Meanwhile, toast fennel seeds in a dry sauté pan over medium heat until they are slightly tan, then pulverize in a spice mill, or mortar and pestle. Combine with oregano, basil, and thyme; set aside.

Add the garlic to the vegetable mixture and sauté for 1 minute. Add the wine and vinegar; continue cooking until liquid is reduced by half. Add reserved dried herbs and the tomatoes, bring to a boil, reduce heat, and simmer for at least 2 hours. Blend with an immersion blender, or by batches in a standard blender. Only then, adjust salt to taste.

Makes about 18 cups. Freeze any leftover sauce in recipe-size portions.

PASTA:

Makes 1 serving
1 (5-ounce) Italian sausage
1 tablespoon vegetable oil
1 teaspoon minced garlic
2 tablespoons red wine
¾ cup sauce
2 tablespoons butter
1½ cups hot cooked orecchiette pasta
1 teaspoon chopped fresh basil, for garnish
Grated pecorino Romano cheese, for serving

Slice 1 sausage per person into fork-size pieces. Gently sauté in vegetable oil over medium heat until cooked, about 5 to 6 minutes. Add garlic and warm for 30 seconds. Add wine and reduce by half. Add sauce and bring to a simmer. Remove from heat and swirl in the butter for a creamy consistency. Toss with hot pasta and serve garnished with fresh basil and cheese.

— From Brian Quinn, Ivy House

LAMB RAGU

MAKES 2 TO 3 SERVINGS

This pasta sauce is a delicious way to tenderize an inexpensive lamb shoulder. Fooddday ran the recipe after it won second place in the professional division of the 2002 Flock and Fleece Festival cook-off. It's a great dish for casual entertaining.

2 ounces pancetta, diced
10 ounces lamb shoulder, trimmed and cubed
    (1½ cups raw cubed lamb)
½ to 1 teaspoon crushed red pepper flakes
1½ teaspoons dried oregano
1 clove garlic, chopped
Salt
¼ cup olive oil
1½ cups chopped fresh mushrooms
1 small onion, finely chopped
¼ cup red wine
3 tablespoons red wine vinegar
1 tablespoon all-purpose flour
1½ tablespoons tomato paste, diluted with
    ¼ cup warm water
Up to 1 cup water (divided)
8 ounces fresh tagliatelle or pappardelle pasta
2 tablespoons chopped fresh Italian (flat-leaf)
    parsley

In a large skillet or small Dutch oven, cook the pancetta until it is limp and has rendered some of its fat. Add lamb and season with red pepper flakes, oregano, and garlic. Brown meat well on all sides. Sprinkle with salt and remove all with slotted spoon; set aside.

Add oil to the pan and heat. Add mushrooms and sauté for 5 minutes. Remove and place with lamb.

Add onion to pan and gently sauté until soft. Pour in wine and vinegar; boil briskly until almost evaporated.

Stir the flour into the diluted tomato paste and add to onions. Cook, stirring for 2 minutes or so. Add a pinch of salt, then return lamb and mushrooms to the pan. Cook, covered, until the lamb is very tender, 1½ to 2 hours, adding water ¼ cup at a time if necessary to prevent ragu from sticking. Taste for salt.

Cook pasta until tender but firm to the bite, and place in a heated bowl with a tablespoon of pasta water. Toss with ragu and top with parsley.

Make ahead: Ragu can be prepared a day ahead and refrigerated.

— From Paul Zerkel, Gino's Restaurant

FETTUCCINE WITH SAGE BUTTER, BACON, AND ARTICHOKES

MAKES 4 SERVINGS

Browned butter and sage make beautiful partners. And with bacon added in, the final dish is certainly not diet fare. But we think it's worth every bite. Be sure to use canned artichoke hearts, not marinated hearts.

½ cup unsalted butter (1 stick)
½ cup very coarsely chopped fresh
    sage leaves
8 ounces cooked bacon, cut crosswise into
    thin strips
1 (8- to 9-ounce) package frozen artichoke
    hearts, thawed and cut in large dice or
    thin wedges
12 ounces dried fettuccine
1 cup freshly grated parmesan cheese
    (4 ounces)
Freshly ground black pepper and salt

Bring a large pot of salted water to a boil for pasta.

Melt butter in large skillet over medium-low heat. Add sage leaves and cook, stirring often, until butter begins to brown very slightly and sage begins to crisp, about 3 to 4 minutes. Add bacon and artichoke hearts; cook until heated through, about 1 minute.

Boil fettuccine until just barely tender to the bite. Drain, reserving 1 cup of cooking liquid. To the skillet, add the fettuccine and half of the reserved cooking liquid, tossing the pasta well with tongs. Add additional cooking liquid as needed to achieve a silky sauce. Sprinkle in cheese and a generous grinding of black pepper, and toss with tongs. Taste and season with salt, if necessary. Tilt pasta out onto a large, warm platter or divide it among individual pasta bowls.

— Adapted from chef Jerry Traunfeld

COMING TO TERMS WITH YOUR GRATER

Fooddday recipes frequently use the terms "grated" and "shredded," but not interchangeably. We use "grated" to refer to the tiny bits you get on the smallest holes of a box grater or Microplane-style tool. Citrus zest, fresh ginger, and hard cheeses, such as parmesan, are some of the foods that are frequently grated. We reserve "shredded" to refer to the larger and longer shreds you typically need for cheddar and mozzarella cheese, or vegetables like zucchini and carrots.

BLT BOW TIES

MAKES 6 SERVINGS

This recipe goes together quickly, but it's loaded with flavor thanks to the savory bacon and the peppery arugula. The small green leaves last only about two days in the refrigerator, so don't let them sit around.

1 pound farfalle (bow-tie pasta)
12 bacon slices, cut into 1-inch pieces
1 (28-ounce) can diced tomatoes, drained
¼ teaspoon crushed red pepper flakes
3 cups chopped arugula
1 cup thinly sliced scallions

1 cup thinly sliced fresh basil (divided)
¼ cup dry white wine
½ cup grated fresh parmesan cheese
    (2 ounces; divided)
Salt and freshly ground black pepper

Cook farfalle in a large pot of boiling salted water until tender but still firm to the bite. Drain farfalle.

Meanwhile, cook bacon in large, heavy skillet over medium heat until crisp, stirring often. Using a slotted spoon, transfer the bacon to paper towels. Drain all but 3 tablespoons of the fat from the skillet. Add tomatoes and red pepper flakes to skillet; cook until tomatoes soften, about 2 minutes. Add arugula, scallions, ½ cup basil, and the bacon; cook until arugula and basil just wilt, about 2 minutes. Stir in wine; bring to simmer. Add farfalle to sauce and toss to coat. Mix in ¼ cup parmesan cheese and remaining ½ cup basil; cook until cheese melts and coats pasta, tossing often, about 2 minutes. Season to taste with salt and pepper, sprinkle with remaining ¼ cup cheese, and serve.

— Adapted from *Bon Appétit* magazine, September 2003

SPAGHETTI WITH TUNA, LEMON, AND OLIVES

MAKES 2 SERVINGS

We adapted this recipe to use Northwest tuna packed in its own juices; look for that phrase on the label, or the words "raw pack." The only ingredients listed should be tuna and salt. However, we also tested this recipe with a national brand of tuna packed in oil and had wonderful results.

2 (5- to 6-ounce) cans tuna (see note)
8 ounces spaghetti or other dried pasta
¼ cup olive oil
1 cup thinly sliced red onion
2 tablespoons grated lemon zest
1 to 2 teaspoons lemon juice
4 teaspoons minced garlic
2 teaspoons capers, rinsed well and drained
10 kalamata olives, pitted and roughly
    chopped
Salt and freshly ground black pepper
¼ to ½ teaspoon crushed red pepper flakes
    (optional)
2 tablespoons chopped fresh parsley

If using tuna canned in its own juices, put the tuna and its juices into a bowl, and flake well with a fork. If using a regular brand canned in oil or water, drain off the liquid and flake the tuna without it.

Cook the spaghetti in a large pot of generously salted boiling water until tender but still firm to the bite.

Meanwhile, heat the olive oil in a medium sauté pan over high heat. Add the onions and cook, stirring frequently, until tender but not soft. Stir in the lemon zest and juice, garlic, capers, olives, and tuna with its juices. Heat through and season with salt and pepper to taste, and red pepper flakes, if using. Toss the tuna sauce with the cooked spaghetti and sprinkle with the parsley.

Note: For best flavor, use a premium tuna, preferably Northwest tuna canned in its own juices. Otherwise, our next choices, in order of preference, would be: an imported oil-packed tuna; domestic oil-packed tuna; water-packed tuna.

— Adapted from *The Mediterranean Kitchen*,
   by Joyce Goldstein (William Morrow)

SPAGHETTI WITH CLAM SAUCE

MAKES 6 SERVINGS

Linda Faus, Foodday's former test kitchen director, developed this recipe for her "Fit for Dinner" column, and it weighs in at a very sensible 22 percent of calories from fat. Keep a few cans of clams in the pantry and you can whip this up almost any night.

4 (6¼-ounce) cans chopped clams in juice
1 pound spaghetti
Salt
¼ cup olive oil
6 cloves garlic, minced
½ to ¾ teaspoon crushed red pepper flakes
1 teaspoon dried basil
1 tablespoon all-purpose flour
1½ teaspoons fresh lemon juice
½ teaspoon grated lemon zest
¼ cup chopped fresh parsley

Over a small bowl or measuring cup drain clams; reserve juice and clams separately.

Bring a large pot of salted water to a boil, add the spaghetti and cook just until tender but still firm to the bite. Drain and keep hot.

Heat the olive oil in a large skillet over medium heat. Stir in the garlic, pepper flakes, and basil; cook for 30 to 45 seconds. Stir in the flour and cook, stirring, for 1 minute. Add the lemon juice, lemon zest, and reserved clam juice and bring to a simmer; cook for 1 to 2 minutes. When the spaghetti is done, drain it, and add it to the skillet along with the reserved clams and parsley. Toss well and serve immediately.

— From Linda Faus

LINGUINE WITH SALMON AND ASPARAGUS

MAKES 6 SERVINGS

This is another recipe from Linda Faus' "Fit for Dinner" column. It calls for just 2 tablespoons of added fat, but you'd never know it because the shallots, capers, and lemon juice add plenty of zing.

1 pound salmon fillet
1 pound thick asparagus spears, tough ends discarded
Salt and freshly ground black pepper
1 pound linguine
1 tablespoon olive oil
½ cup minced shallots (about 3 shallots)
¼ cup drained capers, chopped
½ cup dry white wine

¼ cup fresh lemon juice
1 tablespoon all-purpose flour
2 tablespoons water
1 tablespoon grated lemon zest
6 tablespoons half-and-half
¼ cup fresh basil leaves, thinly sliced

Preheat oven to 400 degrees. Place the salmon and trimmed asparagus spears on a large baking sheet and season with salt and pepper. Bake for 10 to 15 minutes or until the salmon is opaque and flakes easily and the asparagus spears are tender crisp. Remove from the oven and break the salmon into large chunks, and cut the asparagus into 1½-inch pieces. Set aside and keep warm.

▶

While the salmon is cooking, bring a large pot of salted water to a boil and cook linguine until barely tender to the bite, about 9 to 10 minutes. Drain and keep warm.

In a large skillet, heat the olive oil over medium-high heat. Add the shallots, reduce the heat to medium, and cook until they are tender but not browned, about 3 to 4 minutes. Increase heat to high, add the capers, white wine, and lemon juice; bring to a boil. Boil briskly until the sauce is reduced to about ¼ cup.

Meanwhile, make a slurry by stirring together the flour and the 2 tablespoons water; whisk slurry into the sauce and return to a boil. Cook for 1 minute or until the sauce is thickened and the flour no longer tastes raw. Whisk in the lemon zest and half-and-half. Taste for seasoning and add salt and/or pepper, if necessary. Add the cooked linguine and toss and cook for about 1 minute to finish cooking the linguine. Carefully toss in the salmon, asparagus, and basil; serve.

— From Linda Faus

SPAGHETTI WITH CURRIED SEAFOOD MARINARA

MAKES 6 SERVINGS

When it comes to Italian food, curry powder just doesn't compute. But we love the flavor of this dish, and its simplicity, too.

1 pound spaghetti
2 tablespoons extra-virgin olive oil
3 cloves garlic, minced
1 tablespoon curry powder
½ teaspoon crushed red pepper flakes
Salt
½ cup dry white wine
2 (8-ounce) cans plain tomato sauce
12 ounces medium shrimp, shelled and deveined
12 ounces sea scallops, quartered
½ cup chopped fresh Italian (flat-leaf) parsley

In a large pot of boiling salted water, cook the spaghetti until tender but still firm to the bite.

Meanwhile, in a large, deep skillet, heat the olive oil over medium heat. Add the garlic and cook until golden, about 1 minute. Add the curry powder, crushed red pepper flakes, and a pinch of salt and cook, stirring, for 1 minute. Add the wine and cook over high heat until wine evaporates, about 2 minutes. Add the tomato sauce and cook over high heat, stirring occasionally, for 4 minutes. Add the shrimp and scallops to the skillet; simmer, stirring, until just cooked through, about 3 minutes.

Drain the spaghetti, add it to the skillet, and toss well. Season to taste with salt and sprinkle on the parsley. Transfer the spaghetti to bowls and serve.

— Adapted from *Food & Wine* magazine, February 2004

SPICY RIGATONI "ALL'ETNA"

MAKES 4 SERVINGS

Contributor Ivy Manning re-created this dish after enjoying it at a pensione near Mount Etna in Sicily. The innkeeper told her that the blobs of fresh mozzarella that melt on top of the pasta are its "lava."

2 tablespoons extra-virgin olive oil
½ cup grated onion
1 large clove garlic, minced
1 (28-ounce) can crushed tomatoes with basil
¾ cup black oil-cured olives (pitted, if desired)
½ teaspoon smoked Spanish paprika
    (pimentón de la Vera)
¼ teaspoon cayenne pepper
1 tablespoon sea salt
12 ounces rigatoni pasta
1 (4-ounce) ball fresh mozzarella, torn into
    small pieces

In a large skillet, heat the oil over medium-high heat. Add the onion and sauté until golden brown, 3 minutes. Add the garlic and cook, stirring constantly, until fragrant, 45 seconds. Add the tomatoes, olives, paprika, and cayenne. Bring to a simmer and cook on medium-low heat for 15 minutes.

Meanwhile, bring 10 cups of water to a boil in a medium pot. Add salt and rigatoni. Cook until the pasta is tender but still firm to the bite, about 14 minutes. Drain the pasta and add to the skillet with the sauce. Place the pasta and sauce in a large, warm serving bowl; sprinkle with the cheese. Cover with an inverted bowl and let the pasta sit for 5 minutes to allow mozzarella to melt. Serve immediately.

—From Ivy Manning

PASTA ALLA PUTTANESCA

MAKES 6 SERVINGS

There are many versions of puttanesca, but this one from popular Italian cooking authority Giuliano Bugialli is among the simplest, partly because the sauce is uncooked. Only use best-quality, in-season tomatoes. And absolutely do not add grated cheese.

1 pound very ripe tomatoes
4 cloves garlic
25 large leaves fresh basil, approximately
½ cup olive oil
Salt and freshly ground black pepper
1 pound dried pasta, such as chiocciole
    (shells or snails) or penne

Cut tomatoes into small pieces and put in a bowl. Chop the garlic coarsely and add to bowl, then tear the basil leaves into thirds and add to the bowl, along with oil, and salt and pepper to taste. Mix all the ingredients together, then cover the bowl with aluminum foil, and refrigerate for at least 2 hours.

About 30 minutes before serving time, bring a large amount of salted water to a boil. Cook the pasta until tender but still firm to the bite, about 12 minutes. Drain quickly and place it in a serving bowl.

While the pasta is still extremely hot, pour the refrigerated sauce over it. It is the reaction of very hot to very cold that releases the unique flavor of this dish. Toss very well and serve at once.

— Adapted from *The Fine Art of Italian Cooking*,
    by Giuliano Bugialli (Clarkson Potter)

PASTA ALLA SIRACUSANA

MAKES 4 LARGE SERVINGS

This dish is from a Cedar Mill-area restaurant, Pasta Prima, and tastes better the second day. When the recipe first ran in our "Restaurant Request" column, we called it vegetarian in spite of its 1 teaspoon of anchovy paste. Boy, did we ever hear protests from the purists. You can always omit the paste.

½ cup olive oil
1 teaspoon anchovy paste
2 cloves garlic, peeled and cut in half lengthwise
1 medium eggplant, peeled and cubed
2 (14½-ounce) cans diced tomatoes
½ green bell pepper, seeded and cut into strips
½ yellow bell pepper, seeded and cut into strips
10 kalamata olives, pitted and chopped
1 tablespoon capers
5 fresh basil leaves, shredded
¼ teaspoon freshly ground black pepper
Salt
Crushed red pepper flakes (optional)
1 pound angel hair or other dried pasta
Grated pecorino Romano cheese

Whisk together the olive oil and anchovy paste. Heat the oil mixture in a large skillet and sauté the garlic until soft, then discard garlic. Add the eggplant cubes and sauté until tender and golden, not browned, about 10 minutes. Eggplant will at first absorb all the oil, but as it cooks, it begins to release it—almost a third of the original measure. Drain this oil and add the tomatoes to the skillet; cook, covered, for 5 to 6 minutes. Stir in the bell pepper strips, olives, capers, basil, black pepper, and salt to taste. Add red pepper flakes to taste, if using. Cover and continue cooking about 20 minutes.

Meanwhile, cook pasta in generously salted boiling water until tender but still firm to the bite. Drain and serve eggplant mixture over cooked pasta. Top with grated Romano cheese.

— From Maria Gross, Pasta Prima, Cedar Mill

PASTA WITH SPRING VEGETABLES IN LIGHT, LEMONY CREAM SAUCE

MAKES 2 TO 3 MAIN-DISH SERVINGS

Too often pasta primavera is a sad affair, with a heavy, rich sauce and incompatible vegetables. But former Foodday editor Martha Holmberg developed a light yet luscious recipe that really lives up to the meaning of "alla primavera," which in Italian cooking means "spring style."

1 tablespoon butter

1 tablespoon sliced scallions, white and light green parts

1 (14½-ounce) can reduced-sodium chicken broth

½ cup whipping cream or crème fraîche

1 teaspoon grated lemon zest

Salt and freshly ground black pepper

2 medium carrots, peeled and cut into ⅛-inch slices (about 1 cup)

½ medium fennel bulb, cut into ¼-inch dice (about ¾ cup)

12 medium asparagus spears, woody ends snapped off, cut into 1-inch lengths (about 1 cup)

1 cup shelled fresh or frozen peas (1 pound fresh English pea pods will yield about 1 cup)

8 ounces dried fettuccine or linguine

1½ cups freshly grated good-quality parmesan cheese

1 tablespoon chopped fresh herbs, such as parsley, dill, mint, tarragon, or basil (don't use a strong herb such as rosemary, oregano, or thyme)

Bring a large pot with at least 4 quarts of water to a boil. As it's coming to a boil, melt the butter in a medium heavy-based sauté pan, add the scallions, and cook over medium-high heat until fragrant, about 1 minute. Add the broth, turn the heat to high, and boil until reduced to about 1 cup, about 6 minutes.

Add the cream and continue boiling until you have about 1 cup of sauce, another 4 or 5 minutes. Remove the pan from the heat and add the lemon zest. Taste and season with salt and pepper (remember, you'll be adding salty cheese later). Set aside, but keep hot.

Once the pasta water is boiling, add 2 tablespoons salt and get a strainer or large slotted spoon handy. Add the carrots, fennel, and asparagus and boil for 1 minute, then add the peas or snap peas; boil 1 minute longer. Scoop out all the vegetables with the strainer or spoon, shake off the water, and put them in a bowl. Set aside and keep warm.

Let the water come back to a boil, add the pasta, and cook according to the package instructions. Just when the pasta is ready, dip a measuring cup into the water and pull out about ½ cup liquid. Drain the pasta and return it to the pan. Pour in the sauce, add the vegetables and the cheese and toss well, so all the pasta is coated and the cheese melts. The pasta will absorb a bit of liquid as it sits, so it should be fairly liquidy at first. Add a few spoonfuls of the reserved pasta water to get a light, creamy consistency, then toss in the herbs, taste again, and correct seasoning. Serve immediately, with more cheese at the table if you like.

— From Martha Holmberg

►

MAKING PRIMAVERA SAUCE

 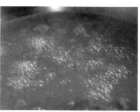 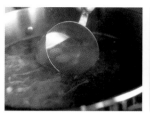 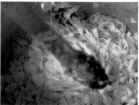

Trim asparagus by snapping, not cutting. Boil the broth several minutes to deepen the flavor. Set aside a cup of the starchy pasta water and use it to loosen the creamy sauce as you toss it with the pasta.

SKILLET LASAGNA

MAKES 6 SERVINGS

When you're craving lasagna but not all the work, this short-cut recipe fits the bill. It's especially nice for casual entertaining. If you don't like red pepper flakes, just omit them.

- 1 pound mild Italian sausage (casings removed if sausage is in links)
- 1 red bell pepper, stemmed, seeded and minced
- 2 cloves garlic, minced
- ¼ to ½ teaspoon crushed red pepper flakes
- Salt
- 8 curly-edged lasagna noodles (6 ounces; do not use no-boil variety), broken into 2-inch pieces
- 1 (26-ounce) jar marinara sauce (about 3 cups)
- 2 cups water
- ½ cup shredded part-skim mozzarella cheese (divided)
- ¼ cup grated parmesan cheese (divided)
- Freshly ground black pepper
- ¾ cup ricotta cheese (part-skim or whole milk—not nonfat)
- ¼ cup chopped fresh basil

Cook meat in a 12-inch nonstick skillet over high heat, breaking it into pieces with a wooden spoon.

Add red bell pepper and cook until fat from the sausage renders, 5 to 7 minutes. Drain fat from meat mixture and return meat to skillet.

Stir in garlic, red pepper flakes, and ½ teaspoon salt; cook over medium-high heat until garlic is fragrant, about 30 seconds.

Add broken noodles to skillet, marinara sauce, and 2 cups water. Cover and cook, stirring often, and adjusting heat as needed to maintain vigorous simmer, until noodles are tender, about 20 minutes. If mixture seems too dry, add a few tablespoons water.

Off heat, stir in half of mozzarella and half of parmesan. Season with salt and pepper. Dot heaping tablespoons of ricotta over noodles, then sprinkle with remaining mozzarella and parmesan.

Cover and let stand off heat until cheeses melt, 3 to 5 minutes. Sprinkle with basil before serving.

— Adapted from *The Best 30-Minute Recipes*, by the editors of *Cook's Illustrated* magazine

PUMPKIN LASAGNA

MAKES 12 SERVINGS

This vegetarian lasagna is heavenly. Thanks to canned pumpkin and no-boil noodles, it's also much easier than many other lasagna recipes. We apologize that you'll have ½ cup of pumpkin purée left over.

    2 tablespoons olive oil
    2 onions, chopped
    2 pounds Swiss chard, tough stems removed,
        leaves washed and chopped
    2¼ teaspoons salt (divided)
    1 teaspoon freshly ground black pepper
        (divided)
    1 teaspoon dried sage (divided)
    ½ teaspoon ground nutmeg (divided)
    3 cups canned pumpkin purée (one 28-ounce
        can minus ½ cup; divided)
    1½ cups whipping cream (divided)
    1½ cups grated parmesan cheese (divided)
    ½ cup milk
    9 no-boil lasagna noodles
    1 tablespoon butter

In a large nonstick frying pan, heat the oil over medium-low heat. Add the onions and cook, stirring constantly, until translucent, about 5 minutes. Increase the heat to medium-high and add the chard, carefully pressing it into the pan. Cook, stirring, until the chard is wilted. Add 1 teaspoon salt, ½ teaspoon pepper, ½ teaspoon sage, and ¼ teaspoon nutmeg; continue cooking and stirring until there is no liquid left in the pan, 5 to 10 minutes.

Preheat the oven to 400 degrees.

In a medium bowl, mix 2 cups pumpkin, ¾ cup cream, ½ cup parmesan, and the remaining 1¼ teaspoons salt, ½ teaspoon pepper, ½ teaspoon sage, and ¼ teaspoon nutmeg.

In a small bowl, combine the remaining 1 cup pumpkin with remaining ¾ cup cream. Set aside.

Pour the milk into a 9-by-13-inch baking dish. Place 3 noodles in the dish and spread half the pumpkin-parmesan mixture over them. Spread half the chard mixture over the pumpkin and add a second set of 3 noodles. Top with remaining half of the pumpkin-parmesan and the remaining chard mixture. Place remaining 3 noodles on top. Pour the reserved pumpkin-cream mixture over the top and sprinkle with remaining 1 cup parmesan. Cut butter into 3 pieces and place on top of the cheese.

Cover with aluminum foil and bake 20 minutes. Uncover and bake until golden, about 15 minutes more. Like most lasagna, this one is easier to cut if left to set for about 10 minutes before serving.

— Adapted from *Quick from Scratch Vegetable Main Dishes*, by Food & Wine Books

ACINI DE PEPE

MAKES 8 SERVINGS

Acini de pepe is a pasta variety shaped like tiny beads. Combined with wild rice, it makes a lovely pilaf. This dish can be made ahead and refrigerated, and it reheats nicely.

⅓ cup uncooked wild rice

3 quarts plus 1 cup water (divided)

8 ounces uncooked acini de pepe pasta (1 cup)

2 tablespoons butter

½ cup diced onion

¾ cup sliced fresh mushrooms

¼ teaspoon salt

¾ teaspoon dried garlic granules

¾ teaspoon freshly ground black pepper

2½ teaspoons dried basil

Wash wild rice thoroughly; place in small saucepan with 1 cup water. Bring to boil; lower heat and simmer, covered, until tender, about 45 minutes.

Meanwhile, in a 4- to 6-quart saucepan, bring remaining 3 quarts water to a boil. Add pasta and boil 10 to 12 minutes. Drain and set aside.

In a large skillet, melt the butter and sauté the onion until translucent. Add the mushrooms and sauté until tender. Add the pasta, wild rice, salt, garlic granules, pepper, and basil. Toss and cook until heated through.

— From McCormick's Fish House & Bar, Beaverton

PAD THAI WITH CHICKEN

MAKES 4 SERVINGS

Foodday contributor Ivy Manning says restaurant versions of pad Thai served in the U.S. are never nearly as good as the pad Thai she enjoyed in Thailand. So she developed her own recipe, and readers loved it. Ivy uses cherry tomatoes and green beans in her dish, but she says you can look to your own vegetable crisper or garden for inspiration.

10 ounces dry rice noodles, preferably about ⅓ inch wide

2 tablespoons firmly packed brown sugar

1 tablespoon granulated sugar

1 tablespoon tamarind concentrate (preferably Tamicon brand)

1 tablespoon sriracha chili sauce

3 tablespoons plus 1 teaspoon fish sauce (divided)

1 small boneless, skinless chicken breast half, thinly sliced (about 6 ounces)

¼ teaspoon freshly ground black pepper

3 tablespoons vegetable oil (divided)

½ cup thinly sliced onions

1 tablespoon minced garlic

½ cup cherry tomatoes, halved

½ cup green beans, trimmed and cut into ½-inch pieces

2 eggs, lightly beaten

½ cup (loosely packed) roughly chopped fresh basil

3 tablespoons chopped roasted peanuts

2 limes, cut into wedges

Place the noodles in a large bowl and cover them with very hot tap water. Set aside and soak until the noodles are pliable, 30 minutes. While the noodles are soaking, prepare the other ingredients.

In a glass measuring cup, combine the brown sugar, granulated sugar, tamarind concentrate, sriracha sauce, and 3 tablespoons fish sauce; stir until the sugars dissolve. In a medium bowl, toss the chicken with the remaining teaspoon of fish sauce and the black pepper.

Drain the noodles and pat them dry. Line up all the ingredients next to the stove. Heat 1 tablespoon oil in a wok or large skillet over medium-high heat. Add the chicken and stir-fry until cooked through, about 5 minutes. Transfer chicken to a large serving bowl; set aside.

Return the wok to medium-high heat and add 1 tablespoon oil. Add the onions and stir-fry until they begin to brown, 1 minute. Add the garlic and stir-fry for 20 seconds. Add the tomatoes and green beans; stir-fry until the tomatoes begin to soften and collapse, 2 minutes. Pour in the eggs and stir vigorously with a spatula until they are just set, 1 minute. Transfer mixture to the serving bowl with the chicken.

Return the wok to medium-high heat and add the remaining tablespoon of the oil to the wok. When the oil is hot, add the rice noodles. Stir-fry until they begin to sear on the edges, 2 minutes. Add the sugar-tamarind mixture and contents of the serving bowl; toss everything together. Transfer the noodles to the serving bowl; toss with the basil and peanuts. Squeeze half of the lime wedges over the noodles and serve, passing remaining lime wedges on the side.

— From Ivy Manning

CHICKEN YAKISOBA

MAKES 4 SERVINGS

This is a basic and mildly flavored yakisoba that has been popular with readers. It also makes very generous servings. If you don't have time to marinate the chicken, simply cut it across the grain in ¼-inch-thick slices and sauté separately before sautéing the vegetables. Add the cooked chicken to the vegetables and noodles when you add the reserved soy sauce mixture.

½ cup soy sauce
½ cup water
½ cup granulated sugar
5 tablespoons dark sesame oil (divided)
1 tablespoon minced garlic (3 cloves)
1 tablespoon peeled and grated fresh ginger
4 boneless, skinless chicken breasts halves
4 (7-ounce) packages fresh yakisoba noodles, uncooked

1 large carrot, peeled and julienned
1 large yellow onion, julienned
Sesame seeds, to garnish
Thinly sliced scallions, to garnish

In a medium bowl, mix together soy sauce, water, sugar, 1 tablespoon sesame oil, garlic, and ginger. Place the chicken in a plastic bag and add 6 tablespoons of the soy sauce mixture; close bag and marinate in the refrigerator for 24 hours. Reserve remaining soy sauce mixture for cooking the noodles.

To cook, remove the noodles from the packages and gently separate. Reserve seasoning packets for another use.

In a large skillet or wok, heat 2 tablespoons sesame oil over high heat. Add carrot and onion; sauté until almost brown. Reduce heat to medium and add noodles. Stir-fry 3 to 4 minutes or until they begin to stick to the pan. Add the reserved soy sauce mixture and stir-fry for 1 to 2 minutes longer.

Meanwhile, in a separate skillet, heat remaining 2 tablespoons sesame oil. Sauté the chicken breasts 3 to 4 minutes per side or until just cooked through. Cut cooked breasts against the grain into thin slices.

Divide the noodles evenly among 4 bowls and fan the chicken breast over the top. Garnish with sesame seeds and scallions.

— From Hallmark Inn, Hillsboro

WE'RE LUKEWARM ON WOKS

In an ideal world, we would all have powerful stoves and scads of pans for every purpose, like a wok. But on the average home cooktop, a relatively small area of the wok touches the burner. This means it can be difficult to get the pan hot enough to achieve a good sear, which is essential for a stir-fry. We have found that a large skillet, with its big, flat bottom, can give better results. Just make sure you use a skillet without a Teflon-type coating, which isn't intended for use over high heat.

If you have success with your wok, by all means use it. Here's how to season and care for it:

A brand-new carbon-steel wok, or one that hasn't been used in a long time, needs to be seasoned before use. But first, a new wok needs to be scoured to remove the coating that manufacturers apply to prevent rust. Scrub the wok vigorously with a scouring pad and hot soapy water, then rinse and repeat.

Next, set the pan over low heat until all the water droplets evaporate. Once it's completely dry, you can start the seasoning process. Preheat the wok over high heat until it's hot enough to instantly vaporize a drop of water. Now add 2 tablespoons of peanut oil, ½ cup sliced unpeeled ginger, and 1 bunch of scallions (not wet), cut into 2-inch lengths. Reduce heat to medium and stir-fry these ingredients for 20 minutes, repeatedly pressing the ginger and scallions against the bottom and sides of the pan. Add a little extra oil if things seem to be drying out.

Remove the pan from the heat and allow it to cool completely before discarding the onion and ginger. Wash the wok with a nonabrasive sponge and hot water, but don't use soap. Set it on a burner over low heat to dry.

Remember, you don't want to scrub off the browned or blackened stuff—that's the start of the wok's seasoned patina, which will get deeper, darker and more nonstick with use. A blackened wok also absorbs more heat and radiates it into the food, so the pan cooks faster and more efficiently.

Avoid using a new wok to heat water, which breaks down the new seasoning. That means no steaming, boiling, or poaching. If you do a lot of Chinese cooking, consider doing what traditional cooks do: have a wok designated only for cooking with water and another separate wok reserved for stir-frying, pan-frying and deep-frying. Also avoid using acidic ingredients in a newly seasoned wok. After it's well-seasoned, you can cook acidic ingredients, but don't leave them in the pan for long.

To clean your wok, scrub it under hot tap water and use very little, if any, soap. Don't put it in the dishwasher, and don't use abrasive detergents or harsh scrubbing sponges.

If your wok has stuck-on bits or a stubborn stickiness, give it a "facial": preheat the pan until hot, then remove from heat, and add 2 teaspoons salt and 1 teaspoon peanut or vegetable oil. Use a double thickness of paper towel to rub the salt scrub around the pan (be careful not to burn yourself). Rinse, then dry the pan over low heat.

SPICY COLD SOBA NOODLES

MAKES 4 SERVINGS

Unlike the yakisoba recipe in this chapter, these soba noodles pack a kick from the sriracha sauce. If you like your food less spicy, cut back on this ingredient.

8 ounces dry soba noodles

½ large red bell pepper, cut in julienne strips

1½ cups fresh sugar snap peas, sliced on the bias

3 scallions, thinly sliced on the bias

2 tablespoons vegetable oil

2 tablespoons dark sesame oil

2 tablespoons red wine vinegar

2 tablespoons plus 2 teaspoons soy sauce

2 tablespoons plus 2 teaspoons granulated sugar

1 to 2 tablespoons sriracha chili sauce (or other hot chile sauce), or to taste

Cook soba noodles a minute or two less than the time indicated on the package. You want them to still be a little firm to the bite. Rinse with cold water and drain completely.

Toss noodles in a large bowl with red bell pepper, snap peas and scallions; set aside.

Combine vegetable oil, sesame oil, vinegar, soy sauce, sugar and chili paste with a whisk. Pour over noodle mixture and toss until evenly coated. Chill until ready to serve.

— Adapted from Benji's Deli Express

AUSTRIAN BACON AND CHIVE BREAD DUMPLINGS

MAKES 4 SERVINGS

Dumplings go with more than just chicken. Contributor Ivy Manning makes nockerl—hearty dumplings made with day-old bread—and pairs them with kielbasa and sauerkraut or braised red cabbage seasoned with caraway seeds.

1 egg

½ cup milk

2 tablespoons minced fresh chives

¾ teaspoon salt

¼ teaspoon freshly ground black pepper

1 tablespoon olive oil

2 slices thick-cut bacon, finely diced (about ½ cup)

¼ cup finely chopped onion

3 to 4 slices of hearty day-old white bread cut into ¼-inch cubes (2¾ cups)

½ cup all-purpose flour

2 quarts water

2 chicken bouillon cubes

2 tablespoons butter

In a large bowl, whisk together the egg, milk, chives, salt, and pepper; set aside.

In a large skillet, heat the olive oil over medium heat. Add the bacon and onion; cook until the bacon is crisp and the onion is tender, 4 minutes. Add the bread cubes and fry, stirring constantly, until the bread is lightly toasted, 3 to 6 minutes. Remove the bread mixture to a large bowl; set aside the unwashed skillet. Pour the egg-milk mixture over the bread mixture and let stand for 10 minutes. Stir in the flour. Cover and refrigerate for 30 minutes or up to 1 day.

In a large saucepan, bring the 2 quarts of water to a boil with the bouillon cubes. Reduce the heat to maintain a gentle simmer. With wet hands, form the bread cube mixture into 12 golf ball-size dumplings. Add the dumplings to the saucepan and cook until the dumplings have puffed slightly and are firm in the center, 15 minutes.

In the pan used to sauté the bacon and onions, melt the butter over medium heat, scraping up any browned bits with a wooden spoon. With a slotted spoon, transfer the cooked dumplings to the pan and toss well to coat dumplings with butter.

— From Ivy Manning

FISH AND SHELLFISH

6

GINGER AND BLACK SOY-GLAZED SALMON

MAKES 4 SERVINGS

You'll need a few Asian cooking staples to make this dish, but the only one that's not available at most supermarkets is the black soy sauce, and we've provided a substitute for that. For the best results, look for salmon fillets at least 1 inch thick.

1 (1-inch) knob fresh ginger, peeled and finely grated (preferably on a Microplane-style grater)

1 large clove garlic, finely grated

⅓ cup mirin (sweetened rice wine)

3 tablespoons unseasoned rice vinegar

3 tablespoons black soy sauce (also called kecap manis or sweet soy sauce; see note)

½ to 1 teaspoon sambal or sriracha hot sauce (optional)

4 (4- to 6-ounce) thick-cut salmon fillets, patted dry and pin bones removed

2 scallions, trimmed, sliced very thin on the bias

In a bowl, blend together ginger, garlic, mirin, vinegar, black soy sauce, and hot sauce, if using. Pour into a dish large enough to contain the fish; submerge fillets, flesh side down. Refrigerate for 6 to 8 hours.

Remove fish from marinade. Pour marinade into a small saucepan and simmer over medium-high heat until thick and syrupy, 5 to 7 minutes, stirring occasionally to prevent scorching.

Meanwhile, adjust oven rack to within 6 inches of broiler and heat broiler. Broil fish on a rimmed baking sheet about 4 minutes. Brush fish liberally with the reduced marinade and cook 3 to 5 minutes longer, until fish is done inside to your liking and the outside glossy. Brush fish with any remaining sauce and serve immediately, topped with scallions.

Note: Black soy sauce, or kecap manis, is a sweet Indonesian soy-based sauce that tastes like a synthesis of soy sauce and mild molasses. Find it at most Asian stores or at grocery stores that have a wide variety of Asian products. If black soy sauce is unavailable, you can make it by combining 2¼ teaspoons regular soy sauce with 2 tablespoons plus ¾ teaspoon mild molasses.

— From Matthew Card

THE WIDE WORLD OF RICE WINE AND ASIAN VINEGAR

The world of Asian ingredients can be a bit bewildering. But it's worth getting to know some essential staples. With the exception of sake and shao hsing, all are sold in the Asian foods aisle of most supermarkets.

Sake: Japanese rice wine. This is a beverage and is sold with other wines.

Mirin: Japanese low-alcohol rice wine that contains 40 to 50 percent sugar, and sometimes salt.

Rice vinegar/rice wine vinegar: Vinegar made from rice wine; milder and less acidic than Western vinegars. Unless otherwise specified, Foodday recipes use the Japanese style, which is mellow and almost sweet.

Seasoned rice vinegar: Japanese rice vinegar that has been sweetened with corn syrup or sugar.

Shao hsing/shaoxing: Chinese rice wine used for drinking as well as cooking. Sometimes referred to as "yellow wine." The style of shao hsing used for cooking is easily found at Asian markets, usually with vinegars. Dry sherry makes a good substitute.

SALMON BURGERS

MAKES 7 PATTIES

Although it's easy to find salmon burgers at most seafood counters, making your own takes very little effort. Serve them on toasted buns with your favorite accompaniments, or alongside a salad tossed in vinaigrette. Note that Danielle Centoni, editor of *The Oregonian's MIX* magazine, developed this recipe to have leftover patties to use to make a second meal: Salmon and Spinach Pasta (recipe follows).

> 2 (14¾-ounce) cans pink or red salmon
> 3 eggs
> ⅓ cup sliced scallions
> ¼ cup chopped fresh Italian (flat-leaf) parsley
> 2 tablespoons capers
> 2 teaspoons Dijon mustard
> Grated zest of 1 lemon
> Juice of ½ lemon
> 2 cloves garlic, grated
> Salt and freshly ground black pepper
> ⅔ cup dry breadcrumbs
> Vegetable oil

Drain the salmon in a fine-mesh sieve. Pick through the meat to remove the bones and dark pieces of skin. Set meat aside.

Beat the eggs in a medium mixing bowl. Add the scallions, parsley, capers, mustard, lemon zest, lemon juice, garlic, and salt and pepper. Stir to combine. Add the salmon and breadcrumbs; gently mix to combine.

Place a large sauté pan over medium heat. Add 2 teaspoons oil. Working in batches, scoop the salmon mixture using a ½ cup measuring cup, and add to the pan. Press to flatten each scoop into a patty. Cook until golden brown on one side, about 2 to 3 minutes. Flip and cook the other side until golden, about 2 to 3 minutes more. Repeat with the remaining mixture.

Serve 4 patties on toasted buns or alongside a tossed salad. Save the remaining patties to make the following recipe for Salmon and Spinach Pasta.

— From Danielle Centoni

SALMON AND SPINACH PASTA

MAKES 4 TO 6 SERVINGS

Danielle Centoni developed this recipe to use patties from the previous recipe, but you could also make it with salmon patties bought from a seafood counter and cooked at home.

> 1½ cups chicken broth
> ½ cup whipping cream
> 3 leftover salmon patties, crumbled
> 2 cups fresh spinach leaves
>   Juice of ½ lemon
> Salt and freshly ground black pepper
> 1 pound dried fettuccine

In a medium sauté pan, boil broth until reduced to 1 cup, about 6 minutes. Add cream and boil until mixture is reduced to 1 cup, about 4 or 5 minutes. Remove from heat and add salmon and spinach; stir until combined. Add lemon juice, and season with salt and pepper to taste.

▶

Meanwhile, cook fettuccine in salted boiling water just until tender to the bite; drain pasta, reserving 1 cup pasta water. Toss cooked pasta with the salmon cream sauce, adding some of the reserved pasta water to smooth out the sauce if necessary.

— From Danielle Centoni

PANCETTA-WRAPPED ROAST HALIBUT

MAKES 4 SERVINGS

Look for a large halibut fillet at least 1 inch thick; anything thinner is liable to overcook before the pancetta crisps. Fattier pancetta works well here. You may have some left over, but some of the pieces may rip while wrapping the fish and you can use the extras.

Kosher salt and freshly ground black pepper
1½ teaspoons minced fresh thyme
1½ pounds halibut fillets, 1 inch thick,
    skinned and cut into 4 equal pieces
⅓ pound thinly sliced pancetta
1 tablespoon chopped fresh parsley
1 lemon, quartered

Adjust oven rack to middle position and preheat oven to 550 degrees. Place a heavy-duty rimmed baking sheet or roasting pan on rack to heat.

Season each fillet liberally with salt, pepper, and thyme. Starting ½ inch in from the tip of the fillet, wrap fillet with slices of pancetta, overlapping slightly. Wrap to within ½ inch of end of fillet.

Remove baking sheet from oven and place fish fillets, at least 2 inches apart, on sheet. Roast until pancetta has crisped and fish is opaque and beginning to flake, 12 to 15 minutes. Serve immediately, sprinkled with parsley and accompanied by lemon wedge.

— From Matthew Card

JUDGING DONENESS WHEN COOKING FISH

The general rule of thumb for cooking fish is 10 minutes per inch of thickness. But the thickness of fish fillets is often uneven, and the rate of cooking depends on the method and temperature. So use your recipe as a guide, but test the fish a few minutes early to be safe. You can try these methods and find the one that works best for you:

- Make a small incision at the thickest part. As soon as the fish is opaque inside, take it off the heat. Some fish are even better removed from the heat while still a little translucent inside, especially leaner types of salmon.
- Insert the tip of a knife or a metal skewer into the fish. If it meets resistance, the fish is still too rare.
- Some chefs insert the tip of a knife or metal skewer into the fish, hold it there for 15 seconds, and then touch the metal to their hand or upper lip. If the blade is cool or just warm, the fish needs to cook longer.
- Press the fish at its thickest part with your index finger; over time you will begin to learn how a nicely cooked fillet feels: like the tip of your nose, not too mushy and not too hard.
- Use an instant-read thermometer to measure the internal temperature at the thickest part of the fish. The USDA recommends 145 degrees, but many chefs prefer 140 degrees or lower.

ROASTED HALIBUT WITH ORANGE-CHILE GLAZE

MAKES 4 SERVINGS

After halibut marinates in a sweet, spicy citrus mixture, the marinade is reduced to a glaze that you spoon over the fish when it comes out of the oven. The result is easy and delicious, with just 215 calories per serving. Since halibut is a firm fish, you could also do this on the grill instead of in the oven.

⅓ cup orange juice
2 teaspoons vegetable oil
Grated zest of 1 lime
3 tablespoons lime juice
1 serrano chile, stemmed, seeded
    and minced
1 tablespoon firmly packed brown sugar
½ teaspoon ground paprika
Pinch ground allspice
1 (1⅓-pound) halibut fillet, cut into 4 portions
¼ teaspoon salt

Whisk together the orange juice, oil, lime zest and juice, chile, brown sugar, paprika, and allspice.

Put the fish into a glass dish and pour half of the orange mixture over it. Refrigerate 1 hour. Refrigerate the remaining orange mixture separately.

Preheat oven to 450 degrees. Remove fish from marinade; discard marinade. Place fish on a foil-lined broiling pan and sprinkle with salt. Roast 10 minutes per inch of thickness, or until the fish is barely opaque in the thickest part.

While the fish is cooking, put the remaining orange mixture into a small saucepan; reduce at a high simmer until thick and syrupy.

Spoon the glaze over the fish and serve.

HALIBUT PICCATA

MAKES 2 SERVINGS

Pan drippings, lemon juice, and capers are the classic ingredients for a piccata-style dish, usually done with veal. But in this version from chef Peter Roscoe, halibut stands in beautifully.

¼ cup all-purpose flour
½ teaspoon salt
½ teaspoon black pepper
1 tablespoon olive oil
2 (6½- to 7-ounce) halibut fillets, about
    1 inch thick
3 tablespoons dry white wine (such as
    chardonnay or pinot gris)
Juice of 2 lemons (about ⅓ to ½ cup)
3 cloves garlic, thinly sliced
1 tablespoon drained capers
5 to 8 tablespoons unsalted butter
Salt and freshly ground black pepper
Chopped fresh parsley, to garnish

Preheat oven to 350 degrees.

In a wide, shallow bowl, whisk together the flour, salt and pepper.

▶

Preheat a large nonstick sauté pan over medium-high until hot and add the olive oil. Lightly coat the halibut fillets in the seasoned flour and place in the pan. Sear until golden brown, about 1 minute per side. Flip the fillets to sear the underside, then transfer them to a baking sheet and place in the oven to finish cooking, about 5 minutes more. The halibut should be just cooked through.

Meanwhile, add the wine and lemon juice to the pan, stirring to scrape up any browned bits. Add the garlic and capers, and cook the liquid over medium-high until reduced by two-thirds. Remove pan from heat and whisk in 5 tablespoons butter to create a creamy, piquant sauce. Taste and whisk in more butter, if desired. Season with salt and pepper to taste.

Place fillets on two plates and drizzle each with the piccata sauce. Garnish with a sprinkle of chopped parsley.

— From chef-owner Peter Roscoe, Fulio's Pastaria & Tuscan Steak House, Astoria

LEMON AID FOR COOKS

Lemon is a cook's secret weapon. When food tastes too bland, sometimes all it needs is a spritz of fresh lemon juice to brighten the flavors and bring the dish alive. Other acidic foods, like brined olives, capers or a splash of vinegar, can often work a similar magic.

HAZELNUT-CRUSTED HALIBUT WITH FOREST MUSHROOMS AND SHERRY VINAIGRETTE

MAKES 4 SERVINGS

Chef Marco Fife combines firm, sweet halibut, hazelnuts, and sautéed forest mushrooms in a simple but sublime recipe that defines Northwest cuisine.

HALIBUT AND MUSHROOMS:

2 tablespoons vegetable oil (divided)
1 medium shallot, thinly sliced
1 pound mixed fresh mushrooms, such as oyster, maitake, shiitake, and chanterelles, torn or cut into pieces
6 sage leaves, cut into thin ribbons
Salt and freshly ground black pepper
4 (6- to 7-ounce) halibut fillets
¼ cup finely chopped hazelnuts, toasted (see note)

VINAIGRETTE:

¼ cup plus 2 tablespoons sherry vinegar
1 tablespoon Dijon mustard
2 tablespoons olive oil
Salt and freshly ground black pepper

To make halibut and mushrooms: In a large sauté pan, heat 1 tablespoon vegetable oil over medium-high heat. Add the shallot; sauté until it begins to brown. Add mushrooms and cook until mushrooms are quite brown and beginning to crisp. Add sage and a pinch of salt and pepper. Cook until sage begins to wilt. Remove to a bowl and keep warm. Don't rinse the pan yet; you'll use it to make the vinaigrette.

In a large skillet, heat remaining tablespoon vegetable oil over high heat. Season fish with salt and pepper. Place fish in pan, skin side up, and cook until the fish releases itself when the pan is shaken, 2 to 3 minutes. Reduce heat to medium-high, turn fish over, and sprinkle with hazelnuts. Cook another 4 minutes or more, depending on the thickness of the halibut, until just cooked through.

To make vinaigrette: Add the vinegar to the mushroom pan and place over medium-high heat. Scrape up any browned bits with a wooden spoon and incorporate into the liquid. Remove from heat and pour into a small bowl. Add mustard and olive oil, and whisk until smooth. Season with salt and pepper to taste.

To serve, place mushrooms in the center of 4 plates, place fish on top, and drizzle with vinaigrette.

Note: To toast hazelnuts, spread the shelled nuts in a shallow pan and roast in a 350-degree oven for 8 to 10 minutes, or until the skins crack. To remove skins, rub warm nuts with a rough cloth or between your palms.

— From chef Marco Shaw, Fife restaurant

BACON-WRAPPED BARBECUED TROUT

MAKES 4 TO 6 SERVINGS

Compared to many fish, trout is very affordable. It's also a sustainable choice you can feel good about buying. Its mild flavor takes beautifully to this simple preparation of Old Bay seasoning, bacon, lemon, and thyme.

> 4 small trout (dressed, but head left on)
> 2 tablespoons Old Bay seasoning
> ¾ lemon, very thinly sliced and then cut in half-moons
> 1 small bunch fresh thyme
> 8 thin slices bacon

Start charcoal briquettes, or preheat half of a gas grill to medium-high (see note) and leave the other half off. Rinse the fish inside and out; pat dry with paper towels. Rub the inside of each trout with ½ teaspoon of the seasoning, and lay a few lemon slices and a quarter of the thyme in each cavity. Rub the outsides of the fish with the remaining seasoning. Carefully wrap two bacon slices around each fish from the tail to the head, affixing the ends of the bacon with toothpicks.

If using charcoal, spread the ashed-over briquettes under half of the grill grate, creating a hot zone and a cool zone. Rub the grill grates with a bit of oil and place the fish on the cool side. Cover and grill for 5 minutes. Using two spatulas, carefully flip the fish over, cover and cook for 5 more minutes. The fish is cooked through when the eyes are opaque white and a knife inserted near the dorsal fin (the top of the fish) reveals flaky, opaque white at the backbone.

Transfer the trout to the hot side of the grill and cook uncovered until the bacon is crisped, about 40 seconds per side. Serve immediately.

Note: To check grill temperature, count the seconds you can hold your hand, palm side down, 2 to 3 inches above the rack, until it feels uncomfortable: 3 seconds for medium-high.

— From Ivy Manning

STEAMED FISH WITH SIZZLED GINGER AND GREEN ONIONS

MAKES 5 SERVINGS

Steaming is a great way to gently cook fish without a lot of added fat. This Chinese dish is a very simple preparation, but the fresh ginger and scallions, lightly sizzled with a dousing of hot oil, gives the mild fish a jolt of flavor. Cutting the scallions into thin slivers makes them curl up like flowers when hit with the hot oil, but you can just slice them crosswise if you prefer.

    2 pounds firm white fish steaks or fillets
        (such as sea bass, tilapia, halibut, or carp)
    1 (1-inch) knob ginger, sliced into coins, plus
        2 tablespoons peeled and julienned
        (divided)
    1 teaspoon Chinese cooking wine (shao hsing)
        or dry sherry
    1 tablespoon granulated sugar
    2 tablespoons soy sauce
    1 teaspoon dark sesame oil (optional)
    4 scallions, thinly sliced
    3 tablespoons vegetable or peanut oil

Dry the fish with paper towels. Place the fish on a heatproof platter, with the coins of ginger scattered throughout. In a deep saucepan or a wok, place a steam rack (or a couple of empty metal cans or some wadded up foil). Pour 2 to 3 inches of water in the pan, place the plate of fish on top of the steamer/cans, and cover. Bring to a boil, and cook until the fish is done, 7 to 8 minutes. When done, remove from the steamer, and drain any accumulated water. Discard the ginger coins.

In a small bowl, add the julienned ginger, wine, sugar, soy sauce, sesame oil, and scallions; stir until sugar is dissolved. Spread over fish.

Heat the vegetable oil in a skillet until it is just barely smoking. Pour the hot oil evenly over the fish, which will lightly cook the ginger and scallions. Serve immediately.

— From Sally Li

BUYING FRESH FISH AND SHRIMP

The first step in any seafood recipe is buying the freshest fish or shellfish you can find. Here's how:

- Make sure the fish is refrigerated or kept on fresh ice that is not melting.
- Ask the fishmonger to let you sniff the fish: It should smell fresh and briny, without fishy or ammonia odors.
- Look for shiny flesh, bright red gills, and clear eyes that have not turned dull and sunken into their sockets.
- The flesh should spring back when pressed. Avoid fish that has begun to darken or turn dry around the edges.
- Shrimp should look translucent and shiny with little or no odor.

CRUNCHY CATFISH WITH REMOULADE SAUCE AND PECAN PILAF

MAKES 4 SERVINGS

Although this isn't the fastest recipe, the oven-"frying" method works beautifully, and with the remoulade and rice pilaf, it makes an incredible meal.

PILAF:

2 tablespoons olive oil
½ cup finely chopped onion
¼ cup finely chopped carrot
¼ cup finely chopped celery
1 cup basmati rice
½ teaspoon Cajun seasoning (see note)
1¾ cups hot chicken broth
2 tablespoons chopped, toasted pecans
    (see note)
1 tablespoon finely chopped fresh dill
Salt and freshly ground black pepper

REMOULADE SAUCE:

6 tablespoons mayonnaise
1 tablespoon finely chopped fresh dill weed
2 tablespoons finely chopped scallions
1 teaspoon Cajun or coarse-grain mustard
1 teaspoon hot sauce
1 teaspoon ketchup
2 teaspoons fresh lemon juice
2 teaspoons capers

FISH:

1 cup fresh breadcrumbs
⅓ cup corn flour or finely ground cornmeal
    (see note)
1½ teaspoons Cajun seasoning
4 (5- to 6-ounce) catfish fillets
Salt and freshly ground black pepper
1 egg, beaten
4 teaspoons melted butter

Place oven rack in the center of the oven and preheat oven to 450 degrees. Line a rimmed baking sheet with foil and spray with nonstick cooking spray; set aside.

To make pilaf: In a medium saucepan, heat the oil over medium heat; sauté the onion, carrot, and celery until vegetables are tender but not browned, 8 minutes. Add the rice and Cajun seasoning, and sauté for 2 minutes, stirring frequently. Add the broth, reduce heat to maintain a gentle simmer, cover, and cook for 20 minutes. Fold in the pecans and dill immediately before serving, and taste to see if it needs salt and pepper.

To make sauce: In a medium bowl, whisk together the mayonnaise, dill weed, scallions, mustard, hot sauce, ketchup, lemon juice, and capers.

To make fish: On a large plate, combine the breadcrumbs, corn flour, and Cajun seasoning. Season the fish with salt and pepper. Dip the fish, one fillet at a time, in the egg, and then the breadcrumbs. Place the fish on the prepared baking sheet; bake for 5 minutes. Turn fish over with a spatula, drizzle with the butter, and bake until the fish easily flakes when pierced with a fork, about 6 minutes. Turn the broiler on until the breading is crisped and golden, about 1 minute. Serve the fish with rice and remoulade sauce.

Note: Many Cajun seasonings have quite a bit of salt, so if you can, choose one where it's not listed as the first ingredient on the label.

Note: To toast nuts, spread on a baking sheet and bake in a 350-degree oven for 5 to 8 minutes or until they start to brown.

Note: Alber's and Bob's Red Mill both make corn flour, but you can substitute a finely ground cornmeal.

— From Ivy Manning

FRESH CRUMBS ARE WORTH YOUR TIME

We know that store-bought breadcrumbs are convenient, but if a recipe calls for fresh breadcrumbs, don't substitute store-bought. Fresh are much lighter and fluffier, and the difference in texture will be noticeable in the finished dish. Small amounts of fresh breadcrumbs can be grated from an artisan loaf on a box grater. For larger amounts, use a food processor.

FISH TACOS

MAKES 6 SERVINGS

Too many fish tacos rely on tomato-based salsas that mask the fish's delicate flavor and yield a generic south-of-the-border taste. But in this recipe, contributor Matthew Card substitutes a dressing that has a potent chipotle chile and balances it with a carrot- and radish-driven slaw to cut through the heat. It's a delicious combination that really showcases the tasty fried fish.

DRESSING:

1 large clove garlic, minced
1 canned chipotle chile in adobo sauce, minced
2 teaspoons lime juice
2 tablespoons sour cream
3 tablespoons mayonnaise
Pinch granulated sugar
Salt

SLAW:

1 medium carrot, shredded
4 to 6 radishes, halved and thinly sliced crosswise
2 tablespoons chopped fresh cilantro
2 cups thinly sliced green cabbage
2 teaspoons lime juice
Salt

FISH:

¼ cup finely ground cornmeal
2 tablespoons cornstarch
½ teaspoon ground cumin
½ teaspoon freshly ground black pepper
2 teaspoons chili powder or paprika
2 teaspoons kosher salt
1½ pounds firm white fish fillets (such as tilapia, true cod, lingcod, or halibut), patted dry and cut crosswise into ½- to ¾-inch-wide strips
3 to 5 tablespoons vegetable oil
12 to 16 small corn or flour tortillas, warmed
Chopped fresh cilantro, to garnish
1 lime, cut into wedges, for serving

To make dressing: Whisk together garlic, chile, lime juice, sour cream, mayonnaise, and sugar. Season to taste with salt, and additional sugar, if needed. Refrigerate for at least 30 minutes before serving.

To make slaw: In a bowl, combine carrot, radishes, cilantro, cabbage, lime juice, and salt to taste; set aside.

To make fish and tacos: In large mixing bowl, blend together cornmeal, cornstarch, cumin, black pepper, chili powder, and salt. Toss fish to coat evenly and transfer to plate. In a large nonstick skillet, heat oil over medium-high heat until shimmering; add fish in a single layer and cook each side until lightly browned and cooked through, 5 to 7 minutes. Smear each tortilla with dressing; top with slaw and fish. Sprinkle with cilantro and serve immediately accompanied by lime wedges.

— From Matthew Card

CATAPLANA SHRIMP WITH GREEN CURRY SAUCE AND SUMMER VEGETABLES

MAKES 4 SERVINGS

In Portuguese cooking, a cataplana is a copper pot designed specifically for steaming shellfish over an open fire or grill. But you don't need one to do this dish. If you want to cook outdoors, we'll tell you how to fashion a substitute using foil and disposable pie plates, but the recipe also works on a stove using a skillet with a lid.

1 pound jumbo shrimp, peeled, deveined, and tails removed
8 ounces skinless halibut fillet, cut into 1½-inch chunks
1 cup halved cherry tomatoes
4 ounces sugar snap peas, cut into ½-inch pieces (1 cup)
1½ cups fresh or frozen corn kernels
⅔ cup coconut milk
1 tablespoon fish sauce
1½ tablespoons fresh lime juice
2 teaspoons Thai green curry paste
1 teaspoon firmly packed brown sugar
¼ teaspoon kosher salt
4 sprigs fresh cilantro plus 2 tablespoons roughly chopped (divided)
1 tablespoon chopped fresh basil
4 lime wedges, to garnish

Preheat grill to high (see note). Set a 9-inch foil pan on enough heavy-duty foil to fully enclose pan and food (see note and photos on page 118).

In a large bowl, toss the shrimp, halibut, tomatoes, snap peas, and corn. In a small bowl, whisk together the coconut milk, fish sauce, lime juice, curry paste, brown sugar, and salt. Pile the seafood and vegetables into the foil pan, pour the coconut sauce over, and add the cilantro sprigs.

Fold the foil around the pan and its contents to create a pouch; crimp to seal tightly. Place the pouch on the grill, close the lid and cook, shaking occasionally, until the shrimp and halibut are opaque and just cooked through, 5 to 6 minutes. (You'll need to open the pouch to check on the seafood, so be careful of escaping steam.)

When the shrimp and fish are cooked, remove the pouch from the grill and let rest for a couple of minutes, then open the foil. To serve, transfer to one large or four individual serving bowls, add the chopped cilantro and basil, and serve immediately with lime wedges.

Note: To check grill temperature, count the seconds you can hold your hand, palm side down, 2 to 3 inches above the rack, until it feels uncomfortable: 2 seconds for high.

Note: A 9-inch foil pan works fine, but we preferred the 9-by-9-by-2-inch "Ultimate Poultry pan," which we found at Fred Meyer with other disposable foil pans.

— From Martha Holmberg

HARRIS WINE CELLAR'S SHRIMP SANDWICH

MAKES 6 SANDWICHES

VERMOUTH SAUCE:

1 (8-ounce) package cream cheese, softened
¼ to ⅓ cup dry vermouth

SHRIMP:

2 cups bay shrimp (tiny cooked shrimp)
½ cup diced celery
½ cup chopped scallions
⅔ cup mayonnaise
⅛ teaspoon celery salt
⅛ teaspoon garlic salt
⅛ teaspoon onion salt
Dash cayenne pepper
Dash angostura bitters (see note)
Butter
Mayonnaise
1 loaf dill rye bread
Cucumber, peeled and sliced
Lettuce, shredded

To make sauce: In a medium bowl, blend together the cream cheese and vermouth until smooth.

To make sandwiches: In a large bowl, stir together the shrimp, celery, scallions, mayonnaise, celery salt, garlic salt, onion salt, cayenne pepper, and angostura bitters.

Spread butter and mayonnaise on one side of dill rye bread. Spread Vermouth Sauce on the other side, followed by a large spoonful of shrimp mixture, and a layer of cucumbers. Top with shredded lettuce and place the other slice of bread on top.

Note: Angostura bitters are available in the liquor supply section of most supermarkets as well as in liquor stores.

— From Art and Sidney Thomas, Harris Wine Cellar

GOAN-STYLE CRAB CURRY

MAKES 4 TO 6 SERVINGS

Goa is on India's coast, where seafood is frequently used in coconut milk curries like this one. This dish offsets the rich coconut and sweet crab with tart tamarind paste and savory Indian spices. Like most curry recipes, this improves with time, so feel free to make in advance.

2 tablespoons vegetable, peanut, or grapeseed oil
1 yellow onion, chopped fine
2 teaspoons peeled and finely chopped fresh ginger
2 teaspoons finely chopped garlic
1 teaspoon cayenne pepper, or to taste

1 tablespoon paprika

1 tablespoon ground cumin

1 tablespoon ground coriander

1 teaspoon turmeric

2 cooked Dungeness crabs (about 4 pounds total), cleaned, broken into pieces and shells cracked, but left on

1⅓ cups water

1 tablespoon plus 1 teaspoon tamarind paste (see note)

2 (14-ounce) cans coconut milk

Salt

½ bunch cilantro, chopped

Fresh chiles (such as red serranos), sliced

Hot cooked rice

In a large saucepan, heat oil over medium heat and stir-fry onions until softened and starting to brown, about 5 to 7 minutes. Add the ginger and garlic; stir-fry for a minute longer. Add the spices and cook another minute.

Add Dungeness crab and cook for another minute. Add the water, tamarind paste and coconut milk. Bring to a strong simmer and cook for 10 more minutes, until the crab is heated and the flavors have blended. Adjust seasoning to taste. Garnish with cilantro and chiles, and serve with hot rice.

Note: Tamarind paste is available at Asian or Latin American markets.

— From Camille Heilman and Jesse Zamora, Vindalho Restaurant

SEA SCALLOPS WITH PEACHES IN BASIL CREAM SAUCE

MAKES 4 SERVINGS

The marriage of peaches and basil with sweet and delicate sea scallops is a perfect way to celebrate summer. The Hands On Cafe is located at the Oregon College of Art & Craft.

1 pound medium sea scallops

All-purpose flour for dusting

4 tablespoons clarified butter (divided; see note)

2 tablespoons minced shallot

2 teaspoons peeled and grated fresh ginger

1 teaspoon ground fennel seeds

3 tablespoons peach balsamic vinegar (see note)

Grated zest and juice of 1 orange (divided)

Grated zest and juice of 1 lemon (divided)

½ fish bouillon cube (see note)

½ cup hot water

¾ cup whipping cream

1 bunch fresh basil, julienned (reserve a few leaves for garnish)

3 to 4 tablespoons anisette liqueur

3 peaches, peeled and sliced (divided; see note)

Salt and freshly ground white pepper

Dust scallops with flour. Heat 2 tablespoons clarified butter over medium-high heat; sauté scallops on both sides until golden brown and just barely opaque in the center—do not overcook. Remove from pan and set aside.

Add remaining 2 tablespoons butter to the same pan and sauté shallot, ginger, and ground fennel until shallot is soft. Add vinegar, orange juice, and lemon juice to pan, stirring to loosen browned bits. Dissolve the ½ bouillon cube in the ½ cup hot water and add to pan along with orange and lemon zests and cream. Bring to a boil, reduce heat, and simmer for a few minutes to reduce slightly.

Add basil, anisette, and half of peaches. Adjust seasoning with salt and white pepper. Add scallops and heat through. Remove to plates and garnish with remaining peaches and basil leaves.

Note: To make clarified butter, melt butter over low heat. When completely melted, let stand for a few minutes, allowing the milk solids to settle to the bottom. Skim the butter fat from the top and place in a container; this clarified, drawn butter is ready for use.

Note: Peach balsamic vinegar is available at some specialty stores, such as Sheridan Fruit Co. and Strohecker's. If unavailable, substitute white balsamic vinegar.

Note: Knorr Fish Bouillon cubes are available at some grocery stores such as Fred Meyer and Zupan's.

Note: To peel peaches, submerge in boiling water for 30 to 60 seconds, then plunge into cold water for 20 seconds. Skins should slip right off.

— Adapted from *The New Ark Cookbook* by Nanci Main and Jimella Lucas (Chronicle Books)

CLASSIC FRIED RAZOR CLAMS WITH PAN SAUCE

MAKES 3 TO 4 SERVINGS

Sweet and rich razor clams are some of the Northwest's finest seafood. With a delicate breading of crispy panko crumbs and a simple pan sauce, they are heaven on a plate.

CLAMS:
1 cup all-purpose flour
1 tablespoon kosher salt
1 teaspoon freshly ground black pepper
1 teaspoon freshly ground white pepper
1 tablespoon granulated garlic
3 eggs, beaten
2¼ cups panko (Japanese-style crumbs)
1 pound shelled and cleaned razor clams
1 cup vegetable or peanut oil

SAUCE:
¼ cup minced shallots
1 medium tomato, chopped
½ cup dry white wine
Juice of 1 lemon
3 tablespoons butter
Kosher salt
Chopped fresh parsley, basil, thyme or chives, or a combination (garnish)

To make clams: In a pie pan, place the flour and season with salt, peppers and granulated garlic. In a second pie pan, whisk the eggs; place the panko crumbs in a third pie pan.

Tenderize clams by pounding with the textured side of a meat mallet; pay particular attention to the tough siphon end. Dredge a clam in seasoned flour, dip in beaten egg, then coat both sides with panko. Place breaded clam on a rack or plate and repeat with remaining clams. Let clams stand for 20 to 30 minutes to let breading set up. Preheat oven to 200 degrees. Put two wire cooling racks over a baking sheet and place in oven.

➤➤

115

In a heavy 10-inch skillet (cast iron is ideal, but stainless steel works well, too), heat oil over medium-high heat. When oil just begins to smoke (400 to 425 degrees) use tongs or a spatula to carefully add clams. Do not crowd; there may be room for only two, depending on the size of the clams. Fry for no more than 30 seconds, then flip clams and cook for 30 seconds on the second side. Transfer cooked clams to warming rack in the oven.

Repeat until all clams are cooked, making sure oil temperature stays between 400 and 425 degrees.

To make sauce: Remove all but 1 tablespoon oil from pan. Reduce heat to medium. Add shallot and tomato; sauté until softened. Deglaze pan by adding wine and lemon juice, and scraping up any browned bits of food. Bring to boil; cook until liquid is reduced to a thin syrup. Add butter to pan; whisk to emulsify. Season to taste with salt. Place fried clams on a platter or divide among individual plates. Drizzle with pan sauce and sprinkle with herbs.

— Adapted from Jeff Keuchle

CLEANING RAZOR CLAMS

Grasp clam by the neck and hold in hot water until you feel the shell release and begin to open. Dip quickly in cold water. Work the shell loose and dislodge the muscle from the shell with a small sharp knife. Slice open the neck cavities and remove all grit and brown matter from inside. Carefully cut lengthwise through the body and foot, opening like a butterfly.

SKILLET CLAMS

MAKES 2 MAIN-COURSE SERVINGS

Jimella Lucas and Nanci Main, formerly of the legendary Ark Restaurant, are now owners and chefs of Market Cafe, in the Klipsan Beach area of Ocean Park, Washington. This dish is served at the bistro as both an appetizer and an entree, but we think you'll want to make a meal of them. Serve with warm garlic bread.

2 pounds manila clams in the shell, rinsed
2 teaspoons fresh minced garlic
⅔ cup diced tomatoes (drained if using canned)
1 cup sliced leeks
10 (¼-inch-thick) slices smoked chorizo sausage (not the raw Mexican variety)
⅛ to ¼ teaspoon crushed red pepper flakes
1½ teaspoons chopped fresh basil (½ teaspoon dried)
2 lemon wedges
4 tablespoons butter, softened

Heat a large skillet or a Dutch oven over high heat until it is very hot. Add the clams, garlic, tomatoes, leeks, chorizo, red pepper flakes, and fresh basil. Squeeze the lemon wedges over the clams and toss the wedges into the skillet with the clams. Add the butter, cover pan with a lid, and cook on high heat for 3 to 4 minutes, just until clams open (occasionally ▶

shaking the pan helps the shells open). You do not want to overcook them! Serve in a deep bowl with crusty bread.

— Adapted from Jimella Lucas and Nanci Main,
Market Cafe, Ocean Park, Washington

MUSSELS IN CATAPLANA

MAKES 4 MAIN-COURSE OR 6 APPETIZER SERVINGS

This is one of another of our cataplana-inspired recipes. But as with the previous version using shrimp, this one can be done in a skillet on the stove if you'd rather not bother with a grill.

SAUCE:

¼ cup olive oil

8 ounces smoked chorizo sausage (not the raw Mexican variety), diced

1 medium yellow onion, sliced

1 small red bell pepper, cored and cut into ⅛-inch julienne

1 small yellow bell pepper, cored and cut into ⅛-inch julienne

4 medium cloves garlic, minced

2 bay leaves

1 teaspoon sweet paprika

1 teaspoon smoked paprika (pimentón de la Vera)

½ teaspoon crushed red pepper flakes

½ cup dry white wine

1 (14-ounce) can good-quality tomatoes (preferably San Marzano variety), drained and chopped

½ cup roughly chopped fresh Italian (flat-leaf) parsley

½ cup roughly chopped fresh cilantro

Salt and freshly ground black pepper

MUSSELS:

2 pounds scrubbed and debearded fresh mussels

½ cup dry white wine

¼ cup roughly chopped fresh cilantro

To make sauce: In a saucepan, heat the olive oil over medium-high heat, and sauté the chorizo until some fat has rendered out and the sausage is lightly crisped around the edges, about 2 minutes; remove and set aside, leaving the fat in the pan. Add the onion, peppers, and garlic, and sauté until soft, 4 to 5 minutes. Add back the chorizo, followed by the bay leaves, sweet paprika, smoked paprika, and pepper flakes.

Add the white wine and chopped tomatoes, and bring to a gentle simmer; cook, stirring occasionally, until thickened, 10 to 15 minutes. Add the parsley and cilantro, and season to taste with salt and pepper. Cool until ready to assemble.

To make mussels: Preheat grill to high (see note). Set a 9-inch foil pan on enough heavy-duty foil to fully enclose pan and food (see note).

Spoon about half of the sauce into the foil pan. Pile the mussels on top and spoon on the remaining sauce; pour in the ½ cup white wine. Fold the foil around the pan and its contents to create a pouch; crimp to seal tightly. Place the pouch on the grill, close the lid and cook, shaking occasionally, until the mussels have opened, 12 to 15 minutes. (You'll need to open the pouch to check on the mussels, so be careful of escaping steam.)

➤➤

When they're cooked, remove the pouch from the grill (sliding a sheet pan under it makes it easy to transport), and let rest for a couple of minutes. Open the foil and discard any mussels that haven't opened. Taste the sauce and adjust the seasoning, then carefully transfer the contents to a large serving bowl, taking care to get all the juices. Toss the chopped cilantro over the mussels and serve immediately.

Make ahead: You can make the sauce up to a day ahead, but don't add the fresh herbs until an hour or so before use.

Note: To check grill temperature, count the seconds you can hold your hand, palm side down, 2 to 3 inches above the rack, until it feels uncomfortable: 2 seconds for high.

Note: A 9-inch foil plate works fine, but we preferred the 9-by-9-by-2-inch "Ultimate Poultry Pan," which we found at Fred Meyer with other disposable foil pans.

— Adapted from David Machado, Nel Centro and Vindalho

ASSEMBLING SEAFOOD CATAPLANA-STYLE

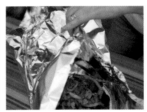

Place a pie plate over large sheets of foil. Add seafood and wine, then enclose the parcel by folding foil edges together. To check for doneness, open the packet part way to make sure shellfish have fully opened.

POULTRY

7

ROASTED CHICKEN THIGHS WITH TOMATOES AND HERBS

MAKES 4 SERVINGS, PLUS LEFTOVERS

If rising grocery prices have taken chicken breasts off your shopping list, consider this lower-cost alternative, using flavorful thighs. The secret is to make sure the ingredients have room to spread out, so use more than one pan if needed so that you're not crowding things. Suitable pans are heavy rimmed baking sheets, or roasting pans that aren't extra deep.

> About ¾ of a large (12-ounce) onion, cut in ¼-inch-thick slices
> 6 to 8 cloves garlic, crushed but not chopped
> 1½ pounds cherry or other small tomatoes, halved
> ¼ cup olive oil
> ¼ teaspoon crushed red pepper flakes or ⅛ teaspoon cayenne pepper
> 3 tablespoons roughly chopped fresh marjoram or thyme (divided)
> Kosher salt
> 3 pounds bone-in chicken thighs (about 12 medium)

Preheat oven to 450 degrees.

In a large bowl, combine the onion, garlic, tomatoes, olive oil, pepper flakes, 2 tablespoons herbs, and 1 teaspoon salt; toss until everything's nicely mixed.

Season the chicken thighs on both sides with salt to taste; arrange on two rimmed baking sheets, with space between the chicken pieces. Distribute the tomato mixture and any juices around the chicken so it's in an even layer, but not covering the chicken.

Roast until the chicken is totally tender when pierced with a knife (or reaches 165 degrees on an instant-read thermometer), 35 to 45 minutes. During roasting, check that the tomato mixture isn't burning.

You want the vegetables to release juices, collapse, and brown slightly but not to burn onto the pan. If they're getting too dark, pour in a few spoonfuls of water or chicken broth.

When the chicken is done, transfer to a serving platter. Put a large sieve or colander over a bowl and carefully scrape the tomato mixture into the sieve. Make sure you catch all the juices, which are delicious. If there are browned juices on the baking sheets, deglaze them by pouring on a bit of water or juice and scraping to dissolve. Add this liquid to the vegetable juices in the bowl.

After the vegetables drain for a few minutes, arrange on the chicken platter as an accompaniment. Sprinkle everything with the remaining 1 tablespoon herbs and serve. Pass a bowl of the reserved juices at the table to drizzle over the chicken and vegetables, if desired, or refrigerate them for use in another recipe, such as a soup.

To reserve leftovers, pour the vegetable juices into a measuring cup, cover and refrigerate (the fat will solidify on the top for easy removal the next day). Depending on appetites, you should have about 4 thighs left over; wrap and refrigerate, along with the reserved tomato mixture.

— From Martha Holmberg

MAPLE ROAST CHICKEN WITH WINTER VEGETABLES

MAKES 8 SERVINGS

This recipe, from restaurateur and cookbook author Jim Dodge, was a hit with Foodday readers and staffers. The maple syrup (be sure to use the real stuff) helps the chicken skin get crisp and dark, while the vegetables turn sweet and soft.

2 tablespoons butter
1 (5- to 6-pound) roasting chicken
½ teaspoon kosher salt
¼ teaspoon freshly ground black pepper
4 carrots, peeled, trimmed and cut into
    3-inch chunks
4 parsnips, peeled, trimmed and cut into
    3-inch chunks
4 ribs celery, trimmed and cut into
    3-inch chunks
4 onions, quartered
½ teaspoon dried rosemary
⅓ cup pure maple syrup

Place rack of oven on lowest level and preheat oven to 400 degrees.

Melt butter in a small saucepan. Brush over breast of chicken, and sprinkle with salt and pepper. Spread carrots, parsnips, celery, and onions evenly in a roasting pan. Place chicken on top and sprinkle with rosemary. Place in oven and baste about every 10 minutes with maple syrup. When you run out of syrup, use pan juices for basting. Roast until tender, when thigh reaches 165 degrees on a meat thermometer. Skin will be golden brown and crisp in about 1 to 1½ hours.

Let stand 10 minutes before carving. Remove chicken and vegetables to a large serving platter and serve.

— Adapted from *Sweet Maple*, by James M. Lawrence and Rux Martin (Diane Publishing)

FORTY-CLOVES-AND-WHO'S-COUNTING CHICKEN

MAKES 4 SERVINGS

For many years Sara Perry wrote a column for the *Sunday Oregonian* called "Taste Makers." She selected this recipe from her own cookbook to make with host Al Roker on NBC's Today show. Although 46 cloves sounds like overkill, most of the garlic is used unpeeled, and it roasts along with the chicken until it's mild and buttery. James Beard often taught students how to make chicken with forty cloves of garlic, but his recipe is quite different from Sara's.

46 plump, unpeeled garlic cloves (divided)
1½ teaspoons or more coarse salt
About 1½ cup coarsely chopped fresh herbs, such as tarragon, thyme, oregano, and sage
Freshly ground black pepper
⅓ cup extra-virgin olive oil
1 (3½- to 4-pound) chicken, cut into serving pieces
Thinly sliced French bread or toast, heated, for serving

Preheat oven to 400 degrees.

Peel 6 of the garlic cloves, slice in half, place on a cutting board and sprinkle with the salt. Mince, pressing and moving the garlic into the salt with the knife to form a rough paste. Transfer to a large bowl and stir in the chopped herbs, pepper, and the olive oil.

Add the chicken pieces, one at a time, to the bowl, and spread the garlic-herb mixture over each piece. Set the pieces in a roasting or baking pan skin side up. Add the remaining 40 unpeeled cloves to the bowl that contained the garlic mixture, and toss to lightly coat with the oil remaining on the sides of the bowl. Tuck the cloves in and around the chicken pieces.

Roast chicken for 30 minutes, and then baste with the pan juices. Continue to roast, basting as desired, until the chicken is fork-tender and just browned, 45 minutes to 1 hour, or until an instant-read thermometer inserted in the middle of a breast reaches 165 degrees.

Serve the chicken with the pan juices and garlic cloves. Pass the French bread. Squeeze the caramelized cloves of roasted garlic from the root end onto the bread and spread. Enjoy with the chicken. Squeeze or pop the more caramelized garlic from the root end onto the plate and eat whole, seasoned with salt and pepper.

— Adapted from *Everything Tastes Better With Garlic*, by Sara Perry (Chronicle Books)

ALWAYS TAKE A CHICKEN'S TEMPERATURE

Older recipes told readers to cook chicken "until juices run clear," or until the meat is no longer pink inside, or until a drumstick wiggles freely. These methods can be unreliable. The best way we have found to determine doneness is to use an instant-read thermometer inserted in the innermost part of the thigh or the deepest part of the breast, without touching bone. The USDA says the safe minimum temperature is 165 degrees, although some people prefer the texture of meat cooked slightly higher, to 170 degrees.

CHICKEN CACCIATORA

MAKES 4 SERVINGS

In Italy, food cooked *alla cacciatora* is done "hunter-style," with mushrooms, onions, tomatoes. Chicken is its most popular rendition. Note that the sauce for this dish only takes 30 minutes and can even be made the day before.

MARINARA SAUCE:

¼ cup olive oil
8 cloves garlic, chopped
1 teaspoon chopped fresh parsley
2 tablespoons chopped fresh basil
½ teaspoon crushed red pepper flakes
2 (28-ounce) cans whole Italian tomatoes
    (preferably San Marzano variety)

CHICKEN:

1 whole 3- to 4-pound chicken
Salt and freshly ground black pepper
¼ cup olive oil (do not use extra-virgin
    olive oil)
1 medium onion, thinly sliced
3 cloves garlic, sliced
⅓ cup dry sherry
2 to 4 cups marinara sauce
8 to 12 ounces sliced fresh mushrooms
15 to 20 pitted gaeta olives (substitute
    kalamata olives if gaeta are unavailable)
4 fresh basil leaves, chopped

To make sauce: Heat the oil in a large saucepan over medium heat. Add the garlic and cook until soft. Add the parsley, basil, and red pepper flakes; heat to release flavors, about 10 seconds.

Drain the liquid from the canned tomatoes and reserve. Crush the tomatoes with your hands and add to the garlic mixture. Add the reserved juice, bring to a gentle simmer and cook 30 minutes (cover pan if sauce looks like it is reducing). Refrigerate until needed. Makes 6 cups.

To make chicken: Cut the chicken into 8 pieces, and season with salt and pepper. In a skillet large enough to hold the chicken pieces without crowding, heat oil over medium-high heat. When the oil is hot, carefully add the chicken pieces, being careful as oil will splatter. Brown the chicken on both sides and remove from the pan. Add the onion and cook for 1 to 2 minutes, or until soft. Add the garlic and cook for 1 minute more. Drain off the oil and add the chicken back to the pan. Add the sherry and cook over high heat, scraping any browned bits from the bottom of the pan, until reduced by half.

Add 2 cups of the marinara sauce. Use 4 cups if you want extra sauce for a side dish of pasta. (Freeze any remaining sauce.) Reduce heat and gently simmer for about 30 minutes, turning chicken pieces once or twice. Add the mushrooms, olives, and basil; continue simmering for 15 minutes more. Turn off heat and let rest for 15 minutes. Skim fat from the surface. Taste and adjust seasoning. Serve hot.

Make ahead: Prepare sauce as directed the day before and refrigerate or freeze until needed.

— From Tuscany Grill

Remove leaves from woody stems by pinching the stem and pulling back from top toward root end. To cut basil chiffonade style, stack the leaves, roll compactly and then thinly slice crosswise. To avoid excessive darkening of herbs, don't mince too finely (far right).

CHICKEN MILANESE

MAKES 4 SERVINGS

Danielle Centoni, editor of *The Oregonian's MIX* magazine, developed this recipe for our "Simply Affordable" column. Although boneless chicken breasts aren't usually considered economical, they are if you use fewer of them and serve them thinly pounded and breaded. If you don't have fresh oregano and parsley on hand, you can get away with seasoning the breading with just salt and pepper.

2 to 3 large boneless, skinless chicken breast halves (about 1 pound)
Salt and freshly ground black pepper
2 eggs
1 cup panko (Japanese-style breadcrumbs)
½ cup all-purpose flour
1 teaspoon grated lemon zest
1 tablespoon chopped fresh herbs such as oregano and/or parsley (optional)
Vegetable oil for frying
2 tablespoons olive oil
1 tablespoon fresh lemon juice
1 teaspoon chopped fresh shallot (optional)
4 cups mesclun mix, arugula, or baby spinach
1 cup cherry or grape tomatoes, halved

Spread a large piece of plastic wrap on a work surface. Place a chicken breast on top and cut it in half horizontally (with the flat side of knife blade parallel to the kitchen counter). Lay another sheet of plastic on top of the breast pieces and use a meat mallet, or large, heavy skillet, to pound them to ¼-inch thickness. Repeat with the remaining chicken.

Season the chicken on both sides with salt and black pepper. Beat the eggs in a shallow bowl and add a pinch each of salt and pepper. Place panko and flour in two separate shallow bowls. Stir the lemon zest, oregano, and a pinch each of salt and pepper into the flour.

Dip a piece of chicken into the flour, coating it on all sides. Shake the excess off, then dip in the eggs and let the excess drip off. Last, dip it in the panko crumbs and set it on a platter or baking sheet while you repeat with the remaining pieces.

Set a large sauté pan over medium-high heat and add vegetable oil ⅛ inch deep. When hot (a piece of bread tossed into the oil should immediately start to sizzle), arrange the chicken in a single layer (you may have to cook it in batches). Cook until golden brown, about 3 minutes per side. Remove with a slotted spatula, and place on a cooling rack set over paper towels to allow the excess oil to drip off (the rack helps keep the underside crispy instead of soggy).

While the chicken cooks, whisk together the olive oil, lemon juice, shallot, and a pinch each of salt and pepper in a salad bowl. When ready to serve, add the salad greens and tomatoes; toss to coat. Divide the chicken among the plates, top with the salad, and serve.

— From Danielle Centoni

CHICKEN ROSEMARY

MAKES 4 SERVINGS

Most people go to a dinner theater for the drama, not the food. But Sylvia's Italian Restaurant and Class Act Dinner Theatre manages to do both beautifully. This dish is simple to prepare and comes together easily. It's also moist and flavorful, and it's easy to understand why the recipe has been passed down for generations in owner Sylvia Posedel's family. Sylvia recommends serving this chicken dish with the pasta or rice of your choice.

½ cup all-purpose flour
1 teaspoon salt
Freshly ground black pepper
6 (6-ounce) boneless, skinless chicken
    breast halves
⅓ cup extra-virgin olive oil
6 cloves garlic, minced (about 2 tablespoons)
1 cup chicken broth
¼ cup dry sherry
½ teaspoon dried rosemary, crumbled
1 tablespoon butter, at room temperature
    (optional)
2 tablepoons chopped fresh parsley

In a shallow bowl, combine flour, salt and pepper to taste. Dredge each chicken piece in the flour mixture, shaking off excess. Place on a platter lined with a sheet of wax paper.

In a very large skillet, heat oil over medium heat. Cook chicken until lightly browned, approximately 4 minutes per side. Remove chicken to a platter and keep warm. Add minced garlic to the skillet and sauté until the garlic is aromatic, about 30 seconds. Stir in chicken broth and sherry, and with a wooden spoon, scrape the browned bits off the bottom of the pan, boiling the mixture for about 2 minutes. Return chicken to skillet and sprinkle with rosemary. Cover skillet with a lid, and simmer slowly for about 15 minutes, or until the chicken is cooked through, basting the breasts with the sauce a few times. Do not overcook the chicken.

If you wish, and just before serving, add 1 tablespoon of butter to the pan in pieces and continue to cook another minute to thicken the reduced sauce and give it some shine. Sprinkle with parsley and serve.

— Adapted from Sylvia's Italian Restaurant and
    Class Act Dinner Theatre

RESERVE CHICKEN AND DUMPLINGS

MAKES 8 SERVINGS

Traditional chicken and dumplings usually means an all-day stint in the kitchen, but this homespun bowl of goodness can be on the table in a couple of hours. If you don't have a bamboo steamer, use a steamer inset in a rice cooker, or a rack set over a pot.

½ cup butter (1 stick)
1 medium onion, cut into 1-inch pieces
2 carrots, cut in half lengthwise and sliced diagonally into 1-inch pieces
2 celery stalks, sliced diagonally into 1-inch pieces
4 large boneless, skinless chicken breast halves, cut into 1-inch cubes (about 2 pounds)
1 teaspoon dried thyme
1 tablespoon herbes de Provence
2 potatoes, peeled and cut into 1-inch cubes
4 cups chicken broth
½ cup all-purpose flour
3 cups whipping cream
4⅔ cups all-purpose baking mix (Bisquick)
1½ cups water
½ cup frozen peas
Salt and freshly ground black pepper
Fresh parsley for garnish

In a large, deep-sided pan, melt the butter over low heat. Add the onion, carrots, and celery; sauté without browning for about 10 minutes or until the onion is translucent.

Add the chicken, thyme, and herbes de Provence; sauté another 10 minutes or until the chicken is almost done. Do not brown the chicken. Add the potatoes and chicken broth, and simmer 10 to 15 minutes or until the potatoes are tender.

In a medium bowl, whisk the flour into the cream until smooth. Add the cream mixture to the simmering stew and stir until incorporated. Bring to a simmer and cook for about 10 minutes or until the mixture is thickened and all of the vegetables are tender. (If the sauce becomes too thick, thin with a little milk.)

While the stew is simmering, combine the baking mix with the water in a medium bowl; stir just until a stiff batter forms. Line the layers of a bamboo steamer (see note) with parchment paper. Drop the dumpling dough onto the parchment with a ¼-cup scoop, leaving about 1 inch between dumplings. Stack the layers and cover. Steam over boiling water 10 to 12 minutes, or until the dumplings are done in the center.

When the stew is thickened, add the peas and season to taste with salt and pepper. Simmer briefly until the peas are hot.

Place 2 dumplings in a shallow bowl and ladle stew over the top. Garnish with parsley and serve hot.

Note: If a bamboo steamer is unavailable, set water to boil in a deep pot with a lid. While water is boiling, use a piece of parchment paper to line a flat steamer rack, cake rack or wire mesh splatter shield that's large enough to rest atop the pot. Steam dumplings by placing them on the parchment paper and covering them with the pot's lid. Use the same method with a steamer inset in a rice cooker.

— From Vintage Room and Restaurant, The Reserve Vineyards and Golf Club, Aloha

SPICY CHICKEN THIGHS WITH APRICOTS AND OLIVES

MAKES 4 SERVINGS

Linda Faus developed this sweet-and-spicy chicken dish for Foodday's "Fit for Dinner" column. Served with whole-wheat couscous or brown rice, and a steamed vegetable, it's almost "health" food, but no one will know it. If you're leery of 1 teaspoon of red pepper flakes, start with ¼ teaspoon and add more to taste.

⅓ cup fresh lemon juice

⅓ cup honey

2 teaspoons ground cinnamon

1 teaspoon crushed red pepper flakes, or to taste

1½ teaspoons kosher salt

1 teaspoon freshly ground black pepper

2 teaspoons ground cumin

1 teaspoon smoked paprika (pimentón de la Vera)

½ cup pimiento-stuffed green olives, coarsely chopped

⅓ cup dried apricots, coarsely chopped

⅓ cup chopped fresh cilantro, plus extra to garnish

1½ pounds skinless chicken thighs (4 large thighs)

In a small bowl, whisk together the lemon juice, honey, cinnamon, pepper flakes, salt, pepper, cumin, and smoked paprika. Stir in the olives, apricots, and cilantro.

Trim any excess fat from the chicken thighs and place in a large zip-top plastic bag. Pour the marinade over and seal the bag. Turn to coat all of the chicken; refrigerate for 2 to 24 hours, turning occasionally.

Preheat oven to 375 degrees. Arrange the chicken thighs in a single layer in a shallow 2-quart baking dish. Pour the marinade over the chicken. Bake for 45 to 50 minutes, or until the chicken registers 165 to 170 degrees on an instant-read thermometer. Garnish each portion with a little chopped cilantro.

— From Linda Faus

DON'T WORRY ABOUT DARKENING NEAR THE BONES

Some people notice that even after roasting or baking, a chicken will have dark-colored meat near the bones. This darkening occurs primarily in young broiler-fryers; since their bones have not calcified completely, pigment from the bone marrow can seep through the porous bones into the meat. Freezing can also contribute to this seepage. When the chicken is cooked, the pigment turns dark. It's perfectly safe to eat this darkened meat, as long as the chicken has been cooked to an internal temperature of at least 165 degrees.

CHICKEN TAGINE WITH APPLES AND RAINBOW CHARD

MAKES 4 TO 6 SERVINGS

Tagine may sound fancy, but it's really just a simple, seasonal stew enriched with a heady blend of dried, ground spices. For this variation, the chicken and apples are simmered with earthy rainbow chard and onion. As the tagine simmers, the apples dissolve into the sauce and thicken it.

If you prefer, a whole chicken, cut into 8 pieces, may be substituted for the thighs, though you'll need to reduce the cooking time by 10 minutes to accommodate the white meat.

> 8 bone-in chicken thighs, trimmed of excess skin and fat
> Salt and freshly ground black pepper
> 1 tablespoon butter
> 1 bunch rainbow chard, stems removed and cut into ½-inch pieces, leaves well-rinsed
> 1 medium onion, halved lengthwise and then cut crosswise into ½-inch slices
> ¼ teaspoon ground cinnamon
> ½ teaspoon ground coriander
> ¼ teaspoon cayenne pepper
> ¼ teaspoon ground cumin
> Large pinch saffron threads, crumbled
> 3 bay leaves
> 4 cloves garlic, thinly sliced
> 2 tablespoons honey
> 2 cups chicken broth
> 2 large or 3 medium semi-tart apples, peeled, cored, and cut into quarters or sixths, depending on size
> Lemon juice to taste
> Hot, cooked couscous (optional)

Adjust oven rack to middle position and preheat oven to 300 degrees.

Pat chicken dry with paper towels and season generously with salt and pepper. Melt butter in large Dutch oven set over medium-high heat. Working in two batches, place chicken skin side down in a single layer and cook, without moving, until well-browned, 5 to 7 minutes. Flip and cook second side until browned, about 5 minutes longer. Transfer to a plate and drain off all but 2 tablespoons of fat from pot. When cool enough to handle, pull skin off chicken and discard skin.

Place the same pot over medium heat. Add chard stems, onion, and a large pinch salt; cook, stirring frequently until softened, 5 to 7 minutes. Stir in cinnamon, coriander, cayenne, cumin, saffron, bay leaves, and garlic; cook, stirring constantly, until very fragrant, about 30 seconds. Stir in honey. Return chicken to pan and pile onion mixture on top. Add broth and bring to simmer; spread apples on top, cover, and transfer pot to oven. Cook for 1 hour.

Meanwhile, bring large pot of water to boil. Add a generous amount of salt; cook chard leaves until just tender, 2 to 4 minutes. Drain, rinse in cool water, squeeze dry, and chop coarsely; set aside.

Remove chicken from pot and transfer to plate. Simmer sauce over medium-high heat until reduced in volume and thick, about 5 minutes. Adjust seasoning and add lemon juice to taste. Remove bay leaves, stir in reserved chard leaves, and return chicken to pot. Serve immediately accompanied by couscous, if desired.

— From Matthew Card

BASIL CHICKEN IN COCONUT-CURRY SAUCE

MAKES 4 SERVINGS

This curry is quick-cooking and delicious. To save about 14 grams fat and 130 calories per serving, substitute lite coconut milk for the regular.

4 skinless, boneless chicken breast halves
2 teaspoons curry powder
½ teaspoon salt
½ teaspoon freshly cracked black pepper
¼ teaspoon chili powder
1 large red onion, chopped (1 cup)
5 cloves garlic, minced
2 fresh jalapeño chiles, seeded and finely chopped
1 tablespoon olive oil, plus more as needed
1 (13½- or 14-ounce) can coconut milk
1 tablespoon cornstarch
3 tablespoons snipped fresh basil
1 teaspoon peeled and grated fresh ginger
3 cups hot cooked rice

Cut chicken in 1-inch pieces and place in a medium bowl. In a small bowl, stir together the curry powder, salt, black pepper, and chili powder. Sprinkle spice mixture over chicken, tossing to coat evenly. Cover and chill for 1 to 2 hours to allow spices to penetrate meat.

In a large nonstick wok or skillet, heat oil over medium-high heat and sauté onion, garlic, and jalapeño chiles for 2 minutes. Remove onion mixture from wok. Add half of the chicken to wok and cook, stirring, for 3 to 4 minutes, or until chicken is no longer pink. Remove chicken from wok. (If necessary, add additional oil.) Repeat with remaining chicken and remove from wok.

Combine coconut milk and cornstarch. Carefully add to wok. Cook and stir until slightly thickened and bubbly. Return chicken and onion mixture to wok. Stir in basil and ginger. Cook and stir about 2 minutes more or until heated through. Serve over hot rice.

— From *Better Homes and Gardens New Cook Book*, 12th edition (Meredith Books)

POK-POK-STYLE VIETNAMESE FISH SAUCE WINGS

MAKES 4 TO 6 SERVINGS

"Get the wings," is what you'll often hear when talking to locals about Pok Pok, the hugely popular Thai restaurant in Southeast Portland. True enough, owner/chef Andy Ricker's fried chicken wings coated in caramelized fish sauce are terrific. We've adapted his recipe from *Food & Wine* to include alternate cooking methods.

½ cup fish sauce (preferably Viet Huong brand fish sauce, also known as Three Crabs)
½ cup superfine sugar (see note)
4 cloves garlic, 2 crushed and 2 minced
3 pounds chicken wings (12 to 14 whole wings), tips trimmed, halved at the joint
2 tablespoons vegetable oil
1 tablespoon chopped fresh cilantro
1 tablespoon chopped fresh mint

In a large bowl, whisk the fish sauce, sugar, and crushed garlic. Add the wings and toss to coat. Refrigerate for 3 hours, tossing occasionally. Remove wings and drain on rack over baking sheet, reserving marinade.

Cook wings using one of these methods:

Bake: in foil-lined pan at 425 degrees on lowest oven rack for 20 to 25 minutes until crispy, turning once;

Broil: 6 inches from heat 15 to 20 minutes, turning once;

Grill: over medium heat 20 to 25 minutes, turning often;

Deep-fry: Pat wings dry and coat in 1 cup cornstarch. Heat vegetable oil (2 inches deep) to 350 degrees. Fry wings in batches for 10 minutes, or until golden and cooked through.

Meanwhile, heat the 2 tablespoons oil in a small skillet. Add minced garlic; cook over moderate heat until golden. Drain on paper towels.

Simmer reserved marinade in a small saucepan over moderately high heat until syrupy, 5 minutes. Strain over cooked wings and toss. Top with cilantro, mint, and fried garlic and serve.

Note: Superfine sugar dissolves more easily than regular granulated sugar. C&H Baker's is one brand. You can make your own by processing granulated sugar in a food processor or blender and then measuring out the amount you need.

— Adapted from *Food & Wine Cocktails 2010* by the Editors of Food & Wine (Food & Wine)

CHEZ JOSÉ LIME CHICKEN ENCHILADAS

MAKES 8 ENCHILADAS

These enchiladas differ from many other recipes in that the meat is cooked in a flavorful broth before it's rolled with the tortillas. This might be one reason why the dish has been on the menu at Chez José Mexican Grill for many years.

1 (3½- to 4-pound) chicken, cut into pieces
1 cup diced onion
⅓ cup dry white wine
⅔ cup chicken broth
2½ tablespoons chopped garlic
2 teaspoons freshly ground white pepper
2 teaspoons dried oregano leaves
2½ teaspoons kosher salt (divided)
Juice of 2½ limes (divided)
1 (16-ounce) container sour cream (2 cups)
½ cup half-and-half
Pinch cayenne pepper, or to taste
Grated zest of 1 lime
Vegetable oil for softening tortillas
8 corn tortillas
1 cup shredded cheddar cheese (4 ounces)

In a medium stockpot, combine the chicken, onion, wine, broth, garlic, white pepper, oregano, 2 teaspoons salt, juice of 1½ limes, and enough water to cover the chicken. Bring to a boil, reduce heat, and simmer until the chicken is tender and comes off the bone easily, about 45 minutes.

Cool chicken 15 minutes and remove from broth. Strain broth and refrigerate or freeze for another use. Remove skin and bone from chicken, and dice chicken meat into ½-inch pieces. Refrigerate until ready to use.

131

In a medium bowl, stir together the sour cream, half-and-half, remaining ½ teaspoon salt, cayenne, the remaining juice of 1 lime, and the grated lime zest. Refrigerate until ready to use.

Preheat oven to 400 degrees. Lightly grease a 9-by-13-inch baking pan.

Over medium-high heat, heat about ⅛ inch vegetable oil in a large skillet. Soften each tortilla in the hot oil, turning once. This should only take a few seconds on each side. Add more oil to the skillet if necessary. Pat the excess oil from each tortilla with a paper towel.

Fill each softened tortilla with ½ cup chicken. Roll tortilla into an enchilada and place into the prepared pan. Top with the lime/sour cream mixture. Sprinkle with cheddar cheese and bake for 20 to 25 minutes or until heated through. Serve immediately.

Make ahead: Chicken can be cooked and refrigerated 1 to 2 days in advance.

— From Chez José Mexican Cafe

YUCATAN CHICKEN

MAKES 6 TO 8 SERVINGS

In rainy Portland, a visit to Salvador Molly's can restore your sunny mood with its relaxed Caribbean vibe and a menu full of vivid, often spicy, flavors. This dish is no exception. The achiote paste—an essential ingredient—gives the chicken its heat and bright red color. The restaurant serves this stew over rice, as well as in burritos and tostadas.

3 pounds boneless, skinless chicken thighs
1 tablespoon olive oil
1 large onion, diced
1 tablespoon minced garlic
2 to 4 tablespoons achiote paste (see note)
½ cup warm water
1 (14½-ounce) can diced tomatoes, undrained
1 bay leaf
¼ teaspoon ground cinnamon
¼ teaspoon ground nutmeg
1 teaspoon dried oregano
½ teaspoon ground cumin
Freshly ground black pepper
1 tablespoon apple cider vinegar or sherry vinegar
1 teaspoon salt or to taste

Trim any fat off the chicken thighs and cut the thighs into chunks. Set aside.

In a large, heavy pot, heat the olive oil over high heat. Add the onion and chicken thighs, and sauté until lightly browned. Stir in the garlic.

In a small bowl, combine the achiote paste and water; stir until smooth. Add to the chicken mixture along with the tomatoes, bay leaf, cinnamon, nutmeg, oregano, cumin, pepper to taste, and vinegar. Stir well, reduce heat to a simmer and cook 45 to 60 minutes, or until chicken is very tender. Taste and add salt as needed. Remove bay leaf before serving.

Note: Achiote paste is a blend of ground annatto seeds, salt, vinegar, and spices. Sold in 3½-ounce bricks in most Mexican markets and at Uwajimaya in Beaverton, it is sometimes labeled "Yucatan recado," "achiote rojo," or "condimento yucateco." Some brands are saltier than others, so taste the stew before adding salt. There is no substitute.

— From Salvador Molly's

AUNTIE ALICE'S TEOCHEW BRAISED DUCK

MAKES ABOUT 4 SERVINGS, DEPENDING ON SIZE OF DUCK

With duck, crispy skin usually gets all the glory. But this recipe is more about moist, tender, flavorful flesh. Serve it with steamed white rice and grilled green onions or sautéed bok choy for an unusual but wonderful meal.

- 1½ to 2 tablespoons Chinese five-spice powder
- 1½ to 2 tablespoons salt
- 1 whole duck
- 1½ to 2 tablespoons granulated sugar
- 10 to 15 thick slices peeled fresh galangal or ginger
- 15 cloves garlic, peeled and lightly bashed
- 1 cup dark soy sauce (see note)

Mix together the five-spice powder and the salt; rub it all over the outside and inside of the duck. Let the duck sit for at least 2 hours in the refrigerator.

Heat a wok or large pot over low heat and add the sugar, stirring until it melts. Add the galangal or ginger and the garlic; fry the mixture until it is brown. Add the soy sauce.

Lightly rinse the seasoned duck—this will make the end product less salty. Carefully slide the duck into the wok, then coat the top of the duck with the sauce and turn it over. Add enough water so that the liquid comes halfway up the sides of the duck. Bring the mixture to a boil and cover.

Uncover and turn the duck over every 15 minutes. After 50 to 60 minutes, see if you can poke a chopstick through the fleshiest part of the duck. If the chopstick goes through fairly easily, the duck is ready. If not, cover and continue boiling until the chopstick pokes through easily.

Once it's ready, turn off the heat and let the duck sit, covered, for 10 minutes. Then slice it up and serve it with rice, and some of the defatted cooking liquid on the side as a sauce.

Note: Dark soy sauce is a thicker, richer style of soy sauce that clings nicely to the duck. Find it at any well-stocked Asian market.

— From *A Tiger in the Kitchen*, by Cheryl Lu-Lien Tan (Voice)

TURKEY BREAST STUFFED WITH CORN BREAD-APRICOT DRESSING

MAKES 6 SERVINGS

Turkey parts are easy to find these days, but if you want a boneless breast, it's easiest to ask your butcher to bone it for you. Be sure to ask for the skin to be left intact. Contributor Ivy Manning explains how to cut the breast so that it opens like a business letter folded in thirds.

- 1 (2½- to 3-pound) boneless turkey breast half (skin on)
- 3 tablespoons butter, softened (divided)
- ¾ cups minced onion
- 2 stalks celery, chopped
- 2 medium cloves garlic, finely chopped
- 1 tablespoon poultry seasoning
- 1½ cups low-sodium chicken broth

4 cups stale corn bread, cubed
3 tablespoons finely chopped fresh Italian
    (flat-leaf) parsley
2 ounces dried apricots, chopped (about ¼ cup)
Salt and freshly ground black pepper

Take the turkey breast out of the refrigerator and allow it to sit at room temperature for 30 minutes.

In a large sauté pan, melt 1 tablespoon butter over medium-high heat, add the onion and celery, and cook until the onion is translucent, about 5 minutes. Add the garlic and poultry seasoning; sauté until fragrant, 30 seconds. Add the broth, bring to a boil, scraping up browned bits on the bottom of the pan, and simmer for 5 minutes. Pour contents of sauté pan into a large bowl with the corn bread, parsley, and apricots. Stir well to combine and season to taste with salt. Cover and set aside in a warm place.

Preheat the oven to 350 degrees. Place the turkey breast skin-side up on a large cutting board and carefully detach the skin from the breast; set aside. Arrange the turkey breast with the narrow end toward you. Using a boning knife, insert the tip of the knife into the thickest part of the breast about a third of the way from the top of the breast. With the knife running parallel to the cutting board, cut into the breast lengthwise to make a 1½-inch-thick flap in the meat, stopping 1 inch before cutting through the meat entirely at the opposite edge. Flip the top flap of meat to the left, as if you were opening a book.

Just to the right of the seam where the "page" opens, make a ½-inch cut straight down into the breast meat (be sure not to cut all the way through to the bottom of the roast). Turn the blade of the knife to face the right side of the remaining roast, and cut it in half to make another flap of meat, stopping ½ inch before you reach the right edge of the roast. Open the flap of meat to the right, thus creating a rough rectangle of meat. Cover with plastic wrap and pound with a meat mallet so that the meat is of an even thickness.

Remove the plastic wrap and sprinkle the meat with salt and pepper. Spread the stuffing over the turkey breast, leaving a 1-inch border at the edges. Fold the end nearest you up and over, tucking your fingers under. Roll up into a cylinder, tucking in the ends if necessary. Place the roast seam-side down and smear the top with the remaining butter. Wrap the reserved skin around the outside of the roast. Tie at 2-inch intervals with butcher's string.

Transfer to the oven and roast, basting occasionally, until an instant-read thermometer registers 165 degrees when inserted in the center, about 1 hour and 15 minutes to 1 hour and 45 minutes. Remove the turkey from the oven and transfer to a platter, tent with foil and allow meat to rest for 20 to 30 minutes. Using a sharp carving knife, cut the roast crosswise into 2-inch-thick slices, discarding string as you carve.

— From Ivy Manning

SALSA VERDE TURKEY (OR CHICKEN) SOFT TACOS

MAKES 4 SERVINGS

After Thanksgiving, leftover turkey tends to linger like houseguests who have worn out their welcome. But instead of serving yet another sandwich, former Fooday contributor Matthew Card likes to pair it with a tangy salsa verde made from tomatillos, serrano chiles, and cilantro. The sauce takes only minutes to pull together, after which the turkey is briefly simmered in it to absorb its flavor and to soften to the succulent texture of braised meat. A quick sauté of poblano chiles and red onions, with whole cumin seeds and a splash of lime juice, finishes the dish.

- 12 to 16 corn tortillas
- 1 pound tomatillos, husked, rinsed well and quartered
- 2 to 3 serrano chiles, seeded and coarsely chopped
- 1 small white onion, coarsely chopped
- 4 cloves garlic, coarsely chopped
- Salt
- 1 cup water
- ¼ cup packed chopped fresh cilantro
- Pinch granulated sugar
- 2 to 3 cups chopped cooked turkey or chicken (preferably dark meat, or mix white and dark)
- 1½ tablespoons extra-virgin olive oil
- 1 medium-large red onion, halved lengthwise and then cut crosswise into ¼-inch slices
- 3 large poblano chiles, cored, seeded and sliced into ¼-inch slices
- 1 teaspoon cumin seeds
- 2 limes (juice of 1 lime, the other quartered)
- Sour cream
- Hot sauce

Wrap tortillas in a damp towel and warm in microwave or a 250-degree oven.

Meanwhile, in a large saucepan, combine tomatillos, serrano chiles, white onion, garlic, pinch of salt, and 1 cup water. Bring to a simmer over medium-high heat, cover, reduce heat to low and cook until vegetables are very tender, about 15 minutes. Strain, reserving a few tablespoons of the cooking liquid, and process mixture with cilantro in a blender until smooth. Add 1 to 2 tablespoons of the reserved liquid if necessary to loosen the consistency. Add sugar and salt to taste; return sauce to pan.

Add turkey to sauce and bring to simmer. Reduce heat to low, cover, and cook until turkey is soft and has absorbed flavor of sauce, about 10 minutes.

Meanwhile, heat oil in large skillet over medium-high heat. Once shimmering, add red onion, poblano chiles, cumin seeds, and a large pinch salt. Cook, stirring occasionally, until soft and browned, 12 to 14 minutes (add splash of water if necessary to prevent sticking). Sprinkle liberally with lime juice.

Divide onion mixture among tortillas and top with turkey. Garnish with sour cream; serve immediately accompanied by lime wedges and hot sauce.

— From Matthew Card

MEXICAN TURKEY MOLE

MAKES 6 TO 8 SERVINGS

Turkey legs are one of the best bargains in the meat department, and their mild flavor is the perfect foil for the Latin American sauce known as mole. This version is thickened with dried red chiles and Mexican chocolate, available in most grocery stores where Mexican ingredients are sold. (If you can't find Mexican chocolate, substitute 2 ounces of bittersweet chocolate and 1 tablespoon of brown sugar.) Serve this rich stew over rice or with corn tortillas, diced avocado and shredded cheese.

This recipe was developed using a 6.5-quart slow-cooker, but you can scale the ingredients down for a smaller appliance.

4 dried New Mexican or ancho chiles
3 cups boiling water
1 tablespoon vegetable oil
1½ cups chopped yellow onion
2 teaspoons dried oregano leaves, preferably Mexican oregano
1½ teaspoons cumin seeds
5 whole cloves
1 bay leaf
1 tablespoon finely chopped garlic
½ cup toasted pumpkin seed kernels (pepitas)
¼ cup sesame seeds
⅓ cup raisins
1 teaspoon salt
1 (14½-ounce) can fire-roasted diced tomatoes with green chiles
2 cups chicken broth
2 turkey drumsticks, skin removed
2 turkey thighs, skin removed
3 ounces (1 tablet) Mexican chocolate, such as Ibarra brand, finely chopped
1 canned chipotle chile, chopped, plus 2 teaspoons adobo sauce from can
1 teaspoon ground cumin

Salt and freshly ground black pepper
½ medium red onion, thinly sliced
⅔ cup chopped fresh cilantro

To reconstitute the chiles, snap the stems off the chiles and shake out the seeds. Place the chiles in a small bowl, cover with the boiling water, weigh down with a small bowl to keep them submerged, and soak while preparing the other ingredients.

In a large sauté pan, heat the oil over medium-high heat. Add the yellow onion, oregano, cumin seeds, cloves, and bay leaf; sauté until the onion has softened,

TIPS FOR USING A SLOW-COOKER

- Never use frozen or partially thawed meat in a slow-cooker, which can cause food to remain too long at temperatures (the danger zone is 40 degrees to 140 degrees) that allow harmful bacteria to grow.

- Put slow-cooking root vegetables on the bottom and sides of the slow-cooker. Put tender vegetables like eggplant, mushrooms and peppers on the top of the other ingredients.

- Add tender ingredients such as fresh herbs, shrimp, cooked rice, and red bell peppers at the end of the cooking time to help preserve flavors and texture.

- Resist the urge to lift the lid and peek inside, which reduces the internal temperature and can delay cooking times by as much as 30 minutes. Sniff near the edge of the lid to get an idea of how things are going.

- To boost flavor at the end of the cooking time, add additional seasonings such as ground spices, lime juice, and Tabasco. Don't forget to taste and season with salt and pepper, if necessary.

5 minutes. Add the garlic and sauté until fragrant, 45 seconds. Transfer the mixture to a slow-cooker.

Add the pumpkin seed kernels, sesame seeds, raisins, salt, tomatoes, and chicken broth. Drain the reconstituted chiles, tear them into pieces (discard any remaining seeds), and place in the slow-cooker. Nestle the turkey pieces into the slow-cooker (they should be nearly submerged in liquid). Cover and cook on low heat for 7 hours.

Carefully lift the turkey out of the slow-cooker with a slotted spoon or spatula, and place on a large plate and set aside. Stir the chopped chocolate, chipotle chile, and ground cumin into the cooking liquid; cook for 1 minute to melt the chocolate.

Using an immersion blender, purée the cooking liquid until smooth. Alternatively, use a regular blender and work in batches, filling the blender only half full and keeping the lid slightly ajar to allow steam to escape. Taste the sauce, and season with salt and pepper, if needed.

Pull the turkey meat from the bones, making sure to avoid the long, thin bones in the drumsticks. Discard bones. Place turkey meat in a large serving dish, pour mole sauce over the meat, and garnish with the onions and cilantro.

— From Ivy Manning

CHEZ PANISSE TURKEY BRINE

MAKES ENOUGH BRINE FOR A 12- TO 16-POUND TURKEY

A basic brine is water and salt, and often sugar. But the extra ingredients in this recipe from the famed Chez Panisse restaurant in Berkeley will add flavor to the stuffing and gravy (if it's made with the drippings). While there won't be a distinct flavor difference in the turkey meat itself, the sugar will promote browning. If the bird is getting too dark during roasting, you can cover it with a tent of foil.

2½ gallons cold water
1½ to 1¾ cups kosher salt
1 cup granulated sugar
2 bay leaves
1 bunch fresh thyme (or ¼ cup dried)
1 whole head garlic, cloves separated and peeled
5 whole crushed allspice berries
4 juniper berries, smashed

In a large food-grade container, add the cold water, salt, and sugar; stir until the salt and sugar have dissolved. Add the bay leaves, thyme, garlic, allspice, and juniper berries.

If there's enough room in your refrigerator, place the turkey in a large stockpot (stainless steel, not aluminum, because the salt could cause pitting) or a food-grade bucket (available at some bakeries and restaurants for a nominal charge). You can also use a plastic oven-roasting bag (be sure to double them as they can break), extra large zip-top bag or special turkey-roasting bag, sold at gourmet stores.

Pour in enough brine so all the bird is covered. (If using a bag, pressing out extra air makes this easier. Seal the bag securely with kitchen twine or the plastic tab seals that come with the bags. Set the bag in a wide bowl or a roasting pan to stabilize the bird and catch any leaks.) Refrigerate on the bottom shelf of your refrigerator for 12 to 24 hours, but no more; it can get mushy if left longer.

If the refrigerator isn't an option, use a picnic cooler to hold the bird-in-a-bag. Surround it with ice or freezer packs, and remind yourself to check on it frequently, because the temperature inside the container needs to be below 40 degrees the whole time (use a refrigerator or instant-read thermometer). When you're ready to roast the turkey, remove it from the brine, and rinse it well inside and out with cool water.

The brine will do most of the seasoning, so don't salt the turkey after brining; also don't add salt to your stuffing if you plan to put it inside the bird. Some of the salt from the brine remains in the cavity and can season the stuffing. To be safe, some cooks recommend baking the stuffing separately.

Ditto for the gravy: you can make gravy using the drippings, but don't add any salt until you taste it first. You will probably need little or none. If you need to extend the gravy with chicken broth, only use low-sodium or unsalted broth, or the gravy could become too salty. Or just add water.

Watch your timing because a brined turkey cooks faster than a non-brined one by about 30 minutes. Use a meat or instant-read thermometer to determine when it's reached 165 degrees in the deepest part of the thigh, but not touching the bone.

— Adapted from Chez Panisse

TWO METHODS FOR BRINING YOUR BIRD

For years we've been telling readers to brine their turkey. It really does help ensure moist, tender meat. But there are two methods, and both have their benefits and drawbacks. Wet brining requires submerging meat in a generous amount of salted liquid (and sometimes sugar and other seasonings) and keeping it cold, either in a refrigerator or a cooler with ice. Unless you have a very large pot, you'll have to place the turkey and brine solution in a large plastic bag, and secure it with kitchen twine or twist-ties, which can be tricky for one person to handle. The benefit is that wet brining is done in 12 to 24 hours; any longer and the meat can turn out spongy.

Dry brining requires applying a salt-based rub and allowing the meat to sit in the refrigerator. There's no fussing with bowls or bags full of water, and the roasted meat doesn't have the sponginess that wet brining can sometimes cause. The downside is that with larger meats, like a turkey, you'll need to keep it refrigerated or cold for as long as three days. This can be a real headache if you don't have a spare refrigerator.

After a bird has been wet-brined, it needs to be rinsed well with cool water. With a dry-brined bird, you only need to dry the skin with paper towels.

Note that brined meats can cook faster than non-brined meats, so be sure to monitor the internal temperature with a meat or instant-read thermometer.

DRY-BRINED TURKEY

MAKES ABOUT A POUND PER PERSON

Most recipes for dry-brining credit chef Judy Rodgers of San Francisco's Zuni Café, where for years the restaurant has used the method on its popular roast chicken. But as many chefs have learned, dry brining is brilliant for turkey, too, and in recent years recipes have been published by Martha Stewart, Alton Brown, the New York Times, the Los Angeles Times, Fine Cooking magazine and others. Instead of just using a basic salt rub, you can use almost any combination of the suggested flavorings that follow. But for best results, be sure to apply the salt four days ahead. A shorter brining period will work, but not as well.

> 1 (12- to 16-pound) turkey
> 3 to 4 tablespoons kosher salt
> ½ cup butter (optional)
> 1½ cups water

Remove turkey from wrapper; remove giblets and neck and save for gravy or another use. Pat turkey dry. Using about 1 tablespoon salt per 4 pounds of bird, rub turkey all over with salt, slipping it under the skin where possible and concentrating more of the salt on the thicker parts. Season the cavity lightly. Place turkey in a large oven bag or food-safe plastic bag and seal tightly, removing any trapped air. Place breast side up on a rimmed baking sheet, and refrigerate for 3 days, turning it over once a day and massaging the salt into the bird (no need to remove it from its bag).

The day before turkey is to be roasted, remove it from the bag and dry it well with paper towels. Do not rinse the bird. Return turkey to the baking sheet and refrigerate it uncovered until the next day. This helps the skin dry and will encourage crisper skin after roasting.

Remove turkey from refrigerator 1 hour before it's time to roast. Preheat oven to 425 degrees. Place turkey breast side up in a roasting pan. Rub butter under breast skin and onto thigh meat, if desired. Tuck wing tips behind the neck and tie legs together with kitchen twine. Roast for 30 minutes. Pour 1½ cups water into the roasting pan, reduce oven temperature to 325 and roast until a thermometer inserted in the deepest part of the thigh reads 165 degrees, about 2 hours longer. Tent turkey loosely with foil if it starts to darken too much.

Remove turkey from oven, transfer to a platter, tent loosely with foil and allow to rest for 30 minutes before carving. You can make gravy with the pan drippings, but be sure to taste before seasoning with any salt.

RUB OPTIONS:

Pick and choose from these suggested flavorings to customize your salt rub. If you want to use whole herbs or spices, such as bay leaves or allspice berries, grind them in a spice grinder or mortar and pestle.

- Freshly ground black pepper
- Ground cumin
- Ground allspice
- Onion powder
- Garlic powder
- Dried bay leaves
- Rubbed sage or minced fresh sage
- Thyme (minced; fresh or dried)
- Rosemary (minced; fresh or dried)
- Smoked paprika (pimentón de la Vera)
- Freshly grated lemon or orange zest

MEAT

8

PERFECT PRIME RIB ROAST

MAKES 6 TO 8 SERVINGS

For a special meal, it's hard to top a prime rib roast. The ideal standing rib roast should contain three to five ribs, and we think three is the perfect size for dinner for six to eight. Ask for a small-end (or first-cut) roast, meaning a roast cut from the loin end of the steer, where the meat is tender, flavorful, and leaner than at the large end. Also, Fooday developed this recipe for a roast that has had the bones cut off the meat and then tied back on. If your roast has not been prepared in this manner, ask the butcher to cut and tie it for you.

> 1 (3-bone) beef rib roast (prime rib), about
>   6 pounds
> 2 tablespoons kosher salt
> 1 tablespoon freshly ground black pepper
> 1 teaspoon dry mustard
> 2 teaspoons chopped fresh rosemary
> 6 to 8 sprigs fresh rosemary (optional)

CREAMY HORSERADISH SAUCE:
> ¼ cup prepared horseradish sauce
> 1 cup sour cream
> 2 teaspoons Dijon mustard (optional)
> ¼ cup finely chopped scallions or fresh chives

At least one day ahead of time, unwrap roast and pat dry with paper towels. Combine salt, pepper, dry mustard, and chopped rosemary; rub mixture generously all over roast, especially in spaces between meat and bones. Refrigerate, uncovered.

Up to 2 hours before cooking the roast, remove from refrigerator and let sit at room temperature, loosely covered.

Position a rack in the center of oven and preheat to 450 degrees. (For grass-fed beef, start at 350 degrees.) Place roast bone side down in a large, shallow roasting pan on a bed of rosemary sprigs, if using (for boneless roasts, line the pan with a roasting rack). Place meat in the oven and roast for 20 minutes, then, without opening the door, reduce oven temperature to 350 degrees. After about another 45 minutes, start checking the internal temperature of the roast with an instant-read probe or meat thermometer. Remove the roast at 115 degrees for rare (10 to 15 minutes per pound), 120 to 125 degrees for medium-rare, and 130 degrees for medium. If using a convection oven, remove it at 110 degrees for rare, 115 to 120 degrees for medium-rare, and 125 degrees for medium.

Tent roast with foil and let sit for 15 to 20 minutes; as roast rests, the juices will be redistributed and the internal temperature will rise by about 10 degrees. Carve the roast at the table and serve with Creamy Horseradish Sauce.

USE A THERMOMETER TO PROTECT YOUR INVESTMENT

Internal temperature, not time, is the best test for doneness, and you don't want to blow it on something as expensive as prime rib. Once removed from the oven, your roast will keep cooking the longer it sits, from about 10 degrees with a resting time of 15 to 20 minutes (Fooday's preference), to as much as 20 degrees or more if allowed to rest as long as an hour. If roasted in a convection oven, the resting temperature of the meat can rise as much as 30 degrees, so be sure to follow the recipe directions for removing the roast a bit earlier.

To make sauce: In a medium bowl stir together horseradish sauce, sour cream, Dijon mustard, if desired, and scallions or chives.

— Adapted from Molly Stevens, Bruce Aidells, and Ben Dyer

HERBED ROAST BEEF IN SALT CRUST

MAKES 12 SERVINGS

Every now and then a recipe takes on a life of its own. And this was one of those recipes. The preparation doesn't make the roast salty at all, it just helps ensure very succulent, juicy meat. After running the recipe four times, we've got it down to a science. Still, it's important to stress a few things, so be sure to read the accompanying tips.

⅓ cup olive oil
¼ cup grated onion
1 teaspoon garlic salt
1 teaspoon dried basil
¼ teaspoon dried marjoram
½ teaspoon dried thyme
¼ teaspoon pepper
1 (4- to 6-pound) boneless beef roast (prime rib, rib-eye, eye of round; see note for roasting information)
1 (3-pound) box kosher salt (more if roast is larger)
1¼ cups water (divided)

In a zip-top plastic bag, combine oil, onion, garlic salt, basil, marjoram, thyme and pepper. Mix well, add roast and coat well with marinade. Refrigerate 2 hours or overnight.

Preheat oven to 425 degrees.

Line a roasting pan with heavy-duty aluminum foil. In a large mixing bowl, combine kosher salt and 1 cup water; mix with hands until salt is well-moistened.

Adding remaining ¼ cup water only as needed to reach a consistency similar to fluffy snow. (Caution: If salt is too wet, it will slide off the meat.)

In the bottom of the roasting pan, pat enough moistened salt to make a rectangle slightly larger than the roast. Pat roast dry with paper towels. Place on salt bed. Insert meat thermometer into middle of roast. Pat rest of moistened salt all over roast, encasing it. (A reader suggests pressing aluminum foil onto salt as you pat it, to make a temporary mold that helps keep salt mixture in place.) Wiggle thermometer around to make sure salt isn't resting against probe.

Place the roast in oven and roast until meat reaches an internal temperature of 115 degrees for rare (10 to 15 minutes per pound), 120 to 125 degrees for medium-rare, and 130 degrees for medium. Remove roast from oven and use a hammer to crack away salt crust; whisk away any remaining salt with a pastry or vegetable brush. Tent roast with foil and let sit for 15 to 20 minutes before carving; as roast rests, the juices will be redistributed and the internal temperature will rise by about 10 degrees.

TIPS FOR SUCCESSFUL SALT-CRUSTED BEEF

- Our roasting times are only guidelines; you'll need a meat thermometer, instant-read thermometer, or the kind that connects the probe to a separate base with a cord.

- Roasts smaller than 4 pounds, such as tri-tip, don't work well because the roast doesn't spend enough time in the oven to form a hard salt crust.

- Be sure to use kosher salt, not rock salt, regular table salt, or pickling/canning salt. Rock salt may have impurities; table salt and pickling/canning salt are too fine.

- Do not pat salt on meat until immediately before roasting; it will not hold well.

- Pat on a thin layer of wet salt first—almost sprinkle it like meal. By the time you have a thin layer in place, it will have dried ever so slightly, making it easier to apply a second layer. This technique is far easier than putting on a thick layer all at once.

- If using a meat or leave-in thermometer, swivel it around a bit before putting the roast in the oven, so the moistened salt isn't packed directly against the metal stem. The hot salt can give you false high readings.

- If using an instant-read thermometer (the kind that doesn't stay in the meat while it cooks), you may have to poke a hole in the salt crust before inserting it into the middle of the roast.

- Check temperature 15 minutes before the estimated time to be done. Remove meat from the oven when thermometer registers 5 degrees below desired doneness.

- Length of roasting time is not directly proportionate to size. Heavier roasts aren't that much bigger around—they're simply longer. In other words, a 6-pound roast takes about 20 minutes per pound to get to medium doneness, or 2 hours. But a 12-pound roast won't take 4 hours—more likely 3.

- If you are using tenderloins, ask the butcher to tie two butt tenderloins (the ends) end-to-end—one small end lapped onto the other's large end—to create a 4½-pound roast, roughly 5 inches long and 4 inches across. (Order these ahead during the holiday season to be sure the butcher has tenderloins.) Salt-encased tenderloins take 1 hour and 15 minutes at 425 degrees to hit medium-rare.

- Note that there are no pan drippings to serve when you bake in salt.

ENCASING BEEF IN SALT CRUST

Pat salt in place, making sure that the meat thermometer isn't touching the layer of salt. After the meat is done cooking, crack off the crust and brush away any excess, and let meat rest for 15 to 20 minutes.

COFFEE-AND-FENNEL-RUBBED STRIP STEAKS WITH ORANGE-THYME BUTTER

MAKES 6 SERVINGS

Coffee is a brilliant flavoring for beef, adding complexity and a bitter edge that balances so many other ingredients. For this dish, avoid very dark-roasted beans, which can make the spice rub taste too bitter.

COFFEE-FENNEL RUB:

2 tablespoons whole coffee beans
2 teaspoons whole fennel seeds
2 teaspoons whole black peppercorns
2 teaspoons firmly packed brown sugar
1 tablespoon kosher salt
2 teaspoons paprika
⅛ teaspoon cayenne pepper (optional)

ORANGE-THYME BUTTER:

6 tablespoons unsalted butter, softened
2 teaspoons minced fresh thyme
1 tablespoon minced fresh Italian (flat-leaf) parsley
1 tablespoon minced shallot
1 heaping teaspoon grated orange zest
Salt and freshly ground black pepper

STEAKS:

4 strip steaks, 1 to 1¼ inches thick (about 3 pounds total), trimmed of excess fat and patted dry
2 teaspoons vegetable oil

To make rub: In a spice grinder, combine coffee beans, fennel seeds, and peppercorns; process until finely ground. Transfer to a small bowl and blend well with brown sugar, salt, paprika, and cayenne, if using.

To make butter: In a small bowl, use a fork to blend butter, thyme, parsley, shallot, and zest; season to taste with salt and pepper and set aside.

To make steaks: Adjust oven rack to middle position and preheat oven to 350 degrees. Thoroughly coat each side of steaks with spice rub and press so mixture adheres. In a large, oven-safe skillet, add oil and heat over medium-high heat until oil is smoking. Place steaks in pan and arrange so they're not touching, and cook until well-browned but not burned, 2½ to 3 minutes. Flip and cook second side until browned, about 2 minutes. Transfer skillet to oven and cook 4 to 6 minutes for medium-rare, 7 to 9 minutes for medium.

Transfer steaks to serving platter, spread each with some Orange-Thyme Butter, and allow to rest for at least 5 minutes. Cut into ¼-inch slices, arrange on warm plates, and top with a little more butter.

— From Matthew Card

TO THAW SAFELY, KEEP MEAT OUT OF "DANGER ZONE"

Smaller pieces of frozen meat, chicken, fish, or other foods can be safely thawed in warm water because they thaw all the way through fast enough to avoid sitting too long in the "danger zone"—between 40 degrees and 140 degrees—when dangerous bacteria multiply quickly. Larger roasts and birds should be thawed in the refrigerator or in cold water (changing the water when it gets icy). Thawing food on the counter is not safe because the outer portion reaches the danger zone before the inside has thawed.

FILET OF BEEF IN PORT-GARLIC SAUCE

MAKES 4 SERVINGS

Over the years, Fooday received several requests for this recipe from Cafe des Amis, but since it was the restaurant's signature dish, chef Dennis Baker declined. However, when he decided to retire and close the restaurant, he generously shared his wonderful recipe with us.

1 tablespoon unsalted butter
2 tablespoons sliced garlic
2¼ cups ruby port
1½ cups veal stock (see note)
½ cup seasoned consommé (see note)
Salt and freshly ground black pepper
1 to 2 teaspoons vegetable oil
4 (6- to 7-ounce) beef tenderloin steaks

Melt the butter in a medium saucepan over low heat. Add the garlic, cover and sweat until the garlic is tender (do not brown).

When the garlic is tender, raise the heat to high and add the port, veal stock and consommé. Bring to a boil and continue boiling until the sauce is reduced to 1 cup (about 30 minutes). Season to taste with salt and pepper. Strain the sauce and keep hot while cooking the steaks.

Heat a cast-iron skillet over medium-high heat. Add enough oil to barely film the pan. Add the steaks and cook to desired degree of doneness, turning once (4 to 5 minutes per side, depending on thickness, for medium-rare). Season steaks with salt and pepper. Add ¼ cup of sauce to the pan and turn the steaks to coat.

Serve the steaks on heated plates, topping each with 3 tablespoons of sauce.

Note: We used More Than Gourmet Glace de Veau, a concentrate for veal stock. Half of a 1.5-ounce package will make 2 cups stock. Find it at stores that carry a wide assortment of gourmet foods. You can also purchase veal stock by the quart at Chop Butchery & Charcuterie (see Resources chapter).

Note: We tested this recipe using undiluted Campbell's Condensed Beef Consommé.

— From Dennis Baker, Cafe des Amis

KOREAN-STYLE BEEF SHORT RIBS

MAKES 4 TO 6 SERVINGS

Not all short ribs are the same. The ones you braise long and slow in the winter are cut into meaty single 3- to 4-inch ribs with a large bone running down the middle. Flanken-cut ribs, the kind used here, are cut crosswise from multiple ribs into long thin strips. Each strip has a couple of thin slices of bone. Flanken-cut ribs are richly marbled and quick-cooking—and fabulous grilled.

1 cup soy sauce
½ cup firmly packed light brown sugar
2 tablespoons ketchup
¼ cup minced garlic (about 12 cloves)
¼ cup peeled and minced fresh ginger (3- to 4-inch piece)
¼ cup rice vinegar
¼ cup dark sesame oil
¼ cup Asian chili paste (such as sambal oelek or sriracha)

2 bunches scallions, thinly sliced
4 pounds flanken-cut beef short ribs
Suggested accompaniments: lettuce wraps,
    steamed rice, kimchi, and bean sprouts

In a bowl, whisk together the soy sauce, brown sugar, ketchup, garlic, ginger, vinegar, sesame oil, chili paste, and scallions. Pour marinade over the short ribs, making sure to coat all the ribs. Let marinate for at least two hours, but preferably overnight. To cook the ribs, remove them from the marinade and shake off any excess. Preheat grill to high (see note). Oil grates well and grill ribs 1 to 2 minutes on both sides. Remove from the grill and serve immediately, with accompaniments.

Note: To check grill temperature, count the seconds you can hold your hand, palm side down, 2 to 3 inches above the rack, until it feels uncomfortable: 2 seconds for high.

— From chef/owner Jon Beeaker, Acme Food and Drink

OVEN-BARBECUED BEEF

MAKES ABOUT 10 SANDWICHES

"Barbecue" assumes outdoor cooking. But in Oregon, that's not always an appealing option. This recipe, from Donna Morgan, a retired food editor of the Salt Lake Tribune, is done entirely in the oven.

Salt and freshly ground black pepper
1 (5-pound) boneless beef roast (chuck,
    rump, sirloin tip, or whatever's cheapest)
2 cups chopped onions
2 cups chili sauce
1 cup ketchup
1 teaspoon Worcestershire sauce
2 cups water
2 tablespoons cornstarch
1 tablespoon chili powder
1 teaspoon paprika
¼ teaspoon black pepper
½ cup firmly packed brown sugar
½ teaspoon ground allspice
10 hamburger buns

Preheat oven to 325 degrees.

Rub salt and pepper over roast, and place on rack in roasting pan. Roast 2½ hours (no basting, no covering). Remove from oven and let stand 1 hour to cool, or refrigerate overnight, depending on when you want to finish baking.

In a large bowl, mix onions, chili sauce, ketchup, Worcestershire sauce, the water, cornstarch, chili powder, paprika, pepper, brown sugar, and allspice.

Slice roast into very thin slices and layer in large baking pan with sauce, ending with sauce. Cover with foil and bake at 325 degrees for 3 hours, or until meat is very tender. Serve on buns.

Make ahead: The initial baking period can be done a day ahead. On the day you plan to serve, slice and cook the meat in the sauce. This dish also freezes beautifully.

— From Donna Morgan

FIRE BRIGADE CHILI

MAKES ABOUT 1½ QUARTS, OR 6 SERVINGS

For years, Marie and Ted Keyes competed on the chili circuit, winning Oregon state chili championships three times, and often placing in the top three spots at the Great Pacific Northwest Chili Cook-off. Their recipe is very spicy and goes well with a bowl of rice and/or beans.

3 pounds trimmed chuck, cubed finely (¼- to ½-inch dice)
1 tablespoon vegetable oil
1 cup beef broth
2 cups water
1 (8-ounce) can tomato sauce
¼ cup hot chili powder
¼ cup mild chili powder
2 tablespoons garlic powder
3 tablespoons minced onion
1 tablespoon granulated sugar
1 tablespoon cayenne pepper
3 tablespoons ground cumin
2 teaspoons salt
2 tablespoons paprika

In a large saucepan or Dutch oven, heat oil over high heat and brown meat. Add beef broth and water, bring to a simmer and cook for 20 to 30 minutes. Add tomato sauce, chili powders, garlic powder, onion, sugar, cayenne, cumin, salt, and paprika. Cook, uncovered, until the liquid is reduced to desired thickness, at least 1½ hours.

— From Ted and Marie Keyes

PUTTING OUT THE FLAMES

If you've ever gone overboard with cayenne pepper or hot chiles, we're sorry to say that there's no easy remedy. You can add more beans or tomatoes, or serve it over rice. If it still is too hot, make another batch—without any spices—and mix the two together. If you end up with much more than you can use, chili freezes well.

RICH'S MEDITERRANEAN LAMB SHANKS

MAKES 6 SERVINGS

A real Foodday favorite, and a perfect dish for fall or winter entertaining. Although Rich's Northwest Bistro in Tualatin served the shanks with roasted new potatoes, they go just as nicely with polenta or couscous, which soak up the delicious sauce.

2 large heads garlic (6 ounces)
1 large onion, diced
2 tablespoons plus ¼ cup vegetable oil (divided)

4 teaspoons dried thyme
4 teaspoons dried oregano
3 to 4 teaspoons salt
2½ teaspoons freshly ground black pepper
2½ teaspoons peeled and grated fresh ginger
2½ cups canned diced tomatoes
1 (8-ounce) can tomato sauce
1 cup water
6 lamb shanks
½ cup all-purpose flour
½ cup chopped kalamata olives

Peel the garlic, leaving each clove whole; you will have about 36 to 42 whole cloves. (A great trick to loosen the skins is to put the cloves in a metal bowl, cover with another metal bowl, and then, holding the bowls together, rapidly and forcefully shake the cloves for about 15 seconds.) In a large saucepan, heat 2 tablespoons oil over medium heat and sauté the onion and garlic until onion is translucent. Add the thyme, oregano, salt, pepper, ginger, tomatoes, tomato sauce, and water. Simmer gently for a few minutes.

Meanwhile, season the lamb shanks with salt and pepper; dredge with flour. In a large skillet, heat the remaining ¼ cup vegetable oil over medium-high heat, and brown the lamb shanks well. Arrange the lamb shanks in one or two shallow baking pans and pour the tomato-ginger sauce over. Cover and bake at 325 degrees for 3½ to 4 hours or until very tender.

Remove lamb shanks and pour the sauce into a large bowl. Let stand a few minutes and then skim off any fat that has risen to the surface. Serve lamb shanks with sauce; sprinkle with chopped olives to garnish.

Make ahead: Shanks can be cooked the day before and refrigerated. Remove congealed fat before re-heating.

— From Rich's Northwest Bistro, Tualatin

RACK OF LAMB WITH HERBED CRUMB CRUST

MAKES 2 SERVINGS

This simple dish has been a longtime favorite of former Foodday columnist Barbara Durbin. Be sure to use an instant-read or meat thermometer to avoid overcooking the lamb.

1 frenched rack of lamb (about 8 chops, ¾ to 1 pound; see note)
1 tablespoon Dijon mustard
1 tablespoon coarse-grain mustard
2 teaspoons minced fresh thyme leaves or ½ teaspoon dried leaves
¼ cup finely minced fresh parsley
Salt and freshly ground black pepper
1 clove garlic, minced (optional)
2 slices artisan-style bread, crusts removed, processed in food processor to make fresh breadcrumbs
1 tablespoon melted butter

Remove any excess fat still on surface of lamb rack. Preheat oven to 375 degrees.

In small bowl, mix two mustards, thyme, parsley, dash of salt and grinding of fresh pepper, and garlic.

Place a rack inside roasting pan, and place lamb on the rack. Slather mustard mixture over lamb. Press crumbs into mustard, drizzle with melted butter.

Roast about 25 minutes, until internal temperature is 125 to 130 degrees for medium-rare.

Note: If the meat is frenched, the butcher has already removed most of the outside layer of fat and has cut fat between each set of bones down to the chops.

— From Barbara Durbin

SHEPHERD'S PIE UNDER CHAMP

MAKES 6 SERVINGS

Shepherd's pie is a frugal British pie that traditionally makes great use of tough mutton. But here it's made with tender ground lamb and topped with fluffy champ (mashed potatoes with scallions), which adds a nice spring green flavor to the dish. If your family doesn't like lamb, substitute lean ground beef, and you've made what the British call a cottage pie.

CHAMP:

1½ pounds (about 4 large) Yukon Gold
   potatoes, peeled and quartered
Salt
⅔ cup milk
1 bunch scallions, thinly sliced
2 tablespoons butter
¼ teaspoon ground nutmeg
1 pinch cayenne pepper
Freshly ground black pepper

LAMB FILLING:

1 pound ground lamb or beef
2 tablespoons olive oil
1½ cups finely chopped onion
1 large carrot, finely chopped
6 ounces cremini mushrooms, sliced (2 cups)
2 tablespoons all-purpose flour
1 heaping tablespoon tomato paste
1 teaspoon fresh thyme leaves, or ¼ teaspoon
   dried thyme
3 tablespoons dry sherry
2½ cups beef or lamb broth
Salt and freshly ground black pepper

To make champ: In a 4-quart saucepan, add the potatoes, 2 teaspoons salt, and cold water to cover by 2 inches. Bring to a boil and cook until the potatoes are tender when pierced with a fork, about 20 minutes. Meanwhile, in a small saucepan, combine the milk and scallions and bring to a simmer; reduce heat to low until ready to mash.

Drain the potatoes into a colander set in the sink and allow steam to evaporate for 10 minutes. Return potatoes to pan. Add the milk/scallion mixture, butter, nutmeg, and cayenne, and mash until potatoes are smooth. Season to taste with salt and pepper, and set aside.

To make filling: Preheat oven to 375 degrees. Line a rimmed baking sheet with foil; set aside. Heat a large sauté pan over medium heat. Add the lamb and cook until it is no longer pink. Drain and transfer lamb to a 2-quart baking dish; set aside.

Return the pan to medium heat and add the oil. Add the onions, carrot, and mushrooms, and sauté, stirring occasionally, until the vegetables are tender, about 10 minutes. Stir in the flour and cook 1 minute. Add the tomato paste, thyme, sherry, and broth, and bring to a simmer over medium-high heat, stirring constantly. Stir in the lamb; simmer uncovered until the stew is thick and bubbly, 15 minutes. Season to taste with salt and pepper.

Pour the lamb mixture into the baking dish. Spoon the champ over the lamb mixture and place baking dish on the prepared baking sheet. Bake until the stew is bubbly around the edges, about 30 minutes. Allow the pie to cool for 10 minutes before serving.

— From Ivy Manning

DOUBLE-CUT PORK CHOPS WITH PUMPKIN-SAGE BREAD PUDDING AND PAN GRAVY

MAKES 6 HUGE SERVINGS OR 12 AVERAGE SERVINGS

Foodday taste testers went nuts for this dish. And the bread pudding was so good our test kitchen director served it as stuffing at Thanksgiving. Note that each chop is 1 to 1½ pounds, so if you don't have a very large appetite, we suggest you plan on sharing.

If you don't have two ovens, make sure your oven will accommodate the pans for both the pork and bread pudding at the same time. If one dish is done before the other, it can sit, covered, while the second dish finishes cooking.

6 double-cut pork chops, rib ends frenched, about 1 to 1½ pounds each (see note)
1 gallon water (16 cups)
1 cup kosher salt, plus extra for seasoning (divided)
¼ cup plus 2 tablespoons granulated sugar
Pumpkin Sage Bread Pudding (recipe follows)
Freshly ground black pepper
3 cups chicken broth
1 cup whipping cream

Place the pork chops in a single layer in a large, deep bowl or nonreactive pan. In a large container, stir together the water, kosher salt, and sugar until the salt and sugar are dissolved. Pour the brine over the pork chops to cover and weigh the chops down with a plate. Cover and refrigerate for 24 hours.

The next day, begin preparation of the bread pudding as directed below, and while bread cubes are soaking in the custard, preheat the oven to 375 degrees.

Remove the chops from the brine and pat dry. Place the chops in a roasting pan and season with pepper. Roast for 1 to 1½ hours or until chops reach 140 degrees on a meat thermometer. Bake bread pudding alongside chops or in a separate oven. When chops are done, remove from the oven and let rest in the pan for about 10 minutes.

Drain the pan juices into a saucepan. Using the chicken broth, deglaze the roasting pan, scraping up all the bits of pork from the bottom. Add the deglazing liquid to the saucepan.

Bring the liquid to a boil, and boil until reduced by half. Add the cream and return to a boil; reduce by one-third to half, or until thick and bubbly. (If the pan gravy is not quite thick enough, stir 1 tablespoon of all-purpose flour into ¼ cup cold water or chicken broth and stir into the gravy. Bring to a boil and cook for 1 to 2 minutes to thicken.)

Keep warm until bread pudding is ready.

To serve, place a large scoop of bread pudding in the center of the plate and place the pork chop on top of the pudding. Drizzle pan gravy over all and serve hot.

Note: Double-cut pork chops with frenched rib ends are available at some specialty groceries such as Zupan's. Call ahead to order to be sure they're available.

PUMPKIN SAGE BREAD PUDDING
1 (16-ounce) crusty French baguette, cut into cubes
¼ cup unsalted butter
1 large onion, diced
1 cup diced celery
2 tablespoons minced garlic
1 cup freshly grated parmesan cheese (4 ounces)
1½ cups canned pumpkin purée
4 eggs plus 3 egg yolks

3 to 4 cups milk (divided)
1½ tablespoons salt
1 tablespoon ground black pepper
½ cup chopped fresh sage leaves

Preheat the oven to 375 degrees. Grease a 9-by-13-inch baking pan. Place the bread cubes in a large bowl and set aside.

In a large skillet, melt the butter over low heat and sauté the onion, celery, and garlic until onion is translucent, about 5 to 7 minutes. Add to the bread cubes along with the parmesan cheese.

In a medium bowl, whisk together the pumpkin, eggs, egg yolks, 3 cups milk, salt, pepper, and sage. Pour mixture over bread cubes and toss to combine. Let sit for 30 to 45 minutes to allow bread to absorb the liquid. If mixture seems dry after sitting, add remaining 1 cup milk and mix well. Pour mixture into the prepared baking pan; cover with greased aluminum foil. Bake for 1 to 1½ hours or until the pudding is set and still moist.

— From Blue Sky Cafe, Manzanita

DEGLAZE TO CAPTURE ALL OF THE FLAVOR

Deglazing is basic technique used by chefs and home cooks. When a food, such as chops, are seared in a skillet, they leave behind what's called a "fond," the caramelized substance that adds so much flavor to food. To incorporate the fond into a dish, the meat and/or vegetables is removed from the skillet and a liquid—usually wine or broth—is added. The cook then stirs and scrapes up the fond to release it from the pan and allow it to dissolve into the liquid. This flavorful liquid can then become the basis of a sauce.

SICILIAN PORK CHOPS WITH PEPPERONCINI

MAKES 4 SERVINGS

Although the Tuscany Grill is no longer open, readers still fondly remember its signature dish. Pork chop recipes are sometimes stodgy affairs. This one is anything but, thanks to pecorino Romano cheese, fresh herbs, garlic, and piquant pepperoncini. Be sure to test the chops and remove them from the oven while they're still pink and juicy inside.

1 cup plain dry breadcrumbs
¼ cup freshly grated pecorino Romano cheese
3 cloves garlic, finely minced
¼ teaspoon crushed red pepper flakes, or to taste
1 tablespoon minced fresh Italian (flat-leaf) parsley
2 to 3 fresh basil leaves, minced
1 teaspoon minced fresh rosemary
4 thick center-cut pork chops (with bone)
Salt and freshly ground black pepper
⅓ cup extra-virgin olive oil
8 whole bottled pepperoncini peppers
½ to 1 cup juice from drained pepperoncini peppers
½ cup water or chicken broth
2 tablespoons butter
Fresh rosemary sprigs for garnish

Preheat oven to 475 degrees.

In a small bowl combine the breadcrumbs, cheese, garlic, red pepper flakes, parsley, basil, and rosemary. Stir to mix well.

Season pork chops with salt and pepper. Dip each pork chop into the olive oil, turning to coat both sides. Dredge the oil-coated chops in the breadcrumb mixture, pressing crumbs into the chops. Use some of the remaining oil to lightly grease a shallow baking pan (do not use a glass dish). Arrange the chops in the oiled pan and add the pepperoncini.

Bake in preheated oven for 15 minutes, then turn chop over. Add the juice from the pepperoncini to the pan and return to the oven. Bake for another 15 minutes or until the chops register 140 degrees on a meat thermometer. Place pan under a preheated broiler until the chops are golden brown and crisp.

Remove chops and pepperoncini to warm platter to rest, and place pan over medium heat. Add water or chicken broth to pan drippings and stir to combine. Whisk butter into the pan sauce until slightly thickened. Serve over the chops. Garnish with sprigs of fresh rosemary.

— From Tuscany Grill

MONTE'S HAM

MAKES 30 SERVINGS

For many families, Easter demands a baked ham. This method cooks the meat low and slow with lots of cloves and a delicious glaze, for truly succulent results.

    1 (15-pound) smoked ham, on the bone
    1½ cups orange marmalade
    1 cup Dijon mustard
    1½ cups firmly packed brown sugar
    1 rounded tablespoon whole cloves

Preheat oven to 300 degrees.

Trim tough outer skin and excess fat from ham. Put ham in a large roasting pan and score, making crosshatch incisions all over it with a sharp knife. Roast for 2 hours. Meanwhile, make a glaze by combining the marmalade, mustard and brown sugar in a medium bowl.

Remove ham from oven and stud with cloves, inserting one at the intersection of each crosshatch, then brush entire surface of ham generously with glaze and return to oven. Cook ham 1 more hour, brushing with glaze at least three times. Turn heat up to 350 degrees and cook 30 minutes more. Carve and serve warm or at room temperature.

—Adapted from *Saveur Cooks Authentic American*, by the editors of Saveur magazine (Chronicle Books)

MEATLOAF STUFFED WITH BASIL, CHEESE, PROSCIUTTO, AND SUN-DRIED TOMATOES

MAKES 8 SERVINGS

This delicious meatloaf is definitely worthy of company. It's from former Foodday home economist Sharon Maasdam, who says, "You can put it together early in the day and then bake it before serving. It's a large recipe, so if you're not serving eight people, freeze the remainder or use it for sandwiches."

1 tablespoon olive oil

1 tablespoon butter

1 small red onion, chopped

2 large cloves garlic, minced

8 ounces roughly chopped fresh mushrooms (3 cups)

Salt and freshly ground black pepper

1¾ cups fresh sourdough breadcrumbs (see note)

1½ pounds lean ground beef

¾ pound sweet Italian sausage, casings removed and discarded

2 eggs, lightly beaten

⅓ cup minced fresh parsley

¾ cup grated parmesan cheese

1 teaspoon minced fresh thyme or ½ teaspoon dried

3 ounces sliced prosciutto

8 ounces thinly sliced havarti cheese

1¼ cups fresh basil, cut into thin strips

⅓ cup drained oil-packed sun-dried tomatoes, cut into strips

Sprigs of fresh basil (optional)

Place oven rack in middle position and preheat oven to 350 degrees. For easiest cleanup, line a jellyroll pan with parchment paper. Aluminum foil will work, but you must remove the meatloaf from the pan within 4 or 5 minutes of removing it from the oven, or it may stick to the foil.

In a large skillet, heat oil and butter over medium-high heat, and sauté onion until softened, about 4 minutes. Add garlic and mushrooms; cook until mushrooms are soft and liquid has evaporated. Season to taste with salt and pepper; set aside to cool slightly before proceeding.

In a large bowl combine breadcrumbs, cooled mushroom mixture, ground beef, sausage, eggs, parsley, cheese, thyme, and a little pepper. Gently mix by hand.

To taste your meat mixture, pull out about 1 tablespoon and microwave it for about 1 minute or until it is cooked. Allow it to cool enough so you can taste it. Correct seasonings if necessary.

Gently pat meat mixture into a 10-by-15-inch rectangle on a sheet of wax paper. With a longer end facing you, layer the prosciutto, havarti cheese, fresh basil, and sun-dried tomatoes on the bottom two-thirds of the meat. Grab the edge of the wax paper closest to you and roll up the loaf. Once meatloaf is rolled up, seal ends and press down slightly to seal lengthwise seam. Place seam side down on prepared jellyroll pan.

Bake, uncovered, for 65 minutes or until the center of the meatloaf registers 160 degrees on a meat thermometer. Slice and garnish with basil sprig, if desired.

Make ahead: The uncooked meatloaf can be assembled, wrapped well and refrigerated up to one day ahead. Bake and serve as directed.

Note: To make fresh breadcrumbs, tear the bread into fourths and place in food processor fitted with the metal blade. Process until medium-size breadcrumbs are formed. This process also can be accomplished in a blender, but with smaller quantities.

— From Sharon Maasdam

MARY McCRANK'S MEATLOAF

MAKES 6 TO 8 SERVINGS

Mary McCrank's has been serving comfort food in Chehalis since 1935, and this traditional meatloaf has been on the menu for years. Chef Gerd Schopp told Foodday that the key to tender, juicy results is to use ground beef with between 15 percent and 20 percent fat and to not overcook the loaf. Schopp uses a meat thermometer and takes the loaves out of the oven when they reach 160 to 165 degrees.

2½ pounds ground beef
4 eggs
¾ cup cracker meal or crushed saltines
¾ cup water
1½ heaping teaspoons beef base (see note)
¾ teaspoon onion salt
¾ teaspoon garlic salt
1½ teaspoons Worcestershire sauce
10 tablespoons ketchup (divided)
6 tablespoons finely diced onion

Preheat oven to 325 degrees. Lightly grease a 9-by-5-inch loaf pan.

In a large mixing bowl, combine the ground beef, eggs, and cracker meal.

In a small bowl, stir together the water and beef base until dissolved. Add the beef broth (water and beef base) to the meat mixture and then add the onion salt, garlic salt, Worcestershire sauce, 6 tablespoons ketchup, and onion. Mix well with a wooden spoon or with clean hands.

Spoon the meatloaf mixture into the prepared loaf pan, packing lightly to remove air pockets. Spoon the remaining 4 tablespoons ketchup over the top and bake for about 1½ hours or until an instant-read or meat thermometer reaches 165 degrees.

Let stand for 15 to 20 minutes before slicing.

Note: Beef base is a bouillon paste similar to bouillon cubes or powder. It is available in many grocery stores in the soup section. One brand is Better Than Bouillon.

— From Mary McCrank's, Chehalis, Washington

PORK TINGA

MAKES 6 TO 8 SERVINGS

Pork shoulder is richly marbled and more deeply flavored than chops or ribs—and it's much less expensive. It requires long, slow cooking to render the connective tissue and ribbons of fat that interlace it, and this classic Mexican stew is a delicious way to do it.

2 (28-ounce) cans whole tomatoes,
    1½ cups juice reserved
1 medium white onion, coarsely chopped
10 cloves garlic, peeled
1 tablespoon plus 1 teaspoon olive oil
    (divided)
Salt and freshly ground black pepper
1 teaspoon dried oregano
⅛ teaspoon ground cloves
⅛ teaspoon ground cinnamon
3 to 4 chipotle chiles canned in adobo sauce
2 tablespoons firmly packed brown sugar
3 pounds pork shoulder, trimmed of excess
    fat and cut into 1-inch cubes
1 cup water
1 pound fresh (uncooked) chorizo sausage,
    casing removed if links
2 tablespoons chopped fresh cilantro
Suggested accompaniments: sour cream,
    lime wedges, diced avocado, hot cooked
    rice, and corn or flour tortillas

Adjust oven rack to within 4 inches of broiler element and heat broiler to high. Press the drained tomatoes flat to remove as much water as possible, reserving the juice (otherwise they won't brown well). Line a rimmed baking sheet with aluminum foil. On the sheet mix together the tomatoes, onion, garlic, and 1 tablespoon olive oil. Season with salt and pepper and broil, stirring frequently, until tomatoes and onions are well-browned and blackened in spots, 15 to 20 minutes. Discard any bits that have burned to a crisp.

Transfer tomato mixture to blender jar, add reserved tomato juice, oregano, cloves, cinnamon, chipotle chiles, and brown sugar; blend until smooth.

Meanwhile, adjust oven rack to lower-middle position and set oven to 300 degrees. Dry pork with paper towels and season liberally with salt and pepper. Add remaining teaspoon olive oil to large Dutch oven set over medium-high heat and, once smoking, add half of the pork in a single layer. Cook, without moving, until well-browned, 4 to 5 minutes. Using tongs, turn pieces and brown second side, about 4 minutes longer. Transfer browned meat to bowl; repeat process with remaining pork.

Add the 1 cup water to pan, scraping up any browned bits adhered to the bottom. Add reserved meat and any juices, pour in tomato mixture, and bring to boil. Cover, transfer to oven, and cook until pork is very tender, about 1½ hours.

Brown sausage in large skillet over medium heat. Drain browned sausage on paper towels and stir into stew. Return to oven and cook until flavors have blended, about 15 minutes. Stir in cilantro, adjust seasoning to taste, and serve with desired accompaniments.

Make ahead: The sauce may be prepared up to two days ahead of time and refrigerated.

— From Matthew Card

EASY OVEN-ROASTED RIBS

MAKES 6 SERVINGS WITH SPARERIBS OR 4 TO 6 SERVINGS WITH BABY-BACK RIBS

These ultra-easy ribs are perfect when you have a craving for 'cue but don't relish standing outside tending a grill. They may not be the smokiest ribs you've ever had, but they'll probably be the easiest.

SPICE RUB:
2 tablespoons kosher salt
2 tablespoons paprika
4 teaspoons chili powder
4 teaspoons granulated garlic or garlic powder
2 teaspoons dry mustard
2 teaspoons freshly ground black pepper

RIBS:
2 racks pork spareribs or baby-back ribs
Bottled barbecue sauce of your choice
(we like Sweet Baby Ray's)

To make rub: Mix together all rub ingredients. Store for up to several months in a tightly closed container.

To make ribs: Preheat oven to 325 degrees.

Using a dull dinner knife, slide the tip under the membrane covering the back of each rack of ribs. Lift and loosen the membrane until it breaks, then grab a corner of it with a paper towel and pull it off. Season the ribs all over with spice rub, putting more on the meaty side than the bone side. On a hot grill or under the broiler, sear the ribs on both sides until they're brown. (You can skip this step, but it gives them a nice crusty exterior.) Transfer ribs to a roasting pan or a baking sheet lined with a rack and cover with aluminum foil.

Roast for 1½ hours (spareribs will take longer to cook), or until the meat has shrunk back about ½ inch from the ends of the bones and is tender enough to tear with your fingers. Uncover ribs, brush them on both sides with sauce and bake, uncovered, an additional 30 minutes. Remove from oven and let rest for at least 15 minutes. Serve warm.

— Rib recipe adapted from Brett Meisner, SP Provisions;
Rub recipe from *Weber's Way to Grill*,
by Jamie Purviance (Oxmoor House)

SOUTHWESTERN GRILLED PORK TENDERLOIN WITH POTATO AND CORN SALAD

MAKES 4 SERVINGS

Meat and potatoes don't have to make a heavy meal. Linda Faus developed this recipe for her "Fit for Dinner" column and kept the fat content low by using vibrant seasonings like cumin, smoked paprika, garlic and lime.

SPICE RUB AND TENDERLOIN:
1½ teaspoons ground cumin
1 teaspoon kosher salt
1 teaspoon smoked paprika (pimentón de la Vera)
½ teaspoon garlic powder

½ teaspoon dried oregano, preferably Mexican oregano

¼ teaspoon freshly ground black pepper

1 pork tenderloin (about 1¼ pounds)

SALAD:

3 tablespoons fresh lime juice

1½ teaspoons reserved spice rub

3 tablespoons olive oil

2 ears yellow corn

2 cups peeled diced red or Yukon Gold potatoes (12 ounces)

½ cup diced red bell pepper

1 jalapeño chile, diced small (seed it first if you want less heat)

⅓ cup diced red onion

3 small scallions, minced

¼ cup chopped fresh cilantro

Salt and freshly ground black pepper

To make spice rub and tenderloin: In a small bowl, stir together the cumin, salt, smoked paprika, garlic powder, oregano, and black pepper. Measure 1½ teaspoons of the spice rub and set aside.

Rub the remaining spice rub all over the pork tenderloin; set aside (if you are not going to grill the tenderloin within 30 minutes, refrigerate until needed).

To make salad: In a small bowl, whisk together the lime juice, reserved spice rub, and olive oil; set aside.

Bring 2 medium pots of water to a boil. Add the corn to one pot and cook for 5 minutes. Drain and let cool. When cool enough to handle, cut the corn off of the cobs.

Preheat a grill to medium-high (see note).

Add a large pinch of salt to the second pot and add the diced potatoes. Return to a boil and cook for 5 to 6 minutes or until the potatoes are just tender, Drain and place in a large bowl. Toss the warm potatoes with 2 tablespoons of the dressing and let stand for a few minutes so the potatoes can absorb the dressing.

Add the cut corn to the potatoes along with the red pepper, jalapeño, red onion, scallions, and cilantro. Toss and add the remaining dressing. Toss again and set aside to allow the flavors to blend. Just before serving, taste and add additional salt and pepper if necessary.

Brush the prepared grill with oil and place the tenderloin in the center of the grill. Grill for 12 to 14 minutes, turning every 2 minutes, or until the pork reaches an internal temperature of 140 degrees. Remove from grill, tent with aluminum foil and let stand for 10 minutes. Slice pork and serve with the salad.

Note: To check grill temperature, count the seconds you can hold your hand, palm side down, 2 to 3 inches above the rack until it feels uncomfortable: 3 seconds for medium-high.

— From Linda Faus

WHEN THE SOLUTION IS THE PROBLEM

A lot of pork tenderloins sold at major markets have been "enhanced" with a salt solution. Although some producers say this helps ensure moist meat, we find this kind of pork far too salty—especially if you use the meat in a recipe that calls for more salt. It also means you're paying for added water and salt. For best quality, carefully read the label and make sure there's no fine print that says "salt solution." Or shop at a store that carries unenhanced pork. If you want to ensure moist pork, make sure it's still rosy pink inside when you remove it from the oven. The USDA recommends cooking pork roasts, tenderloins, and chops to an internal temperature of 145 degrees, followed by a 3-minute rest.

CORPENY'S TAMALE PIE

MAKES 12 SERVINGS

Suzanne Ziegler, chef and co-owner of Corpeny's Restaurant in Seaside, adapted this recipe from *The Fannie Farmer Cookbook*. Suzanne says the key to serving this pie is to make it the day before so it has time to set up.

2 (12-ounce) packages Jimmy Dean Original Flavor Sausage
1 cup diced onion
½ diced green bell pepper
½ diced red bell pepper
¾ cup diced celery
4 cloves garlic, minced
3 jalapeño chiles, seeded and diced
2 cups canned diced tomatoes
½ cup plus 2 tablespoons canned diced green chiles
½ cup plus 2 tablespoons sliced black olives
3 tablespoons chili powder
1 tablespoon ground cumin
4 cups water plus 2 cups cold water (divided)
¼ cup butter
1½ cups cornmeal
1½ to 2 teaspoons salt (divided)
1½ cups shredded cheddar cheese (divided)
1½ cups shredded Monterey jack cheese (divided)
Salsa

Crumble the sausage into a large pan and brown over medium-high heat, stirring frequently. When the sausage is almost browned, add the onion, green and red bell peppers, celery, garlic, and jalapeños. Continue cooking until the vegetables are tender, about 7 to 10 minutes.

While the sausage and vegetables are cooking, place the tomatoes, diced green chiles, and olives in a large colander to drain. When the cooked vegetables are tender, pour the sausage mixture over the tomatoes in the colander and drain. Return the mixture to the pan, and add the chili powder and cumin. Bring to a simmer and cook for 20 to 30 minutes. The mixture could be frozen at this point if desired.

While the sausage mixture is simmering, bring 4 cups water and the butter to a boil in a large saucepan.

Meanwhile, stir the 2 cups cold water together with the cornmeal and 1½ teaspoons salt. When the water-butter mixture has come to a boil, stir in the cold water-cornmeal mixture. Return to a boil, stirring constantly, then reduce the heat to as low as possible, cover, and simmer for 35 minutes. Taste and add remaining ½ teaspoon salt, if needed.

Preheat the oven to 350 degrees. Lightly grease a 9-by-13-inch baking pan.

Spread half of the cooked cornmeal in the prepared pan. Allow to stand for 10 to 15 minutes or until cooled and slightly firm (you could refrigerate the mixture to speed the cooling). Spread the sausage mixture evenly over the cornmeal layer, making sure to spread to the corners. Top with half of the cheddar and Monterey jack cheese. Spread remaining cornmeal mixture over the cheese and top with the remaining cheeses. Bake for 1 hour or until heated through and golden brown on top. For easiest serving, refrigerate until firm (2 to 3 hours or overnight), then cut into squares and reheat in the microwave oven. Serve with salsa.

— From Corpeny's Restaurant, Seaside

VEGETARIAN AND VEGAN FARE

RIBOLLITA

MAKES 4 TO 6 SERVINGS

Born from the renowned thrift of Tuscan cooks, ribollita (literally, "reboiled") is a rib-sticking stew of white beans, vegetables, hearty kale, and stale bread flavored with lashings of garlic and olive oil. It's a great way to recycle those toothy bits of stale baguette sitting in the bread box. If you can't find lacinato kale (also called dinosaur, Tuscan, cavolo nero, or black kale), you can substitute regular kale. Although there are several components to this dish, they are easy to make, and the Spicy Garlic and Herb Oil keeps for three weeks.

Salt
1 large bunch lacinato kale, stemmed, rinsed, and chopped coarsely
½ to ¾ cup drained canned diced tomatoes
4 to 6 cups Tuscan White Beans (see accompanying recipe)
3 or more cups Rosemary Croutons (see accompanying recipe)
Spicy Garlic and Herb Oil (see accompanying recipe) or extra-virgin olive oil
Garnishes: lemon wedges, coarse salt, crushed red pepper flakes, and grated dry Vella Monterey jack or Parmigiano-Reggiano cheese

Bring large pot of water to boil over high heat and season liberally with salt. Add kale and cook until tender, 5 to 7 minutes. Drain and cool under running water. Squeeze dry.

In a Dutch oven, heat tomatoes and beans over medium heat, and bring to a slow simmer (add splash of broth or water if necessary to loosen consistency). Stir in greens and croutons to combine. Divide equally among bowls and drizzle liberally with olive oil or Spicy Garlic and Herb Oil, and serve with other desired garnishes.

TUSCAN WHITE BEANS

MAKES 6 TO 8 SIDE-DISH SERVINGS

These can be served alone with a grating of cheese or drizzle of oil, or used as a sidedish. Dry, sharp Vella Monterey jack cheese is less expensive than Parmigiano-Reggiano, and domestically produced. According to the producer, it was developed as a substitute for the imported parmesan before it became widely available.

2 tablespoons extra-virgin olive oil
1 medium red onion, diced fine
1 large carrot, diced fine
½ large fennel bulb, cored and diced fine, or 1 stalk celery, diced fine
Pinch crushed red pepper flakes
Pinch fennel seeds
Salt
1 pound Great Northern beans, soaked in water overnight
1 head garlic, top ⅛ cut off to expose cloves
1 bay leaf
6 cups mushroom or vegetable broth and/or water
Granulated sugar (if necessary)
Garnishes: extra-virgin olive oil, coarse sea salt, grated Vella Monterey jack, or Parmigiano-Reggiano cheese

In a large Dutch oven, heat olive oil over medium-high heat. Add onion, carrot, fennel or celery, red pepper flakes, fennel seeds, and large pinch salt; cook, stirring occasionally, until mixture begins to brown and stick to the bottom of the pot, 12 to 15 minutes. Stir in the beans, garlic head, bay leaf, and broth and/or water; bring to boil, then reduce heat to low and simmer, partially covered, until beans are soft and tender (adding additional liquid as necessary to cover), 1½ to 2 hours.

Remove garlic and bay leaf from pot. Discard bay leaf. When cool enough to handle, squeeze garlic cloves from papery skins, mash to paste with back of knife, and stir into beans. Adjust seasoning to taste with salt and a pinch of sugar, if needed. Serve with desired garnishes.

ROSEMARY CROUTONS

MAKES 3 TO 5 CUPS

Croutons are best made with hearty bread that's two to four days old. It should be firm, but still sliceable. If the bread is fresh, skip the water. A well-seasoned cast-iron skillet is the best choice, though a nonstick skillet should work well, too. The moist bread cubes may stick a bit to a traditional skillet. A sprig of sage may be substituted for the rosemary. Leftovers may be added to soups, salads, or frittatas.

> Half to three-quarters of a stale baguette or rustic loaf, cut into ¾-inch cubes (3 to 5 cups)
> 3 to 4 tablespoons extra-virgin olive oil
> 1 sprig rosemary or sage
> Coarse salt and freshly ground black pepper

In a large bowl, toss cubes with enough water to make bread soft, moist, and pliable, but not crumbly. Squeeze bread and drain excess water from bowl.

In a large skillet, heat oil over medium-high heat until just shimmering. Reduce temperature to medium, add bread and rosemary sprig, and cook,

stirring infrequently, until bread cubes are lightly browned, 7 to 10 minutes (you may need to use spatula to scrape any stuck-on bits of bread free). Remove rosemary and season bread generously with salt and pepper.

SPICY GARLIC AND HERB OIL

MAKES ABOUT 1 CUP

This oil can be used to flavor everything from beans and greens to grilled cheese sandwiches and vinaigrettes. Feel free to experiment with different kinds of hot dried chiles, such as habanero or dundicut, a Pakistani chile that just plain rocks. Milder varieties like ancho or New Mexico don't add much of a kick. You can also use fresh bird's-eye chiles.

> 1 cup olive or vegetable oil
> 6 cloves garlic, smashed and coarsely chopped
> 6 sprigs thyme
> 4 bay leaves, crumbled
> 1 tablespoon sweet or hot paprika
> 4 to 8 dried red chiles (such as arbol, California, or dundicut), stemmed and crumbled
> 2 tablespoons extra-virgin olive oil

In small saucepan, combine olive or vegetable oil, garlic, thyme, bay leaves, paprika, and dried chiles; cook over medium-low heat until rapidly sizzling, 4 to 7 minutes. Remove from heat and cool to room temperature. Strain through fine-meshed strainer set over a bowl, pressing on solids to extract as much oil as possible; discard solids. Stir in extra-virgin oil. Store in an airtight container in the refrigerator (use within 3 weeks). Stir before use.

— Adapted from Matthew Card

A PRIMER ON PAPRIKA

These days, recipes can call for one or more of several kinds of paprika. Here are the varieties you'll see in most stores in the U.S. And remember that as with most herbs and spices, after about six months, paprika will begin to lose its punch:

Sweet paprika: This is the type of mild, sweet paprika that most of us have in our spice cupboard.

Hungarian paprika: Has a more pungent or pronounced flavor than regular paprika; comes in sweet, hot, and smoked varieties.

Smoked paprika: Now sold by large labels such as McCormick's and Spice Islands. Spanish version is called pimentón de la Vera and comes in three varieties: sweet (dulce), medium-hot (agridulce) and hot (picante).

ROASTED CAULIFLOWER AND DELICATA SQUASH WITH HARISSA AND YOGURT

MAKES 4 SERVINGS

In this simple main course, the heat comes not only from cranking up the oven to roast the squash and cauliflower, it also comes from the harissa, a spicy condiment from northern Africa. But store-bought harissa can be extremely spicy, so contributor Ivy Manning makes a milder version with dried chiles, lemon juice, herbs, and spices.

HARISSA:

8 dried guajillo chiles (see note)
8 dried New Mexican chiles (see note)
8 cups boiling water
1 teaspoon ground caraway
½ teaspoon ground cumin
1 teaspoon dried mint
3 tablespoons extra-virgin olive oil
1 teaspoon kosher salt
3 large cloves garlic
Juice of 1 lemon

ROASTED VEGETABLES:

2 medium delicata or butternut squash
1 medium head cauliflower (about
    1½ pounds), cut into large florets
4 medium shallots cut lengthwise into
    ½-inch-thick slices

3 tablespoons extra-virgin olive oil
Kosher salt and freshly ground black pepper
Steamed basmati rice or couscous
½ cup plain Greek yogurt
¼ cup chopped fresh cilantro or Italian
    (flat-leaf) parsley

To make harissa: Place the dried chiles in a large bowl. Pour the boiling water over the chiles, place a saucer on top of them to keep them submerged; soak for 1 hour. Remove the stems and seeds, and discard soaking liquid.

In a food processor, combine the chiles, caraway, cumin, mint, olive oil, salt, garlic, and lemon juice. Process, stopping to scrape down the sides of the work bowl, until smooth. Transfer to a bowl and set aside.

To make roasted vegetables: Preheat the oven to 400 degrees. Using a sharp vegetable peeler, peel away most of the skin on the squash (leaving a bit of skin in the indentations of the squash is fine; it is edible). Halve the squash lengthwise and scoop out the seeds. Cut the squash crosswise into ½-inch-thick slices.

▶▶

165

In a large bowl, combine the squash, cauliflower, shallots, and olive oil, stirring to coat the vegetables. Spread the vegetables in an even layer on a rimmed baking sheet and sprinkle with salt and pepper. Bake until the squash pieces are pierced easily with a fork, 30 to 40 minutes.

Serve the roasted vegetables over rice or couscous with a few tablespoons of harissa and yogurt spooned over the top of each serving. Garnish with cilantro or parsley; serve.

Note: Guajillo chiles have an earthy, complex flavor. New Mexican chiles are mild and fruity. You can find both types at Latin grocery stores and many supermarkets. In a pinch, you can use easier-to-find California chiles instead, perhaps increasing the heat by adding a pinch or two of hot paprika.

Make ahead: Harissa can be made a week or two ahead, covered with a thin layer of additional olive oil in an airtight container, and refrigerated.

— From Ivy Manning

SOUTHERN TOMATO PIE

MAKES 6 TO 8 SERVINGS

This Southern classic won the 2008 Portland Pie-Off and the following year was voted one of Foodday's favorite recipes. Tricia Butler of Sassafras Southern Kitchen says the recipe is very forgiving, and that you can use any cheese or seasoning blend you like.

2 tablespoons butter
1½ large onions, sliced in ¼-inch rings
    (Walla Walla Sweets work best)
Salt
5 large tomatoes, peeled, cored and cut in
    bite-size chunks (see note)
2 cups shredded medium-sharp cheddar
    cheese
½ cup mayonnaise or sour cream
½ teaspoon freshly cracked black pepper
    (divided)
1 (10-inch) pie shell
1 teaspoon granulated sugar (divided)
½ teaspoon dried basil (divided)
1 tablespoon dried Italian herb blend, herbes
    de Provence or other favorite seasoning

Melt butter in a sauté pan and add onions. Cook at medium-low for about 30 minutes until lightly caramelized, stirring every few minutes to avoid burning.

Meanwhile, lightly salt tomatoes and drain in colander for 20 to 30 minutes. Preheat oven to 425 degrees.

Mix cheddar with mayonnaise or sour cream and ¼ teaspoon of the pepper and set aside.

Line pie shell with parchment paper or foil, fill with beans or pie weights (to avoid bubbles), and bake for 15 minutes or until golden brown. Reduce oven temperature to 350 degrees.

Firmly squeeze the tomatoes between your hands or against the colander to remove most of their liquid (too much liquid will make the filling watery). Remove pie shell from oven and carefully remove paper or foil and pie weights. Add half of the tomatoes to the pie shell and sprinkle with a pinch of salt, then half of the pepper, sugar, and basil. Add the rest of the tomatoes, another pinch of salt, then the remaining pepper, sugar, and basil.

Spread cheese mixture over tomatoes. Sprinkle herb blend on top of cheese. Add caramelized onions to the top of the pie in an even layer; bake for 30 minutes. Cover with foil if the crust starts to brown too much. Allow pie to set for 10 to 15 minutes to firm up before serving.

Note: To peel tomatoes, plunge into boiling water for 30 seconds to 1 minute. Remove immediately and plunge into cold water. Skins should slip off easily.

Make ahead: If you want to freeze the pie, use sour cream instead of mayonnaise and freeze the pie unbaked. Bake it straight from the freezer without thawing, at 350 degrees for 45 minutes to 1 hour, or until the cheese is melted and the center is fully heated through.

— From Tricia Butler, owner, Sassafras Southern Kitchen

ROASTED CHERRY TOMATO TART

MAKES 6 SERVINGS

This tart is crazy elegant, with jewel-like cherry tomatoes studding a pillow of goat cheese. While the tart is best with lovely late-summer tomatoes, it can be made year-round using cherry tomatoes. Slow roasting in the oven concentrates their flavor and reduces the moisture content, so your tart won't be soggy.

- 1½ to 2 cups cherry tomatoes (the exact amount can vary, depending upon the size and shape of your tomatoes—if you roast too many, it's not a bad thing)
- Olive oil
- 1 tablespoon Dijon mustard
- 1 (9-inch) tart crust or puff pastry crust, par-baked
- 8 ounces chèvre or other soft goat cheese
- 2 eggs
- ½ cup half-and-half or milk
- 2 teaspoons chopped fresh thyme or other herb of your choice (divided)
- Salt

Preheat oven to 200 degrees. Halve the cherry tomatoes along their equators, and place them cut-side up in a baking dish. Drizzle with a bit of olive oil, and put them in the oven for 3 hours. They should shrink to about two-thirds their original size, but still be juicy. Set aside. (You can skip the slow-roasting step, if you like, and your tomatoes will be a bit prettier and less shriveled, but not nearly so oh-my-goodness rich.)

Raise oven temperature to 375 degrees. Spread the mustard over the bottom of the tart shell in a very thin layer. In a mixer (or using a whisk or fork and a lot of patience), blend together the chèvre, eggs, half-and-half, and half the thyme. Pour mixture into the tart shell. Gently arrange the tomatoes on top, cut-side up.

Gently transfer the tart to the oven and bake 45 minutes, until the filling has puffed and begun to brown and the tomatoes are slightly caramelized on top. Remove from the oven and let cool slightly. Sprinkle the remaining fresh herb and a light sprinkling of salt across the top, and serve.

— From Deena Prichep

WELSH RABBIT WITH TANGY WATERCRESS SALAD

MAKES 4 SERVINGS

In England, the poor man's meat was once rabbit, while in Wales, the poor man's meat was cheese. Hence the name Welsh rabbit, or Welsh rarebit, for the simple open-faced sandwiches eaten by poor Welsh dairy farmers. Despite its humble ingredients, this simple dish can be a culinary triumph if you choose aged cheddar cheese, such as extra-sharp Tillamook or Kerry Gold Irish cheddar, and a hoppy ale for an intriguing note of bitterness.

1 (15-ounce) loaf crusty bread, cut into
    8 slices (about 1 inch thick)
1 bunch watercress, tough stems removed
1 teaspoon lemon juice
2 teaspoons extra-virgin olive oil
Salt and freshly ground black pepper
3 tablespoons butter
3 tablespoons all-purpose flour
¾ cup pale ale
2 teaspoons Worcestershire sauce
½ teaspoon dry mustard
8 ounces aged extra-sharp cheddar cheese,
    shredded
2 tablespoons minced fresh chives

Place the oven rack 3 inches below the broiling element and preheat the broiler. Place the bread slices in one layer on a rimmed baking sheet. Broil until browned, about 3 minutes. Remove the baking sheet from the oven; leave the broiler on.

Toss the watercress with the lemon juice and olive oil and season with salt and pepper; set aside.

In a small saucepan over medium heat, melt the butter. Whisk in the flour and cook for 1 minute. Gradually add the ale, whisking constantly, and cook until the mixture is thick and bubbly, 3 minutes. Add the Worcestershire sauce, dry mustard and a handful of the cheese. Cook, always stirring in one direction to prevent the sauce from becoming stringy, until the cheese has melted. Continue to add cheese gradually until all the cheese has been added and the mixture is smooth. Remove from heat and stir in the chives.

Spread the cheese mixture liberally on the untoasted sides of the bread, place under the broiler and cook until the cheese is bubbly and browned in places, about 4 minutes. Place 2 slices of bread on each dinner plate and top with a big mound of watercress. Serve immediately.

— From Ivy Manning

RYE PANADE

MAKES 4 TO 6 SERVINGS

Rye bread is much more flavorful than white bread, but it can do a lot more than just make a pastrami sandwich. Layered with caramelized onions and sautéed kale, and bound with broth and nutty gruyère cheese, it becomes a casserole with real character.

 8 ounces stale rye bread, cut into cubes
  (about half of a standard loaf, a third
  of a large loaf)
 2 cups chicken or vegetable broth (divided)
 8 tablespoons olive oil (divided)
 2 onions, sliced into thin half-moons
 3 cloves garlic, thinly sliced
 3 tablespoons red wine
 1 tablespoon balsamic vinegar
 1 teaspoon fennel seeds
 Leaves from a few sprigs fresh thyme
 1 bunch kale, washed and roughly torn
 1 teaspoon salt
 1 cup shredded gruyère cheese (4 ounces)

Toss the rye bread cubes with ¼ cup broth and 2 tablespoons olive oil. Set aside.

Heat 4 tablespoons olive oil in a large skillet over a medium-high heat. Add the onions and cook until lightly caramelized, about 30 minutes. When almost done, add the garlic, red wine, balsamic vinegar, and fennel seeds; cook until liquid has evaporated, but do not let the garlic burn. Add the thyme leaves and turn off the heat.

While the onions are caramelizing, heat 1 tablespoon olive oil in a large pot over a medium heat. Add the kale, 1 tablespoon broth, and the salt. Cook until the kale is wilted, about 5 minutes. Set aside.

Preheat oven to 350 degrees.

Coat a large casserole dish (about 9-by-13-inch capacity) with the remaining 1 tablespoon olive oil. Layer half of the rye bread cubes, half of the onion mixture, half of the kale, and half of the cheese. Repeat with remaining bread, onion, kale, and cheese. Pour the remaining broth over the casserole. Cover loosely with foil, and bake for 1 hour, until the panade is golden and bubbling.

— From Edgar Loesch, Fressen Artisan Bakery

REGULAR, KOSHER, AND COARSE SALT

These days, salt is no longer simple. In addition to table salt and kosher salt, there are all kinds of specialty salts, from Oregon sea salt to pink salt from the Himalayas. At Foodday, we like to cook with Diamond Crystal kosher salt, because of the way the flaky crystals cling to food. We think you should save those expensive artisanal salts for finishing a dish or for placing on the table.

If you want to substitute one type of salt for another, you'll need to adjust the measurement, because coarse salts—such as kosher or specialty sea salts—are flakier or have irregular grains, which means the salt doesn't compact as tightly when you measure it. You end up with less salt in a measure, so substituting the same measure of table salt might make your food too salty.

Experts say to substitute 1 teaspoon table salt for 1½ to 2 teaspoons kosher salt. As for sea salts, the grains vary widely in size and weight, so it's difficult to give an exact equivalent.

If you're making something savory, such as a soup or stew, you can taste as you go, so getting an exact conversion isn't crucial. But too much salt can really spoil the flavor of cookies and other baked goods, so it's a good idea to start with a smaller amount, taste a tiny bit to see if tastes good, or "flat." If it tastes flat, add a bit more salt.

LAYERED TORTILLA CASSEROLE

MAKES 8 SERVINGS

Casseroles aren't as popular as they once were, but they have many virtues, not the least of which is that they can be great comfort food. This one-pot winner is brimming with tomato salsa, cheese, and chiles, layered with corn tortillas and a savory custard mixture. It's a great dish for using up stale, leftover corn tortillas.

1 tablespoon olive oil
1 large onion, chopped
3 cloves garlic, minced
1½ cups prepared tomato salsa, plus
    additional for serving
12 corn tortillas
1½ cups shredded pepper jack cheese
    (6 ounces; divided)
1 (7-ounce) can diced mild green chiles,
    undrained (divided)
4 eggs
1 cup buttermilk
1 (8¾-ounce) can creamed corn
1 teaspoon dried oregano or 1 tablespoon
    minced fresh oregano
½ teaspoon ground cumin
Salt and freshly ground black pepper
Chopped fresh cilantro, to garnish (optional)

Preheat oven to 350 degrees. Spray a 9-by-13-inch baking dish with nonstick cooking spray; set aside.

In a medium skillet, heat oil over medium-high heat, add onion and garlic, and sauté until onion is softened. Remove from heat and stir in 1½ cups salsa.

Place 6 tortillas in bottom of prepared baking dish. Top with half of the cheese and half of the canned chiles. Top with onion-garlic-salsa mixture.

Cut remaining 6 tortillas into quarters and place on top. Place remaining cheese and chiles on top of the tortillas.

In a large bowl, whisk together the eggs, buttermilk, corn, oregano, cumin, and salt and pepper to taste. Pour over top of casserole. Using a fork, lift and jiggle some of the top layer of tortillas so some of the egg mixture settles into the layers. Bake for 45 to 50 minutes, or until top is set and browned.

Allow to rest 15 minutes. If desired, garnish with fresh cilantro and additional salsa.

— From Cathy Thomas

SQUASH ENCHILADAS WITH SPICY PEANUT SAUCE

MAKES 4 TO 6 SERVINGS

Butternut squash and sautéed vegetables, rolled in tortillas and topped with a spicy peanut sauce, transcend ordinary enchiladas. If you prefer, tortillas may be softened in the microwave: place four or five between two damp microwave paper towels and heat on high for 45 seconds. Fill these tortillas, then repeat with remaining tortillas.

FILLING:

1 small butternut squash (about 1 pound)
2 tablespoons vegetable oil
1 medium carrot, peeled, quartered, and sliced
¼ pound fresh mushrooms, diced (about 1¼ cups)
½ cup diced onion
½ cup diced jicama
1 small Granny Smith apple, peeled and diced
¼ cup sunflower kernels, chopped
1 tablespoon white vinegar
½ teaspoon salt
2 tablespoons chopped fresh cilantro

SPICY PEANUT SAUCE:

2 cups water
1 tablespoon vegetable-flavored instant bouillon granules
½ teaspoon salt
½ teaspoon ground cumin
½ teaspoon minced garlic
2 canned chipotle chiles in adobo sauce, chopped
3 tablespoons New Mexican chili powder (see note)
1 tablespoon vegetable oil
½ teaspoon dried oregano
1 tablespoon minced onion
1 tablespoon all-purpose flour
¾ cup creamy peanut butter

TO ASSEMBLE:

Vegetable oil for softening tortillas
8 to 10 corn tortillas
1 cup shredded cheddar cheese (4 ounces)
1 cup shredded Monterey jack cheese (4 ounces)

To make filling: Preheat oven to 400 degrees.

Cut the butternut squash in half and scoop out seeds. Place cut side down on a baking pan with a small amount of water, and bake about 1 hour or until tender. Or, microwave on high 6 minutes, turning once, or until tender. When cool enough to handle, scoop cooked squash out of shell and set aside.

In a large skillet, heat oil over medium-high heat and sauté carrot, mushrooms, and onion until the carrot is tender-crisp. Add the cooked squash, jicama, apple, sunflower kernels, vinegar, salt, and cilantro; mix well and set aside while preparing sauce.

To make sauce: In a medium saucepan, combine water, vegetable bouillon, salt, cumin, garlic, chiles, and chili powder. Bring to a boil.

Meanwhile, in a small sauté pan, heat oil over low heat. Add oregano and onion, and sauté until onion is soft. Add flour and cook, stirring, for 1 minute.

Stir the onion mixture into the chile mixture. Bring to a boil and cook about 2 minutes; remove from heat. Strain and discard solids. Add peanut butter to strained sauce and stir until well-combined; set aside.

To assemble: Preheat oven to 350 degrees.

Heat a small amount of oil in a shallow skillet. Dip each tortilla in the oil for a few seconds to soften. Lay softened tortillas on paper towels to drain.

Place a spoonful of squash mixture down the center of each tortilla. Roll up and place seam side down in a lightly oiled 9-by-13-inch baking pan. Pour the sauce over the rolled tortillas, and sprinkle with cheddar and jack cheeses. Bake for 15 to 20 minutes or until cheese is melted and enchiladas are hot in the center.

Note: New Mexican chili powder is available in the Hispanic foods section of most supermarkets.

— From Chez José Mexican Cafe, Portland

BLACK BEAN, CORN, AND ANAHEIM CHILE TAMALES

MAKES ABOUT 30 TO 35 TAMALES

There's no denying that making your own tamales is a labor of love. But when there are friends and family to help, it's nothing less than a party. And the results—especially when you make them with homemade masa—are well worth the work.

40 dried corn husks (about 5 to 6 ounces)

FILLING:
3 fresh Anaheim chiles
1 tablespoon vegetable oil
1 cup frozen corn, defrosted
1 (15-ounce) can black beans, drained
   and rinsed
½ cup prepared tomato salsa (medium spicy)
Salt and freshly ground black pepper
1 cup crumbled queso fresco cheese

HOMEMADE MASA:
⅓ cup nonhydrogenated shortening
1⅔ cups unsalted butter, at room temperature
4 teaspoons salt
5 pounds fresh masa (see note)
2 cups chicken or mild vegetable broth
Tomato salsa, to serve

Soak the corn husks in a large pot of hot tap water for 15 minutes to make them pliable enough to separate. Drain the husks and pick them apart, discarding any corn silk you find. Rinse the husks well and return to the pot, cover with hot water, and soak for 30 minutes. While husks soak, prepare filling and masa.

To make filling: Place the chiles directly over a gas flame set on medium-high and cook, rotating the chiles with tongs occasionally, until charred all over, about 3 minutes per side. Alternatively, place on a baking sheet and broil 6 inches below broiling element until blistered on both sides, about 10 minutes. Transfer to a bowl, cover with a plate or plastic wrap, and allow to steam for 30 minutes. Remove the skin, seeds, and stem. Chop the flesh and set aside.

In a sauté pan, heat the vegetable oil over medium-high heat and sauté the corn until it begins to brown. Add the beans; cook and mash lightly with a spoon until you have a chunky mixture that is slightly sticky. Add the salsa, chiles, and salt and pepper to taste. Remove from heat and let mixture cool to room temperature. Stir in the cheese. Makes 4 cups.

To make masa: Soak husks as directed below. Meanwhile, in a large (6-quart) stand mixer, whip the shortening, butter, and salt until pale and fluffy, 2 minutes. (If you have a smaller stand mixer, make the dough in two batches.) Scrape down the sides of the bowl with a rubber spatula and switch to the paddle attachment. Put the mixer on low speed and add golf ball-size wads of the fresh masa alternately with broth (the consistency should be between spackle and Play-Doh). Add warm water, if necessary, to get the right consistency. Increase speed to medium-low, and whip the dough until it is fluffy and a pea-size amount floats when dropped into a glass of cold water, about 5 minutes. Keep covered until ready to use.

To assemble and cook: Drain the husks and pat dry. Open a corn husk in the palm of your hand with the tapered end toward your wrist. Spread about ¼ to ⅓ cup masa dough (depending on the size of the husk you're working with) and spread edge to edge over the top half of the husk, leaving ¼ inch at the top end and about 4 inches at the bottom (tapered) end uncovered. Put 2 to 3 heaping tablespoons of filling in a vertical line on the dough. Fold in first the left side and then the right side of the husk so the edges make an overlapping seam in the center that encloses the filling. Fold the tapered end of the husk up so that it is even with the top end of the tamale.

Put a few coins in a large soup pot. Place a metal steaming rack in the pot and fill the pot with water to just below the bottom of the rack. Overlap enough corn husks to line the rack and go partially up the sides of the pot. Place the tamales vertically in the steamer with open end up, propping them against the side of the pot and each other. (Depending on the size of your pot, you should be able to fit in about 20 tamales at one time; for more tamales, either set up more than one pot or steam the tamales in batches.) Cover the tamales with a few corn husks and cover with a tightly fitting lid.

Bring the water to a boil over medium-high heat. Reduce heat to a gentle simmer, cover, and steam without peeking, for 1 hour. (Monitor the water level by listening carefully: if the coins stop rattling, you need to increase the heat, or the water has boiled off and you need to add a few cups of boiling water to the pot.)

To check for doneness, carefully remove a tamale from the pot and allow it to cool for 1 minute. Unwrap it and cut it open; the tamale is done if the dough is firm. If the dough is still raw and soft, steam the tamales longer. Depending on the size of your tamales, they may take as long as 2 hours total to cook.

Carefully remove the tamales and place them on a platter. Serve with salsa and sour cream.

Note: Fresh masa, also labeled "unprepared masa," can be found refrigerated in Latin markets, often in 5-pound bags. It does not keep for long, so buy it the day you plan to make tamales, if possible.

Make ahead: The filling can be made up to 2 days in advance and refrigerated in an airtight container until ready to use. Finished tamales can be stored in the freezer for up to three months wrapped in plastic and then foil. Reheat in the microwave covered with a damp paper towel, or steam over simmering water until hot throughout.

— From Ivy Manning

Using wet fingers, spread the prepared masa over the top half of a soaked corn husk. Spoon on the filling and fold both long sides over the filling so they meet in the middle.

ROASTING CHILES OFFERS A BIG REWARD

Roasting gives chiles and bell peppers a wonderful smoky flavor that can add so much depth to a recipe. The process is simple: char the skins on a grill, over a gas burner on your stove, or under the broiler, until the chiles are well-blackened. Then place them in a bag or covered bowl, and let them steam until the skins are loosened and the chiles cool enough to handle. Use your fingers to peel off the blackened skin, without worrying about a few stubborn pieces left behind. Some people rinse the peeled chiles, but we think that washes away some of the smoky flavor. To simplify things, you can core the raw peppers and cut them into halves so you can avoid having to turn them as they char on the grill or under the broiler.

SAVORY MUSHROOM STRUDEL

MAKES 4 MAIN COURSE, OR 12 APPETIZER, SERVINGS

Strudels are not just for dessert. Here, Ivy Manning makes a savory version by wrapping thin layers of crisp, buttery pastry around mixed fresh mushrooms. Sheets of frozen store-bought phyllo are a delicious and time-saving stand-in for traditional strudel dough. Just be sure to allow time to let the phyllo defrost in the refrigerator.

1 pound mixed fresh mushrooms, such as
   shiitake, portobello, oyster, and/or morel
2 tablespoons olive oil (divided)
¾ cup thinly sliced yellow onion
1 tablespoon minced garlic
1 teaspoon chopped fresh thyme
4 teaspoons soy sauce
3 tablespoons water
1 cup shredded jarlsberg or gruyère cheese
   (4 ounces)

Salt and freshly ground black pepper
10 sheets phyllo dough, thawed
⅓ cup butter, melted
½ cup rye breadcrumbs (from about
   1 slice of bread)

Preheat oven to 375 degrees.

Line a baking sheet with parchment paper. Brush the mushrooms clean with a soft-bristled mushroom brush and rinse briefly under cold running water. Remove the tough stems from shiitake and portobello mushrooms; discard. Thinly slice mushrooms.

In a large skillet, heat 1 tablespoon of the oil over medium-high heat. When it is hot, add the onion and sauté, stirring frequently, until golden brown, 4 minutes. Add the garlic, thyme, and half of the mushrooms. Cook until the mushrooms have released their liquid, 4 minutes. Continue to cook until all of the liquid has cooked off, 1 minute. Transfer mixture to a large bowl. Return the skillet to medium-high heat and add remaining tablespoon of oil. Sauté the remaining mushrooms until tender. Add the soy sauce and simmer, stirring constantly, until all the liquid has cooked off, 1 minute. Add to the mushrooms in the bowl. Add the 3 tablespoons of water to the pan and cook, stirring up any bits from the bottom of the pan, until the water has reduced to about 1 tablespoon. Scrape into the bowl with the mushrooms and chill for 10 minutes. Combine mushrooms with cheese, and season with salt and pepper.

Place one piece of phyllo dough with the long side toward you on a large cutting board. Brush with some melted butter, and sprinkle with some breadcrumbs. Top with another sheet of phyllo dough, brush with butter, and sprinkle with crumbs. Repeat, buttering and sprinkling the remaining phyllo sheets, but do not add crumbs to the final sheet. Spread the mushroom mixture over the phyllo, leaving a ½-inch border on all sides. Starting from a long side, roll phyllo up tightly around filling and place seam-side down on the prepared baking sheet. Brush with butter and bake until golden brown, 35 minutes. Let cool for 5 minutes. With a sharp serrated knife, slice the strudel into eight slices.

— From Ivy Manning

LEEK BREAD PUDDING WITH CHANTERELLES

MAKES 10 SIDE-DISH SERVINGS OR 6 MAIN-COURSE SERVINGS

Chanterelles are among the most abundant of the edible wild mushrooms in the Northwest, and many people forage their own in the fall. But they're also readily available at many stores and farmers markets. Here they add their mild, earthy flavor to a savory bread pudding, also known as a strata. This is a superb dish for a special occasion.

2 cups well-rinsed and sliced (½-inch) leeks
    (white and pale green parts only)
Kosher salt
¼ cup butter
8 ounces cleaned, sliced fresh chanterelle
    mushrooms
10 cups cubed baguette; 1½ to 2 loaves
1 tablespoon chopped fresh chives
1 teaspoon fresh thyme leaves

3 eggs
6 cups half-and-half
Ground nutmeg
1 cup shredded emmentaler cheese (4 ounces)

In a large, heavy skillet, on medium-high heat, add the leeks and sauté for 5 minutes (leeks might stick a little, but when the butter is added it will help them release). Season to taste with salt, lower the heat to medium-low and stir in the butter. Partially cover the pan and cook, stirring now and then, until the leeks are starting to soften, about 20 minutes. Stir in the chanterelles and continue to cook another 10 minutes.

While the leeks are cooking, toast the bread cubes by putting them on a parchment-lined baking sheet, in a single layer, and baking for about 20 minutes until lightly brown. Put bread cubes in a large

175

mixing bowl. Add the leeks and chanterelles to the bread, then toss with the chives and thyme.

In another mixing bowl, make a custard by whisking the eggs, then whisking in the half-and-half, 1 to 1½ teaspoons salt (less if using table salt) and a pinch of nutmeg.

Sprinkle ¼ cup of the cheese in the bottom of a 9-by-13-inch baking dish. Spread half the leek/bread-cube mixture and sprinkle with another ¼ cup of cheese. Spread the rest of the leek/bread mixture, topping with another ¼ cup of cheese. Pour enough of the custard to cover the bread and press gently on the bread so it soaks up the custard. Let stand for 15 minutes.

Meanwhile, preheat oven to 350 degrees.

Add the remaining custard and sprinkle with the remaining cheese (it's OK if some of the bread sticks out). Sprinkle with salt, and bake for 1½ hours or until set and browned.

— Adapted by Donna Litvin from *Ad Hoc at Home*,
by Thomas Keller (Artisan)

MUSHROOM AND BRUSSELS SPROUTS RAGÔUT WITH CREAMY POLENTA

MAKES 4 SERVINGS

Ragôuts are rich, savory mixtures of meat and/or vegetables cooked slowly in stock or water to create something that's thinner than a stew but thicker than a soup. In this version, browned Brussels sprouts and wild mushrooms are seasoned with herbs, aromatics, and white wine to create a dish that holds its own quite nicely without meat.

2 tablespoons butter (divided)
2 tablespoons plus 2 teaspoons olive oil (divided)
8 ounces small Brussels sprouts, quartered or cut into sixths
Salt and freshly ground black pepper
8 ounces wild mushrooms, sliced (such as shiitake, oyster, chanterelle, or hedgehog)
1½ cups finely chopped onion
1 teaspoon minced garlic
¾ teaspoon dried savory or thyme
½ cup dry white wine
1 tablespoon low-sodium soy sauce
2 tablespoons all-purpose flour
3 cups mushroom broth, or broth of your choice
1½ teaspoons Dijon mustard
1 cup low-fat milk
3 cups water
1 cup quick-cooking polenta
1 (3-inch) sprig fresh rosemary
2 tablespoons butter, at room temperature

In a large sauté pan, melt 1 tablespoon butter over medium-high heat. Add 1 tablespoon oil. When the oil is hot, add the Brussels sprouts, sprinkle with salt and pepper, and sauté until the sprouts are browned and tender, 3 minutes. Transfer to a bowl.

Return the pan to medium-high heat, and add the remaining tablespoon butter and 1 tablespoon of the oil. Add the mushrooms, sprinkle with salt and pepper, and sauté until mushrooms are browned and have given off their liquid, about 3 minutes. Transfer to the bowl with the Brussels sprouts.

▶

Add the remaining 2 teaspoons oil to the pan, and the onions. Sauté until golden brown, about 4 minutes. Reduce the heat to medium, add the garlic and savory, and sauté for about 45 seconds.

Add the white wine and soy sauce, and sauté until the wine has evaporated, 1 minute. Stir in the flour and cook for 1 minute, stirring constantly. Gradually whisk in the mushroom broth and mustard. Bring to a simmer and cook until thickened slightly and bubbly, 10 minutes. Fold in the Brussels sprouts and mushrooms, and reduce the heat to low.

In a medium saucepan, combine the milk and water, and bring to a boil. Gradually whisk in the polenta and add the sprig of rosemary. Reduce heat and simmer, stirring constantly, until the polenta is thick and smooth, 5 to 8 minutes, depending on the package instructions. Remove the rosemary sprig and stir in the butter. Divide the polenta among bowls, top with the ragôut and serve.

Note: If you can't find instant polenta, you can use a tube of precooked polenta, which is usually easier to find. Cut the polenta into chunks, place it in a saucepan and heat it with about 1¼ cups of milk and the rosemary sprig, stirring until it becomes soft, smooth, and warm. Remove the sprig and stir in the 2 tablespoons of butter before serving.

— From Ivy Manning

ROASTED RED PEPPER-CASHEW SPREAD

MAKES ABOUT 2 CUPS

This versatile spread is perfect on toast points or crackers for a party appetizer, but it also would make a good sandwich filling or dip for pita triangles and veggie sticks. You can roast the red peppers yourself, but by using store-bought, the dish can be assembled in less than five minutes. [*VEGAN*]

½ cup raw, unsalted cashews
2 jarred roasted red bell peppers, well-drained
1 tablespoon lemon juice
1 teaspoon salt
½ cup nutritional yeast

In a food processor or blender, place cashews, bell peppers, lemon juice, salt, and yeast. Blend until smooth, approximately 1 minute.

— From Chelsea Lincoln, www.flavorvegan.blogspot.com

TOMATO-COCONUT-BASIL SOUP

MAKES 6 SERVINGS

At his now-closed Kalga Kafe, chef Sukhdeep Singh took tomato soup—an American cold-weather standby—and gave it global flair. The coconut milk makes the soup creamy and smooth, while olive oil and fresh basil gives it herbal interest. It's also a brilliantly simple recipe. [VEGAN]

¼ cup vegetable oil
1¾ cups diced onion
¼ cup whole peeled garlic cloves
2 (28-ounce) cans diced tomatoes
1 (14-ounce) can coconut milk
1 vegetable bouillon cube
3 tablespoons evaporated cane sugar (see note) or granulated sugar
1 tablespoon sea salt, or to taste
Extra-virgin olive oil
Chopped fresh basil, to garnish

In a large saucepan, heat vegetable oil over medium heat, and sauté onions and garlic until onions are lightly golden, approximately 8 minutes. Add canned tomatoes and their juice, coconut milk, and bouillon cube and stir; turn heat to high, bring to a boil, then turn down to low and simmer for 20 minutes.

Stir in sugar and salt and remove from heat. Purée in a blender or with an immersion blender. Ladle soup into bowls and drizzle with olive oil. Garnish with chopped basil leaves.

Note: Evaporated cane sugar is available at stores that have a wide selection of natural foods.

— From chef Sukhdeep Singh

POTATO-ASPARAGUS SOUP

MAKES 6 SERVINGS

Sautéed, steamed, grilled . . . Is there another way to enjoy Oregon's wonderful local asparagus? Indeed. Author Isa Chandra Moskowitz briefly boils it and then purées it for a simple and satisfying soup. [VEGAN]

3 pounds russet potatoes, peeled, cut into 1-inch pieces
1 pound asparagus
2 tablespoons olive oil
1 large onion, cut into ½-inch dice
3 cloves garlic, minced
1 teaspoon salt
Freshly ground black pepper

4 cups vegetable broth, or 2 vegetarian bouillon cubes dissolved in 4 cups water
2 bay leaves
Juice of 1 lemon
¼ cup chopped fresh dill weed

In a stockpot, add potatoes and cover with cold water. Cover the pot and bring to a boil, then lower the heat and simmer for 20 minutes or until potatoes are tender.

Meanwhile, snap the tough ends off the asparagus and discard. Cut the tips of the stalks into 2-inch pieces and the remainder of the stalks into ½-inch

▶

pieces. When potatoes are just about tender, add the asparagus and simmer for 3 minutes; drain potatoes and asparagus; set aside.

Rinse out the pot and return to stove over medium heat. Add the oil and heat, then add onion and sauté for 5 to 7 minutes. Add the garlic, salt, and pepper and sauté 2 more minutes. Add the broth and bay leaves, bring to a boil, and cook for 10 minutes,

then discard the bay leaves. Add the potatoes and asparagus, and heat through. Purée three-quarters of the soup in a blender or food processor, return to the pot and reheat, if necessary. Add a squeeze of lemon and serve garnished with fresh dill.

— From *Vegan with a Vengeance*, by Isa Chandra Moskowitz (Da Capo Press)

SPICY ASIAN ZUCCHINI SLAW

MAKES 6 SERVINGS

This Asian-inspired salad is light and lively and a wonderful change of pace from the usual mixture of cabbage and mayo. Be sure to serve the slaw right after adding the dressing, since the zucchini will soften as it sits. [**VEGAN**]

SALAD:

1 large zucchini, julienned or shredded
1 orange bell pepper, julienned
2 scallions, thinly sliced
1 cup fresh bean sprouts
⅓ cup raw cashews

DRESSING:

3 tablespoons rice wine vinegar
1 tablespoon tamari or soy sauce
1 tablespoon dark sesame oil
1 teaspoon peeled and grated fresh ginger
1½ teaspoons lightly toasted sesame seeds
   (see note)
¼ teaspoon crushed red pepper flakes

To make salad: In a large bowl, toss together zucchini, bell pepper, scallions, bean sprouts, and cashews.

To make dressing: In a small bowl, whisk together the vinegar, tamari, oil, ginger, sesame seeds, and pepper flakes. Dress the salad just before serving and toss to coat.

Note: To toast seeds, place in a small dry skillet and cook over medium heat, stirring often, until lightly browned.

— From Grant Butler

WHAT WE MEAN BY "JULIENNE"

Recipes sometimes call for the cook to "julienne" something, which is a pretty way of saying to cut it into matchstick-size pieces. Chefs are usually adept at this, but it can be slow going for the rest of us. It helps to have sharp knives, and also to cut the food into ¼- to ⅛-inch-thick planks before slicing into thin sticks. Many mandolines have a julienne setting, but if the food is dense and hard—like a carrot—the work can get tricky, even dangerous. There are also hand tools, used like a peeler, that will cut julienne strips. You may have to experiment before you find your most effective method. Just try not to be OCD about your efforts!

CLASSIC MACARONI AND "CHEEZE"

MAKES 10 SERVINGS

A vegan version of rich and creamy mac-and-cheese seems impossible without butter, cream, and cheddar. But instead of incorporating faux cheese or margarine, as many vegan recipes do, the richness here comes from the raw cashew and macadamia nuts that are blended into the sauce. The starch of the Yukon Gold potatoes thickens the sauce nicely. [*VEGAN*]

1 pound macaroni or rotini pasta
2 medium Yukon Gold potatoes, peeled and diced
1 medium carrot, peeled and diced
⅔ cup diced white or yellow onion
2½ cups water
⅔ cup vegetable oil
⅓ cup raw cashews
⅓ cup raw macadamia nuts
2 teaspoons fine sea salt
2 cloves garlic, chopped
¼ teaspoon dry mustard
2 tablespoons fresh lemon juice
½ teaspoon freshly ground black pepper
¼ teaspoon cayenne pepper
¼ cup unseasoned breadcrumbs (optional)

Preheat oven to 350 degrees. Cook pasta in salted boiling water just until it's tender to the bite. Drain and set aside.

While the pasta is cooking, combine the potatoes, carrot, onion, and water in a small saucepan over medium heat. Bring to a boil, reduce the heat, cover, and simmer for 10 minutes or until the vegetables are tender.

In a blender, add the vegetable oil, cashews, macadamia nuts, salt, garlic, mustard, lemon juice, black pepper, cayenne, and the vegetables and their cooking water; process until completely smooth.

Toss the cooked pasta with the sauce until completely coated. The mixture will appear quite soupy, but don't worry: the pasta will absorb much of the sauce as the dish bakes, and the sauce will thicken considerably. Transfer macaroni and sauce to a lightly oiled 3-quart casserole dish. Sprinkle with the breadcrumbs, if using. Bake for 30 minutes or until bubbling.

— From *Quick and Easy Vegan Celebrations,* by Alicia C. Simpson (The Experiment)

MUSHROOM BURGERS WITH BARLEY

MAKES 6 BURGERS

Vegans like burgers, too. Cooked barley makes this burger wonderfully chewy, and you can mix up the flavor combinations with different mushrooms, substituting hedgehog, trumpet, or oyster mushrooms for the cremini and shiitakes. The patties will be quite wet when assembled, but the starch from the potato helps bind the ingredients, and the burgers will firm up as they cook. [**VEGAN**]

> 1 medium Yukon Gold potato, peeled and
>   cut into ½-inch pieces
> 1 portobello mushroom
> 10 fresh shiitake mushrooms
> 12 fresh cremini mushrooms
> 3 tablespoons olive oil (divided)
> ½ teaspoon dried thyme
> 2 tablespoons balsamic vinegar
> 1 cup cooked barley (see note)
> ½ teaspoon salt
> ¼ teaspoon freshly ground black pepper

Steam or boil the potato until tender. Drain and place in a large bowl; mash with fork and set aside.

Trim the stem off the portobello mushroom and scrape off the gills. Chop stem and mushroom cap into ½-inch pieces. Stem the shiitake mushrooms and thinly slice the caps. Thinly slice the cremini.

Preheat oven to 375 degrees.

In a large oven-safe skillet, heat 1 tablespoon oil over medium heat. Cook the portobello slices and dried thyme for 6 to 8 minutes, until the mushroom slices begin to soften and release their moisture. Add the cremini and shiitake slices, and cook for 10 minutes until they too have sweated and pan juices have cooked off. Add vinegar and stir to deglaze pan; stir this liquid into the mushrooms.

Transfer mushrooms to a food processor (do not wash skillet); process until mixture is a coarse purée (or chop finely by hand). In a mixing bowl combine the mushroom mixture, the reserved mashed potato, cooked barley, salt, and pepper. Shape into 6 patties.

In the same skillet you used to sauté the mushrooms, heat the remaining 2 tablespoons oil over medium-high heat. Add the patties and cook until browned on both sides, 6 to 10 minutes total. Transfer the pan to the oven and bake for 12 to 15 minutes, until the burgers are firm and cooked through.

Note: To cook hulled (whole-grain) barley, simmer ½ cup dried barley in 1 cup water until water is absorbed and barley is tender, about 40 minutes.

— From *Veggie Burgers Every Which Way*, by Lukas Volger (The Experiment)

SAME MUSHROOM, DIFFERENT AGE

Portobello mushrooms are the mature and much larger form of the brown variety called cremimi. Portobellos are more expensive than their smaller cousins, but the large size is perfect for burgers and for grilling. Because portobellos are more mature, the gills on the underside of the cap are exposed and more moisture has evaporated. This gives the mushrooms a wonderful meaty texture.

FORBIDDEN RICE AND VEGETABLES IN AGAVE-CAYENNE DRESSING

MAKES 8 TO 10 SERVINGS

Deep purple, nutty-tasting forbidden rice is so named because in China it once was served only to members of the emperor's court. Now everyone can eat it, but it takes patience, requiring nearly an hour to cook, and you mustn't crack the pot lid until it's done. The nearly black, chewy grains are wonderfully satisfying in this colorful salad, which makes a delicious light lunch or side dish for grilled meats. This vegan recipe can also be wheat-free if you substitute wheat-free soy sauce in the dressing. [*VEGAN*]

AGAVE-CAYENNE DRESSING:

½ cup agave nectar
½ cup red wine vinegar
2 tablespoons soy sauce
1½ teaspoons salt
1 teaspoon dark sesame oil (or to taste)
½ teaspoon cayenne pepper
½ teaspoon freshly ground black pepper
1 tablespoon sherry
⅛ teaspoon ground cloves
½ cup vegetable oil

RICE AND VEGETABLES:

2 slender carrots, peeled and cut into
    thin coins
¼ cup white vinegar
2 tablespoons plus 1 teaspoon granulated
    sugar
Pinch of salt
2 cups uncooked forbidden rice (see note)
4 cups water
3 cups mixed vegetables: pea pods, cut into
    ½-inch pieces or frozen peas; broccoli,
    cut into small florets; red and yellow bell
    peppers, diced

¾ cup pecans, toasted (see note)
½ cup thinly sliced scallions
Pomegranate seeds, to garnish (optional)

To make dressing: In a small bowl, whisk together agave, vinegar, soy sauce, salt, sesame oil, cayenne, black pepper, sherry, and cloves. Drizzle in oil, stirring constantly, until combined. Makes about 1¾ cups.

To make rice: In a bowl or glass jar, add carrots, vinegar, sugar and salt; mix well to dissolve sugar. Allow to stand for at least 1 hour, or refrigerate for up to one day.

Meanwhile, in a medium pot, add rice and the 4 cups water, cover with a tight-fitting lid, and bring to a boil over high heat; liquid will turn purple. Turn heat to low and simmer for 50 to 60 minutes. Do not peek or lift lid.

Transfer rice to a large stain-resistant bowl and stir lightly to break up clumps. Set aside to cool. Meanwhile, strain carrots and place in a medium bowl. Add mixed vegetables and half of dressing and toss well. Just before serving, add vegetables to cooled rice and stir gently, adding more dressing as needed.

Mix in toasted pecans and scallions. Garnish with pomegranate seeds, if desired. Serve at room temperature or chilled.

Note: Forbidden rice is available at Whole Foods Market, some Safeway stores, Uwajimaya, and other Asian and specialty groceries, and in bulk at WinCo.

Note: To toast nuts, spread on baking sheet and bake in 350-degree oven for 5 to 8 minutes or until they start to brown.

— From Elaine Low, Kitchen Goddess Catering, Vancouver, Washington

MINCED SEITAN AND HERB SALAD WITH SPICY THAI DRESSING (LARB)

MAKES 4 SERVINGS

Cooking vegetarian Thai cuisine can be tricky, since dishes often call for fish sauce, a pungent amber liquid made from small, salted fish. To get a similar, salty-fermented flavor, Ivy Manning substitutes Bragg Liquid Aminos. The golden brown condiment is made from fermented soybeans and adds a savory punch that regular soy sauce can't quite manage. You can find it in the natural foods section at many grocery stores.

[VEGAN]

8 ounces seitan (see note)
2 tablespoons vegetable oil
1 large clove garlic, thinly sliced
2 shallots, thinly sliced (about ¼ cup)
1 medium red Thai chile, minced, or
    1 teaspoon crushed red pepper flakes
    (see note)
3 tablespoons lime juice
2 tablespoons Bragg Liquid Aminos
1 teaspoon soy sauce
1½ teaspoons firmly packed brown sugar
¼ teaspoon freshly ground black pepper
2 tablespoons finely chopped fresh mint leaves
2 tablespoons finely chopped fresh cilantro
1 cucumber, peeled
4 green leaf lettuce leaves, torn

Finely chop the seitan until it looks like cooked ground beef crumbles. Alternatively, pulse the seitan pieces in a food processor.

In a medium sauté pan, heat the oil over medium-high heat. When the oil is hot, add the seitan and garlic, and sauté, stirring with a spatula, until the seitan begins to brown and the garlic is fragrant, about 2 minutes. Set aside.

In a medium bowl, combine the shallots, chile, lime juice, liquid aminos, soy sauce, brown sugar, and pepper; stir until the sugar dissolves. Add the sautéed seitan mixture and chopped herbs to the dressing; toss to combine.

Cut the cucumber lengthwise and cut it into thin slices. Arrange the slices around the edges of a small platter. Place the torn lettuce in the center of the platter, top with the seitan mixture and serve.

Note: Find seitan near the tofu in the refrigerated section of many grocery stores.

Note: Thai red chiles, sometimes called "Thai bird" or "bird's eye" chiles, are tiny—about 1 inch long—and very hot and spicy. You can find them at Asian markets.

— From Ivy Manning

SPICY BLACK BEAN SAUTÉ

MAKES 6 SERVINGS

This versatile dish is perfect on its own with a side of quinoa or long-grain brown rice. Or you can use it as an alternative to taco meat, folding spoonfuls of it into warmed corn tortillas.

[VEGAN]

- 1 tablespoon light olive oil
- ½ medium yellow onion, diced
- 2 medium carrots, peeled and diced
- 6 cloves garlic, minced
- ½ large jalapeño chile, minced
- 1 (15-ounce) can black beans, drained and rinsed
- 3 large cremini mushrooms, cleaned and thinly sliced
- 1 Field Roast vegan Mexican chipotle sausage, casing removed and discarded, and sausage crumbled
- ½ teaspoon dried oregano
- ½ teaspoon ground cumin
- ½ teaspoon salt or to taste

In a large skillet, heat olive oil over medium heat until it starts to shimmer. Add onions and carrots and sauté until they soften and start to brown, 4 to 5 minutes.

Add garlic and jalapeño; cook an additional 1 to 2 minutes, until garlic starts to brown. Add beans, mushrooms, crumbled sausage, and spices. Cook an additional 4 to 5 minutes, stirring frequently so seasonings are dispersed and flavors mingle.

— From Grant Butler

MEXICAN QUINOA WITH PEPITAS AND CILANTRO

MAKES 4 SERVINGS

Leftovers of this spicy side dish make a great addition to a lunchtime wrap. Just toss warmed-up spoonfuls into a whole-grain tortilla along with cubes of baked tofu, avocado slices, and salsa.

[VEGAN]

- 1½ cups water
- 1 cup red quinoa
- ½ cup raw pumpkin seed kernels (pepitas)
- 1 cup chopped fresh cilantro
- 2 cloves garlic
- ½ jalapeño chile
- ½ teaspoon salt
- 1 teaspoon ground cumin
- 2 tablespoons olive oil
- 1 teaspoon fresh lime juice
- 1 small red bell pepper, chopped
- 2 scallions, chopped

In a 2-quart pot with a tight-fitting lid, bring the water to a boil. In a medium bowl, soak quinoa in cold water for about 5 minutes, then drain using a fine-mesh strainer. When the water boils, add the quinoa, and return to a boil. Reduce heat to low, cover, and simmer for 15 minutes. The water should all be absorbed, and small holes should have formed on the surface of the grain. Let stand, covered, for 5 minutes to finish steaming.

In a large sauté pan over high heat, dry-toast the pumpkin seed kernels, shaking the pan, until they begin to pop. Remove from heat and put into a food processor or blender. Add the cilantro, garlic, jalapeño, salt, and cumin, and process, frequently stopping to scrape down the sides of the bowl, until all the ingredients are well minced. Gradually add the olive oil and lime juice, processing until smooth.

Stir the cilantro mixture, bell pepper, and scallions into the quinoa while still warm and serve.

— From *The New Whole Grains Cookbook*, by Robin Asbell (Chronicle Books)

ACORN SQUASH WITH PECAN-CHERRY STUFFING

MAKES 6 SERVINGS

Fooddav first ran this recipe at Thanksgiving as a vegan entree. But there's no reason why it has to be a holiday dish, or that it can't be served in smaller portions as a side dish. [**VEGAN**]

- 3 medium acorn squash, halved and seeded
- 3 tablespoons olive oil, plus more, if desired (divided)
- 1 cup unsweetened rice or almond milk
- 2 teaspoons ground sage
- 1 teaspoon dried oregano leaves
- 10 slices stale, whole-grain bread, cubed (we used Dave's Killer Bread 21 Grains)
- 4 stalks celery, minced
- 2 medium yellow onions, minced
- ½ cup shredded carrot
- ¼ to ½ cup dried cherries or fresh or dried cranberries
- 2 tablespoons toasted pecans, roughly ground (see note)
- Salt and freshly ground black pepper
- 6 tablespoons maple syrup or agave nectar

Preheat oven to 400 degrees.

Rub the insides of the cut squash with 1 tablespoon olive oil. On a silicone baking mat or greased baking sheet, bake the squash, cut side down, for about 25 minutes, or until soft. Remove from oven and allow it to rest until cool enough to handle.

Meanwhile, in a large bowl, mix milk with the herbs. Add the bread cubes and let them soak in this mixture for about 15 minutes. The bread should absorb all the liquid.

In a large saucepan over medium-low heat, add remaining 2 tablespoons oil. When oil is hot, add the celery, onions, and carrot; slowly sauté until soft, about 15 minutes. Add the sautéed vegetables to the bread mixture, along with the cherries and pecans. Season with salt and pepper to taste.

Once the squash is cool, cut a small slice from the rounded side of the halves, creating a flat base so they will stand securely. Place squash on the baking sheet, with cavities facing up. Drizzle 1 tablespoon of maple syrup or agave nectar in each squash half, then fill evenly with the stuffing, forming a slight dome with a kitchen spoon. Drizzle with additional olive oil, if desired.

Return to oven and bake for 15 to 25 minutes, until heated through. Be careful not to burn.

Note: To toast nuts, spread on a baking sheet and bake in a 350-degree oven for 5 to 8 minutes or until they start to brown.

— From *The Urban Vegan*, by Dynise Balcavage (Three Forks)

BARBECUE TOFU SANDWICHES WITH SWEET AND SOUR SLAW

MAKES 4 SERVINGS

If you're craving the flavor of barbecue but want to stick to vegan fare, these tofu sandwiches are just the thing. Non-vegans can substitute honey for the agave nectar. [**VEGAN**]

SANDWICHES:

1 (20-ounce) package of extra-firm tofu
¼ cup sliced shallots
2 cloves garlic, peeled
¾ cup ketchup
6 tablespoons water
1½ tablespoons dark sesame oil
1½ tablespoons walnut or hazelnut oil
3 tablespoons agave nectar
1½ tablespoons coarse-grain mustard
½ tablespoon chili powder

SWEET-AND-SOUR COLESLAW:

5 cups finely shredded green cabbage
5 cups finely shredded red cabbage
1 carrot, shredded
3 scallions, thinly sliced
1 teaspoon salt
⅓ cup white wine vinegar
⅓ cup granulated sugar
½ teaspoon celery salt
Freshly ground black pepper

4 hamburger buns

To make sandwiches: One hour before you bake the tofu, wrap it in paper towels and place it on a dinner plate. Place another plate on top of the tofu and put a heavy object on top to squeeze out as much liquid as possible. Meanwhile, in a food processor, add the shallots, garlic, ketchup, water, sesame oil, walnut oil, agave nectar, mustard, and chili powder; blend until smooth.

Preheat oven to 350 degrees. Line a rimmed baking sheet with parchment paper.

Cut the tofu into 2-inch cubes. Pour the sauce over the tofu, tossing gently to coat the tofu with sauce. Spread the tofu evenly on prepared baking sheet. Bake for 1 hour, until the edges of the tofu have crisped slightly.

To make slaw: Meanwhile, place the cabbage, carrot, and scallions in a large serving bowl. Toss vegetables with the salt and let it sit for 5 minutes. Meanwhile, place the vinegar and sugar in a small microwave-safe measuring cup; microwave for 2 minutes, until the sugar dissolves.

Toss the hot vinegar mixture over the vegetables, and add celery salt and pepper to taste. Allow the slaw to rest for at least 30 minutes while the tofu bakes.

Put the tofu on buns, top with coleslaw, and serve. The remaining coleslaw can be served on the side.

Make ahead: The baked tofu filling freezes well for up to 3 months. Defrost in the refrigerator for about 24 hours.

— From Ivy Manning

QUICK AND EASY

10

HALIBUT AND MANGO SALSA IN PACKETS

MAKES 4 SERVINGS

A great way to cook fish is by baking it in parchment or aluminum foil packets (the French call this technique en papillote). The packets minimize fishy kitchen odor and make cleanup super easy, while the wet ingredients—in this case, salsa and lime juice—create steam that helps keep the fish moist. Oh, and there's little or no added fat involved. Brilliant.

4 (6-ounce) halibut fillets
Salt and freshly ground black pepper
1 cup prepared mango-and-peach salsa
2 tablespoons fresh lime juice
1 ripe mango, peeled and cut into ¼-inch dice
2 tablespoons chopped fresh cilantro

Preheat oven to 425 degrees. Set out four sheets of foil or parchment, each about 12 by 24 inches. Place one halibut fillet on each sheet. Season fish with salt and pepper. If any of the halibut pieces are very thin, tuck the ends under themselves.

In a medium bowl, stir together the salsa, lime juice, mango, cilantro, and salt and pepper to taste. Divide the salsa mixture evenly among the four fillets. Fold foil or parchment over the fish and crimp edges to completely enclose packets. Place packets on a rimmed baking sheet and bake for 15 minutes.

Remove fish from oven and place unopened packets on dinner plates. To serve, let each diner open his or her own packet, being careful to avoid the hot steam.

MISO-GLAZED SALMON

MAKES 4 SERVINGS

Miso and salmon pair beautifully, especially when you add Asian flavors such as ginger, soy sauce, and sesame oil. Miso paste keeps in the refrigerator for months, so even though this dish only uses 2 tablespoons, the rest need not be wasted.

4 (6-ounce) salmon fillets
Salt and freshly ground black pepper
2 tablespoons white miso paste
¼ cup mirin (seasoned rice wine)
1 teaspoon peeled and finely minced
   fresh ginger
2 teaspoons soy sauce
¼ teaspoon dark sesame oil

Place oven rack about 4 inches from broiler element, and preheat broiler to high.

Season the salmon with salt and pepper.

In a small bowl, whisk together the miso, mirin, ginger, soy sauce, and sesame oil. Brush the miso mixture on the salmon and broil for 6 to 8 minutes, depending on the thickness of the salmon. Baste one or two times while fish broils and one last time when you remove it from the oven. Serve immediately.

— From Karen Thompson

RED SNAPPER VERACRUZ

MAKES 4 SERVINGS

"Veracruz" typically describes a dish prepared with seafood, tomatoes, chiles, onion, and seasonings. This quick version includes lime juice, piquant green olives, and capers for plenty of zip.

1½ pounds red snapper fillet, or cod or halibut
2 to 4 tablespoons lime juice
½ teaspoon salt
¼ teaspoon freshly ground black pepper
2 tablespoons olive oil
1 medium onion, thinly sliced
2 large cloves garlic, minced
4 cups chopped fresh or canned tomatoes
12 pimiento-stuffed green olives, cut in half
2 tablespoons drained capers
1 teaspoon dried Mexican oregano
1 bay leaf
Pinch crushed red pepper flakes, or to taste
Steamed long-grain rice
Chopped fresh cilantro, to garnish (optional)

Brush fish with lime juice, and season with salt and pepper. Place in a large skillet and set aside.

In a large saucepan, heat oil over medium heat, add onion and garlic; cook until onion is tender but not browned. Add tomatoes, olives, capers, oregano, bay leaf, and red pepper flakes, if using. Bring to a boil, reduce heat, and simmer 10 minutes. Pour sauce over fish in skillet, place over medium-high heat, and bring to a boil. Reduce heat, cover and simmer 8 to 10 minutes, or until fish flakes easily when tested with fork. If sauce is not thick and chunky, remove fish to a platter and keep warm; continue to cook sauce until thickened. Serve fish and sauce over hot rice, garnished with cilantro, if desired.

PUTTING THE SQUEEZE ON CITRUS

You'll get more juice from limes and lemons that are at room temperature instead of cold. You can take this a step further by microwaving the fruit whole on high setting for 15 to 30 seconds. Don't overdo it and cook the fruit! Then, remove the fruit from the microwave, place it on the counter, press firmly with your palm and roll it back and forth a few times. This helps break the cells that hold the juice.

QUICK FISH TACOS WITH LIME MAYONNAISE AND GREEN CHILE SALSA

MAKES 4 SERVINGS

Breaded and frozen fish fillets aren't usually in our grocery basket, but they're excellent in these tacos. You just pop the fish in the oven to bake while you toss together a quick cabbage slaw and a lime-flavored topping, then warm the tortillas and chop a little cilantro. They may not be authentic, but they're really delicious.

    4 tablespoons fresh lime juice (divided)
    1½ teaspoons granulated sugar
    1½ teaspoons salt
    1½ cups finely shredded cabbage (see note)
    8 whole pieces frozen breaded fish fillets
        (not the sticks made from minced fish)
    ½ cup mayonnaise
    ½ teaspoon grated lime zest
    8 corn tortillas
    ⅓ cup roughly chopped fresh cilantro
    ½ cup green salsa (salsa verde)
    ½ cup crumbled cotija, feta, or, in a pinch,
        shredded Monterey jack cheese (optional)

In a medium mixing bowl combine 3 tablespoons lime juice with the sugar and salt; add cabbage and toss. Continue to toss cabbage occasionally as you prepare the rest of the dish.

Bake fish as directed on the package. While the fish is baking, stir together the mayonnaise, lime zest, and the remaining 1 tablespoon lime juice. Just before serving, wrap the tortillas in paper towels; heat in the microwave on high for 1 minute.

To assemble, lay a fish fillet in a tortilla (cut the fish in half, if it fits better that way). Top with lime mayonnaise, cilantro, salsa, cabbage, and cheese, if using. Repeat, to make a total of eight tacos. Serve immediately.

Note: Many stores sell a finely shredded cabbage often called "angel hair." If you prefer to slice your own, cut a whole cabbage in half and slice into very thin shreds.

— From Martha Holmberg and Shannon Wheeler

SEARED SHRIMP WITH GREEN CHILE-CILANTRO RICE

MAKES 4 SERVINGS

Our inspiration for this dish is what's sometimes called "green rice," which is white rice flavored with generous amounts of minced cilantro and lime zest. Although we're generally not fans of converted rice, here it's a good choice because it cooks up so fluffy. While the rice cooks, all you do is toss the shrimp with three seasonings and sear them in a hot skillet.

1 (7-ounce) can green salsa (salsa verde)
1 (4-ounce) can diced mild green chiles
1½ cups converted rice (Uncle Ben's Original)
¼ cup chopped fresh cilantro
½ teaspoon grated lime zest
1 pound large raw shrimp, peeled and
  deveined
¼ teaspoon garlic salt
¼ teaspoon ground cumin
¼ teaspoon chili powder
1 tablespoon vegetable oil
Garnishes: sour cream, salsa, and
  tortilla chips

In a 1-quart measuring cup, combine the salsa, diced chiles, and enough water to make 3⅓ cups liquid. Pour into a medium saucepan and bring to a boil. Stir in the rice. Reduce heat to low, cover, and simmer for 20 minutes. Remove from heat and let stand for 5 minutes with the cover ajar. Stir in the cilantro and lime zest. Cover and set aside until needed.

When the rice is almost done, toss the shrimp with the garlic salt, cumin, and chili powder. In a large skillet, heat the oil over medium-high heat until it's almost smoking. Add the shrimp and sear for about 1½ minutes, then turn and sear the other side for another 1 minute. Remove from heat.

Divide the rice among 4 bowls, top with shrimp. Drizzle with sour cream. Serve with salsa and tortilla chips.

— From Linda Faus

BOK CHOY WITH SHRIMP AND BLACK BEAN SAUCE

MAKES 4 SERVINGS

Stir-fries often call for a long list of sauce ingredients. But a jar of black bean-garlic sauce makes a good shortcut, and it's sold in the Asian foods aisle of most supermarkets. The sauce is rich and thick, and has a relatively mild garlic flavor. The other shortcut we use here is frozen peeled shrimp, something for which we are forever grateful. We always keep a bag in the freezer and defrost just the number we need in a colander under cool water.

- 2 tablespoons vegetable oil (divided)
- 1 small onion, halved lengthwise and sliced crosswise
- 1 red bell pepper, seeded and cut into ¼-inch strips
- 4 large stalks bok choy, including leaves, sliced ¼-inch thick
- ¾ pound peeled shrimp (thawed if frozen)
- ¼ cup black-bean-garlic sauce (see note)
- ⅛ teaspoon chili paste
- 1½ teaspoons cornstarch
- 1 tablespoon water
- Sesame seeds or chopped nuts, to garnish (optional)
- Hot cooked rice

Heat a large heavy skillet or wok over high heat. Add 1 tablespoon oil and when hot, add onion and bell pepper; cook, stirring constantly, just until tender-crisp, 1 to 2 minutes. Transfer to a large bowl and keep warm.

Return skillet to heat, add remaining tablespoon oil, bok choy, and shrimp; cook, stirring constantly, just until shrimp turn opaque. Add black bean sauce, chili paste, and vegetables from bowl, and stir until everything is well-incorporated with sauce and heated through.

Whisk the cornstarch into the water and pour over the stir-fry, stirring constantly until the sauce is shiny and has thickened slightly. Serve over hot rice, garnished with sesame seeds or nuts, if desired.

Note: We used Sun Luck Black Bean Garlic Sauce, which comes in an 8-ounce jar and is sold in most supermarkets in the Asian foods aisle.

POT STICKER-SPINACH-CHICKEN SOUP

MAKES 3 SERVINGS

Foodday ran two contests for recipes that use five ingredients or less, and some of the entries were brilliantly simple. This one, from Betty Robbins, won first place in "Five Easy Pieces, the Sequel" in 2001. Even though it's made with just canned broth, frozen pot stickers, and a few seasonings, it makes a truly soothing meal in just minutes. Betty says of her dish: "This is a complete meal when served with crispy, hot French or sourdough bread, and a glass of your favorite wine."

2 (14½-ounce) cans reduced-sodium chicken broth or one 32-ounce box
2 cloves garlic, minced
1 fresh green or red jalapeño chile, seeded and minced
16 to 18 frozen pork pot stickers (or substitute other pot stickers; see note)

1½ cups fresh baby spinach or regular spinach, torn (about 1 ounce) or ⅓ cup frozen leaf spinach (one-fourth of a 10-ounce box), thawed, drained, and squeezed to remove excess liquid
Hot chili oil (optional)

In a medium saucepan, simmer chicken broth with garlic and jalapeño over low heat for 5 minutes. Add frozen pot stickers and simmer an additional 5 minutes. Add spinach and simmer just until wilted, but still bright green.

Serve hot, with chili oil on the table for those who prefer it.

Note: Pot stickers come in various sizes and packages. We used Trader Joe's frozen Pork Gyoza Pot Stickers (also labeled Pork and Vegetable Dumplings); there are 24 to 26 per 1-pound package.

— From Betty Robbins

SAFETY AND CANNED FOODS

Most canned foods have a very long "safe life" when properly stored at cool room temperatures. Unless a can is bulging or leaking, its contents are perfectly safe to eat. However, quality diminishes with long-term storage, and the food will slowly start losing nutrients, flavor, and texture. This is why the recommended storage time for canned food is a year. Low-acid foods, such as meat, fish, stews, beans, and most vegetables, maintain quality longer than high-acid foods and are edible for up to two years. High-acid canned foods, such as tomato products, citrus juices, pineapple, peaches, pears, and other fruit, react with the metal container, so storing them longer than eighteen months will result in a metallic taste. However, the food is safe to eat.

Sometimes there's a packing date on the bottom of the can or a "best if used by" stamp to indicate the age of the product. If the label doesn't list "nutrition facts," the product was packed or canned in 1994 or before.

Examine all home-preserved and store-bought canned foods before using them. As you open the can or jar, notice whether air rushes out. Don't eat food if it does, or if the liquid spurts, because spoilage has occurred and the food is not safe to eat.

The exception is tomato products, because the acid in the tomatoes can react with the metal in the can. This creates a gas, causing a spurt. The tomatoes are safe to eat.

Always smell the contents at once. The odor, color, and texture should be typical of the food. An off odor probably means spoilage. Do not taste and do not give to animals.

GINGER-SCENTED BUTTERNUT SQUASH SOUP

MAKES ABOUT 6 CUPS

Few products compare to cooked butternut squash for convenience. Peeling and seeding a whole winter squash is a time-consuming task, whereas opening the package takes but moments. The amount of ginger recommended is conservative. Add more if you like your soup spicy.

- 3 cups low-sodium chicken broth
- 2 (10-ounce) packages frozen cooked butternut squash
- 1 cup unsweetened applesauce
- About 1 teaspoon salt, or to taste
- 3 tablespoons granulated sugar
- 1 teaspoon ground ginger, plus additional to taste
- ½ cup whipping cream

In a medium pot over medium heat, combine the broth and frozen squash. Cook, spooning the broth over the squash, until the squash has defrosted, about 12 minutes. Add the applesauce, salt to taste, sugar, and ginger; whisk to combine. Increase the heat to medium-high and bring the mixture to a boil. Reduce the heat to medium-low, add the cream, and simmer gently for 30 minutes. Taste and season accordingly.

— From Stephanie Witt Sedgwick, *Washington Post*

SALMON AND CORN CHOWDER

MAKES 3 TO 4 SERVINGS

Cooking with condensed cream soups is very old school, but there are times when it works quite nicely. We use it here as the basis for a lovely creamy chowder that doesn't taste at all like something from a can.

- 2 (10¾-ounce) cans condensed cream of potato soup
- 2¾ cups whole milk
- ½ cup dry white wine
- ¾ teaspoon dried dill weed
- ½ teaspoon freshly ground black pepper
- 8 ounces smoked salmon
- ¾ cup frozen corn kernels
- Chopped fresh parsley (optional garnish)

In a medium saucepan, combine soup, milk, wine, dill, pepper, and salmon. Cook over medium heat, stirring, until well-blended and slightly thickened, 5 to 10 minutes. Add corn and cook until heated through. Divide among bowls and garnish with parsley, if desired.

CHICKEN PAPRIKASH IN A PINCH

MAKES 4 SERVINGS

Chicken paprikash is one of those classics that deserves to be made more often—and if you use leftover rotisserie chicken, it's super simple. The tangy sour cream balances the pungent paprika (we use both sweet and hot varieties) and when combined with chicken and some broth, it makes a magical sauce for hot egg noodles. You can whittle the calories a bit by substituting reduced-fat sour cream, but we don't recommend using nonfat sour cream (for anything, really).

¼ cup butter
1 cup chopped onion
½ cup diced red bell pepper
1½ cups reduced-sodium chicken broth
1 tablespoon sweet paprika
1 teaspoon hot paprika (see note)
1 teaspoon kosher salt
1 tablespoon all-purpose flour
1 cup sour cream
3 cups shredded or diced cooked chicken
2 to 3 cups hot cooked egg noodles
    (4 to 5 ounces dry)

In a large skillet, melt the butter over medium-high heat. Add the onion and sauté for 5 minutes, or until tender and beginning to turn golden. Add the red pepper and continue cooking until tender, about 3 to 4 minutes longer. Stir in the chicken broth and bring to a boil; continue boiling until the sauce has reduced by half, about 3 minutes.

Stir in the sweet and hot paprika, and the salt. Stir the flour into the sour cream and whisk into sauce until smooth; bring to a simmer. Taste and adjust seasoning if necessary. Fold in the chicken and noodles. Serve hot.

Note: Hot paprika can pack some heat, so if you prefer your paprikash mild, substitute more sweet paprika. Note, however, that the flavor of the dish will be sweeter.

— From Linda Faus

LINGUINE WITH CHICKEN AND ASPARAGUS IN PESTO CREAM SAUCE

MAKES 8 SERVINGS

Prepared pesto is fabulous convenience food. But some people prefer a milder, less intense sauce. By mixing in a little half-and-half, you get a creamy sauce that suggests basil instead of clobbering you with it. Even though we used chicken tenders here, you could substitute leftovers from a rotisserie chicken, or use shrimp or scallops instead.

1 pound dry linguine
1 tablespoon olive oil
2 teaspoons minced garlic
1 (8-ounce) package sliced fresh mushrooms
1 pound chicken tenders, cut into bite-size
    pieces
1 pound asparagus, ends trimmed
1 (8-ounce) container pesto
1 cup half-and-half
1 tablespoon fresh lemon juice
Salt
Grated parmesan cheese

Cook the linguine in boiling salted water just until tender to the bite. Drain and keep warm.

While the pasta is cooking, heat the olive oil in a large skillet over medium-high heat. Sauté the garlic and mushrooms for 3 to 4 minutes or until the mushrooms are almost tender. Add the chicken and asparagus and continue cooking until the chicken is almost cooked through and the asparagus is tender-crisp, about 5 minutes more.

Stir in the pesto and half-and-half and bring to a simmer. Add the lemon juice and season to taste with salt. Toss the pesto cream sauce with the pasta and serve with parmesan cheese.

— From Linda Faus

BROWN BUTTER GNOCCHI WITH SPINACH AND PINE NUTS

MAKES 4 SMALL SERVINGS

It takes longer to boil the water to cook the gnocchi for this dish than it takes to whip up the sauce and assemble. And it's really delicious. There's plenty of spinach to make you feel like you were eating something healthy, and just enough butter and cheese to make it all taste wonderful.

If you're serving this as an entree for hungrier folks, consider doubling it, or adding a chop or sausage alongside.

1 (16-ounce) package vacuum-packed gnocchi
2 tablespoons butter
2 tablespoons pine nuts
2 cloves garlic, minced
1 (10-ounce) package fresh spinach
¼ teaspoon salt
¼ teaspoon freshly ground black pepper
¼ cup finely shredded parmesan cheese

Cook gnocchi according to package directions; drain.

In a large nonstick skillet, heat butter over medium heat. Add pine nuts; cook 3 minutes or until butter and nuts are slightly browned, stirring constantly. Add garlic; cook 1 minute. Add drained gnocchi and spinach; cook 1 minute or until spinach wilts, stirring constantly. Stir in salt and pepper. Sprinkle with parmesan cheese.

— Adapted from *Cooking Light* magazine

MINI MEATLOAVES

MAKES 6 SERVINGS

Meatloaf isn't the easiest meal to serve on a weeknight. But when you make the loaves in individual portions, dinner comes together a lot quicker. We also trimmed some of the work by using a store-bought pasta sauce to moisten and help season the ground beef.

1 teaspoon vegetable oil
¾ cup chopped onion
1¼ pounds lean ground beef (about 85 percent lean)
½ cup Italian seasoned dry breadcrumbs
½ cup roasted garlic pasta sauce
1 egg, lightly beaten
¾ teaspoon salt

Preheat oven to 375 degrees. Spray 6 muffin cups with nonstick cooking spray.

In a small skillet, heat the oil over medium heat and sauté the onion until tender, about 3 to 4 minutes. Set aside to cool.

In a medium bowl, combine the ground beef, breadcrumbs, pasta sauce, egg, salt, and cooled onions. Using clean hands, mix until well-combined.

Divide the meat mixture into 6 equal portions and press into 6 prepared muffin cups, shaping a smooth, rounded top on each mini meatloaf. If your muffin pan holds more than 6 muffins, fill the remaining empty cups with water. Bake for about 25 minutes or until an instant-read or meat thermometer inserted into the center of a mini meatloaf reads 160 degrees. Remove from oven and let stand for 5 minutes

— From Linda Faus

IS PREHEATING THE OVEN ESSENTIAL?

If a recipe says to preheat your oven, the cooking timing is based on the oven being at temperature, but preheating isn't just important to the timing. The initial temperature that the food is exposed to can make a difference in the final result. Many roast recipes, for example, call for the meat to be "seared" by a blast of very hot air right at first, to develop a browned surface.

Preheat the oven for baked goods that contain baking powder, baking soda, or yeast. They will brown more evenly. And, since the rising for cakes, cookies, quick breads, yeast breads, and yeast rolls is affected by heat, putting those items in a preheated oven will result in a lighter product. Although brown-and-serve rolls and breads have already risen, they will brown more evenly in a preheated oven.

Casseroles may be placed in a cold oven and the heat turned on.

SIMPLE BRAISED BEEF

MAKES 4 SERVINGS

We would never call this boeuf bourguignon. For starters, there's no red wine, onions, or mushrooms. But when you're in the mood for tender, slow-cooked beef, this is a simple alternative. And it soothes our conscience that even some chefs use demi-glace concentrate as a shortcut.

1 (2- to 3-pound) beef chuck roast
Salt and freshly ground black pepper
1 tablespoon vegetable oil
1 (1½-ounce) cup Demi-Glace Gold
    concentrate (classic flavor made with
    veal and beef stock; see note)
1¼ cups hot water, plus more as needed

Preheat oven to 350 degrees. Season chuck roast with salt and pepper. Heat a skillet over medium-high, add oil and heat until it's almost smoking. Brown the chuck roast on the first side, without disturbing, for 3 to 4 minutes. Roast should release from the pan if it is well-browned. Turn roast over and brown the second side for another 3 minutes.

Place the roast in a pot that's a relatively tight fit. In order to properly braise, the cooking liquid needs to come at least halfway up the sides of the roast. Whisk together the demi-glace and hot water. Pour over chuck roast. Cover and bake for 2 hours or until the roast is tender. Check once or twice during cooking and add a little water if the sauce is starting to look too thick. You don't want it watery, but you don't want it to be as thick as tomato sauce either.

When roast is done, transfer to a platter, cover loosely with foil and let sit for 10 to 15 minutes before serving. Skim the fat from the sauce and serve the de-fatted liquid over slices of roast.

Note: Find Demi-Glace Gold brand at stores that carry a wide selection of gourmet foods.

ORANGE-DIJON PORK CHOPS

MAKES 4 SERVINGS

Pork adores fruit, even when it's from a jar of preserves. After searing bone-in chops (they're more flavorful than boneless) we serve them with a simple pan sauce made with a little brandy, orange marmalade, some mustard, and a pat of butter. If you prefer, you can substitute wine, broth, or even juice for the brandy.

> 4 bone-in rib pork chops, about 1¾ pounds
> Salt and freshly ground black pepper
> 1 teaspoon olive oil
> 1 tablespoon brandy, other liquor or chicken broth
> ¼ cup orange marmalade
> 2½ tablespoons Dijon mustard
> ½ teaspoon garlic salt
> 1 tablespoon butter

Season the pork chops on both sides with salt and pepper. In a large nonstick skillet, heat oil over medium-high heat; brown the chops on one side for about 3 to 4 minutes. Turn chops and cook on the second side for another 3 to 4 minutes, or until barely pink in the center. Remove to a plate and keep warm.

Reduce the heat to medium and stir the brandy or other liquid into the pan juices. Whisk in the marmalade, mustard, and garlic salt; cook for 1 to 2 minutes, or until the sauce comes together. Whisk in the butter and any juices that have collected on the plate of pork chops. Plate the chops, drizzle with the sauce, and serve.

LAMB GYROS

MAKES 4 SERVINGS

A gyro sandwich has a magical combination of Mediterranean flavors: garlicky lamb, salty feta, cool tzatziki, and rich hummus, all tucked into a folded pita bread with lettuce and tomato. But instead of buying gyros from a food cart, you can easily make them at home using ground lamb. And with all the delicious garnishes, you'll need relatively little meat.

> 12 ounces ground lamb (see note)
> ¼ teaspoon dried oregano leaves
> ¼ teaspoon dried thyme leaves
> ⅛ teaspoon dried dill weed
> 1 to 2 large cloves garlic, minced
> Salt and freshly ground black pepper

> 4 whole pita breads or Greek flat breads
> ½ cup hummus
> 4 large leaves lettuce
> 2 Roma tomatoes, sliced crosswise about ¼ inch thick
> 1 (6- to 8-ounce) container tzatziki (cucumber-yogurt sauce)
> ¼ to ⅓ cup crumbled feta cheese
> Pitted kalamata olives or dill pickle slices (optional)

Gently combine lamb with oregano, thyme, dill, garlic, and salt and pepper to taste. Portion mixture into golf-ball-sized rounds and flatten slightly. In a skillet or on a grill, cook the little patties over medium-high heat, turning often, until they reach 165

201

degrees on an instant-read thermometer, about 10 minutes.

Warm the pita breads in a 350-degree oven (or grill them until hot). Spread about 2 tablespoons of hummus on each pita (we serve them uncut, like a tortilla), add lettuce leaves and tomato slices. Top with a quarter of the lamb. Spoon tzatziki over the lamb, and sprinkle with feta cheese and olives. Fold pita to enclose the fillings and serve.

Note: Some markets, such as New Seasons, sell gyros lamb patties or garlic-lamb sausages in the meat case. Either makes a great shortcut for the plain ground lamb, oregano, dill, thyme, black pepper, salt, and garlic.

— From Linda Faus

PULLED PORK ON CHEESY POLENTA

MAKES 4 SERVINGS

Enchilada sauce and polenta might sound like fusion-cooking-run-amok, but remember that polenta is made from corn, which isn't far removed from corn tortillas. The biggest time-saver for this dish is using a tub of precooked pulled pork, which is sold in the meat case. For the polenta, we chop up a tube of prepared polenta and simmer it with milk, which quickly renders it soft and luscious. Alternatively, you could skip the simmering step and instead brush slices of polenta and grill or fry them.

1 (17-ounce) package prepared pork roast with au jus, rinsed (we used Hormel brand)
1 cup red enchilada sauce
1 chipotle chile canned in adobo sauce, minced
½ teaspoon ground cumin
½ teaspoon dried Mexican oregano

Juice of 1 lime
1 (17- to 18-ounce) tube prepared polenta
1 to 1¼ cups whole milk
¾ cup shredded Monterey jack cheese
2 tablespoons chopped fresh cilantro

Using two forks, pull the rinsed pork into large shreds. In a medium saucepan, combine pork, enchilada sauce, chipotle chile, cumin, oregano, and lime juice. Bring to a simmer; cook until heated through and flavors have blended, about 5 to 6 minutes.

Meanwhile, in a medium saucepan over medium heat, combine the polenta and milk. Heat, mashing and stirring the polenta, until smooth and creamy. Add additional milk if needed to reach the desired consistency. Stir in the cheese.

To serve, spoon polenta onto each plate, then top with pulled pork. Sprinkle with cilantro and serve.

— From Linda Faus

MEDITERRANEAN LENTIL SALAD

MAKES 4 SERVINGS

Refrigerated pre-cooked lentils are a wonderful convenience product, and we find the texture and flavor superior to canned lentils. Here we turn them into a quick main-dish salad with the help of a simple vinaigrette, marinated artichoke hearts, onion, feta cheese, and herbs.

- 8 large leaves romaine lettuce
- 2 (8-ounce) packages refrigerated steamed lentils (about 2 cups; see note)
- 2 teaspoons sherry or apple cider vinegar
- ¼ cup extra-virgin olive oil
- Freshly ground black pepper
- 1 (6½-ounce) jar marinated artichoke hearts
- ⅓ cup chopped red onion or ½ cup chopped sweet onion
- 6 ounces feta cheese, crumbled or cut into cubes
- Salt
- 1 handful mixed fresh herbs, such as parsley, basil, and marjoram, coarsely chopped

Tear two lettuce leaves on each of four large plates. In a large bowl, mix together lentils, vinegar, oil, and pepper to taste. Drain artichokes (reserve marinade for another use, if desired). Add artichokes to lentils along with onion and feta; toss gently. Add salt to taste and additional pepper, if desired. Stir in herbs, spoon over plates of torn lettuce, and serve.

Note: We used Earth Exotics Cooked & Ready to Eat Lentils, which we found in the refrigerated case at Fred Meyer. Trader Joe's carries its own brand.

LEMON-GINGER ICE CREAM SANDWICHES

MAKES 16 SANDWICHES, FOR 8 SERVINGS

Cool lemon and the warmth of ginger are the yin and yang of this refreshing treat. If you like making your own lemon curd, this is a great way to enjoy it.

- 1 pint premium vanilla ice cream, softened
- ½ cup lemon curd
- 32 thin, crisp ginger cookies (we used Anna's Ginger Thins; see note)

In a medium bowl, stir together the ice cream and lemon curd; return to the freezer for 15 minutes to firm.

Lay 16 cookies, bottom-side up, on a rimmed baking sheet. Using a small ice cream scoop, scoop about 2 tablespoons of the ice cream mixture onto each cookie and top with the remaining 16 cookies, pressing to flatten slightly. Freeze for at least 3 hours before serving. To freeze longer, wrap each sandwich tightly in plastic wrap, and place carefully in a plastic freezer bag. Use within 2 weeks.

Note: Anna's Ginger Thins are available at New Seasons Markets, Ikea, and other specialty stores.

— From Linda Faus

RHUBARB CUSTARD CAKE

MAKES 15 SERVINGS

When reader Mara Nesbitt-Aldrich e-mailed her Rhubarb Custard Cake recipe to former Food-day editor Chris Christensen, Chris made it, took a bite, fell in love, then passed the recipe on to our readers. The cake has a layer of tart rhubarb and a sweet custard that falls to the bottom of the pan, with the cake rising to the top.

1 (18¼-ounce) box white cake mix (any kind that requires oil as an ingredient)
¼ teaspoon freshly grated nutmeg (optional)
3 cups diced rhubarb, cut in ½-inch pieces
1½ cups granulated sugar
1 pint whipping cream (2 cups)

Preheat oven according to cake package directions. Cut rhubarb into pieces and set aside.

Prepare cake as directed on package. Add nutmeg to batter. Pour batter into an 11-by-15-inch baking pan (a 9-by-13-inch pan won't work unless it is very deep; add 5 minutes or so to the cooking time).

At the last minute, toss the sugar with the rhubarb and sprinkle over the cake batter. Drizzle the entire pint of whipping cream over the batter and fruit; do not mix it in.

Bake about 35 minutes, or until the top of the cake turns a light golden brown and begins to leave the sides of the pan. A toothpick stuck into the cake part of the dessert should come out clean.

Note: This recipe was tested using a glass baking dish. If you use a metal pan, increase the temperature 25 degrees.

— From Mara Nesbitt-Aldrich

PEANUT BUTTER CUP BARS

MAKES 54 BARS

These bars are another winner from our "Five Easy Pieces" contest. As the name says, they're like Reese's Peanut Butter Cups in bar form.

1 cup butter, melted (2 sticks)
1½ cups graham cracker crumbs
2 cups powdered sugar
2 cups peanut butter (divided)
1 (12-ounce) bag semisweet chocolate chips (2 cups)

In a large bowl, mix butter, graham cracker crumbs, powdered sugar, and 1 cup peanut butter. Spread into a 9-by-13-inch pan. In the microwave oven or in a saucepan over medium-low heat, melt chocolate chips and remaining 1 cup peanut butter; stir.

Spread evenly over cracker crumb mixture; refrigerate until firm. Cut into 54 bars. Store in the refrigerator.

— From Ana M. Brown

BEAVERTON BAKERY POPPY SEED CAKE

MAKES 12 SERVINGS

One of Beaverton Bakery's most popular items is its poppy seed cake. Although it uses both a cake mix and instant pudding, our home economist loved it. Perhaps it's due to that little bit of cream sherry?

3 cups white cake mix (see note)
3 eggs
½ cup vegetable oil
1 (3½-ounce) package vanilla instant pudding
⅓ cup water
1 teaspoon almond extract
¼ cup plus 2 tablespoons cream sherry
¼ cup poppy seeds

CREAM CHEESE FROSTING:
1 pound cream cheese, at room temperature
½ cup unsalted butter, at room temperature (1 stick)
1½ cups powdered sugar
1 teaspoon vanilla extract
1 teaspoon lemon juice
⅓ cup whipping cream

Preheat oven to 350 degrees. Grease two 9-inch cake pans or 1 tube or Bundt pan.

In large mixing bowl, add cake mix, eggs, oil, pudding, and water. Blend on low speed until moistened. Then add almond extract, sherry, and poppy seeds; mix at medium speed for 2 minutes. Pour batter in prepared pan and bake immediately.

Two 9-inch layer cakes will bake about 25 to 30 minutes, tube or Bundt pan, about 40 to 50 minutes. Cool in pan on rack, then remove and frost.

To make frosting: With an electric mixer, beat the cream cheese and butter together on medium speed until well-combined. Add the powdered sugar and mix until just blended, scraping down the sides of the bowl with a rubber spatula as needed.

Add the vanilla and lemon juice; beat on low speed until just combined. Slowly mix in the cream on low speed until just combined. Once all the cream is incorporated, beat the frosting on medium-high speed for a few seconds. Use the frosting immediately or store in the refrigerator until ready to use. Allow frosting to come to room temperature before spreading.

Note: An 18¼-ounce package cake mix has 4 cups of cake mix. Beaverton Bakery suggests using the leftover cup of cake mix to make a streusel topping for another dessert.

— Adapted from Beaverton Bakery, Beaverton

NEED PLENTY OF POPPY SEEDS?

Poppy seeds can be costly if you buy them in small spice jars at a supermarket. If you want larger amounts you can save money by buying them locally at Penzeys or Bob's Red Mill (see Resources chapter), and in bulk at WinCo.

BREAKFAST AND BRUNCH

11

BREAKFAST FRIED RICE

MAKES 2 SERVINGS

This creation of contributor Deena Prichep is vaguely inspired by garlicky Mexican red rice but is unabashedly inauthentic. It's also really delicious and a great way to use up leftover rice. Don't try this with hot, freshly cooked rice or it will clump together in a gooey mess.

> 1 tablespoon olive oil
> ½ teaspoon achiote seeds (also labeled annatto seeds; optional; see note)
> 1 large, or 2 small, cloves garlic, chopped
> 1 small tomato, chopped (optional)
> 2 cups leftover rice (cold or room temperature)
> 2 handfuls chopped fresh cilantro
> Salt and freshly ground black pepper
> 2 eggs
> Hot sauce, for serving
> Lime wedges, for serving

Place the oil and achiote seeds in a heavy skillet, and heat over medium-high. As the oil warms, it will take on color from the seeds. When the oil is very hot (but not smoking) and reddish from the achiote, quickly spoon the seeds out and discard them.

Add the garlic to the hot red oil in the skillet, and stir quickly as it sizzles. When garlic is lightly browned (be careful not to let it burn), add the tomato; sauté until the heat comes back up and the tomato softens a bit, but doesn't break down, about a minute or so. Add the rice and cilantro. Stir frequently with a spatula or spoon, breaking up the rice clumps and coating grains with the garlicky red oil (without mashing them too much). Season to taste with salt and pepper. When the rice is well-oiled and heated through, remove to two plates.

Quickly crack the eggs in the pan, fry them as you like them, and slide one on top of each plate of rice. Season with a few shakes of hot sauce, a squirt of lime, and additional salt and pepper.

Note: Achiote, also known as annatto or curry korn, contributes a reddish-orange color and a slightly peppery, nutmeg flavor. You can find the seeds at Latin American or Asian markets or at Penzeys stores (see Resources chapter and online).

— From Deena Prichep

BACON AND EGG BRUSCHETTA

MAKES 2 SERVINGS

This dish is very rustic and not meant to be fancy fare. It's messier than most bruschetta, so you'll probably want to eat it with a knife and fork.

> 4 (½-inch-thick) slices soft ciabatta bread (see note)
> Extra-virgin olive oil
> 2 medium handfuls baby mixed greens (approximately 1½ cups; frisée works great)
> 4 thick slices bacon, cooked crisp
> 4 eggs, poached (see note)
> Sea salt and freshly ground black pepper
> Parmigiano-Reggiano cheese shavings
> Aged balsamic vinegar

Lightly brush both sides of the ciabatta slices with about 1 tablespoon oil. Grill until lightly toasted on each side.

Place grilled bread on a big plate. Arrange the greens evenly over the four slices of bread. Break each slice of bacon in half and place two halves on each slice of bread. Carefully place the poached eggs on top of the bacon and season with salt and black pepper. Shave a few pieces of cheese over the top of each egg, and drizzle some of the balsamic vinegar and additional olive oil over the dish. Serve warm.

Note: A soft ciabatta works best; bread with a thick crust makes the bruschetta difficult to eat.

Note: To poach eggs, fill a large skillet with 2 to 3 inches of water. Set pan over medium heat and bring to a simmer. Add 3 tablespoons apple cider vinegar or white vinegar. Crack an egg into a cup, then gently slide the egg into the water; use a spoon to nudge the whites to help them gather around the yolk instead of trailing off. Adjust heat as you add additional eggs so that water stays at a gentle simmer. Poach eggs, uncovered, until whites are set and yolks have started to thicken but are not hard, 1½ to 2 minutes for runny yolks, 3 to 5 minutes for firmer eggs. Remove each egg with a slotted spoon.

— From chef Ian Duncan, Vino Paradiso

MAKING BETTER BACON

- To discourage curling, add bacon to the cold skillet before turning on the heat. A cast-iron skillet, or one with a heavy bottom, helps the meat cook more evenly.
- Use medium to medium-low heat. Don't turn it until the bacon releases easily from the pan, then turn frequently.
- In our experience, older bacon cooks more quickly and can burn more easily than fresh bacon. The National Pork Board told us this might be due to moisture loss, which would cause the bacon to cook faster.
- Baking bacon takes longer than stovetop cooking, but you can leave it to cook untended and the strips will stay flat. Place the bacon on the rack of a broiler pan, and bake in a preheated 400-degree oven for 15 to 20 minutes, or until done to your liking.
- To microwave bacon, place a couple of layers of paper towels on a microwave-safe plate, add bacon, cover with a paper towel, and cook on high for a total of approximately 1 minute for every slice.

BAKED EGGS "ICEHOUSE" (WITH WONDERFUL VARIATIONS)

MAKES 1 SERVING

Former Fooday editor Martha Holmberg learned this recipe while working at the Icehouse restaurant in Telluride, Colorado. But she calls it more a method than a recipe, since you can make it with almost any combination of ingredients you choose, once you understand how the dish is put together.

You'll need individual ovenproof bowls or ramekins, each with about a 12-ounce capacity. If they're a little big, that's OK.

1 half of a toasted English muffin, torn into 1-inch pieces

2 slices bacon, cooked until crisp, drained and crumbled

¼ cup diced cherry tomatoes (or other tomato with some flavor)

1 tablespoon diced roasted and peeled hot green chiles (canned is fine)

1 lightly poached egg (the egg will cook a little more in the oven; see note)

Salt and freshly ground black pepper

¼ cup heavy whipping cream

½ cup shredded good-quality aged cheddar

Preheat oven to 425 degrees. Put half of the muffin pieces, bacon, tomatoes, and chiles in the bottom of an ovenproof ramekin or bowl, nestle the egg on top, and season with salt and pepper. Scatter the rest of the bacon, tomatoes, and chiles on top of the egg, add the remaining muffin pieces, and pour the cream over the top. Sprinkle with cheese. Let the dish sit at least 15 minutes before baking, to let the muffin pieces absorb some of the cream.

Put the ramekin on a sheet pan for easy handling. Bake until the cheese is melted and beginning to brown, and most of the cream has been absorbed, 14 to 15 minutes. Let rest about 5 minutes before serving for the best consistency and flavor.

Note: To poach eggs, fill a large skillet with 2 to 3 inches of water. Set pan over medium heat and bring to a simmer. Add 3 tablespoons apple cider vinegar or white vinegar. Crack an egg into a cup, then gently slide the egg into the water; use a spoon to nudge the whites to help them gather around the yolk instead of trailing off. Adjust heat as you add additional eggs so that water stays at a gentle simmer. Poach eggs, uncovered, until whites are set and yolks have started to thicken but are not hard, 1½ to 2 minutes for runny yolks, 3 to 5 minutes for firmer eggs. Remove each egg with a slotted spoon.

Make ahead: This can be assembled the night before baking. Be sure to cover tightly and refrigerate. Add 1 to 2 minutes to the baking time.

Variations: Use the muffin, egg, and cream as in the main recipe, but replace the bacon, tomatoes, chiles, and cheddar with your choice of the following ingredients:

- 1 ounce thinly sliced ham, cut into ribbons; 1 teaspoon Dijon mustard whisked into the cream, plus 1 teaspoon spread onto the toasted muffin; ½ cup shredded gruyère cheese.
- ¼ cup medium salsa; 1 tablespoon chopped fresh cilantro; ¼ cup drained canned pinto beans; ½ cup crumbled queso fresco.
- 1 teaspoon pesto whisked into the cream; 2 drained and minced oil-packed sun-dried tomatoes; ½ cup crumbled goat cheese; 2 teaspoons freshly grated parmesan cheese.
- 2 to 3 ounces fresh spinach, lightly wilted, seasoned with salt and pepper, squeezed dry, and chopped; ½ cup ¼-inch slices of cooked chicken sausage.

POACHING EGGS

  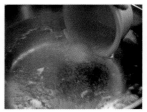 

Bring a pan of water to a very strong simmer and add about 2 tablespoons white vinegar. Gently slip the egg from a cup into the water; with a spoon, nudge the whites to help them gather around the yolk. If cooking multiple eggs, you may need to raise the heat a bit, because adding cold eggs will lower the temperature of the water.

(any flavor); ½ cup shredded fontina cheese.

- 2 marinated artichoke heart quarters, chopped; 1 chopped roasted red pepper from a jar; ½ cup shredded fontina cheese.
- 1 ounce cold-smoked salmon or lox, cut into bite-size pieces; 1 teaspoon drained capers; 1 teaspoon minced red onion, sautéed in olive oil until soft; ¼ cup crème fraîche (you'll still add the ¼ cup cream from the master recipe); no cheese in this one.

— From Martha Holmberg and the Foodday Test Kitchen

DENVER BREAKFAST BAKE

MAKES 6 TO 8 SERVINGS

This egg dish takes the traditional Denver omelet ingredients and bakes them with bread in a savory custard. Not only is it a good way to use leftover artisan bread, it's a smart recipe for entertaining, since it can be made the night before and refrigerated until it's time to bake.

2 tablespoons butter or olive oil
¾ cup diced onion
1½ cups julienne-cut mixed red and green bell peppers
1 tablespoon minced garlic
8 eggs
3 cups half-and-half
1 teaspoon salt
¼ teaspoon freshly ground black pepper
8 cups cubed (1-inch) artisan-style bread
1½ cups julienne-cut ham
2 cups shredded cheddar cheese (8 ounces)
½ cup grated parmesan cheese

In large sauté pan, heat butter over medium-high heat. Add onion and peppers and sauté about 4 minutes. Add garlic and cook 30 seconds more. Remove from heat and set aside.

In large bowl, whisk together eggs, half-and-half, salt, and pepper until well-combined. Add bread, ham, cheddar cheese, and half the parmesan cheese. Place in a buttered 11-by-13-inch baking pan (use a 9-by-13-inch plus an 8-inch if you don't have a larger pan). Sprinkle remaining ¼ cup parmesan cheese over top. Cover and refrigerate at least 1 hour or preferably overnight so that bread soaks up egg mixture.

When ready to serve, preheat oven to 350 degrees and bake until puffy and golden, and knife inserted in center comes out clean, 45 to 50 minutes.

— From Kathy Casey Food Studios, www.kathycasey.com

PLAY IT SAFE WITH GLASS BAKING DISHES

Glassware can be a great choice for some recipes (it's our favorite for pies), but breakage can occur with sudden temperature changes and impact. Be sure to follow these precautions with any glass baking dish:

- Always place hot glass bakeware on a dry, cloth potholder or towel—never on top of the stove, on a metal trivet, on a damp towel, directly on a counter or in a sink.
- Never put glass bakeware directly on a burner or under a broiler.
- Always allow the oven to fully preheat before placing glass bakeware in the oven.
- Add a small amount of liquid sufficient to cover the bottom of the dish prior to cooking foods that may release liquid. Never add liquid to the hot pan.

DRIED APRICOT AND CHERRY GRANOLA

MAKES ABOUT 18 CUPS

After former test kitchen director Linda Faus gave bags of this granola to staffers at Christmas, we were hooked. The magical mixture of several kinds of seeds and nuts, combined with the tart dried fruit and sweet coconut, makes a blissful breakfast. Don't try substituting quick-cooking or instant oatmeal, because it just won't be as good.

- 6 cups old-fashioned oatmeal, uncooked
- 1 cup wheat germ
- 1 cup shredded sweetened coconut
- 1 cup toasted almonds, chopped (see note)
- 1 cup toasted pecans, chopped (see note)
- 1 cup sunflower kernels
- 1 cup toasted sesame seeds (see note)
- 1 cup pumpkin seed kernels
- 1 cup firmly packed brown sugar
- 1 teaspoon ground cinnamon
- ½ teaspoon kosher salt
- ¾ cup honey
- ½ cup vegetable oil
- 1½ cups chopped dried apricots
- 1½ cups chopped dried tart cherries

Preheat oven to 325 degrees.

In a large bowl, stir together the oatmeal, wheat germ, coconut, almonds, pecans, sunflower kernels, sesame seeds, pumpkin seeds, brown sugar, cinnamon, and salt. In a small bowl, whisk together the honey and oil. Pour the honey mixture over the oat mixture; stir until all of the dry mixture is coated with the honey and oil. Spread onto 2 large rimmed baking sheets and bake for 45 minutes, stirring 3 or 4 times. Stir in the dried apricots and cherries and bake for another 15 minutes, stirring once. Remove from oven and let cool, stirring occasionally while cooling.

Note: To toast nuts, spread on baking sheet and bake in 350-degree oven for 5 to 8 minutes, or until they start to brown. To toast seeds, bake for 3 to 5 minutes or until slightly brown.

To store: Granola will keep for up to 2 weeks in an air-tight container before it begins to go stale. Or transfer to a zip-top freezer bag and freeze up to 6 months.

— From Linda Faus

CHERRY SCONES

MAKES 8 SCONES

This is an adaptation of an old English recipe for cream scones. It's the style of scone where the fruit sits in cluster on top of the pastry, rather than being dispersed throughout.

- 2 cups all-purpose flour
- ⅓ cup granulated sugar
- 2 teaspoons baking powder
- ⅛ teaspoon salt
- ⅓ cup chilled unsalted butter
- 2 eggs (divided)
- 1 teaspoon vanilla
- ½ cup whipping cream
- ½ cup fresh or frozen tart cherries, pitted (thawed, if using frozen)
- Approximately 2 tablespoons raw sugar

Preheat oven to 375 degrees.

In a large bowl, combine flour, sugar, baking powder, and salt. Cut the butter into small cubes and, with a pastry blender, mix them into the flour mixture until the mixture resembles coarse crumbs. In a small bowl, beat 1 egg with the vanilla and cream. Add the cream mixture to the flour mixture. Stir until combined, but don't overmix.

Knead dough gently a few times on a lightly floured surface. Shape into a circle approximately 7 inches wide and 1½ inches thick. Carefully cut into 8 wedges. Place scones on a lightly greased baking sheet or parchment paper-covered baking sheet. Make a small indentation in the center of each scone. Place approximately 1 tablespoon cherries in the indentation. Beat remaining egg and brush it on the scones, avoiding the cherries. Sprinkle with raw sugar. Bake for 15 to 18 minutes, or until lightly browned.

— From Delphina's Neighborhood Baking Co.

BLUEBERRY-CORNMEAL SCONES

MAKES 8 SCONES

Cornmeal adds a bit of toothsome crunch to these scones. For optimum tenderness, avoid overworking the dough.

2 cups all-purpose flour
⅓ cup cornmeal
⅓ cup granulated sugar
2 tablespoons baking powder
½ cup butter (1 stick)
2 eggs, plus 1 egg white (divided)
½ cup whipping cream
1 cup fresh or frozen blueberries, thawed and drained if frozen

Preheat oven to 350 degrees.

In a large bowl, combine flour, cornmeal, sugar, and baking powder. Cut in butter with a pastry blender until mixture is crumbly. Beat 2 whole eggs with cream. Add egg mixture to flour mixture; stir gently until the dough is uniform and completely mixed. Fold in blueberries. Place dough on lightly floured surface. Shape into a circle approximately 6 inches wide and 2 inches thick. Cut into 8 wedges. Place scones on a lightly greased baking sheet. Beat egg white and brush on scones. Bake for 15 minutes or until golden brown on top.

— From Three Lions Bakery

MAC BRAN MUFFINS

MAKES ABOUT 24 MUFFINS

This was one of Foodday's top ten "Restaurant Requests" from 1992. The original recipe calls for egg substitute, but we also provide a measurement for real eggs. Be sure to allow batter to sit overnight to allow bran to absorb liquid.

1½ cups firmly packed brown sugar
⅓ cup vegetable oil
2 eggs plus 1 egg white (or ⅔ cup liquid egg substitute)
1 tablespoon light molasses
1¼ cups buttermilk
3½ cups all-purpose flour

2 teaspoons baking soda

1 tablespoon baking powder

3 cups wheat bran

1 (15¼-ounce) can juice-packed crushed pineapple, including juice

1¾ cups warm water

In a large mixing bowl, combine brown sugar, oil, egg substitute, molasses, and buttermilk. In another bowl, mix flour, baking soda, and baking powder. Add flour mixture to large mixing bowl and stir lightly.

Mix in wheat bran and undrained pineapple. Pour warm water over top and stir just until mixed. Do not overmix. Refrigerate overnight or up to 24 hours to give bran time to absorb liquid.

The next day, preheat oven to 350 degrees.

Fill lightly greased muffin tins or paper-lined tins three-quarters full. Bake 22 to 25 minutes or until lightly browned.

— From Multnomah Athletic Club

PUMPKIN MUFFINS

MAKES 18 LARGE MUFFINS

Oregon no longer has an Il Fornaio location, but while this Italian restaurant and bakery existed on Northwest 23rd Avenue, Portlanders loved its hearth-baked breads and baked goods. This was one of them.

3 tablespoons butter, softened

2½ cups firmly packed brown sugar

1 (16-ounce) can pumpkin

¾ cup vegetable oil

3 eggs

½ teaspoon vanilla extract

½ teaspoon grated lemon zest

3½ cups all-purpose flour

¼ teaspoon salt

1 teaspoon baking soda

1 teaspoon ground cinnamon

¼ teaspoon ground nutmeg

¼ teaspoon ground cloves

1 cup chopped walnuts

½ cup raisins

Preheat oven to 350 degrees. Grease muffin tins or line with paper liners.

In a large bowl, combine the butter with the brown sugar until no lumps of butter can be seen. Stir in the pumpkin, oil, eggs, vanilla, and lemon zest.

In another large bowl, sift the flour with the salt, baking soda, cinnamon, nutmeg, and cloves. Stir the walnuts and raisins into the flour. Add the flour mixture to the pumpkin and gently combine. Fill the prepared muffin cups two-thirds full and bake for 25 to 30 minutes, or until a toothpick inserted in the center comes out clean. Remove from pans and cool on a wire rack.

— From Il Fornaio

EGGS: HOW OLD IS OLD?

The date on an egg carton is the last day the eggs can be sold at the supermarket. They should be OK to use a week or two beyond that date. To check the freshness of an egg, place it in a glass of water: if the egg floats, it's starting to go bad and should not be used; if it sinks, it's safe to cook and use. Instead of transferring raw eggs to a holder in the refrigerator door, store them in the carton they came in. This will keep them cooler, and prevent them from losing moisture and absorbing odors.

BLUEBERRY BUCKLE COFFEECAKE

MAKES 9 TO 12 SERVINGS

Is this a true buckle (defined as a single-layer cake made with blueberries)? Or is it a coffee-cake? No matter what you call it, we can't think of a better way to start a Sunday morning.

STREUSEL TOPPING:
½ cup granulated sugar
½ cup all-purpose flour
⅓ cup quick-cooking or old-fashioned oatmeal, uncooked
½ teaspoon ground cinnamon
⅛ teaspoon ground nutmeg
⅓ cup butter

CAKE:
1½ cups all-purpose flour
1 cup quick-cooking or old-fashioned oatmeal, uncooked
2½ teaspoons baking powder
¼ teaspoon salt
½ cup butter
½ cup granulated sugar

1 egg
⅔ cup milk
2 cups fresh or frozen blueberries (do not thaw if frozen)
2 tablespoons lemon juice

To make topping: In medium bowl, combine sugar, flour, oatmeal, cinnamon, and nutmeg. Cut in butter until mixture is crumbly; set aside.

To make batter: Preheat oven to 350 degrees. Grease an 11-by-7-inch baking dish. In medium bowl, combine flour, oatmeal, baking powder, and salt; set aside.

In a large bowl, beat together butter and sugar; blend in egg. Add flour mixture alternately with milk, mixing until well-blended. Spread into prepared pan.

Toss blueberries with lemon juice; sprinkle over batter. Sprinkle streusel topping evenly over blueberries.

Bake 55 to 60 minutes. Serve warm.

CINNAMON BUNS FROM HEAVEN

MAKES 12 LARGE ROLLS

This recipe from Bend resident Nicki Cross was first published in Fooddday in 1992. Since then it's appeared in our section five more times, and was also selected to grace the cover of The Best American Recipes 2000, by Fran McCullough and Suzanne Hamlin.

Nicki uses an 11-by-15-inch Wilton pan to make 12 rolls. If you do not have that size pan, you will need to use 2 pans: 9-by-13-inch and 8-inch square.

DOUGH:
2 packages active dry yeast (4½ teaspoons)
1 cup warm water (110 to 115 degrees)
⅔ cup plus 1 teaspoon granulated sugar (divided)
1 cup warm milk
⅔ cup butter
2 teaspoons salt
2 eggs, lightly beaten
7 to 8 cups all-purpose or bread flour, or more if needed

FILLING:

1 cup melted butter (2 sticks; divided)

1¾ cups granulated sugar (divided)

3 tablespoons ground cinnamon

1½ cups chopped walnuts (optional)

1½ cups raisins (optional)

CREAMY GLAZE:

⅔ cup butter, melted

4 cups powdered sugar

2 teaspoons vanilla extract

4 to 8 tablespoons hot water

To make dough: In a cup, stir together the yeast, warm water, and 1 teaspoon sugar; set aside.

In a large bowl, mix warm milk, remaining ⅔ cup sugar, butter, salt, and eggs; stir well and add yeast mixture. Add half the flour and beat until smooth. Stir in enough of the remaining flour to make a slightly stiff dough (dough will be sticky).

Turn out onto a well-floured board and knead 5 to 10 minutes, or until dough is smooth and elastic.

Place in a well-buttered glass or plastic bowl, cover, and let rise until doubled in bulk in a warm place, free from drafts, about 1 to 1½ hours. When doubled, punch down dough; let rest 5 minutes. Roll out on floured surface into a 15-by-20-inch rectangle.

To make filling: Spread dough with ½ cup melted butter. Mix together 1½ cups sugar and the cinnamon. Sprinkle over buttered dough. Sprinkle with walnuts and raisins.

Roll up jellyroll-fashion and pinch edges together to seal. Cut into 12 slices. Use remaining ½ cup melted butter to coat the bottom of a 9-by-13-inch baking pan and an 8-inch-square pan. Sprinkle remaining ¼ cup sugar over the butter. Place slices close together in pans.

Let rise in warm place until dough is doubled in bulk, about 45 minutes.

Preheat oven to 350 degrees.

Bake for 25 to 30 minutes, or until nicely browned. Let cool slightly, then spread with glaze.

To make glaze: Mix melted butter, powdered sugar, and vanilla; add hot water 1 tablespoon at a time until glaze is of desired spreading consistency. Spread over slightly cooled rolls.

— From Nicki Cross

RICH, HOT ORANGE ROLLS

MAKES ABOUT 32 ROLLS

Former Foodday home economist Sharon Maasdam is renowned for her baking. And when she gets together with family or friends, they often request these orange rolls. If you prefer, you can use half whole-wheat and half white flour, and substitute honey or brown sugar for granulated sugar.

ROLLS:

¾ cup milk

½ cup butter, at room temperature (1 stick)

½ cup granulated sugar

1 teaspoon salt

2 packages active dry yeast

½ cup warm water (110 to 115 degrees)

4¼ to 4½ cups bread or all-purpose flour

2 eggs, at room temperature

217

FILLING:

⅔ cup butter, at room temperature
1 cup granulated sugar
4 teaspoons grated orange zest

To make rolls: Warm milk and add to a large bowl with butter, sugar and salt. Cool to lukewarm.

Sprinkle yeast on warm water and stir to dissolve.

Add 1½ cups flour to milk mixture; beat well by hand or with an electric mixer at low speed about 1 minute. Beat in eggs and yeast mixture. Gradually stir in enough remaining flour, a little at a time, to make a soft dough that leaves the sides of the bowl.

Turn onto lightly floured board; knead until smooth, satiny and no longer sticky, 5 to 8 minutes.

Place in a lightly greased bowl, then turn dough to grease top. Cover and let rise in warm place until doubled, about 1 hour. Meanwhile, make filling.

To make filling: Mix butter, sugar and orange zest together.

Punch dough down and let rest for 10 minutes. Divide the dough in half. Roll each half into a 16-by-8-inch rectangle. Divide filling between the two rectangles and roll lengthwise as for jellyroll; seal edges. Cut in 1-inch slices. Place, cut side down, into greased muffin tins. Cover and let rise until doubled, about 30 to 40 minutes.

Preheat oven to 375 degrees. Bake rolls for 15 to 20 minutes. If using dark muffin tins, place on a baking sheet the last 10 minutes of baking. Cool a few minutes in pans, then invert onto rack.

— Adapted from *Homemade Bread*, by the food editors of *Farm Journal*

AEBLESKIVERS

MAKES ABOUT 30 PANCAKES (4 TO 6 SERVINGS)

Aebleskivers (eh-bleh-SKEE-vors) are the irresistible Danish pancake balls that can be filled with almost anything, from applesauce to gruyère cheese. You'll need either a traditional cast-iron aebleskiver pan, or one of the newer nonstick pans, which eliminate the need for greasing. If you use a cast-iron pan, don't substitute butter or oil for the shortening. The shortening not only keeps the pancakes from sticking, but gives them a crisper shell than oil would and doesn't burn as easily as butter.

We've included two methods for cooking them, one of which is easier for beginners, or for adding a filling. The other method gives you a slightly hollow ball, which is nice for filling with berries, jam or whipped cream at the table.

4 eggs, separated
1¾ cups buttermilk
¼ cup granulated sugar
2 cups all-purpose flour
2 teaspoons baking powder
1 teaspoon baking soda
1 teaspoon salt
¼ cup butter, melted
Vegetable shortening, for cooking
    in cast-iron pan
Optional garnishes: powdered sugar, puréed
    sweetened strawberries (frozen are fine)
    or jam of your choice, whipped cream

In a large bowl, beat egg yolks. Add buttermilk and sugar. In a separate bowl sift flour with baking powder, baking soda and salt. Add to egg mixture and stir in melted butter. In a clean bowl, beat egg whites until very stiff and gently fold into batter.

Heat aebleskiver pan over medium-low heat. When it's hot, spoon a tiny bit (less than ¼ teaspoon) of shortening into each cup. Tilt and turn pan so that the melted shortening coats each cup. Fill and cook using either of the two following methods:

To make solid balls: Fill each mold with batter. As the bottom of each pancake turns golden brown, use a skewer to flip it over. If you want to add a filling, start with a generous tablespoon of batter to each mold, followed by a teaspoon of filling, followed by another tablespoon of batter. Cook on both sides until golden brown, and a skewer inserted into center comes out without any clinging wet batter. Monitor heat carefully: If baked too fast, the pancakes will burn on the outside before the batter on the inside is cooked.

To make hollow balls: Fill cups almost full with batter and allow to cook undisturbed for about 30 seconds. Then, use a skewer to peek at the undersides of the pancakes; when each is golden brown, give it a quarter turn by poking it with a skewer and pulling upward and allowing the uncooked batter to flow down into the cup. Continue rotating each pancake by quarter turns until you have a complete ball. Test for doneness by sticking a skewer into the center of a ball: If it comes out with wet batter, continue to cook and turn, so that one side doesn't get a lot browner than the other. Monitor heat carefully: If baked too fast, the pancakes will burn on the outside before the batter on the inside is cooked.

Note that subsequent batches will not need as much shortening to grease the pan as the first batch. Keep pancakes warm in a low oven as you finish cooking all the batter.

If desired, dust with powdered sugar and serve with puréed sweetened strawberries or your favorite jam, and whipped cream.

MAKING HOLLOW AEBLESKIVERS

A ¼-cup measuring cup is handy for filling the aebleskiver pan cups. After bottoms have browned, use a skewer to pull the half-round up a quarter turn, allowing the uncooked batter to fill in behind it. After the fresh batter is set, give the partial ball another quarter turn. Repeat until you have a complete ball, turning frequently until it's is nicely browned and tests cooked on the inside with a skewer.

OATMEAL PANCAKES WITH WALNUT BUTTER

MAKES 2 TO 4 SERVINGS

Although weekday mornings can be hectic, the flavored butter and a portion of the batter for this recipe are made ahead, and both will keep in the refrigerator for several days.

PANCAKES:

2 cups old-fashioned oatmeal, uncooked
2½ cups buttermilk
2 eggs, lightly beaten
¼ cup melted butter or vegetable oil
½ cup all-purpose flour
1 teaspoon baking soda
1 teaspoon baking powder
½ teaspoon salt
2 tablespoons granulated sugar
½ cup firmly packed brown sugar

WALNUT BUTTER:

1 cup butter, softened (2 sticks; see note)
¼ cup granulated sugar
¼ cup firmly packed brown sugar
½ cup chopped walnuts, toasted (see note)
½ teaspoon vanilla extract
¼ teaspoon walnut extract (optional; see note)

To make pancakes: In a medium bowl, combine the oatmeal and buttermilk. Cover and refrigerate overnight.

The next day, add eggs and butter to oatmeal mixture and stir to combine. In a separate bowl, sift together the flour, baking soda, baking powder, and salt. Stir the sugars into the flour mixture; add to the oatmeal mixture and mix to combine, but do not overmix. Heat griddle, but make sure it's not too hot as it takes time for the oatmeal to cook; a little lower is better. Lightly spray the griddle with nonstick cooking spray. Cook pancakes until golden brown on both sides. Serve with Walnut Butter.

To make butter: The night before, combine the butter, sugars, walnuts, vanilla, and walnut extract, if using. Refrigerate overnight to allow flavors to combine. You can freeze any leftovers. Makes 1½ cups.

Note: To toast nuts, spread on baking sheet and bake in 350-degree oven for 5 to 8 minutes or until they start to brown.

Note: Walnut extract is available at The Decorette Shop (see Resources chapter) or from online retailers.

NOTES ON OATS

Many recipes call for "rolled oats." Those can be "old-fashioned oatmeal" or "quick-cooking oatmeal," since both are whole oat groats that are steamed and rolled to flatten them into flakes. Both types contain all parts of the oat grain, including the bran, endosperm, and germ portion. Quick-cooking oatmeal is simply cut into slightly smaller, thinner pieces so they cook faster.

According to Quaker Oats, these oatmeals can be used interchangeably in most recipes. If you want distinct grains in chewy baked goods, such as a hearty bread, muffins, or cookies, use the old-fashioned variety. Quick-cooking oats tend to blend in with the other ingredients in a recipe. Don't use instant oatmeal unless a recipe calls for it because it absorbs too much liquid and will make your dish mushy.

Make ahead: The batter keeps well for days in the refrigerator, at least a week and a half. You may need to thin it out a little with more buttermilk before cooking the pancakes. The butter can be made and refrigerated up to a week in advance.

— From Morning Glory restaurant, Ashland

DAVID EYRE'S PANCAKE (DUTCH BABY-STYLE)

MAKES 2 TO 4 SERVINGS

Eyre was from a well-known Oregon pioneer family and an editor at the *Oregon Journal*, Portland's afternoon paper. His recipe was popularized more than forty years ago by Craig Claiborne in the *New York Times*, although Eyre credited it to *The St. Francis Hotel Cookbook*, published in 1919. He said he used a heavy aluminum pan, "which results in a delicate texture. An iron frying pan produces a texture more like a popover, but glass baking dishes work fine, too. You can be inventive. You can leave out the nutmeg, lemon, and powdered sugar and have a fine 'shell' for savory fillings. And try it as a dessert pancake by adding peaches or strawberries or other fruits at the very last moment. Or slosh the basic pancake with Cointreau, Triple Sec, dark rum, or whatever you find in the liquor cabinet."

½ cup all-purpose flour
½ cup milk
2 eggs, lightly beaten
Pinch of ground nutmeg (optional)
¼ cup butter
2 tablespoons powdered sugar (optional)
Juice of half a lemon (optional)

Preheat oven to 425 degrees.

In a mixing bowl, combine flour, milk, eggs and nutmeg. Beat lightly. Leave the batter a little lumpy.

Melt the butter in a 12-inch skillet with heatproof handle. Pour in batter and bake 15 to 20 minutes, or until the pancake is golden brown.

Sprinkle with sugar and return to the oven for a minute or two. Sprinkle with lemon juice, then serve with preserves or fresh fruit.

— *The New York Times*

APPLE PUFFED PANCAKE

MAKES 6 TO 8 SERVINGS

This oven-baked "pancake" is much deeper than David Eyre's Dutch baby, and has a very custardy texture. And with the sliced apples and cinnamon, it almost qualifies as dessert.

6 eggs
1½ cups milk
1 cup all-purpose flour
3 tablespoons granulated sugar
1 teaspoon vanilla extract
½ teaspoon salt
¼ teaspoon ground cinnamon
½ cup butter (1 stick)
2 apples, peeled and thinly sliced
2 to 3 tablespoons firmly packed brown sugar

Preheat oven to 425 degrees.

In a blender or large bowl, mix eggs, milk, flour, sugar, vanilla, salt, and cinnamon until blended. (If using an electric mixer, batter will remain slightly lumpy.)

In the oven, melt butter in a 12-inch fluted porcelain quiche dish or a 9-by-13-inch baking dish; add apple slices and return to oven until butter sizzles. Do not let it brown. Remove dish from oven and immediately pour batter over apples. Sprinkle with brown sugar.

Bake in middle of oven 20 minutes or until puffed and brown. Serve immediately.

— From *Cooking for Entertaining*, by Marlene Sorosky (HP Trade)

IRONING OUT WAFFLE ISSUES

If your waffles are sticking to your waffle iron, there may be more than one reason.

Using nonstick cooking spray: This spray becomes too hot when preheated, causing the lecithin in the spray to burn and leaving a sticky residue. Remove this residue by thoroughly washing the grids. If that doesn't work, make a paste of baking soda and water and brush it on the grids. Let the paste dry, then brush off. Coat the grids with vegetable oil, heat the iron and make a waffle, then discard it. Before making your first waffle, use a pastry brush with natural—not plastic—bristles and brush the grids with a light coating of vegetable oil. You don't need to repeat this procedure unless the waffles start sticking again.

Insufficient heat: Waffles also stick if the iron is not hot enough when you add batter. Check waffles for doneness when steam stops coming out the sides of the waffle iron—that means they're cooked through.

Too little fat or too much sugar in the batter: You may need to adjust your recipe by either adding a little more fat, or cutting back on the sugar.

SAUCES, DRESSINGS, AND CONDIMENTS

12

WARM DIPPING SAUCE OF OLIVE OIL, RED ONION, BLUE CHEESE, AND BALSAMIC VINEGAR

MAKES ABOUT 10 SERVINGS (3 TABLESPOONS EACH)

Even if you're short on time, you don't have to fall back on humdrum nuts or chips for an hors d'oeuvre. This brilliant dipping sauce is incredibly easy to make, or, if you prefer, you can do most of the work several hours ahead. And the recipe can easily be increased.

> 1 cup extra-virgin olive oil
> 1 cup finely chopped red onion
> ⅓ cup coarsely chopped kalamata olives
> 2 tablespoons balsamic vinegar
> 4 ounces crumbled blue cheese
> 1 good-quality baguette, cut into ¼-inch slices

In skillet, heat the olive oil over medium heat. Add onion and sauté gently until it softens, about 5 to 7 minutes. Stir in olives and vinegar; remove from heat and let cool slightly.

When ready to serve, crumble the blue cheese into the warm sauce. Stir gently, making sure that most of the cheese remains in identifiable chunks (that will soften as the sauce sits).

Pour the sauce into a shallow container, or individual plates, and serve immediately with baguette slices for dipping.

Make ahead: After stirring in the olives and vinegar, and allowing to cool slightly, cover and refrigerate up to several days ahead. Warm the mixture just before serving and stir in cheese as directed.

— From Jan Roberts-Dominguez

KNOW YOUR BALSAMIC VINEGAR

We're fans of balsamic vinegar, but we like to use it selectively, when it will add an accent of brightness and depth. Used thoughtlessly, balsamic's sweetness can be cloying; for a basic vinaigrette, we prefer to use a lighter red wine vinegar or sherry vinegar. If you have a really top-notch balsamic, like 10-year-old Lucini Gran Riserva, use it like a condiment and drizzle it on:

- Simply prepared flaky fish, such as halibut
- Steamed or roasted green vegetables, such as green beans or asparagus
- Perfectly ripe strawberries
- Vanilla ice cream
- Hunks of Parmigiano-Reggiano cheese
- Slices of pork loin or pork tenderloin

Use less expensive balsamic when you're adding lots of other strongly flavored ingredients to things such as:

- Marinades for grilled beef, pork, chicken, salmon, or mushrooms
- Savory-sweet jams or caramelized onions
- Pan sauces for richer cuts of pork or beef

SOUR CREAM-SCALLION BUTTER

MAKES ¾ CUP

¡Oba! on Northwest 12th Avenue serves this spread with the bread that's brought to your table, but we found that it also makes a very good topping for mashed potatoes or even mild white fish.

½ cup butter, softened (1 stick)
2 teaspoons roasted garlic (see note)
½ teaspoon minced fresh garlic
2 tablespoons sour cream
Scant ¼ teaspoon chili powder
Pinch chipotle chili powder
½ teaspoon kosher salt
1 small scallion, thinly sliced
2 tablespoons minced fresh cilantro

In a small bowl, combine the butter, roasted garlic, and fresh garlic; whip with an electric mixer until creamy. Add the sour cream, chili powders, and salt, and whip at high speed until very fluffy. Add the scallion and cilantro and whip again until well-mixed and fluffy. Refrigerate until ready to serve. Bring to room temperature before serving.

Note: To roast a whole head of garlic, peel away the excess papery skin and cut a thin slice off the top to expose some of the cloves. Drizzle top with 1 teaspoon olive oil. Wrap in foil and bake at 375 degrees for about 45 minutes, or until soft. Cool.

— From executive chef Scott Neuman, ¡Oba!

BOURBON-BROWN SUGAR SALAD DRESSING

MAKES 1½ CUPS

Bima, which once was part of the Northwest Portland restaurant scene, served this wonderfully sweet-and-tangy dressing on a spinach salad. The nip of bourbon gives it complexity, but not enough to make it taste boozy.

5 tablespoons plus 1 teaspoon firmly packed brown sugar
2 tablespoons plus 2 teaspoons molasses
1 tablespoon bourbon
¼ cup balsamic vinegar
1 cup olive oil
Salt

In a small bowl or a food processor or blender, mix the brown sugar, molasses, bourbon, and balsamic vinegar. Slowly whisk in the olive oil. (If using a food processor or blender, slowly pour the olive oil into the vinegar mixture with the machine running.) The dressing should be dark brown and thick. Taste and add salt as needed. Chill and serve.

— From chef Margot Leonard, Bima Restaurant

HONEY-MUSTARD SALAD DRESSING WITH TARRAGON

MAKES 2 CUPS

This dressing, from the family-run restaurant called Perry's, first ran in Foodday in our "Restaurant Requests" column. Our recipe tester's family liked it so much they used it as a dip for chicken as well as a dressing.

1 cup mayonnaise
¼ cup Dijon mustard
1 tablespoon German-style coarse-grain mustard (see note)
¼ cup buttermilk
6 tablespoons honey
2¼ teaspoons dried tarragon
¾ teaspoon prepared horseradish

In a medium bowl, combine mayonnaise, Dijon and coarse-grain mustards, buttermilk, honey, tarragon, and horseradish; stir until smooth. Refrigerate until ready to use.

Note: Perry's uses Inglehoffer brand mustard.

— From Perry's on Fremont

ZUCCHINI PESTO

MAKES 2 CUPS

Where there is zucchini, there are often bushels of basil, too. Combine the two, and you've got a deliciously different pesto. Zucchini lends creaminess and body to this sauce, transforming the basil paste into something tastier and a little less rich. It's a great sauce for grilled fish, as a dressing for a white bean and zucchini salad or drizzled over a salad of heirloom tomatoes and fresh mozzarella.

½ cup plus 1 tablespoon extra-virgin olive oil (divided)
1 large shallot, peeled and sliced (⅔ cup)
6 medium garlic cloves, chopped
3 tablespoons almond slivers, toasted (see note)
1 medium zucchini, cut into ½-inch dice (7 ounces)
1 cup firmly packed fresh basil leaves
2 teaspoons lemon juice

Heat 1 tablespoon oil in a medium sauté pan over medium-low heat. Add the shallot and cook until softened but not browned, about 4 minutes. Add the garlic and sauté until fragrant, 45 seconds. Transfer the shallots and garlic to a blender and add the almonds, zucchini, basil and lemon juice. With the blender running, slowly add the remaining 1/2 cup olive oil, stopping to stir the ingredients occasionally. Blend until smooth and season with salt and pepper.

Note: To toast nuts, spread on baking sheet and bake in 350-degree oven for 5 to 8 minutes or until they start to brown.

Make Ahead: Sauce can be made and refrigerated for up to one week, or frozen for up to two months (re-blend once defrosted to regain the creamy texture).

—From Ivy Manning

TOMATO RELISH

MAKES 4 CUPS

If you like ketchup with your eggs, you'll love this relish. Grand Central Bakery serves it on its bacon-and-egg sandwich, which takes it from basic to bold. The relish keeps for several weeks, so you can always have it on hand for Sunday breakfast.

¼ cup sliced sun-dried tomatoes (dry-packed, not oil-packed)
¼ cup olive oil
1 large white onion, diced
1 large leek, diced
1 (28-ounce) can diced tomatoes (Grand Central uses Muir Glen brand), drained, juices reserved
2 tablespoons firmly packed brown sugar
3 tablespoons balsamic vinegar
1 tablespoon kosher salt

In a small bowl, cover the sun-dried tomatoes with boiling water. Let sit until soft, about 10 minutes. Drain, reserving the soaking liquid, and purée in a food processor. Add a little of the soaking liquid if the purée is too stiff. Set aside.

In a large skillet, heat the olive oil over medium-high heat. Add the onion and cook until it begins to caramelize, about 10 minutes. Turn heat down and add diced leek. Cook until leek is tender, 6 to 8 minutes longer.

Combine the reserved juice from the canned tomatoes with the sun-dried tomato purée. Add to the onion-leek mixture in the pan, and turn up the heat, stirring until the liquid evaporates.

Add brown sugar, balsamic vinegar, and salt. Reduce the heat to low; cook until the sugar and salt are dissolved. Remove from heat, cool, and stir in uncooked canned diced tomatoes. Adjust seasoning to taste.

Make ahead: Relish can be made and stored covered in the refrigerator for up to 4 weeks, or frozen for up to 6 months.

— Adapted from Grand Central Bakery

CLEANING LEEKS

Leeks are related to onions and as such, they have many layers. But unlike onions, leeks are great at trapping dirt. We use two methods for cleaning them:

- If your recipe calls for slices, trim off the dark green portion and the root, and slice crosswise to desired thickness. Then, add to a bowl of cold water, and swish and separate the slices so that the dirt falls to the bottom of the bowl. Scoop the slices out of the bowl and drain in a colander.
- If you require whole leeks, trim off the dark green portion and the root hairs, but leave a little of the root end intact to hold the layers together. Then, make a deep incision down the length of the leek so that you can gently spread the leaves open and rinse well.

KETCHUP

MAKES 3½ CUPS

Think ketchup is ketchup? Not after you've had Bread and Ink Cafe's housemade ketchup, deeply flavored with eight spices, onions, brown sugar, and cider vinegar. Just don't try this with out-of-season or mediocre tomatoes. In fact, you may want to do what the restaurant does and use good-quality canned tomatoes.

2 (28-ounce) cans tomatoes in purée (or
    3½ to 4 pounds fresh)
2 medium onions, coarsely chopped
1 teaspoon whole allspice
1 teaspoon whole cloves
1 teaspoon celery seeds
1 teaspoon peppercorns
1 teaspoon whole coriander seeds
¼ teaspoon ground mace
½ stick cinnamon
½ bay leaf
1⅓ cups firmly packed brown sugar
1 cup apple cider vinegar
1½ teaspoons salt

In a food processor, process the tomatoes and onions until smooth. In a square of cheesecloth, tie up the allspice, cloves, celery seeds, peppercorns, coriander, mace, cinnamon, and bay leaf. Place the tomato mixture in a heavy-bottomed nonreactive pot and add the cheesecloth bag, brown sugar, and vinegar. Bring to a boil, reduce heat to a slow simmer, and cook, stirring often, until thickened and just beginning to turn shiny, about 3½ hours.

If the ketchup sticks to the bottom of the pan, check carefully to see if it is actually beginning to burn; if it is, remove the ketchup to a bowl and clean the pan. Return the ketchup to the clean pan and continue simmering.

When ketchup is thick, dark, and shiny, remove the cheesecloth bag, squeezing it against the side of the pan to remove juices. Stir in the salt. Refrigerate until ready to serve.

— From Bread and Ink Cafe

CAPRIAL PENCE'S ROASTED TOMATO SAUCE

MAKES ABOUT 2 CUPS

Chefs Caprial Pence and her husband, John, have been part of Portland's dining scene since the early '90s, running Caprial's Bistro, publishing several cookbooks and producing successful television programs, including "Caprial and John's Kitchen." The Pences like to serve this sauce not only on pasta, but over grilled polenta with gorgonzola, and as a base for tomato soup.

½ cup olive oil
1 tablespoon chopped fresh herbs (such
    as basil, rosemary and thyme)
½ teaspoon coarsely ground black pepper
1 rib celery, chopped
1 carrot, chopped
1 small onion, chopped
5 cloves garlic, peeled
1½ to 2 pounds fresh tomatoes, cored
¼ cup balsamic vinegar

➤➤

1 teaspoon salt
Freshly ground black pepper
Preheat oven to 475 degrees.

Preheat oven to 475 degrees. In a 7½-by-11-inch roasting pan, place the oil, herbs, pepper, celery, carrot, onion, and garlic cloves. Place the cored tomatoes on top of the vegetables and roast until the tops of the tomatoes are brown, about 45 minutes.

In a food processor, purée the mixture until smooth. Add the vinegar and blend. Season with salt and pepper to taste. Bring to a simmer if using immediately, or to reduce the sauce to the desired consistency. Refrigerate if not using immediately.

Make ahead: This sauce can be made and refrigerated for up to 1 week or frozen for up to 6 months. Seasonings may need to be adjusted if frozen.

—Adapted from *Caprial's Cafe Favorites* by Caprial Pence

ZESTY LEMON BASTING SAUCE

MAKES ABOUT 1 CUP

Although Amanda Stanko first created this sauce for a chicken-grilling contest, it also would be delicious on pork chops, or even seafood. You won't use a lot of limoncello liqueur, but it keeps indefinitely and is nice to have on hand for other recipes.

1½ teaspoons grated lemon zest
⅓ cup fresh lemon juice
¼ cup Dijon mustard
2 tablespoons peeled and minced fresh ginger
2 tablespoons minced fresh rosemary
2 tablespoons minced fresh garlic
2 tablespoons limoncello (Italian lemon liqueur)
Salt
Lemon pepper seasoning

In a medium bowl, stir together the lemon zest, lemon juice, mustard, ginger, rosemary, garlic and limoncello. If not using immediately, cover and refrigerate. Season food with salt and lemon pepper before applying sauce.

— From Amanda Stanko, first place, 2003 Oregon Fryer Commission Big Cluck Great Grill-Off

HEAVENLY SAUCE

MAKES 2½ CUPS

Oregon cookbook author Jan Roberts-Dominguez's inspiration for this recipe was the signature house sauce from the Oregon chain Cafe Yumm!, which uses its savory sauce in hearty rice bowls. Build your own rice bowls with beans, rice, black olives, avocado, and chopped green onions, or use the sauce for fresh or steamed vegetables, on leafy greens, or with grilled meats.

Cafe Yumm! uses almonds instead of hazelnuts in its original sauce, and you can experiment with other varieties of nuts, such as ½ cup of raw slivered almonds or ½ cup of soaked raw cashews, which can yield a smoother texture than roasted hazelnuts. It's easy to play around with the sauce's flavor profile, substituting curry powder for the ground cumin or tossing in a single canned chipotle pepper to ratchet up the heat.

½ cup vegetable oil
½ cup toasted and skinned hazelnuts
    (see note)
⅓ cup cooked garbanzo beans (canned is fine)
¼ cup cooked soybeans (canned is fine;
    see note)
4 cloves garlic
½ cup water
½ cup freshly squeezed lemon juice
⅓ cup nutritional yeast (see note)
1 tablespoon ponzu sauce or soy sauce
½ teaspoon salt
½ teaspoon dried basil
¼ teaspoon ground cumin
⅛ teaspoon ascorbic acid (see note)

In a blender, combine oil, hazelnuts, garbanzo beans, soybeans, and garlic. Run the blender, stopping several times to scrape the sides of the jar and push the mixture into the blades. Once the mixture is a rough purée, add the water, lemon juice, yeast, ponzu, salt, basil, cumin, and ascorbic acid. Continue blending until the mixture is relatively smooth. Scrape into a container and store in the refrigerator for up to two weeks.

Note: To toast hazelnuts, spread the shelled nuts in a shallow pan and roast in a 350-degree oven for 8 to 10 minutes, or until the skins crack. Rub warm nuts with a rough cloth or between your hands to remove as much skin as possible.

Note: Look for soybeans, ascorbic acid, and nutritional yeast in the health and bulk food sections of most well-stocked grocery stores. Nutritional yeast is not the same as active dry yeast or brewer's yeast. Nutritional yeast has a nutty flavor and is used by many vegans as a substitute for cheese on things like pasta dishes or popcorn. It has plenty of B-complex vitamins and is a complete protein.

— From *Oregon Hazelnut Country*, by
Jan Roberts-Dominguez (Hazelnut Marketing Board)

SIMPLE KANSAS CITY-STYLE SAUCE

MAKES ABOUT 2 CUPS

There are high-quality barbecue sauces available commercially. But making a finger-licking homemade sauce doesn't require much effort beyond measuring a few ingredients and perhaps chopping one or two things. This is a thick, red sauce that's great for glazing ribs and chicken. It has plenty of sweetness from brown sugar and molasses, but is mild enough to avoid overpowering the meat.

1 cup ketchup
½ cup firmly packed brown sugar
¼ cup red wine vinegar
2 tablespoons molasses
2 tablespoons dark corn syrup
½ tablespoon butter
½ teaspoon liquid smoke
¼ teaspoon kosher salt
¼ teaspoon coarse black pepper
¼ teaspoon paprika
⅛ teaspoon chili powder
⅛ teaspoon garlic granules
⅛ teaspoon cayenne pepper

➤➤

In a medium saucepan, mix ketchup, sugar, vinegar, molasses, corn syrup, butter, liquid smoke, and spices; heat over medium heat, stirring frequently. As soon as the sauce begins to boil, reduce the heat to low and simmer for 20 minutes. Continue stirring frequently to prevent scorching. Cover and refrigerate if not using right away.

— From *BBQ Makes Everything Better*, by
Aaron Chronister and Jason Day (Scribner)

CHIMICHURRI

MAKES ABOUT 2½ CUPS

This classic from Argentina is a simple mixture of chopped fresh parsley and oregano with vinegar and red pepper flakes. But what it does for grilled steak is phenomenal. You may never go back to A.1. after you've had this.

4 cloves garlic, peeled and crushed
1 teaspoon salt
2 cups lightly packed Italian (flat-leaf) parsley leaves and tender stems, finely chopped
½ cup fresh oregano leaves, finely chopped
½ cup red wine vinegar
1 cup olive oil
1 tablespoon crushed red pepper flakes

Place the crushed garlic on a cutting board and sprinkle salt over it. Wait a minute or so; you will notice some moisture leaching from the garlic. Holding your knife blade almost parallel to the cutting board, scrape the blade over the garlic a few times, turning the garlic into a semi-soft paste. Place the garlic paste in a small mixing bowl.

Add the parsley, oregano, vinegar, oil, and red pepper flakes to the bowl with the garlic paste, and stir until well-combined. Cover and refrigerate if not using right away.

— From *Latin Grilling*, by Lourdes Castro
(Ten Speed Press)

THAI PEANUT SAUCE

MAKES 1¼ CUPS

Peanut butter isn't just kids' stuff. Blended into a savory sauce with other Asian flavors, it's divine for dipping fresh vegetables, or served on pasta, grilled pork or chicken, even tofu.

½ cup creamy peanut butter
2 cloves garlic, minced
3 tablespoons granulated sugar
⅓ cup soy sauce
⅓ cup rice vinegar
1½ tablespoons hot chili oil

1½ teaspoons minced fresh cilantro
Pinch crushed red pepper flakes

In a small mixing bowl, cream the peanut butter, garlic, and sugar until well-blended. Add the soy sauce, vinegar, chili oil, cilantro, and red pepper flakes; mix until blended. Chill for 1 to 2 hours or overnight to blend flavors.

— From Hall Street Grill, Beaverton

ADVANCE-PLANNING TURKEY GRAVY

MAKES 7 TO 8 CUPS

Thanksgiving's not really about the turkey, it's about the gravy, right? It has to be good and there has to be a lot of it. Making it ahead not only means you don't have to fuss too much on T-day itself, but also that you can make a large quantity. We figure about ½ cup per person, so there's enough for the vegetables and stuffing, as well as the turkey and mashed potatoes.

4 turkey wings or other parts (about 3 pounds)
1 cup chopped carrot
1 cup chopped celery
2 medium onions, chopped
8 cups low-sodium chicken broth (divided)
1 cup hot water
½ teaspoon dried thyme
¾ cup all-purpose flour
¼ cup butter, at room temperature
½ teaspoon freshly ground black pepper
Salt

Preheat oven to 400 degrees. In a large roasting pan, arrange the turkey wings in a single layer. Roast until wings are browned, about 1¼ hours.

Transfer the wings to a 5- to 6-quart pot along with the carrot, celery, onions, and 6 cups of chicken broth. Refrigerate the remaining 2 cups of broth.

Deglaze the roasting pan with about 1 cup of hot water, scraping and stirring to release and dissolve all the cooked-on juices. Add this pan juice to the pot along with the thyme. Bring to a boil, reduce heat and simmer uncovered for 1½ hours.

Transfer the wings to a cutting board, remove the skin and bones and save the meat for another use.

Strain the broth into a 3-quart saucepan. Use a wooden spoon to press as much liquid as possible from the vegetables. Discard vegetables. Skim excess fat and discard. Bring the broth to a gentle boil.

In a separate bowl, whisk flour into the 2 cups chilled broth until well-blended. Whisk flour mixture into the boiling broth. Bring the gravy back to a boil and cook until thickened about 3 to 4 minutes. Stir in butter and pepper. Taste and add salt if necessary. Serve immediately or freeze up to 6 months.

— Adapted from *Woman's Day* magazine

PINECREST COMMITTEE CRANBERRY SAUCE

MAKES ABOUT 2½ CUPS

This cranberry sauce is always part of Food-day's online Thanksgiving guide because it's delicious, easy, and keeps for months in the refrigerator. But leftovers may not last that long, because we keep finding ways to enjoy it, such as serving alongside roast pork, over ice cream, or with pancakes.

3¾ cups whole cranberries (one 12-ounce bag)
1½ cups firmly packed brown sugar
½ cup water
Juice and grated zest of 1 orange
    (about ½ cup juice)
⅓ cup brandy
⅓ cup raisins
¾ teaspoon ground cinnamon
½ teaspoon ground nutmeg

►►

In a large saucepan, combine cranberries, brown sugar, water, orange juice and zest, brandy, raisins, cinnamon, and nutmeg. Bring mixture to a boil, reduce heat, and simmer gently for 10 to 15 minutes (the foam will subside, and the liquid will thicken and turn glossy). Remove from heat and let sit at least 15 minutes before serving. Serve warm or chilled.

Make ahead: Prepare up to 1 month ahead and store in the refrigerator.

— From Jan Roberts-Dominguez

PINOT NOIR-POACHED FIGS

MAKES 4 CUPS

These delicious figs are served with a charcuterie plate at Higgins Restaurant. Try them as a nice accompaniment to cheeses, as a dessert topping, or even a hostess gift. We also discovered they're wonderful by themselves, especially when eaten by the light of the refrigerator in the middle of the night.

1 (750-milliliter) bottle pinot noir
1 cup honey
½ cup red wine vinegar
1 tablespoon whole peppercorns
2 cinnamon sticks
1 tablespoon whole cloves
2 pint baskets fresh Black Mission figs,
    halved (2½ pounds)
1 teaspoon salt

In a nonreactive saucepan, bring the wine, honey, vinegar, peppercorns, cinnamon sticks, and cloves to a simmer. Continue cooking at a low boil until the mixture is reduced to a light syrup, 30 to 40 minutes. Strain the mixture and return it to the pan. Add the halved figs and the salt, and stir gently. Cook the figs until just tender, 5 to 10 minutes. Remove from the heat and allow the figs to cool in the wine syrup. Refrigerate if not serving immediately.

Make ahead: For longer storage, figs can be processed in jars in a boiling-water canner for 15 minutes.

— From Higgins Restaurant & Bar

REACTIVE VS. NONREACTIVE COOKWARE

Occasionally recipes that include generous amounts of acidic ingredients—such as wine or tomatoes—will call for "nonreactive" cookware, which includes enamel-coated, anodized aluminum, or stainless steel pans. Do not use copper (even if it's lined with tin), cast-iron, or non-anodized aluminum pots with these recipes, or the metal could react chemically with the acid in the food and cause an off-taste.

BERRY SYRUP

MAKES 5 PINTS OR 9 HALF PINTS

During Oregon's berry season, it's easy to get carried away at a U-pick farm and bring home more than you can use at once. Turning your haul into homemade syrup is a wonderful way to preserve it. This recipe calls for quite a bit of sugar, which gives it a more syrupy consistency. If you're after a lighter version, cut back on the sugar, and extend the boiling time to 5 minutes, then simmer 5 to 9 minutes.

6½ cups fresh marionberries or other caneberries
6¾ cups granulated sugar

Wash 5 pints or 9 half-pint jars. Keep hot until needed. Prepare lids as manufacturer directs.

Wash and stem the fruit, then crush in a saucepan using a potato masher. Heat to boiling and simmer until soft, 5 to 10 minutes. Strain through a colander into a bowl and drain until juice is cool enough to handle. Discard pulp.

Over a bowl, strain the collected juice through a double layer of wet cheesecloth set in a wire mesh strainer or jelly bag. Discard any remaining pulp. You should have about 4½ to 5 cups of juice.

In a large saucepan, combine the juice with the sugar, bring to boil, and simmer 1 minute. Remove from heat, skim off foam, and ladle the hot syrup into one hot jar at a time, leaving ½-inch headspace. Wipe jar rim with a clean, damp cloth. Attach lid. Fill and close remaining jars. Process in a boiling-water canner for 10 minutes (15 minutes at 1,001 to 6,000 feet).

Alternately, pour the syrup into sterilized jars and refrigerate up to 6 weeks. Or pour into ice cube trays and freeze, then pop the cubes into freezer bags and return to freezer for up to 12 months.

— From *The Complete Guide to Home Canning*, by the U.S. Department of Agriculture

FREEZING FRESH CANEBERRIES

When it comes to capturing the berry harvest, the freezer is your friend. Use this guide, from master preserver Jan Roberts-Dominguez, for saving a cache of blackberries, marionberries, or raspberries:

Unsweetened, individually frozen: This is the best method for preparing syrups, toppings, and jams at a later date. However, unsweetened fruit will lose quality faster than those packed in sugar or syrup. You can generally store the fruit for eight months without sacrificing quality.

Place washed, well-drained, sorted berries in a single layer on a cookie sheet; freeze until firm. Pack into plastic freezer bags or containers, cover, and freeze.

Syrup pack: Pack berries into rigid plastic freezer containers or straight-sided jars, covering with a light syrup (heat 5¼ cups water and 2¼ cups granulated sugar to melt the sugar) and leaving 1-inch headspace. Cover and freeze.

Sugar pack: This is the method recommended for making pies. Add ½ cup granulated sugar to each quart of fruit and mix thoroughly. Pack into rigid plastic freezer containers or straight-sided jars, leaving ½-inch headspace. Cover and freeze.

CHOCOLATE HAZELNUT BUTTER

MAKES 2½ CUPS

This luxurious spread/sauce/confection is the homemade version of Nutella—and it has many uses. Warm slightly to soften (set the jar in a pan of warm water), then spoon over ice cream. Bring to room temperature and use as a filling for a layer cake or to make cookie sandwiches, or as a topping for brownies. You can even make instant "truffles" by rolling small balls of the chilled mixture in sifted cocoa (store them in the refrigerator).

> ¾ cup lightly packed Dutch-process cocoa
> 1 cup granulated sugar
> ¼ teaspoon salt
> ½ cup hot water
> ¾ cup unsalted butter, at room temperature
> ½ to 1 teaspoon vanilla extract, or to taste
> ⅛ teaspoon almond extract
> 1 cup toasted and coarsely chopped hazelnuts (see note)

In the top of a double boiler (or use a heatproof bowl that can be placed over a saucepan containing simmering water), combine the cocoa, sugar, and salt. Thoroughly whisk the mixture, then whisk in the hot water. Set the pan over simmering water; stir until the sugar has completely dissolved and the mixture is hot, about 3 minutes. Remove the bowl or saucepan from the simmering water and set aside; cool the contents to lukewarm.

In a small bowl using an electric mixer, or in a food processor, cream the butter with the vanilla and the almond extract just until it is light and somewhat fluffy. With the mixer or food processor still running, gradually add the lukewarm chocolate mixture, continuing to beat or process just until everything is well-combined. Scrape the mixture into a fresh bowl and let it cool completely, stirring or whisking it occasionally to lighten its texture. Add the hazelnuts. Store in clean, dry jars, covered tightly, in the refrigerator. Will keep at least 8 weeks.

Note: To toast hazelnuts, spread the shelled nuts in a shallow pan, and roast in a 350-degree oven for 8 to 10 minutes or until the skins crack. Rub warm nuts with a rough cloth or between your hands to remove as much skin as possible.

— From *Fancy Pantry*, by Helen Witty (Workman Publishing)

PRESERVES AND PICKLES

13

RED PEPPER JELLY WITH VERJUS

MAKES ABOUT 3½ CUPS

This is an easy and delicious jelly with a sweet bite. It looks like confetti in a jar and makes a perfect holiday or house gift, and a delightful accompaniment to roast meats such as lamb or pork.

8 ounces red bell pepper (about 1 large pepper), stemmed, seeded, and finely chopped

4 ounces green bell pepper (about ½ large pepper), stemmed, seeded, and finely chopped

3¼ cups granulated sugar

½ cup verjus (see note)

¼ cup cider vinegar

1 teaspoon crushed red pepper flakes

1 (3-ounce) pouch liquid pectin

In a large pot, combine peppers with sugar, verjus, vinegar, and pepper flakes (jelly will foam up high while cooking). Bring to a boil, stirring, until sugar is dissolved. Add the liquid pectin. Continue to cook, stirring occasionally, over medium heat for about 12 minutes, or until jelly registers 220 degrees on an instant-read or candy thermometer. (Stir jelly before checking temperature to make sure the entire batch is evenly cooked to 220 degrees.)

Carefully pour hot jelly into a flat baking dish and let cool in the refrigerator until jelly is firm. Stir jelly so pepper flakes are evenly distributed. Refrigerate in sterilized jars for up to 3 months.

Note: Verjus (rhymes with au jus), or verjuice, is the unfermented juice of unripe grapes. It has a delicate tartness and flavor that can be used like lemon juice or vinegar in everything from sauces to desserts. Find verjus at specialty food stores such as Pastaworks and Foster & Dobbs, or through the following producers' websites: montinore.com, abacela.com, verjus.com, seufertwinery.com, xthegrape.com, rstuartandco.com, and maggiebeer.com.au/home.

— From Sarah Schafer, Irving Street Kitchen

CLEAN JARS VS. STERILE JARS

All jams, jellies, and pickled products processed less than 10 minutes, or not processed at all, should be put into sterilized jars. Jars used for vegetables, meats, and fruits do not need to be sterilized because the processing time exceeds 10 minutes; for these foods, simply wash the jars well and fill with hot water until needed. If you need to sterilize your jars, place them right side up on the rack in a boiling-water canner. Fill the jars and canner with hot (not boiling) water to 1 inch above the tops of the jars. Boil 10 minutes at altitudes of less than 1,001 feet. Boil 1 additional minute for each additional 1,000 feet of elevation. Keep jars in hot water until needed, then drain. Save the hot water for processing the filled jars.

BLUEBERRY CHUTNEY

MAKES 4 HALF PINTS

This chutney is fabulous over grilled salmon or tuna, poultry, and pork. After making it, simply ladle it into jars and refrigerate. It's not a candidate for boiling-water canning because its acid level may not be high enough to keep it safe at room temperature.

4 cups fresh or frozen blueberries
1 large yellow onion, finely chopped
½ cup red or white wine vinegar
⅓ cup firmly packed brown sugar
⅓ cup dried cherries
2 tablespoons minced fresh ginger
2 tablespoons minced fresh garlic
2 tablespoons curry powder (preferably Madras)
2 teaspoons yellow or brown mustard seeds
½ teaspoon salt
3 tablespoons chopped fresh mint

Sterilize 4 half-pint jars and lids. (Because this chutney will be stored in the refrigerator, you don't have to use canning jars.) Fill with hot water until needed.

In a heavy-bottomed, medium-size pot, combine the blueberries, onion, vinegar, brown sugar, dried cherries, ginger, garlic, curry powder, mustard seeds, and salt. Bring to a boil, then reduce heat; simmer until the onions are very tender and the chutney has thickened, about 20 to 25 minutes. Stir often to avoid scorching. Remove from heat and let cool before adding the mint.

Spoon the mixture into the jars, attach lids, and refrigerate. Chutney will keep for at least 3 to 4 weeks.

— Adapted from a recipe by Greg Higgins, owner/chef of Higgins Restaurant & Bar

PLUM CHUTNEY

MAKES ABOUT 5 PINTS

Foodday readers often ask for ways to use Italian prune plums. This is a delicious solution.

1 cup firmly packed brown sugar
1 cup granulated sugar
¾ cup apple cider vinegar
3½ pounds Italian prune plums, halved and pitted (7 cups)
1 cup seedless golden raisins
⅓ cup chopped onion
1 clove garlic, minced
2 teaspoons mustard seeds
3 tablespoons chopped crystallized ginger
2 teaspoons salt
¾ teaspoon cayenne pepper, or to taste

In a large saucepan, bring the sugars and vinegar to a boil. When sugars have dissolved, add plums, raisins, onion, garlic, mustard seeds, ginger, salt, and cayenne; bring to a boil again. Reduce heat and simmer 45 to 50 minutes, or until thick.

Meanwhile, wash 5 pint jars and keep hot until needed. Prepare lids as manufacturer directs. Ladle hot chutney into 1 hot jar at a time, leaving ¼-inch headspace. Wipe jar rim with a clean, damp cloth.

Attach lid. Fill and close remaining jars. Process in a boiling-water bath 10 minutes (15 minutes at 1,001 to 6,000 feet; 20 minutes above 6,000 feet).

— From *Oregon Sampler: Resorts & Recipes*, by the Assistance League of Corvallis

CRANBERRY-PEAR CHUTNEY

MAKES ABOUT 4 PINTS

Chutney makes a versatile complement to a huge variety of dishes and edibles, including everything from roasted chicken to cheese sandwiches. This chutney features two of our favorite fall fruits.

4 cups fresh or frozen cranberries, picked over and stemmed
2½ cups granulated sugar
1¼ cups water
6 whole cloves
2 cinnamon sticks, each about 3 inches long
1 teaspoon salt
4 firm Bosc or Anjou pears, peeled, halved lengthwise, cored, and cut into ½-inch dice
1 small yellow onion, diced
1 cup golden raisins
⅓ cup diced crystallized ginger
½ cup whole hazelnuts, toasted and halved (see note)

In a deep 6-quart saucepan, combine the cranberries, sugar, 1¼ cups water, cloves, cinnamon, and salt. Bring to a boil over medium heat, stirring frequently to dissolve the sugar. Cook until the cranberries begin to pop, about 10 to 12 minutes. Adjust the heat so the mixture simmers. Stir in the pears, onion, raisins, and ginger. Continue to cook, stirring frequently, until thick, 10 to 15 minutes longer. Remove from the heat, stir in the hazelnuts. Discard the cinnamon sticks and cloves, if you can find them.

Meanwhile, wash 8 half-pint jars or 4 pint jars; keep hot until needed. Prepare lids as manufacturer directs. Ladle hot chutney into 1 hot jar at a time, leaving ¼-inch headspace. Wipe jar rim with a clean, damp cloth. Attach lid. Fill and close remaining jars. Process in a boiling-water canner for 10 minutes (15 minutes at 1,001 to 6,000 feet; 20 minutes above 6,000 feet). Or, if preferred, refrigerate in tightly sealed jars for up to 3 months.

Note: To toast hazelnuts, spread the shelled nuts in a shallow pan, and roast in a 350-degree oven for 8 to 10 minutes or until the skins crack. Rub warm nuts in a rough cloth or between your hands to remove as much skin as possible. You can substitute unsalted cashews. Toast like hazelnuts, until lightly browned.

—From Diane Morgan

GINGERED PEARS

MAKES 4 PINTS

This wonderful preserve is from food writer Frances Price, who likes to give the pears as gifts at Christmas. Winter pears are denser and firmer than "summer" varieties like Bartlett and are better suited for this recipe.

 4 pounds hard winter pears, such Seckel,
  Forelle, Bosc, Comice, or Anjou
 4 pounds granulated sugar (9 cups)
 2 or 3 lemons
 2 ounces peeled and minced fresh ginger, or
  more to taste (about ⅓ cup)
 2 ounces diced crystallized ginger, or more
  to taste (about 3 tablespoons)

Peel, halve, core, and thinly slice large pears (for Seckel pears, peel but leave whole). Place pears in a large mixing bowl, add sugar, and toss to coat pears.

Squeeze lemons, reserving juice. Trim white membrane from lemon halves and cut rind into thin slivers; add juice and rind to sugared pears; let stand several hours to draw out juices.

Wash four pint jars and keep hot until needed. Prepare lids as manufacturer directs.

Place the pear mixture in a large nonreactive pot or canning kettle. Add fresh and crystallized gingers, bring to a simmer, and cook about 45 minutes, or until pears look translucent and syrup is quite thick. You will need to gently stir the pears up from the bottom occasionally to prevent scorching.

Alternatively, you could cook the pears twice: bring mixture to a boil and cook for 15 to 30 minutes; cool for several hours or overnight, then bring the mixture to a boil again. Cook until the pears look translucent and the syrup is quite thick.

Ladle the hot pears and their syrup into 1 hot jar at a time, leaving ¼-inch headspace. Wipe jar rim with a clean, damp cloth. Attach lid. Fill and close remaining jars. Process in a boiling-water canner for 20 minutes (25 minutes at 1,001 to 3,000 feet; 30 minutes at 3,001 to 6,000 feet; 35 minutes above 6,000 feet).

— From Frances Price

PEERLESS RED RASPBERRY PRESERVES

MAKES 3 HALF PINTS

This is a perennial favorite at Foodday. The secret of making the brilliantly colored and fresh-tasting preserves is brief, fast cooking in small batches. A wide, shallow pan—such as a 12-inch skillet—is essential. You can use fresh or frozen unsweetened berries.

 4 cups red raspberries, fresh or frozen
  unsweetened
 3 cups granulated sugar
 ¼ cup strained fresh lemon juice (about
  1 medium)

Sort fresh raspberries, discarding any that are soft, moldy, or otherwise suspect. Rinse them and drain them well. Thaw frozen raspberries, saving all their juice.

▶

In a large bowl, stir the raspberries (including the juice from thawed berries), sugar, and lemon juice together using a rubber spatula; let the mixture stand, stirring gently once or twice, until the sugar has dissolved, about 2 hours.

Wash 3 half-pint jars and keep hot until needed. Prepare lids as manufacturer directs.

Scrape the mixture into a large skillet or sauté pan. Bring it to a boil, stirring constantly with a straight-ended wooden or nylon spatula, and boil it rapidly, stirring often, until it reaches 220 degrees on a candy/jelly thermometer, or passes the cold saucer test (see note). This will take only 3 to 5 minutes, depending on the water content of the berries. Remove from heat.

Skim foam from surface. Ladle hot preserves into 1 hot jar at a time, leaving ¼-inch headspace. Wipe jar rim with a clean, damp cloth. Attach lid. Fill and close remaining jars. Process in a boiling-water bath for 10 minutes (15 minutes at 1,000 to 6,000 feet; 20 minutes above 6,000 feet).

Note: To test preserves with a cold saucer, remove pan from heat; place a spoonful of hot jam on a chilled plate. Place in freezer for 1 minute; draw finger through jam on saucer, if jam does not flow back filling in path, it is thick enough.

— From *Fancy Pantry*, by Helen Witty (Workman Publishing)

STRAWBERRY MARMALADE

MAKES ABOUT 8 HALF PINTS

This marmalade has a gorgeous ruby color and a strong strawberry flavor. It's a wonderful departure from ordinary strawberries preserves.

- 2 medium oranges
- 1 lemon
- ¾ cup water (divided)
- 3½ cups crushed strawberries (about 1 quart whole berries)
- 2 tablespoons strained fresh lemon juice (1 small lemon)
- ½ teaspoon butter
- 7 cups granulated sugar
- 1 (3-ounce) pouch liquid pectin

Wash 8 half-pint jars and keep hot until needed. Prepare lids as manufacturer directs.

Using a zester tool, remove the zest of the oranges and lemon. Or, with a sharp paring knife, thinly slice off the zest, then cut into fine strips. Peel the fruit, removing all of the white pith. Separate the orange and lemon segments from the white membrane; remove any seeds. Discard the membrane. Chop the fruit and set aside.

In a small bowl, combine the orange and lemon zest and ¼ cup of the water. Let soak for 10 minutes. Drain the zest and discard the water.

In an 8-quart nonreactive pot, combine the drained zest, chopped oranges and lemon, and the remaining ½ cup of water. Over medium heat, bring the mixture to a boil. Reduce the heat, cover, and simmer for 15 minutes.

Add the strawberries, lemon juice, and butter to the citrus mixture. Gradually stir in the sugar. Heat, stirring constantly, until the sugar is completely dissolved. Increase the heat to medium-high. Bring the mixture to a full rolling boil, stirring constantly. Stir in the entire contents of the pectin pouch. Return the mixture to a full rolling boil and, stirring constantly, boil for 1 minute. Remove the pan from the heat. Skim off any foam.

To prevent floating fruit, allow the marmalade to cool 5 minutes before filling the jars. Gently stir the marmalade to distribute the fruit.

Ladle the hot marmalade into 1 hot jar at a time, leaving ¼-inch headspace. Wipe jar rim with a clean, damp cloth. Attach lid. Fill and close remaining jars.

Process in a boiling-water canner for 10 minutes (15 minutes at 1,000 to 6,000 feet; 20 minutes above 6,000 feet).

— Adapted from *Blue Ribbon Preserves*, by Linda J. Amendt (HP Trade)

BE PARTICULAR ABOUT PECTIN

If you're using a recipe that calls for commercial pectin, there are several points you need to pay attention to:

- Do not attempt to switch powdered pectin for liquid or liquid for powdered; the two are not interchangeable.
- Make sure you only use the quantity of pectin called for.
- Do not reduce the amount of sugar in a recipe, because it's an integral part of the gelling process. For low-sugar jams, use only those recipes developed for less sugar.
- The steps for combining the sugar and pectin are very specific. When you add the sugar depends on the type of pectin you use. Follow your recipe, adding the ingredients in the order directed.

Here's a simple rule of thumb: when using powdered pectin for cooked jam, add it to the strained juice or chopped fruit before heating. Next, bring the mixture to a full rolling boil (a boil that cannot be stirred down). Then add the sugar. Bring to a boil again and boil for 1 minute.

When using liquid pectin, first combine the chopped fruit (or strained juice) with the sugar, and bring the mixture to a full rolling boil (stir constantly so you won't scorch the mixture). Then add the liquid pectin, return the mixture to a full rolling boil, and boil for 1 minute.

EXQUISITE STRAWBERRY JAM

MAKES 4 HALF PINTS

This recipe needs no commercial pectin and yields a very "soft"—but very luscious—jam. And it only takes only seven minutes to cook. The secret is in the brief, small-batch cooking, so this recipe cannot be doubled. A wide, shallow pan—such as a 12-inch cast-iron skillet—is essential.

4 heaping cups washed and hulled fresh strawberries (1 pound, 6 ounces; to ensure a high pectin content, about a quarter of the berries should be slightly underripe)
3½ cups granulated sugar
⅓ cup strained fresh lemon juice
1 teaspoon butter

▶

In a food processor, coarsely chop the berries in small batches by pressing the pulse button several times (you can also do this by hand, but it goes pretty slow). You should have 3½ cups of coarsely chopped berries.

In a large bowl, combine the berries with the sugar and lemon juice. Gently stir using a rubber spatula until the sugar is evenly distributed and the juices have begun to flow. Let the mixture stand, stirring gently every 20 minutes, for at least 1 hour, but no longer than 2 hours.

Wash 4 half-pint jars. Keep hot until needed. Prepare lids as manufacturer directs.

Scrape the mixture into a 12-inch skillet or sauté pan. Add the butter (this controls the production of foam). Bring mixture to a boil over medium-high heat, stirring constantly with a straight-ended wooden or nylon spatula. Reduce heat as needed to keep mixture from boiling over, and boil for 7 minutes.

Remove the skillet from the burner and let the jam settle for about 20 seconds; if any foam remains, skim it off. Ladle hot preserves into 1 hot jar at a time, leaving ¼-inch headspace. Wipe jar rim with a clean, damp cloth. Attach lid. Fill and close remaining jars.

At this point, the jam may be stored in the refrigerator for up to nine months or longer without the quality suffering. For long-term storage at room temperature, process the jars in a boiling-water canner for 10 minutes (15 minutes at 1,000 to 3,000 feet; 20 minutes at 3,000 to 6,000 feet; 25 minutes above 6,000 feet). Remove the processed jars from the boiling water and let cool on the counter, undisturbed, overnight.

Note: This is going to be a very "loose" jam, so if you don't like such a soft gel, you should choose a different recipe. There's also a stronger likelihood of fruit wanting to float toward the top of the jar, which creates a clear layer of jam at the bottom of the jar. About 3 hours after the jars have been removed from the canner, if the clear space at the bottom of the jars hasn't started to fill in with fruit, turn the jars on their heads for 60 minutes, then gently flip them back for 60 minutes; repeat the process several times during the day or night. This really does seem to work.

—From Jan Roberts-Dominguez

WHOLE CHERRY PRESERVES

MAKES ABOUT 4 PINTS

This is a wonderful recipe. During cooking, the cherries become profoundly sweet and chewy, and every spoonful tastes like fruit and sun reduced to a single flavor. Note that it's a very "soft" preserve. Cherries are naturally low in pectin, and in order for them to gel when cooked with only sugar or honey, they must be simmered long and slowly over very low heat.

2 pounds ripe sweet cherries, such as Bing or Lambert
3½ cups granulated sugar
2 cups water
1 star anise
2 tablespoons honey

Discard any blemished cherries. Remove and discard the stems from the cherries. Remove the pits from the cherries. With some varieties, this can be done by simply squeezing the fruit until the pit pops out, leaving the cherry whole. However, some varieties have more tenacious pits and require the use of a cherry pitter. An alternate method is to slit the cherry open with a knife and pick out the pit. Set the pitted cherries aside.

Put the sugar and water in a large, heavy-bottomed, nonreactive pot. Let stand, stirring occasionally, until the sugar dissolves, 5 or 10 minutes. Add the star anise and simmer over low heat, stirring from time to time, for 15 minutes. Remove the star anise and stir in the pitted cherries and the honey. Raise the heat and bring to a boil. Reduce the heat to low and simmer about 1¾ hours, increasing the heat to medium-low after about 1½ hours. Be careful the preserves do not scorch.

Meanwhile, wash 4 pint jars or 8 half-pint jars and keep hot until needed. Prepare lids as manufacturer directs.

After the first 45 minutes of cooking the preserves, begin to test for the gel point with a thermometer. You're there when the thermometer reads 220 degrees at sea level to 1,000 feet (218 degrees at 1,000 feet; 216 degrees at 2,000 feet; 214 degrees at 3,000 feet; 212 degrees at 4,000 feet; 211 degrees at 5,000 feet; 209 degrees at 6,000 feet; 207 degrees at 7,000 feet; 205 degrees at 8,000 feet).

Ladle the hot preserves into 1 hot jar at a time, leaving ¼-inch headspace. Wipe jar rim with a clean, damp cloth. Attach lid. Fill and close remaining jars. Process pints or half pints in a boiling-water canner for 10 minutes (15 minutes at 1,000 to 6,000 feet; 20 minutes above 6,000 feet).

— Adapted from *The Glass Pantry*, by
Georgeanne Brennan (Chronicle Books)

DOUBLE TROUBLE

When preparing jams, jellies, and fruit spreads, prepare them in single-recipe batches. Do not double recipes, which can prevent the spread from gelling. And do not reduce or increase the measurement for any ingredient.

Remember that soft spreads continue to thicken as they cool. You won't know if it's properly set until it reaches room temperature. To test the seal on your jars, allow to first cool for 12 to 24 hours. If the center of the lid is concave and doesn't pop up and down, the seal has formed.

AMARETTO CHERRIES

MAKES 1 QUART

This recipe is less boozy than classic brandied cherries, and the cherries end up tasting the way maraschinos ought to. Fooddaycontributor Lynne Sampson Curry keeps the cherries firm and fresh-tasting by steeping them in the hot syrup instead of cooking the fruit in it. Add the cherry pits, if you like, for a subtle almond flavor.

For dessert, serve these cherries at room temperature over angel food or other vanilla-flavored cake, and top it all off with whipped cream. For a light cocktail, make a grown-up Shirley Temple using lemon-lime soda – with lots of extra cherries.

1 pound (about 3½ cups) rinsed, stemmed, fresh Bing, Lambert, Van, or other sweet red cherries (pitted or unpitted)
¼ cup reserved pits (optional)
1 cup water

1 cup plus 2 tablespoons granulated sugar
½ cup amaretto liqueur
1 strip lemon zest (about 1 by 2 inches)

In a 1-quart canning jar, place cherries and pits, if using. Set aside.

In a medium saucepan, bring the water and sugar to a boil over medium-high heat, stirring until the sugar dissolves. Stop stirring and boil the syrup uncovered for 1 minute.

Pour the amaretto into the jar and add the lemon zest. Pour enough hot syrup into the jar to cover the cherries. Screw on the lid securely and gently shake to mix. Steep at room temperature until cool and store in the refrigerator for 2 days before using.

— From Lynne Sampson Curry

LIENA'S RASPBERRY LIQUEUR

MAKES ABOUT 2 QUARTS

This super-easy liqueur requires layering raspberries and sugar in jars and shaking them once a week for several months while the fruit ferments. That's it. You can strain out raspberries and serve the liquid as a liqueur, or spoon liqueur and fruit over ice cream. And who says you couldn't try making it with marionberries?

2 pounds unwashed fresh raspberries
(organic or unsprayed; about 7 cups)
2 pounds granulated sugar (about 4½ cups)

Alternate layers of raspberries and sugar in sterilized 1-quart canning jars. Close jars loosely so air can escape, and keep them in a cool place. Sugar and fruit will ferment and bubble; stir each (or temporarily tighten lid and shake, then re-loosen lids) once a week.

After at least 6 months, or when bubbling stops, raspberry liqueur is ready, but it will mellow and improve on keeping. Strain liqueur or enjoy with the fruit.

— From *My Château Kitchen*, by Anne Willan (Clarkson Potter)

RHUBARB LIQUEUR

MAKES AS MUCH AS YOU WANT

This is more of a formula than recipe, easily adapted to any amount of rhubarb. Foodday contributor Deena Prichep likes to mix the liqueur with seltzer for an instant cocktail, or serve it straight up, still cold from the freezer. It's a perfect celebratory toast, reminding you of the sweetness of spring at any time of the year. Remember that the liqueur needs to age for a minimum of a month in order to mellow.

Rhubarb, fresh or frozen
High-proof grain alcohol, such as Everclear
or Clear Spring (these are often held
behind the liquor store's counter)
Granulated sugar

Chop the rhubarb finely to expose maximum surface area, or hack it into rough chunks and then pulse it a few times in a food processor. Place the rhubarb pieces in a glass jar, cover with grain alcohol by an inch or so, screw the lid on, and allow to steep 3 to

▶▶

4 weeks. As the liqueur sits, the flavor and color will leach out of the rhubarb, leaving the alcohol rosy and the rhubarb a sickly yellow-white (the exact amount of time this takes will vary).

When the rhubarb has finished steeping, strain it from the alcohol, and filter the solution through several layers of cheesecloth, or drip it through a coffee filter.

Measure the final amount of alcohol—this is your base number. In a saucepan, heat 1½ times that amount of water, and half to three-quarters of that amount of sugar, depending on how sweet you like things (I tend toward the middle). For example, 4 cups rhubarb alcohol would need 6 cups of water and 2 to 3 cups sugar.

Let the sugar syrup cool, then add it to your filtered alcohol. Taste (the flavors will be a bit harsh), and add more sugar if desired. Let age for at least a month before enjoying. Rhubarb liqueur keeps at any temperature, but is especially delicious enjoyed cold from the freezer.

— From Deena Prichep

JAN'S DAMN GOOD GARLIC DILLS

MAKES ABOUT 4 QUARTS

Refrigerator dills will always be crisper than pickles that are subjected to boiling-water canners, so they turn out especially fresh tasting. Fooddy contributor Jan Roberts-Dominguez adapted this recipe from one by chef and restaurateur Greg Higgins. Feel free to play around with your own seasonings.

4 quarts pickling cucumbers, rinsed well
16 large cloves garlic, peeled and sliced
4 heads fresh dill, halved
About ½ teaspoon crushed red pepper flakes
1 quart apple cider vinegar
1 quart water
¼ cup mixed pickling spices
⅓ cup pickling salt
2 tablespoons granulated sugar
½ teaspoon ground turmeric
1 cup chopped fresh dill

If the cucumbers are too large, you may want to cut them into chunks, slices, or sticks. Otherwise, leave them whole. Pack the cucumbers into sterilized jars or food-grade plastic containers, leaving ½-inch headspace. Divide the sliced pieces of garlic and halved dill heads among the containers. Add a pinch (about ¼ teaspoon per quart) of the pepper flakes to each container (another pinch or two can be used for folks who enjoy more of a "bite" in their pickles).

In a nonreactive pot, prepare the brine by combining the vinegar, water, pickling spices, salt, sugar, turmeric, and 1 cup of chopped fresh dill. Bring to a boil, then reduce heat and simmer for 5 minutes. Strain off the seasonings from the brine, then ladle the hot brine into the containers, leaving ¼-inch headspace. Attach lids. Let cool to room temperature, then store in the refrigerator.

The pickles are "becoming good" after 7 to 10 days of aging, but need at least a month to really blossom in flavor. Even then, they will continue to improve and improve for months, up to as long as a year.

Boiling-water canner method: If you really don't have enough refrigerator space and need to store batches at room temperature, then you'll have to process the jars in a boiling-water canner.

Wash pint or quart canning jars and keep hot until needed. Pack the pickles into the jars, leaving ½-inch headspace. Divide the garlic slices among the jars. Pour the strained hot brine into 1 jar at a time, leaving ½-inch headspace. Wipe jar rim with a clean, damp cloth. Attach lid. Fill and close remaining jars.

Process jars using the Low-Temperature Pasteurization Treatment: Place jars in canner filled halfway with warm water (120 to 140 degrees). Add hot water to a level 1 inch above jars. Heat the water enough to maintain 180 to 185 degrees for 30 minutes. Check with a candy or jelly thermometer to be certain the water temperature is at least 180 during the entire 30 minutes. Temperatures higher than 185 may cause unnecessary softening of pickles.

Note: There is not a processing time for 2-quart jars, so if you are using this size, the jar(s) must be refrigerated.

—From Jan Roberts-Dominguez

PICKLING CALLS FOR PURE SALT

If a recipe calls for pickling or canning salt, it's best not to substitute table salt. Pickling and canning salt is recommended because it is a pure granulated salt that does not contain an anti-caking additive or iodine. If table salt is used, the anti-caking additive can turn the brine cloudy and create sediment in the bottom of the jar, and the iodine can darken the pickles. Canning salt is also fine for baking, cooking, and normal table use.

CRISPY PICKLED CARROTS

MAKES 1 PINT

Lavender lends a pleasing floral note to these bright, crispy carrots. The sticks make a healthful appetizer, quick snack, or a great addition to a meal.

> 1 pound carrots
> 4 fresh unsprayed lavender sprigs with blossoms, each about 4 inches long (or ½ teaspoon dry culinary lavender buds)
> ¾ cup rice vinegar or white wine vinegar
> ½ cup granulated sugar
> ½ teaspoon salt (optional)

Peel carrots and cut lengthwise into ½-inch-thick sticks that fit vertically in a sterilized 1-pint glass jar, coming to about ¾ inch below the rim.

In a 10- to 12-inch frying pan, bring 1 inch of water to a boil over high heat. Add carrots and cook uncovered until they are barely tender when pierced, about 5 to 7 minutes; drain. Lay jar on its side and pack carrots in loosely so that they will be standing upright in the jar; tuck fresh lavender sprigs between carrots. (If you are using lavender buds, sprinkle the buds over the carrots.)

In a 1- to 1½-quart pan, combine vinegar, sugar and salt, if using. Bring to a boil, stirring, until sugar dissolves. Pour hot liquid over vegetables to cover. Reserve extra liquid. Cover jar with lid and shake jar to release any trapped bubbles.

Chill until the next day, then check jar and add reserved marinade, if needed, to cover carrots. Store in the refrigerator up to 2 weeks, turning jar occasionally.

— Adapted from *Discover Cooking With Lavender*, by Kathy Gehrt (Florentia Press)

PICKLED CHERRY TOMATOES

MAKES 1 QUART

Cherry tomatoes are among the most generous plants in the garden. So when you've got more tomatoes than you can handle, turn them into pickles with this easy recipe. The tomatoes remain firm and make a great accompaniment to a meat or tuna sandwich. Or, use them to dress up a plate of cold cuts or other raw vegetables. These are quite tart, so use more sugar, up to ½ cup, if you prefer a less tart pickle. Also, try different herbs, such as thyme or basil.

1 quart water
2 tablespoons coarse sea salt or kosher salt
1 pound firm cherry tomatoes (round and plum varieties of all colors can be used)
2 cups apple cider vinegar
¼ cup granulated sugar or more to taste
2 sprigs fresh summer savory or tarragon
12 black peppercorns

In a large bowl, combine the water and salt, and stir to dissolve the salt.

Prick the bottom of each tomato once with a clean needle. Place the tomatoes in the salt brine, cover, and marinate for 24 hours at room temperature.

In a large saucepan, combine the vinegar and sugar. Stir to dissolve the sugar. Bring just to a boil over high heat. Remove from the heat and cool thoroughly.

Remove the tomatoes from the salt brine and drain thoroughly. Discard the salt brine.

Carefully place the tomatoes in a sterilized 1-quart canning jar. Arrange the herbs and peppercorns around the edges of the jar. Pour the vinegar-sugar mixture over the tomatoes. Secure the jar tightly. Let sit in a cool, dry place—or in the refrigerator—for 3 weeks before tasting. Once opened, the tomatoes can be refrigerated for up to 3 months.

ROASTED SUMMER TOMATOES

MAKES ABOUT 2½ CUPS SMOOTH SAUCE, 4 CUPS CHUNKY SAUCE

Roasting fresh tomatoes until they're soft on the inside and beautifully browned on the outside concentrates their flavor. They come out of the oven gloriously golden and wrinkled, and they are wonderful to have on hand in the refrigerator and freezer for simple sauces and soups. You can purée them into a velvety sauce right after roasting, or freeze them in their chunky state and decide what to do with them later in the year.

Instead of peeling the tomatoes before roasting, you can roast them and then pluck the darkened skins off the flesh after roasting (they come off easily). You can then place the skins in a blender or food processor along with a healthy splash of the liquid from the roasting pan and blend to a purée. Stir this mixture back into the vegetables before refrigerating or freezing.

About 2 pounds tomatoes, peeled if desired (see note), cored and halved, quartered, or cut into 1-inch cubes (to measure 4 cups)

1 Walla Walla sweet onion, peeled, and cut into 1-inch chunks (about 1 cup)

½ cup coarsely chopped fresh basil

8 or 10 cloves of garlic, peeled

About ¼ cup olive oil

About ½ teaspoon salt

About ¼ teaspoon freshly ground black pepper

Preheat oven to 375 to 450 degrees (the hotter the oven, the shorter the roasting time). Prepare the tomatoes as desired. If using cherry tomatoes, simply remove the stems and halve each one. Place the tomatoes in a large roasting pan, jellyroll pan, or any baking sheet with sides. Add the onion, basil, and garlic. You can crowd the vegetables together, but don't go beyond a single layer. Drizzle on a bit of olive oil, then sprinkle with salt and pepper to taste.

Roast until the tomatoes' skins turn golden (if unpeeled). Depending on your oven temperature and the size of your tomatoes, this will take anywhere from 20 minutes to about 1½ hours. When done, they will have collapsed and look quite wrinkled. Alternatively, you can roast the vegetables over indirect heat on a medium to medium-high grill (see note), with the lid on.

Remove the roasting pan from the oven or grill; let the vegetables cool. With a metal spatula or wide, flat-sided wooden spatula, stir and scrape the cooled tomatoes to dissolve all of the cooked-on bits of food. If you plan to purée the tomatoes, add to a food processor and process just until almost completely smooth (with a few chunks remaining).

To freeze, ladle the sauce into freezer containers, leaving about 1-inch headspace. Let cool completely, then attach lids, and freeze.

251

Note: To peel tomatoes (don't peel the cherry variety), cut a shallow X in the bottom of each tomato. Plunge them into boiling water for 30 seconds. Remove immediately and plunge into cold water. Skins should slip off easily.

Note: To check grill temperature, count the seconds you can hold your hand, palm side down, 2 to 3 inches above the rack, until it feels uncomfortable: 3 seconds for medium-high.

BOWLED OVER BY GARLIC

If you need to peel a large quantity of garlic cloves, put them in a medium to large metal bowl. Place another metal bowl upside down on top of the first bowl. Holding the two bowls together, vigorously shake for 20 to 30 seconds. Skins will be loosened and easy to pull off the cloves.

AUNT LOIS' SPICED PICKLED BEETS

MAKES ABOUT 1 QUART

This recipe has been in former staff writer Barbara Durbin's family for four generations. Originally, of course, the pickles were made from fresh beets, not canned. But using small baby beets or sliced beets mean that these can be ready in minutes, though they're better after they've had a couple of days to "pickle." These go especially well with roast beef (and horseradish sauce) or ham.

1½ cups granulated sugar
1 cup apple cider vinegar
½ cup water
1 teaspoon whole cloves
½ teaspoon mixed pickling spices
1 cinnamon stick
½ teaspoon salt
2 (1-pound) cans whole baby beets or sliced beets, drained

In a medium nonreactive saucepan, place sugar, vinegar, water, cloves, pickling spices, cinnamon stick, and salt. Bring to a boil, stirring to dissolve sugar.

Add drained beets and simmer just until heated through. Place beets and pickling juice in a sterile quart jar and refrigerate. For best quality, use within 3 months.

— From Barbara Durbin

GOLDEN PICKLED EGGS

MAKES 1 QUART

With seemingly half of Portland keeping poultry these days, we imagine that many of you are rolling in eggs. One great way to use them is to put them up in flavored brine. After the eggs have pickled for a few days, you can enjoy them dabbed with a little mayo or aioli, or toss them into all kinds of salads, or serve them alongside an Indian curry.

1 tablespoon pickling or kosher salt
1½ cups apple cider vinegar
½ cup water
1 tablespoon granulated sugar
1 (1-inch) cinnamon stick
1 teaspoon crushed white peppercorns
½ teaspoon ground allspice
½ teaspoon ground turmeric
¼ teaspoon whole celery seeds
2 shallots, thinly sliced
About 12 hard-cooked eggs, peeled (see note)

In a nonreactive saucepan, combine all the ingredients except the eggs. Bring mixture to a boil, reduce the heat and cover and simmer for 15 minutes. Let the liquid cool.

Put eggs in a sterilized quart jar. Pour the cooled vinegar mixture over the eggs. Cap the jar and refrigerate it for at least a week before serving. Refrigerated eggs will keep for several weeks.

Note: To hard cook eggs, place in a pan and cover with 1 inch of cold water. Cover the pan, bring to a boil, remove the pan from the heat, and let the eggs rest, still covered, for 11 minutes. Immediately pour off the hot water and fill the pan with cold water. As the water warms, dump and refill with cold water until the eggs are cool.

— Adapted from *The Joy of Pickling*, by Linda Ziedrich (Harvard Common Press)

BREADS

14

NO-KNEAD BREAD

MAKES 1 (1½-POUND) LOAF

Jim Lahey of Sullivan Street Bakery in New York City took the baking world by storm when the New York Times popularized his knead-free method for making bread. With just a few minutes of hands-on work, you get a bakery-quality artisan-style loaf, with a crackly crust and soft, chewy interior. No bread hooks, no kneading until your wrists ache. Just mix, wait, bake and enjoy.

Greg Mowery has adapted the New York Times version and made the method even easier with the help of parchment paper. He says, "don't think about cutting the loaf before it has come to room temperature and no longer feels even a slight bit warm." He adds that it makes fabulous toast, and that it was made for bruschetta or crostini. Note that once the bread is wrapped, the crust will become softer and lose its incredible crunch.

> ### GET THE BEST RESULTS FROM NO-KNEAD BREAD
> - Use instant (such as Fleichmann's RapidRise or Red Star Quick-Rise) yeast.
> - Substitute no more than half whole-grain flour for the white flour in the basic recipe.
> - While you can let the dough rise for as little as a dozen hours, aim for the maximum rise time of 18 hours.
> - Get the right pot: Some swear by Le Creuset pots and cast-iron Dutch ovens, but our best loaves came from a 3½-quart, covered, ceramic baking dish.
> - Be a weekend yeast warrior. No-knead bread requires very little effort, but timing the steps is easier and more enjoyable on days when you're close to home.

3 cups all-purpose or bread flour (up to
  ½ cup can be whole-wheat flour), plus
  more for dusting
½ teaspoon instant yeast (see
  accompanying tips)
2 teaspoons kosher salt
1⅓ cups slightly warm water

In a large bowl combine flour, yeast and salt. Add the water and stir until blended (dough will be shaggy and rather sticky). Cover bowl with plastic wrap, then top with a kitchen towel. Let dough rest at least 12 hours, preferably about 18, at warm room temperature, about 70 degrees.

Dough is ready when its surface is dotted with bubbles. It will be very wet and somewhat difficult to handle. Lightly flour a work surface and place dough on it (a plastic scraper can help get the dough out of the bowl). Sprinkle dough generously with a little more flour (and flour your hands), and fold it over on itself three or four times. Cover loosely with plastic wrap and let rest about 15 minutes.

Using just enough flour to keep dough from sticking to work surface or your fingers, gently and quickly shape dough into a ball. Generously spray an 18-inch length of parchment paper with nonstick cooking spray. Place paper in a shallow 10-inch skillet (like an omelet pan) and put dough seam side down on the paper. Cover with the same plastic wrap you used when raising the dough and let rise for about 2 hours. When it is ready, dough will be more than double in size and will not readily spring back when poked with a finger. It will remain a warm and sticky dough.

At least 30 minutes before dough is ready, preheat oven to 450 degrees. Put a 4-quart heavy covered pot (cast-iron, Pyrex or ceramic) in the oven to heat. (Note that this bread is tough on enameled cast-iron, such as Le Creuset. It's best to use an old pot you don't care too much about.). When oven is at full temperature is, use a razor blade to slash a cross on the top of the loaf. Carefully remove the very hot pot from oven. Pick up the dough using both sides of the paper and gently place dough and paper into the hot pot. Cover with lid and bake 30 minutes, then remove lid and bake another 10 minutes, or until loaf is beautifully browned (be careful not to let the bottom of the loaf burn, although a little char is fine). Remove loaf to a rack and cool, discarding the parchment. Cool on a rack.

— Adapted from Jim Lahey of Sullivan Street Bakery, New York City

IRISH WHEATEN BREAD

MAKES 1 LARGE LOAF OR 2 SMALLER LOAVES

"Wheaten" bread is similar to soda bread in that it uses baking soda for leavening instead of yeast. But unlike its cousin, wheaten bread includes some sugar and whole-wheat flour. The secret to this bread is to use a light touch with the mixing and kneading. Don't beat the dickens out of it, says Mary Loughran, mother of former Foodday staffer Siobhan Loughran, both natives of Ireland.

4 cups all-purpose flour
1⅔ cups whole-wheat flour
1 tablespoon baking soda
1 tablespoon plus 2 teaspoons granulated sugar
1 teaspoon salt
3 tablespoons butter
2½ cups buttermilk

Preheat oven to 350 degrees. In a large bowl, sift together the all-purpose and whole-wheat flours, baking soda, sugar, and salt; rub in butter using your fingertips or cut in using a pastry blender until mixture resembles coarse crumbs. Make a well in the center of the flour mixture and add buttermilk. Mix together with a fork; form into a ball and place on a floured surface. Knead lightly to form a smooth dough, but don't overwork it. Form into a large round loaf; place on a greased and floured baking sheet, or divide dough between two 9-inch pie pans. Mark a cross on the top with a sharp knife. (This makes it easy to divide into quarters, called farls.) If you make one large loaf, bake it for 1 hour. If you make two smaller loaves, bake them 45 minutes.

Note: Mary Loughran likes to add a fistful of bran or ¼ cup pinhead oatmeal to give the bread a nutty texture.

— From Mary Loughran and Siobhan Loughran Taylor

FREEZER LEMON BRIOCHE BREAD

MAKES 2 LOAVES

This is a tender, sweet, lemony bread that's surprisingly easy to make. Since the mixer does most of the work, there's very little kneading required. After you braid the dough you can pop the loaves into the freezer. Later, just thaw, give them a second rising and bake.

5¼ to 6¼ cups all-purpose flour (divided)
½ cup granulated sugar
½ teaspoon salt
2 (¼-ounce) packets active dry yeast
½ cup milk
½ cup water
⅔ cup butter
4 eggs, at room temperature
1 teaspoon lemon extract

GLAZE:
1 egg white
1 tablespoon granulated sugar

In a large bowl, thoroughly mix 1 cup flour, ½ cup sugar, salt, and undissolved dry yeast.

In a saucepan, combine milk, water, and butter over low heat, and heat until liquids are very warm (120 to 130 degrees). Butter does not need to melt.

Gradually add milk mixture to dry ingredients and beat 2 minutes at medium speed with electric mixer, scraping sides of bowl occasionally. Add eggs, lemon extract, and 1 cup flour. Beat at high speed 2 minutes, scraping sides of bowl occasionally. Stir in enough additional flour to make a soft dough.

Turn out onto heavily floured board; knead lightly to form a ball. Cover with a towel; let rest 15 minutes.

Divide dough in half. Divide each half into three equal pieces. Form each piece into a 12-inch-long rope.

Braid three ropes together; pinch ends to seal. Repeat with remaining three ropes. Place on large greased baking sheet. Let rise in a warm place, free from draft, until doubled in bulk, about 1 hour 15 minutes.

To make glaze: Combine egg white and 1 tablespoon sugar; brush mixture on braids.

Preheat oven to 350 degrees and bake loaves about 25 minutes or until done. Remove from baking sheets and cool on wire racks.

To make ahead: After braiding loaves, wrap tightly with plastic wrap; freeze until firm. Transfer to plastic freezer bags. Keep frozen up to 1 month. To bake, remove from freezer; unwrap and place on ungreased baking sheets. Let stand covered with plastic wrap until fully thawed, about 3 hours. Proof, glaze, and bake as directed above.

SPROUTED WHEAT SANDWICH BREAD

MAKES 1 LOAF

Sprouted and ground wheat berries give this bread a nutty texture. With whole-wheat doughs, the bran from the wheat tends to "cut" the gluten strands, so you must knead the dough longer to achieve enough gluten strength to rise the dough nicely and give a lighter finished loaf. The dough will be sufficiently kneaded when it's elastic and springy, and you see strands of dough form between the bran bits. Although this recipe uses a food processor for kneading, you can make it in a stand mixer with a dough hook or by hand kneading. With a mixer it might take 10 minutes; by hand 15 or 20 minutes.

> 1 cup wheat berries, preferably from local hard red wheat
> ¼ cup water
> 2 tablespoons vegetable oil
> ¼ cup molasses
> 1½ teaspoons salt
> 2 teaspoons instant yeast (such as Fleischmann's RapidRise)
> 2 cups whole-wheat flour

The day before you plan to bake your bread, add the wheat berries to a bowl with enough fresh cool water to cover by about 1 inch. Soak the berries for about 12 hours, drain, return to the bowl, and cover. After about 4 hours, you should see a little white nub popping out of the ends of the berries, which is the sprout. (You should have about 1½ cups of sprouted wheat, which is just what you will need for this recipe.) Place the sprouted berries in the bowl of a food processor with a metal blade, add ¼ cup water, process the berries for about 2 minutes until they are well-ground and the mixture is a little creamy, a bit like cooked oatmeal.

Replace the food processor's metal blade with the plastic dough blade. Add the oil, molasses, salt, yeast, and flour. Pulse to combine, then let the processor run until the dough forms a ball around the blade and the sides of the bowl are clean. You may need to stop the processor and redistribute the dough a couple of times to get it to form a ball. Add more water or flour as needed in very small amounts (ours took 2 tablespoons flour), until the dough rolls freely around the bowl. This should take about 2 minutes.

Remove the dough from the processor bowl onto a lightly floured surface and hand knead 3 or 4 minutes to be sure the dough is well-developed. The dough may get a bit sticky; sprinkle a bit of flour as you go to keep it from sticking to your hands, but not so much as to stiffen it. Remember that with 100 percent whole-wheat bread, the more you knead the dough, the lighter and loftier the finished loaf.

Place the dough in an oiled bowl, cover with a cloth, and place in a warm place (such as an oven with the light on). Let the dough rise until doubled in size and a finger pressed gently into it leaves a small indentation, about 2 hours.

Gently turn the dough out (don't "punch" it down—you don't want to de-gas it too much) on a very lightly floured surface and lightly pat into a rectangle about 8 by 6 inches. Gently roll the dough into a log, pinch the seam together and place seam side down in an oiled 9-by-5-inch loaf pan. Cover the loaf with a cloth and place it in a warm spot to rise. The bread is ready to bake when it has doubled in size and a finger pressed gently on the surface leaves a small dent that slowly springs back, about 1 hour.

Bake the loaf in a preheated 350-degree oven for 30 to 35 minutes. Then, immediately turn the finished loaf out of the pan to cool.

— From, Katie McNeil, Pacific Sourdough, Waldport

FOCACCIA WITH ROASTED GRAPES (SCHIACCIATA)

MAKES 12 TO 15 SERVINGS

An old Tuscan recipe typically made during the grape harvest, schiacciata (ski-ah-CHA-tah) adapts nicely to the modern kitchen with no-knead baking techniques. The dough requires overnight resting and relatively little hands-on time. You can make the roasted grapes ahead of time, but do make extra—they're delicious over pancakes, pound cake or ice cream.

3 pounds Red Flame grapes or other
    seasonal seedless grapes
½ cup extra-virgin olive oil (divided)
1 (¼-ounce) packet active dry yeast
1½ cups warm water (85 to 95 degrees)
    minus 2 tablespoons

¼ cup granulated sugar
1 egg, beaten
3½ cups unbleached all-purpose flour
½ cup whole-wheat flour
2 tablespoons rye flour (optional, but gives
    dough a more savory flavor)
2 teaspoons salt
2 to 3 tablespoons coarse sugar (optional)
1 to 2 tablespoons chopped fresh rosemary
    (optional)

Preheat oven to 350 degrees. Wash and pull grapes off stems. Place on baking sheet lined with parchment paper, toss with 2 tablespoons olive oil and roast in oven for 35 minutes, until grapes give up some of their juice. Let cool.

In the bowl of a stand mixer, sprinkle yeast over water. Add ¼ cup granulated sugar and the egg; beat until combined. Add the flours ½ cup at a time, followed by ¼ cup olive oil and the salt. Beat until dough is smooth and satiny and pulls away from sides of bowl. You might need to add more all-purpose flour, but try to use as little as possible; the stickiness will decrease as the dough rises. Place in an oiled bowl, cover tightly with plastic wrap and refrigerate overnight.

The next day, remove dough from refrigerator and cut in half. Place each ball of dough in a lightly oiled bowl, cover and let stand at room temperature until doubled, about an hour. Dislodge one dough ball onto an oiled, large 13-by-18-inch baking sheet. Stretch it out to fill pan. If dough sticks to your hands, oil them or dip hands in cold water. Brush with 1 tablespoon olive oil and scatter half of roasted grapes over dough.

Roll out second ball of dough on a floured surface into a 13-by-18-inch rectangle and gently layer it on top of the other half (like the top slice of a sandwich). Press the 2 halves together to eliminate air pockets. Push with your fingers all the way through to the baking sheet, making holes in the dough, and stretch the dough sideways so that it fills almost the whole sheet. Brush with remaining 1 tablespoon olive oil, then sprinkle with remaining grapes and optional sugar and rosemary. Let rise about 15 minutes while you preheat oven to 500 degrees.

Bake for 5 minutes, then lower heat to 400 degrees and bake for 20 to 30 minutes or until golden brown. Watch that grapes don't burn (lay a sheet of foil over if they get dark). Transfer to large rack to cool for 10 minutes, then remove from pan and continue cooling on wire rack. Serve warm or at room temperature.

—From Marco Flavio, www.cookhereandnow.com, adapted from *No Need to Knead*, by Suzanne Dunaway (Hyperion)

FILLING FOCACCIA WITH GRAPES

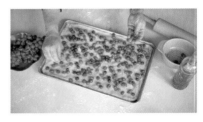  

Place roasted grapes in an even layer over bottom layer of dough. Roll top portion of dough and carefully place over grapes. Press out any air pockets, then use your fingers to make deep dimples in the dough.

GARLIC-PARMESAN BREAD

MAKES 1 MEDIUM LOAF

You think you know garlic bread? Wait until you try this version from former Foodday editor Martha Holmberg. She grates the garlic on a Microplane grater so you don't bite into harsh raw bits, and also adds grated lemon zest, which really makes the flavors sing. Since loaf sizes vary so much, it's hard to say how far the topping will go. You can make a big batch and then freeze what you don't use. If you put the extra topping in a self-sealing freezer bag and smooth it out into a flat packet, the butter will thaw very quickly, and you can have garlic bread without having to plan ahead.

½ cup butter, softened (1 stick)
¼ cup lightly packed finely grated parmesan cheese
1 tablespoon olive oil
1 large clove garlic, very finely minced or grated on a Microplane-style grater (more if you like your bread very garlicky)
1 packed teaspoon finely grated lemon zest
¼ teaspoon kosher salt
⅛ teaspoon freshly ground black pepper
1 medium loaf artisan-style bread (see note)

Preheat oven to 425 degrees. In a food processor or a large bowl, add butter, parmesan, oil, garlic, lemon zest, salt, and pepper. Pulse a few times to blend, but don't overprocess or the butter might separate. If mixing by hand, use a fork or a wooden spoon.

Slice the bread, cutting almost but not all the way through the bottom crust, so it's easy to pull apart. Spread an even coating of topping on each side of each slice. Wrap the bread in foil and put the loaf on a baking sheet to catch any butter that runs out. Heat in the oven for about 25 minutes or until the butter is melted, then open up the top of the foil and bake another 5 minutes or so to slightly crisp the top of the loaf. Serve while it's hot.

Note: Choose a loaf of bread that has a nice crisp crust but that also has enough "inside" so each slice offers both crusty and soft. A baguette is too slender; a fatter loaf such as a batard, Parisian, or other chubbier style works best.

— From Martha Holmberg

GRILLED CILANTRO-MINT NAAN

MAKES 10 BREADS

Jerry Traunfeld was the executive chef for many years at the HerbFarm in Woodinville, Washington, and now owns Seattle's Poppy Restaurant. He created this splendid recipe by filling dough balls for naan—a simple flatbread from India by way of Afghanistan—with flavor-packed herbs and cashews, and baking them on a grill.

DOUGH:
5 cups unbleached all-purpose flour
2 teaspoons granulated sugar
4 teaspoons baking powder
4 teaspoons kosher salt
1 egg
½ cup whole-milk yogurt
1¼ cups warm water (105 to 115 degrees)
¼ cup peanut or vegetable oil

FILLING:
¾ cup fresh mint leaves
2¼ cups coarsely chopped fresh cilantro
1 large clove garlic, chopped
1½ tablespoons chopped fresh ginger
¼ cup plus 2 tablespoons raw cashews
1½ teaspoons kosher salt
½ cup peanut or vegetable oil
Melted butter (optional)

To make dough: In the bowl of a stand mixer fitted with a paddle attachment, combine the flour, sugar, baking powder, and salt. In a separate bowl, whisk together the egg and yogurt, followed by the water and oil. Pour the liquid ingredients into the dry ingredients. Using the dough hook, knead the dough for about 5 minutes. Turn the dough out onto a floured board, form it into a ball, and divide it into 10 equal pieces. Form each piece into a ball, place on a baking sheet lined with parchment paper, cover with plastic wrap, and let it rest for at least 1 hour or up to 1½ hours.

Preheat grill to medium-high (see note).

To make filling: In a food processor, combine the mint, cilantro, garlic, ginger, cashews, and salt. Process until finely chopped. Scrape down the sides, turn the machine back on and pour in the oil. Transfer the filling to a small bowl.

On a floured board, roll a ball of dough into an 8-inch circle. Spread the center with about 2 teaspoons of the filling, spreading to within ½ inch of the edge. Drop another 1 teaspoon of filling in the center of the bread. Gather the edges up, pinching them together in the center, to seal in the filling. Pat the dough packet into a flat round, then turn it over and gently pat it into a 6- to 7-inch circle. Transfer to a parchment-lined baking sheet. Continue forming the dough, layering parchment in between the breads if you stack them (using wax paper between breads will cause them to stick).

Place about 3 breads directly on the grill grate, and lower the lid. Cook for 1 to 2 minutes, until the breads look puffy and are lightly browned on the bottom. Turn the breads over, lower lid, and finish cooking the other side, another 1 to 2 minutes. Brush lightly with melted butter, if desired. Continue to cook the remaining breads. Serve warm, whole or cut in half.

Note: To check grill temperature, count the seconds you can hold your hand, palm side down, 2 to 3 inches above the rack, until it feels uncomfortable: 3 seconds for medium-hot.

— Adapted from *Wood-Fired Cooking*, by Mary Karlin (Ten Speed Press)

FILLING HERBED NAAN

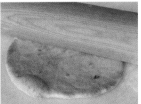

Roll the dough and spread with filling, being sure to leave the border bare. Enclose the filling by pulling the edges of dough together and pinch to secure. Flatten dough into a disk with your hand, then roll and grill as directed.

CHRISTMAS POTICA BREAD

MAKES 2 LOAVES, ABOUT 36 SLICES

Pronounced po-teet-sa, this bread is a Slovenian treat made with a sweetened nut filling wrapped inside yeast dough. Former Foodday home economist Cheri Swoboda serves it to her family on Christmas morning.

SWEET ROLL DOUGH:

1½ packets active dry yeast (scant
    1½ tablespoons)
2 cups milk, lukewarm (divided)
½ cup granulated sugar
½ cup butter, melted (1 stick)
1 teaspoon salt
Grated zest from ½ lemon (about
    1½ teaspoons)
About 6 cups all-purpose flour

NUT FILLING:

¼ cup milk, heated until hot
1 cup ground or crushed walnuts (see note)
½ cup granulated sugar
2 tablespoons honey
½ teaspoon grated lemon zest
1 tablespoon sour cream
1 egg, beaten
1 tablespoon rum, light or dark (or substitute
    2 teaspoons vanilla extract)
10 vanilla wafer cookies, crushed

To make dough: In measuring cup, dissolve yeast in ¼ cup warm milk for 2 to 3 minutes.

In a large bowl, combine dissolved yeast mixture, remaining 1¾ cups milk, sugar, butter, salt, and lemon zest. Add 4 cups of flour and combine. Continue adding enough flour to make a soft dough, beating with a wooden spoon.

Knead lightly on a floured surface for 8 to 10 minutes. Let rise in a greased bowl until doubled in size, about 45 minutes.

To make filling: In a small saucepan, pour hot milk over ground nuts and let rest for a few minutes. Add sugar, honey, lemon zest, and sour cream. Cook over low heat until warm, about 5 minutes. Remove from heat and stir in beaten egg and rum; set aside.

To assemble, spray two 9-by-5-inch loaf pans with nonstick cooking spray.

Divide dough in half. Roll each piece on a floured surface until ¼ to ½ inch thick. Divide nut filling evenly between dough pieces. Sprinkle crushed vanilla wafers on top. Roll up as a jellyroll and pinch edges to seal them. Place in prepared bread pans. Let rise until double.

Preheat oven to 375 degrees. Bake about 45 minutes, or until golden brown.

Note: Use food processor to grind nuts, or crush them with a rolling pin.

— From Cheri Swoboda

SHARON'S FLAKY BUTTERMILK BISCUITS

MAKES 9 (3-INCH) BISCUITS

We've published this recipe from former Food-day home economist Sharon Maasdam so many times that we finally inducted it into our unofficial Hall of Fame. The biscuits are excellent as a base for strawberry shortcake as well as for savory dishes, like biscuits and gravy. If you want to give the biscuits a sweet touch, add 1 tablespoon granulated sugar when you combine the flour and other dry ingredients.

    8 tablespoons butter (divided)
    2 cups all-purpose flour
    2 teaspoons baking powder
    ¼ teaspoon baking soda
    ½ teaspoon salt
    ¾ cup buttermilk

Preheat oven to 450 degrees. Melt 4 tablespoons butter in an 8- or 9-inch square baking pan; set aside.

Into a large bowl, sift together flour, baking powder, baking soda, and salt. Cut in remaining 4 tablespoons butter with a pastry blender or two knives until the mixture resembles coarse cornmeal.

Make a well in the dry ingredients and add buttermilk all at once. Stir only to moisten and until dough is free from sides of bowl.

Knead gently 10 to 12 folds. Use a light hand in kneading. Do not overknead or biscuits will be tough.

Roll or pat out to at least 1 inch thick. Cut with a 2- or 3-inch cutter that has been dipped in flour. Place biscuits in the baking pan with the melted butter; turn biscuits over so both sides are coated. Place close together in baking pan. Bake 12 to 15 minutes. Serve immediately.

Make ahead: Ingredients should be mixed together just before baking. However, if you need to hold the biscuits, the cut dough rounds can be refrigerated for up to 1 hour.

—From Sharon Maasdam

MAKING BISCUITS

Spoon dough into a measuring cup and level with a straight edge (do not level it by tapping or shaking the cup). Cut butter in with a pastry blender or two table knives. Knead gently, then roll to no thinner than 1 inch. As you cut biscuits, avoid twisting the cutter.

BUTTERMILK ROLLS

MAKES 18 ROLLS

These tender rolls are a very popular item at Elephants Delicatessen, especially during the holidays. The secret may be the potato flour, which is readily available in many supermarkets.

    1 tablespoon dry active yeast
    ¾ cup warm water
    1 cup buttermilk, at room temperature
    2 tablespoons vegetable oil
    4½ to 5 cups all-purpose flour
    2 tablespoons plus 2 teaspoons granulated
        sugar
    2 tablespoons potato flour (also marked
        potato starch, see note)
    1½ teaspoons salt

In a small bowl, stir together the yeast and warm water. Let stand until yeast begins to foam, about 5 to 10 minutes.

In a large mixing bowl, combine yeast mixture with buttermilk and oil. Stir in flour, sugar, potato flour, and salt. Dough should come away from bowl and be firm enough to handle with hands. Add additional flour or water if necessary.

Turn dough onto a lightly floured surface and knead for 10 to 15 minutes or until dough is smooth and soft. Place dough in a lightly greased bowl. Cover with a damp cloth or plastic wrap; let rise in a warm place until double, approximately 1 hour.

Shape dough into 18 rolls and place on a lightly greased cookie sheet. Let rise until double, approximately 1 hour.

Preheat oven to 375 degrees.

Carefully cut a cross in the top of each roll with a sharp knife. Sprinkle lightly with flour. Bake 15 to 18 minutes, or until lightly browned.

Note: Potato flour (also marked potato starch) is available in many supermarkets. Depending on the store, however, it can be found with other baking ingredients, or with Asian or kosher foods.

— From Elephants Delicatessen

POPOVERS

MAKES 12 POPOVERS

Popovers are much easier to make than you expect, and they make any meal feel festive. Note there are three secrets to great popovers: make sure the pan is hot before you pour in the batter, fill each section not more than half full, and be sure not to open the oven while they're baking.

    1½ tablespoons unsalted butter, melted, plus
        softened butter for greasing pans (divided)
    1½ cups all-purpose flour
    ¾ teaspoon kosher salt
    3 eggs, at room temperature
    1½ cups whole milk, at room temperature

Preheat oven to 425 degrees.

Generously grease aluminum popover pans or custard cups with softened butter. You'll need enough pans to make 12 popovers. Place the pans in the oven for 2 minutes to preheat.

Meanwhile, in a medium bowl, whisk together the flour, salt, eggs, milk, and melted butter until smooth. The batter will be thin. Open the oven, slide out the rack and fill the popover pans less than half full (this is easiest with a liquid measuring cup) and bake for exactly 30 minutes. Do not peek or they will collapse. Serve immediately.

— Adapted from *Barefoot Contessa Parties!*, by Ina Garten (Clarkson Potter)

QUICKIE OLIVE OIL BISCUITS

MAKES 2 SERVINGS, 3 BISCUITS EACH

These biscuits are easy, good, and heart-healthy because they're made with monounsaturated olive oil instead of butter or shortening. They mix up so quickly you'll go right through that bag of self-rising flour. For color and an extra bit of flavor, add the fresh herb and a couple of chopped pimiento-stuffed olives.

1 cup self-rising flour
1 tablespoon chopped fresh rosemary, basil, or parsley (optional)
A couple of chopped pimiento-stuffed olives (optional)
3 tablespoons extra-virgin olive oil
About ¼ cup 1 percent milk

Preheat oven to 400 degrees.

In a small bowl, stir together the flour, herb, and olives, if using. Make a well and add olive oil and milk; stir until blended and a soft dough is formed.

Add more or less milk to adjust consistency. Do not overwork or biscuits will be tough.

Drop soft dough from spoon onto a baking sheet coated with nonstick cooking spray. Bake until golden, about 10 minutes.

— Adapted from *Entertaining 1-2-3*, by Rozanne Gold (Little, Brown)

MAKE SELF-RISING FLOUR YOURSELF

Self-rising flour is a low-protein flour with baking powder and salt added. It's sometimes seen in recipes for biscuits, quick breads, and cookies. Do not use it for yeast breads. One cup of self-rising flour contains 1½ teaspoons baking powder and ½ teaspoon of salt. You can make your own self-rising flour by combining all-purpose flour, salt, and baking powder in these proportions.

ELAINE DOTY'S BANANA BREAD

MAKES 1 LOAF

Don't let the wholesome ingredient list fool you: this moist banana bread is all treat, with the bonus of potassium, fiber, and calcium in every slice. It's also a great way to use overripe bananas. Expect the loaf to sink a little in the pan as it cools.

1 cup whole-wheat flour
¼ cup wheat germ
1 teaspoon baking soda
5 tablespoons butter
½ cup granulated sugar
1 egg
1¼ cups mashed bananas (about 2½ medium)
¼ cup plain nonfat yogurt
½ cup raisins (optional)

Preheat oven to 350 degrees. Butter an 8-by-4-inch loaf pan. In a medium bowl, stir together the flour, wheat germ, and soda; set aside. In a mixing bowl, cream butter and sugar. Beat in egg. In a medium bowl, combine bananas and yogurt. To the butter mixture, add the flour mixture and banana mixture in several alternating additions. Stir just until dry ingredients are moistened. Mix in raisins. Turn into prepared pan. Bake until well-browned and loaf shrinks from pan, and toothpick inserted into center of loaf comes out clean, about 50 minutes. Cool on rack for 5 minutes. Remove from pan and cool completely before slicing.

— From *San Francisco Chronicle*

ITALIAN PRUNE PLUM NUT BREAD

MAKES 2 LOAVES

The Italian prune plum is more tart than some varieties and is good for baking and cooking. It has a slightly flattened shape with bluish-purplish skin, yellow flesh, and a clingy pit. It's one of the varieties used to make dried plums (producers now prefer that term to "prunes").

1 cup butter (2 sticks)
2 cups granulated sugar
1 teaspoon vanilla extract
4 eggs
3 cups all-purpose flour
1 teaspoon salt
1 teaspoon cream of tartar
½ teaspoon baking soda
¾ cup plain or lemon yogurt
2 teaspoons grated lemon zest
2 cups diced (½-inch) fresh Italian prune plums
1 cup chopped nuts

Preheat oven to 350 degrees.

In a large bowl, cream butter, sugar, and vanilla until fluffy. Add eggs, one at a time, beating after each addition.

Sift together flour, salt, cream of tartar, and baking soda.

Stir together yogurt and lemon zest; add to creamed mixture alternately with dry ingredients. Stir until well-blended. Add diced prune plums and nuts, and mix well.

Divide between two greased-and-floured 9-by-5-inch loaf pans. Bake 50 to 55 minutes or until wooden pick inserted near center comes out clean.

HECETA LIGHTHOUSE ORANGE BREAD

MAKES 2 LOAVES

At Heceta Head Lighthouse Bed and Breakfast on the Oregon coast, guests enjoy a seven-course breakfast every morning, which includes this moist bread. When the recipe ran in Foodday, it received raves from staff and readers.

1 orange
Orange juice, as needed
2 eggs
½ cup vegetable oil
4 cups all-purpose flour
1 cup plus 2 tablespoons granulated
    sugar (divided)
½ teaspoon salt
2 tablespoons baking powder
1 (12-ounce) can evaporated milk
1 teaspoon vanilla extract

Oil two 8-by-4-inch loaf pans.

Wash orange, cut into quarters, and remove seeds (do not peel). Place in a food processor or blender, and process until puréed. Add orange juice if necessary to measure 1 cup.

In a medium bowl, beat eggs until foamy. Add oil and beat 1 minute. Add orange purée and stir to combine.

In another bowl, sift together the flour, 1 cup sugar, salt, and baking powder. To the egg mixture, add the dry ingredients alternately with the evaporated milk and vanilla, beginning and ending with dry ingredients; mix well.

Preheat oven to 400 degrees.

Divide batter evenly between prepared pans. Let batter rest for 20 minutes. Sprinkle 1 tablespoon sugar over both loaves.

Bake 20 minutes. Score the top of each loaf lengthwise with a sharp knife. Reduce heat to 300 degrees and bake another 40 minutes. Bread is done when a cake tester inserted in the center of the bread comes out clean. Let bread rest 20 minutes before turning out of pans.

Note: This batter can be divided among 5 mini bread pans and baked for 20 minutes at 400 degrees. Reduce heat to 300 degrees and score top. Bake another 20 minutes or until bread tests done.

— From *The Lighthouse Breakfast Cookbook,* by
Michelle Bursey and Carol Korgan (WestWinds Press)

MAKE A DATE WITH YOUR BAKING POWDER

Has your baking powder exceeded its freshness date? Check the expiration date on the bottom of the box. If the date has passed, you still may be able to use it for baking. To test whether you need a fresh supply, pour ¼ cup hot tap water over ½ teaspoon baking powder in a measuring cup. The fresher the baking powder, the more actively this mixture will bubble. If the chemical reaction is weak or does not occur, your baking powder will not properly raise whatever you're planning to bake.

ELEPHANT EARS

MAKES 6 PASTRIES

Elephant ears, those floppy fried treats covered in cinnamon sugar, are popular at community events and places such as Portland Saturday Market. But they can be fun to make at home too, especially when you use frozen bread dough as a shortcut. Note that these are best eaten hot from the oil; they are not as good reheated.

    1 (1-pound) loaf frozen Rhodes bread dough
        (whole-wheat or white; half of a 2-pound
        package)
    6 cups vegetable oil for deep frying
        (48 ounces)
    ¾ cup granulated sugar
    1 tablespoon ground cinnamon
    ¼ cup butter, melted

Thaw frozen bread dough in its original plastic bag in refrigerator overnight or at room temperature for 2 hours.

Preheat oven on warm or lowest setting, approximately 150 degrees. Using a serrated knife (to avoid compressing the dough), cut the loaf into 6 equal pieces. Use a rolling pin to roll each piece into a circle 3 to 3½ inches in diameter.

Place dough circles on an ungreased baking sheet and cover with plastic wrap. Turn off preheated oven. Place baking sheet of dough in oven with door propped open for 30 minutes.

Pour oil into a 10-inch or larger skillet, wok, or electric fry pan. Oil should be 1½ to 2 inches deep, and pan should be deep enough to allow oil to bubble.

Heat oil to 375 degrees. Combine sugar and cinnamon in a 7-by-10-inch or 9-inch-square baking pan; mix well and set aside.

Work 1 piece of dough at a time, keeping remaining dough covered. Between fingers and palm, squeeze dough to work out air bubbles all the way around. With fingers spread under dough, stretch dough out to a 10- or 12-by-4-inch ear. Carefully place in hot oil.

With rubber-handled tongs, push dough under surface of oil. Fry until lightly browned on both sides, turning once, about 1 minute. Place elephant ear on paper towels to drain. Blot top with paper towels.

Immediately brush top with melted butter. Invert elephant ear in sugar-cinnamon mixture; press lightly. Repeat with remaining dough. Be sure oil returns to 375 degrees before frying next ear. Eat while they're hot.

Cheese variation: Add 1 clove garlic, minced, or ⅛ teaspoon garlic powder to butter before melting. Brush fried elephant ear with garlic butter. Sprinkle with finely shredded cheese (parmesan, cheddar, or Monterey jack). Set aside several minutes for cheese to melt or toast under broiler until bubbly, about 15 seconds.

Baby-size variation: If you do not have a heavy, 10-inch skillet with 2½- or 3-inch sides, use a smaller skillet or deep fryer. Cut bread dough into 8 pieces. Warm dough in preheated oven only 20 minutes. Shape and fry elephant ears as directed above.

15

CAKES, PIES, AND OTHER DESSERTS

LEMON TART

MAKES 1 (9-INCH) TART

Unlike some lemon tarts that are cloying or simply too intense, this one is light and luscious. It was on the menu at The Arbor Cafe in Salem for many years and is a longtime favorite of both readers and staff.

CRUST:

1¼ cups all-purpose flour
6 tablespoons cold unsalted butter
2 tablespoons granulated sugar
Pinch of salt
1 egg yolk
1½ tablespoons ice water

FILLING:

Finely grated zest of 3 lemons, plus the pared zest of another lemon, cut into slivers, to garnish (divided)
1 cup granulated sugar
½ cup fresh lemon juice
3 eggs
3 tablespoons sour cream
6 tablespoons melted butter
Powdered sugar, to garnish

To make crust: In a food processor, combine the flour, cold butter, sugar, and salt. Pulse 4 or 5 times or until the butter is reduced to the size of small peas.

In a small bowl, mix together the egg yolk and water. Add to the food processor and pulse just until the mixture begins to come together. Form into a flat disk, wrap, and refrigerate about 20 minutes. Roll the dough between sheets of plastic wrap into a 10-inch circle. Invert the dough into a 9-inch tart pan with a removable bottom. Fit the dough into the pan and press into the sides to form a rim. Chill for 30 minutes.

Preheat oven to 375 degrees. Place a sheet of parchment paper in the tart shell and weigh down with pie weights, dried beans, or rice. Bake for 15 minutes. Remove parchment and weights and continue baking until golden brown, about 10 to 15 minutes more. Reduce oven temperature to 300 degrees.

To make filling: In a food processor, add the grated lemon zest and sugar, and process for 30 seconds. Add the lemon juice, eggs, sour cream, and melted butter; process until well-combined. Pour into the baked crust and bake for 15 to 20 minutes, or until set but not browned. Cool slightly and then refrigerate for at least 1 hour. Serve garnished with powdered sugar and slivers of lemon zest.

— From The Arbor Cafe, Salem

LEMON ANGEL PIE

MAKES 1 (9-INCH) PIE

An angel pie is made with a baked meringue crust that softens slightly after the filling is added. Over the years, many of our readers asked for the pie they fondly remembered from Hillvilla restaurant, where the Chart House today overlooks downtown Portland. However, Hillvilla's owner, the late Eddie Palaske, wouldn't part with the recipe for his signature dessert. Ours is a close version. It's great accompanied by fresh Oregon strawberries.

MERINGUE CRUST:

4 egg whites, at room temperature
Pinch of salt
1 teaspoon white vinegar or ¼ teaspoon
   cream of tartar
1 cup superfine sugar (see note)
2 teaspoons cornstarch

FILLING:

4 egg yolks, beaten
½ cup granulated sugar
¼ cup fresh lemon juice
Grated zest of 2 lemons (about 2 tablespoons)
1 cup whipping cream

OPTIONAL GARNISHES:

Sweetened whipped cream, shreds of lemon
   zest, and fresh mint leaves

Preheat oven to 350 degrees. Line a shallow, 9-inch glass, ceramic, or metal pie pan with parchment paper. (Cut out a 12-inch circle and place in pan, pleating paper so it lies flat around the sides.)

To make crust: Place egg whites in a clean bowl (avoid using plastic, which tends to retain a slightly greasy film and prevents the whites from reaching full volume). Beat with an electric mixer (use a whisk attachment if you have one) on medium-low speed until the whites are frothy, about 1 to 1½ minutes. Increase the speed to medium-high, add salt and vinegar, then slowly add the sugar (1 to 2 tablespoons at a time), beating until soft peaks form, about 2 to 3 minutes. (If using a hand-held mixer, this may take longer.)

Increase speed to high; beat until stiff and glossy, about 3 minutes. Sprinkle in the cornstarch during the last minute. Spread meringue on top of parchment paper, and use the back of a large spoon to make the edges higher on the sides.

Place on middle rack of oven and reduce heat to 300 degrees. Bake for 1 hour. Turn off oven; leave the meringue inside with the door shut until completely cool, about 4 hours.

To make filling: In the top of a double boiler, combine egg yolks, sugar, lemon juice, and lemon zest; mix well. Cook over simmering water until mixture is thickened, about 10 minutes. Mixture is thick enough when it mounds slightly when dropped from spoon. Remove from heat and cool to room temperature, about 1 to 1½ hours.

In a medium bowl, whip cream until stiff and fold into cooled filling. Spread mixture in cooled crust. Refrigerate at least 4 hours or up to 24 hours. Just before serving, garnish top with whipped cream, lemon peel shreds, or fresh mint leaves.

Note: Superfine sugar dissolves more easily, which helps keep the meringue from weeping. C&H Baker's Sugar is one brand. You can substitute regular granulated sugar if you place a generous cupful in a food processor or blender and blend for 15 seconds. Measure out 1 cup.

Variations: If you want your crust to be white rather than a pale beige, bake the meringue at 250 to 275 degrees for 1 hour. For a stronger lemon flavor, fold only half of the whipped cream into the filling and use the remainder for garnish. However, the lemon part of the filling makes only about 1 cup, so adding all the whipped cream to the filling makes it fill the crust more completely.

COCONUT-LEMON PUDDING CAKES

MAKES 8 SERVINGS

We offered these delicate cakes as a Mother's Day dessert, but the creamy texture makes them a fitting finale for any special occasion.

¼ cup unsalted butter, melted

1 cup granulated sugar (divided)

3 eggs, separated, at room temperature (divided)

1½ teaspoons grated lemon zest

¼ cup all-purpose flour

¼ heaping teaspoon salt

1¼ cups unsweetened coconut milk

⅓ cup fresh lemon juice

Whipped cream, to garnish (optional)

½ cup flaked sweetened coconut, toasted, to garnish (optional; see note)

Preheat oven to 350 degrees. Butter eight 6-ounce ovenproof ramekins and set aside.

In a large bowl, whisk together the butter, ⅔ cup sugar, and the egg yolks until smooth and fluffy, about 1 minute. Whisk in the lemon zest. Add the flour

TAKE THE CHILL OFF OF EGGS

When it comes to baking, cold eggs do not incorporate well and can make your dish too dense. If you're making sweet yeast breads, such as cinnamon rolls, cold eggs will lower the temperature of the yeast mixture, the yeast will not be properly activated, and the dough won't rise as well.

If you forget to take the eggs out of the refrigerator early, you can bring them to room temperature quickly by placing them in a bowl of warm water for 5 to 10 minutes. If the eggs need to be separated, crack them while they are still cold (they separate more easily cold). Place egg whites in one bowl and yolks in another. Place the bowls in a larger container of warm water until the chill is gone. This will take about 10 minutes, depending on the number of eggs. You can assemble the other ingredients while the eggs are warming.

and salt to the bowl; slowly drizzle in coconut milk, whisking constantly, until mixture is smooth. Whisk in the lemon juice (mixture will be thin).

In a clean bowl using an electric mixer, beat egg whites until soft peaks form when beaters are lifted. Gradually, a few teaspoons at a time, beat in the remaining ⅓ cup sugar. Continue beating until the sugar is completely dissolved and medium-firm peaks form when beaters are lifted.

Gently whisk a third of the egg whites into the batter. Then, using the whisk, gradually fold the batter into the remaining whites. Divide the mixture evenly among the ramekins, filling them to within ⅛ inch of the top. Place the ramekins in a 9-by-13-inch or larger pan (2 inches deep or less). Pour warm water into the pan to reach halfway up the sides of the ramekins. Place pan in the upper third of the oven and bake for 27 to 30 minutes, until the pudding tops are golden and spring back when touched, but leave a shallow indentation.

As with soufflés, there is no good way to judge doneness, so be sure to set a timer. The cakes will settle as they cool. Remove them from the hot water bath and place them on a wire rack to cool. Cool for 30 minutes to set completely and allow layers to form. Serve just warm or, better yet, refrigerate until completely chilled. Garnish with whipped cream and toasted coconut, if desired.

Note: To toast coconut, place on a baking sheet and bake in a preheated 325-degree oven for 15 to 20 minutes, or until lightly browned.

— From Nicole Rees

L'AUBERGE POACHED LEMON CHEESECAKE

MAKES ABOUT 16 SERVINGS

L' Auberge was a lovely restaurant in Northwest Portland, and a wonderful spot for a special-occasion meal. This sublime cheesecake has a very creamy, light filling rather than the much denser New York-style cheesecake.

Finely ground graham cracker crumbs
4 (8-ounce) packages cream cheese, softened
1¾ cups granulated sugar
6 eggs
Grated zest and juice of 1½ lemons
¾ cup whipping cream
1½ teaspoons vanilla extract
Pinch salt

Preheat oven to 325 degrees.

Butter an 8- to 10-cup stainless steel or ovenproof mixing bowl and dust with finely ground graham cracker crumbs. Set aside.

In a large mixing bowl, beat together the cream cheese and sugar. Add the eggs one at a time, scraping down the sides of the bowl frequently. Add the lemon zest, lemon juice, cream, vanilla, and salt; beat until very smooth.

Carefully pour the cream cheese mixture into the prepared bowl. Sprinkle the top of the cream cheese mixture with more graham cracker crumbs. Place the bowl in a large roasting pan, and pour boiling water into the roasting pan deep enough that it will come several inches up the side of the cheesecake bowl. Bake for 1½ hours.

Turn off the oven and let cake sit, without opening the oven door, for another hour. (Set timer so you won't forget it.) Chill poached cheesecake at least 4 hours or overnight.

To unmold, dip the bowl briefly into very hot water and place a serving plate over the top of the bowl. Remove bowl from the hot water and, holding the plate firmly on top of the bowl, invert, and shake gently until the cheesecake unmolds onto the serving plate.

— From June Reznikoff, former chef, L'Auberge

BO'S PUMPKIN CHEESECAKE

MAKES 2 (10-INCH) CHEESECAKES, 32 SERVINGS

This is one of Foodday's most requested recipes. "Bo" was Bo Snyder, a local caterer who produced the cheesecake for restaurants. The recipe is especially great for the holidays because it makes two cakes and freezes beautifully.

CRUST:

2 cups graham cracker crumbs
¾ cup toasted and ground hazelnuts (see note)
½ cup granulated sugar
½ cup melted butter (1 stick)

FILLING:

4 (8-ounce) packages cream cheese, softened
2 cups granulated sugar
1 tablespoon vanilla extract
½ cup sour cream
½ cup whipping cream
1½ teaspoons ground cinnamon
¾ teaspoon ground ginger
¾ teaspoon ground nutmeg
¼ teaspoon ground cloves
¼ cup all-purpose flour
8 eggs
3 cups canned pumpkin purée (slightly less than one 29-ounce can; do not use pie filling)

Preheat oven to 400 degrees.

To make crust: Lightly spray the bottom and sides of two 10-inch springform pans with nonstick cooking spray. Line sides of the pans with parchment or wax paper.

In a small bowl, combine graham cracker crumbs, hazelnuts, sugar, and melted butter. Mix well and divide evenly between prepared pans. Press firmly over the bottom and ½ inch up the sides of the pans.

To make filling: In a large bowl, use an electric mixer to combine cream cheese, sugar, and vanilla. Mix until smooth; add sour cream and whipping cream. Scrape the sides of the bowl and continue beating. Add cinnamon, ginger, nutmeg, cloves, and flour. Add eggs one at a time, beating well after each addition; beat in pumpkin. Divide evenly between prepared pans.

Place pans in oven side by side. Bake 20 minutes, then lower oven temperature to 200 degrees for 1 hour or until the cheesecakes feel firm to the touch. Turn oven off; let cheesecakes cool in the oven with the door slightly ajar for about 1 hour. This helps prevent the cheesecake from cracking (if a crack should appear, blend some sour cream, powdered sugar and vanilla and spread over the top when ready to serve). Cool, cover, and refrigerate or freeze cheesecakes.

➤➤

Note: To toast hazelnuts, spread the shelled nuts in a shallow pan, and roast in a 350-degree oven for 8 to 10 minutes or until the skins crack. To remove skins, rub warm nuts with a rough cloth or between your hands.

Make ahead: If serving fresh, the cheesecake can be made up to 5 days in advance. For longer storage, wrap tightly with aluminum foil, and freeze up to 2 months. To serve frozen cheesecake, unwrap and thaw, either overnight in refrigerator or at room temperature for several hours; cover leftover cake with plastic wrap and store in refrigerator.

— From Bo's Desserts

FRESH BERRY CUSTARD TART

MAKES 1 (9- OR 10-INCH) TART

This recipe is such a winner, and incredibly easy. The crust is whirred up in the food processor, pressed into the pan without rolling, and the custard poured into the hot pastry. We make it with strawberries, raspberries, or blueberries, but you can substitute almost any fresh fruit you like, or even top it with slices of poached pear.

1 cup all-purpose flour
½ cup granulated sugar (divided)
¼ teaspoon baking powder
⅓ cup butter
2 egg yolks
1 cup sour cream
1 teaspoon vanilla extract
½ teaspoon grated lemon zest (optional)
2 pints fresh berries

Preheat oven to 400 degrees.

In a food processor, combine flour, ¼ cup sugar, and baking powder.

Pulse once or twice. Add butter in tablespoons and process until butter is incorporated and mixture is crumbly (it will not form a ball).

Pour into a 9-inch tart pan and press gently over bottom, allowing a little to creep up the sides. Do not pack mixture down firmly. Bake for 10 minutes.

While crust is baking, combine egg yolks, sour cream, remaining ¼ cup sugar, vanilla, and lemon zest, if using.

Remove crust from oven and immediately pour sour cream mixture into hot crust. Return to oven for 10 minutes. Remove from oven, cool, and refrigerate for at least 1 hour.

When ready to serve, arrange fruit on top of custard.

WHICH BUTTER IS BEST?

Unsalted and salted butter can be used interchangeably in most recipes. But unsalted butter has a delicate, creamy flavor that many people prefer. Others think that the salt in salted butter brings out its good flavor. When a recipe calls for butter, it means the salted kind. If unsalted butter is substituted, the amount of salt in the dish should be increased slightly. Although the amount of salt in salted butter varies by brand, we usually figure on slightly less than ½ teaspoon in each stick. The salt acts as a preservative so the butter will keep its fresh taste. Unsalted butter is much more perishable; if not used within a week or two after purchase, it should be frozen.

MARIONBERRY COBBLER

MAKES 12 SERVINGS

Oregon's own marionberries—a cross between the Olallie berry and the Chehalem berry—have rich depth and tangy acidity. It's no wonder it's become the most commonly produced blackberry. We love marionberries in this old-fashioned cobbler, which came to us from Mary Wiese, mother of the owner of Dooger's Seafood and Grill. You'll need a deep-dish 9-by-13-inch pan. As the cake layer rises to the top, it displaces the berry mixture, and a 2-inch high pan won't be deep enough to contain it all without a spillover. We learned this the hard way!

> 2¼ cups water
> 26 ounces marionberries, fresh or frozen
> 2¼ cups granulated sugar (divided)
> 2 tablespoons cornstarch
> 6 tablespoons butter
> 1⅓ cups milk
> 2 cups all-purpose flour
> 2½ tablespoons baking powder
> ½ teaspoon salt

Preheat oven to 350 degrees. Spray an extra-deep 9-by-13-inch pan with nonstick cooking spray.

In a large saucepan bring the water to a boil. Add the marionberries and return to a boil. In a bowl, mix together 1½ cups of the sugar and the cornstarch, stirring until no lumps remain. Stir the cornstarch mixture into the berries and bring back to a boil (mixture will be quite thin). Remove from heat and set aside.

In a large mixing bowl, cream butter with the remaining ¾ cup sugar. Add the milk and beat until well-combined (mixture will look curdled).

Sift together the flour, baking powder, and salt. Add the flour mixture to the milk mixture; beat until well-combined. Spread the cake batter evenly into the bottom of the prepared baking pan. Ladle the berry mixture over the top of the cake (be sure there is at least an inch of space between cobbler and top of pan). Bake for 45 minutes. The cake will rise to the top of the cobbler.

— From Dooger's Seafood and Grill

BLUEBERRY PUDDING

MAKES 6 SERVINGS

This is more like a clafouti than a modern creamy pudding. It came to us from former Foodday editor Chris Christensen, and whatever you want to call it, it's wonderful comfort food. It can be thrown together at a moment's notice—and will disappear just as quickly.

> 2 tablespoons butter
> 1 cup all-purpose flour
> 1 teaspoon baking powder
> 1 cup granulated sugar (divided)
> ¼ teaspoon salt
> Pinch freshly grated nutmeg
> 1 pint (2 cups) fresh blueberries or one
>   12-ounce package frozen blueberries
>   (do not thaw)

½ cup 1 percent milk
1 egg
1 teaspoon vanilla extract
Ice cream (optional)

Preheat oven to 375 degrees.

Melt butter in a 1½-quart casserole and tip dish to coat sides.

In a medium bowl, sift together the flour, baking powder, ½ cup sugar, salt, and nutmeg. In a small bowl, toss berries lightly with the remaining ½ cup sugar.

In another small bowl, lightly beat the milk, egg, and vanilla, then add to the dry ingredients; mix lightly.

Spoon half the berries into batter and fold in lightly. Pour batter into buttered dish. Sprinkle remaining berries on top. Bake 35 minutes.

Serve warm with a scoop of vanilla ice cream, if desired.

MARZIPAN TORTE

MAKES 1 (9-INCH) TORTE

Of all the desserts Foodday has run over the years, former test kitchen director Linda Faus names this as her favorite. She says the torte, which is from now defunct Panini in Southwest Portland, is excellent served with fresh seasonal fruit or a simple sauce made from puréed berries.

12 ounces almond paste (1 cup plus
    3 tablespoons)
2 to 3 teaspoons water
¾ cup butter (1½ sticks)
1 cup plus 2 tablespoons granulated sugar
5 eggs
3 tablespoons kirsch, amaretto, triple sec,
    or brandy
¾ cup all-purpose flour
¾ teaspoon baking powder
Powdered sugar

Preheat oven to 350 degrees.

Butter the sides of a 9-inch round cake pan that is at least 2 inches deep, or use a springform pan, and line the bottom of the pan with parchment paper.

In a food processor, blend the almond paste with the water to form a smooth paste; set aside.

In a large mixing bowl, using an electric beater, cream the butter and sugar until light and fluffy. Add the almond paste and beat until incorporated. Add the eggs, one at a time, beating well after each addition. Add kirsch and mix well.

Sift together the flour and baking powder, and fold the flour mixture into the creamed mixture by hand. Spread in the prepared baking pan and bake for about 1 hour, or until a toothpick comes out clean when inserted in center. If the cake is underdone, it will fall as it cools.

Turn the cake out of the pan and dust with powdered sugar.

— From Panini

SPICED PEAR SKILLET CAKE

MAKES 12 SERVINGS

Baking a cake in a cast-iron skillet gives it a rustic appeal that's irresistible. And when it's made with fresh ginger, warm spices, and fall's finest pears, we can't think of a better way to end a cool-weather meal.

1 cup firmly packed light brown sugar
6 tablespoons unsalted butter, cut into
    4 pieces
1⅓ cups all-purpose flour
1⅓ cups granulated sugar
2 teaspoons ground cinnamon
1¼ teaspoons baking soda
½ teaspoon salt
2 eggs
½ cup vegetable oil
1 small pear, unpeeled, coarsely shredded
1 tablespoon peeled and grated fresh ginger
4 medium pears, peeled, cored, each cut into
    6 wedges (about 1½ pounds)
Vanilla ice cream (optional)

Position rack in center of oven and preheat oven to 350 degrees.

Sprinkle brown sugar evenly over bottom of a heavy 12-inch ovenproof skillet (preferably cast iron) with 2½-inch sides.

Add butter pieces to skillet. Place skillet in oven until butter melts, about 5 minutes.

Meanwhile, in a large bowl, mix flour, granulated sugar, cinnamon, baking soda, and salt. Using an electric mixer, beat in eggs and oil. Mix in pear and ginger.

Using oven mitt, remove skillet from oven; whisk butter and sugar until sugar dissolves. Arrange pear wedges in skillet in a flower pattern, fitting wedges closely together and placing any remaining wedges in center. Pour batter over pears, spreading evenly.

Bake until cake is springy to the touch and tester inserted into center comes out clean, about 1 hour.

Transfer skillet to rack and cool 20 minutes. Loosen edge of cake with knife. Place large plate over skillet. Using oven mitts, firmly grasp plate and skillet. Carefully invert skillet, turning out cake onto plate. Remove skillet.

Serve cake warm with ice cream, if desired.

— From *Bon Appétit* magazine, October 1992

CHERRY CLAFOUTI

MAKES 8 SERVINGS

A clafouti is a traditional French dessert that's a heavenly hybrid of custard, cake, and pudding. Once you've pitted the fresh cherries, it will take less than five minutes to finish preparation. Frozen cherries, or fresh fruit such as berries or plums, can also be used.

1½ teaspoons plus 1 tablespoon unsalted
    butter (divided)
1 pound dark sweet cherries, pitted
½ cup plus 2 tablespoons granulated sugar
    (divided)
4 eggs
Small pinch salt
½ cup all-purpose flour

1 cup 1 percent milk
¼ cup kirsch liqueur (see note)
1 tablespoon powdered sugar

Preheat oven to 400 degrees.

Use 1½ teaspoons butter to grease a shallow 10-inch porcelain or earthenware dish. Spread cherries in a single layer in the dish.

In a mixing bowl, whisk together ½ cup granulated sugar, eggs, and salt until well-blended. Sift in the flour, stirring at the same time with the whisk. Whisk in the milk and kirsch. Pour the mixture over the cherries.

Shave the remaining 1 tablespoon butter over the surface. Sprinkle with remaining 2 tablespoons granulated sugar.

Bake until the surface is golden brown, 25 to 35 minutes. Remove from the oven. Let cool 15 to 30 minutes and sprinkle with powdered sugar. Serve warm.

Note: Kirsch is a clear cherry brandy.

— Adapted from *Provence the Beautiful Cookbook*, by Richard Olney (HarperCollins)

CLEAR CREEK FRUITCAKE

MAKES 8 SMALL LOAVES

Please, no tired fruitcake jokes. This cake, made with pear brandy from Portland's own Clear Creek Distillery, is divine—and it doesn't have any icky green cherries. In fact, you can vary the proportions of the different fruits depending on your taste, as long as they total about 10 cups.

1½ cups chopped dried pineapple
1½ cups chopped dried apricots
2 cups chopped dried pears
2 cups chopped dried apples
2 cups dark raisins or dried cranberries
1 cup golden raisins
1 cup pear brandy, preferably Clear Creek,
    plus additional for aging
3 cups all-purpose flour
2 teaspoons baking powder
2 teaspoons ground cinnamon
1 teaspoon salt
½ teaspoon ground nutmeg
½ teaspoon ground allspice
½ teaspoon ground cloves
2 cups walnut halves

1½ cups whole hazelnuts
1½ cups whole almonds
2 cups pecan halves
4 eggs
1¾ cups firmly packed brown sugar
1¼ cups applesauce
¾ cup butter, melted and cooled
½ cup molasses

Preheat oven to 300 degrees. Grease eight 3½-by-6-inch loaf pans. (Or, to make individual servings, substitute two 8-ounce cleaned pineapple cans for each loaf pan.) Set aside.

In a medium bowl, combine pineapple, apricots, pears, apples, and dark and golden raisins. You should have about 10 cups. Pour brandy over fruit and toss to coat; let stand for 30 minutes.

Into a large bowl, sift together flour, baking powder, cinnamon, salt, nutmeg, allspice, and cloves; stir in walnuts, hazelnuts, almonds, and pecans. Add the brandy/fruit mixture and blend thoroughly.

In a medium bowl, beat eggs until frothy. Add brown sugar, applesauce, melted butter, and molasses; beat until well-blended and smooth. Add the egg mixture to the flour mixture; stir well to evenly coat fruits and nuts with batter.

Pour the batter into prepared loaf pans to three-quarters full and bake 1 hour. The cakes are done when the sides begin to pull away from the edge of the pans and a toothpick inserted in the middle comes out clean. They should be a rich, mahogany color.

Cool fruitcake in pans about 15 minutes, then turn out on a cooling rack. When thoroughly cooled, wrap cakes in cheesecloth that has been soaked in additional pear brandy. Cover with foil and store in an airtight container or refrigerator until ready to serve. The cake is best after it has aged at least 2 to 3 weeks.

— From Marie Hein and Clear Creek Distillery

SHARON'S PERFECT APPLE PIE

MAKES 1 (9-INCH) PIE

Many apple pies end up with a hollow layer between the fruit and top crust, which is caused by the apples collapsing as they bake. But Sharon Maasdam macerates the apple slices with the sugar and spices for several hours (or overnight), which softens the fruit. This eliminates the hollow layer, and allows you to fit a lot more apples into the pie. The result is magnificent.

    9 cups sliced apples (about 9 apples;
        see note)
    ½ cup granulated sugar, plus additional for
        sprinkling over top crust (divided)
    ½ cup firmly packed brown sugar
    1 to 1½ teaspoons ground cinnamon
    ¼ teaspoon ground nutmeg (optional)
    1 teaspoon vanilla
    ¼ teaspoon salt
    2 tablespoons lemon juice
    Pastry for 9-inch, 2-crust pie (see
        accompanying recipe)
    3 tablespoons all-purpose flour
    1 tablespoon butter, cut up

Measure the apples and place in a bowl, or 2-quart measuring cup, with the granulated sugar, brown sugar, cinnamon, nutmeg, vanilla, salt, and lemon juice. Mix well and leave at room temperature, covered, at least 8 hours or up to 12 hours.

When ready to make the pie, preheat the oven to 425 degrees.

Roll out the pastry for the bottom crust and place in a 9-inch pie pan. Using a slotted spoon, place the apples in the pie shell level with the pie pan rim or slightly mounded. Add the flour to the juices remaining in the bowl and mix well. Pour the juice over the apples in the pie pan.

Dot the apples with butter and place the top crust over. Crimp the edge. Make slits in the top crust for air to escape. Sprinkle very lightly with granulated sugar.

Tear 2-inch-wide strips of aluminum foil, fold over once lengthwise and place over the crimped edge, pinching lightly to hold. This prevents the crust edge from browning too much.

Place the pie on a rack in the lower third of the oven. Bake 15 minutes. Reduce heat to 350 and bake another 45 to 60 minutes, or until the apples are tender when the pie is pierced with a fork in the center. Place on a rack to cool.

Note: To fill a 10-inch pie plate, use 11 to 12 cups of sliced apples (11 to 12 apples), ⅔ cup granulated sugar, ⅔ cup firmly packed brown sugar, 2 teaspoons ground cinnamon, a rounded ¼ teaspoon ground nutmeg, 1½ teaspoons vanilla, a rounded ¼ teaspoon salt, 3 tablespoons lemon juice, ¼ cup all-purpose flour, and 1½ tablespoons butter. Add 10 to 15 minutes to the baking time.

— From Sharon Maasdam

PASTRY FOR DOUBLE-CRUST PIE

MAKES 1 (9-INCH) DOUBLE CRUST

2¼ cups all-purpose flour
½ teaspoon salt
½ cup cold butter, cut up (1 stick)
¼ cup cold vegetable shortening
4 to 6 tablespoons ice water

In large bowl, mix flour and salt. With pastry blender or 2 knives used in scissors fashion, cut in butter and shortening until mixture resembles coarse crumbs. Sprinkle in ice water 1 tablespoon at a time, mixing lightly with fork after each addition, until dough is just moist enough to hold together.

Shape dough into 2 disks, one slightly larger than the other. Wrap both in plastic wrap and refrigerate 30 minutes or overnight. If chilled overnight, let stand at room temperature 30 minutes before rolling.

On lightly floured surface, with floured rolling pin, roll larger disk into 12-inch round. Roll dough round gently onto rolling pin; ease into pie plate. Trim edge, leaving a 1-inch overhang. Reserve trimmings for decorating pie, if desired. Fill pie crust.

Roll remaining disk into 12-inch round. Cut 1-inch slits to allow steam to escape during baking; center over filling. Fold overhang under; make desired decorative edge. Bake pie as directed in recipe.

— From *Good Housekeeping Baking,* from the editors of *Good Housekeeping* magazine (Hearst)

PICKING APPLES FOR PIE

Fall and winter apples that are good for pies include Pinova (aka Pinata), Pippin, Melrose, King, Yellow Delicious, Jonathan, Jonagold, Gala, and Rome Beauty. Granny Smith apples are good, too, as long as they're not too tart; taste them first. A mixture of apples is even better. Don't use Red Delicious; they lack the flavor and texture needed for pies.

SHARON'S PEACH COBBLER

MAKES 9 SERVINGS

When peach season is here, there's no better way to enjoy them than in this classic cobbler from former Foodday home economist Sharon Maasdam.

5 to 6 cups peeled and sliced peaches
   (see note)
Few drops almond extract (optional)
1½ cups granulated sugar (divided)
1 cup all-purpose flour

1 teaspoon baking powder
¼ teaspoon salt
½ cup butter, melted (1 stick)
½ teaspoon vanilla
½ cup 2 percent milk
½ cup water

Preheat oven to 350 degrees. Place peaches in a 9-by-13-inch baking dish. Dribble a few drops of almond extract over peaches, if using.

In a large bowl, mix together ½ cup sugar, flour, baking powder, and salt. In a separate bowl, mix melted butter, vanilla, and milk. Combine the two mixtures and stir until blended. Spread over top of peaches.

Mix water with remaining 1 cup sugar and pour over batter in pan. Bake about 1 hour, until topping is golden brown.

Note: To peel peaches, submerge in boiling water for 30 to 60 seconds, then plunge into cold water for 20 seconds. Skins should slip right off.

— From Sharon Maasdam

PEELING PEACHES

Drop peaches into boiling water for 30 to 60 seconds, then immediately transfer to a bowl of cold water. The skins will be loose and easy to pull off. Slice fruit off the pit and prepare as directed.

PEACH MELBA EN PAPILLOTE

MAKES 4 SERVINGS

This version of the classic French dessert comes together in minutes and is served in cute little bundles of parchment tied with butcher's twine. They're great on their own, but in true Melba style, we recommend a scoop of vanilla ice cream or frozen yogurt on top once the bundles are opened.

½ vanilla bean
2 teaspoons lemon juice
4 white peaches, pitted and cut into
    ½-inch-thick wedges
½ pint raspberries (6 ounces)
3 tablespoons granulated sugar
1 tablespoon orange liqueur, such as
    Grand Marnier
2 tablespoons butter
4 (12-inch) lengths parchment paper
4 pieces butcher's twine
1 pint vanilla ice cream

VANILLA BEANS VS. EXTRACT

Vanilla beans are a wonderful addition to many desserts, but they can be expensive. If you want to substitute vanilla extract, use 2 to 4 teaspoons vanilla for a 4-inch vanilla bean. Another approach is to use ½ to 1 teaspoon vanilla for each inch of bean called for in a recipe. We suggest starting with the lesser amount and then adding more extract to taste. Add the extract to cooked mixtures after they have slightly cooled.

If you buy vanilla beans, be sure to wrap them tightly in plastic wrap, place in a glass jar, and keep in the refrigerator for up to six months.

Preheat oven to 425 degrees. Slice vanilla bean lengthwise, scrape out the sticky black seeds and add them to a large bowl. (Either discard the pod, or place it in a container of granulated sugar to make vanilla sugar.) To the same bowl add the lemon juice, peach wedges, raspberries, sugar, and orange liqueur; toss to combine.

Spread the butter in a 4-inch circle in the center of each piece of parchment. Mound the fruit in the center of each piece of parchment. Gather parchment paper edges up and over the fruit and tie the ends together with the twine to create a little bundle. Place the bundles on a baking sheet; bake until you can see the fruit juices bubbling on the inside, 10 minutes.

Place the bundles in dessert bowls, invite diners to cut open their own purses and then plunk down scoops of ice cream on top of the fruit.

— From Ivy Manning

FRESH STRAWBERRIES WITH SABAYON

MAKES 4 TO 6 SERVINGS

Sabayon is the French version of the Italian zabaglione, a light, foamy custard that is exquisite on its own, but even nicer nestled with fresh Oregon berries. Although most versions have to be made just before serving, this one allows you to make the base and whipped cream ahead, and fold them together just before serving.

    3 egg yolks
    ½ cup granulated sugar
    3 tablespoons all-purpose flour
    ½ cup dry white wine
    ½ cup dry sherry
    1 cup heavy whipping cream
    1 quart fresh strawberries, lightly rinsed,
        hulled and sliced
    Fresh mint (optional garnish)

In a medium bowl, whip the egg yolks and sugar with an electric beater until mixture is pale yellow and doubled in volume, about 3 minutes. Add the flour and continue to whip until combined. Stir in the white wine and dry sherry. Transfer the mixture to a double boiler; cook over simmering water, stirring constantly, until thickened. Do not allow the mixture to boil. Remove from heat and refrigerate the mixture in a covered bowl at least 2 to 3 hours.

In a separate bowl, whip the cream until stiff peaks form. (Cream, bowl, and beaters should be very cold.) Refrigerate until ready to assemble dessert.

To assemble, place equal parts of the sabayon base and the whipped cream in a bowl; fold the mixtures together. Place a large dollop of the sauce in the center of a dessert plate and spread it out slightly. Mound a generous serving of berries on top. Garnish with fresh mint.

CREAM DEPENDS ON FAT FOR WHIPPING

You'll notice that some of our recipes call for "heavy whipping cream" and "whipping cream." Heavy cream is at least 36 percent fat while the fat in regular cream ranges from 30 to 35 percent. Both are suitable for whipping, but heavy cream whips up faster and with more volume. It also is more stable and weeps less. In recipes where the cream is not whipped, such as in a soup, you really won't notice a difference.

Make ahead: The sabayon base needs to chill for at least 2 to 3 hours, but it could be done even earlier in the day if you wish. The whipped cream can also be made and refrigerated several hours ahead and folded into the base just before serving.

— From Anthony Demes, Couvron

OUR BEST BANANA WHIPPED CREAM CAKE

MAKES 1 (4-LAYER, 9-INCH) CAKE

Once upon a time there was a Portland bakery called Bohemian, which made a hugely popular banana whipped cream cake. When the bakery closed, readers were bereft. So Foodday worked with a "food engineer" to come up with a copycat cake. Our recipe calls for xanthan gum to give a finer crumb in the cake and to make the filling and frosting more stable, but you can make the cake without it.

We found this cake (like the bakery banana cakes we tasted) had even more banana flavor the second day. This cake must be kept refrigerated because of the whipped cream filling and frosting.

CAKE:

2 cups sifted cake flour (not all-purpose flour)
1 cup granulated sugar
2 teaspoons baking powder
1 teaspoon baking soda
1 teaspoon salt
1 teaspoon xanthan gum (optional; see note)
½ cup corn oil (corn oil produces a better texture)
1 cup mashed very ripe bananas (3 medium)
1 teaspoon vanilla extract
1 teaspoon artificial vanilla (see note)
⅓ cup buttermilk
2 egg yolks

MERINGUE:

2 egg whites
1 teaspoon cream of tartar
½ cup granulated sugar

WHIPPED CREAM FILLING AND FROSTING:

2 cups regular whipping cream if using a stabilizer (otherwise use heavy whipping cream)
¼ to ½ cup powdered sugar
½ teaspoon xanthan gum or all-purpose stabilizer (optional), such as instant ClearJel (see note) or gelatin formula for frosting (see accompanying recipe)
1 teaspoon vanilla (natural or artificial)
2 medium bananas or 1 large, sliced thin
Cake crumbs (optional; see note)
1 maraschino cherry with stem, for garnish (optional)

Preheat oven to 325 degrees.

Grease and flour two 9-inch round cake pans.

To make cake: In a large bowl, sift together sifted cake flour, sugar, baking powder, baking soda, salt, and xanthan gum, if using. Add corn oil, mashed bananas and vanilla. Beat 1 minute with electric mixer. Add buttermilk and egg yolks and beat another minute.

To make meringue: In a separate bowl, with clean beaters, beat egg whites lightly. Add cream of tartar and, while continuing to beat, add sugar gradually. Beat until a stiff meringue forms. Fold the meringue gently into cake batter. (Underfolding will leave white streaks; overfolding will make the cake tough.)

Pour into prepared pans. Bake until toothpick inserted in center comes out clean, about 30 minutes. (See note about cake strips.) Cool on cake racks.

Split each layer horizontally to make a total of four layers.

To make whipped cream filling and frosting: In a large chilled bowl, whip cream with electric mixer, gradually adding powdered sugar mixed with ½ teaspoon xanthan gum or stabilizer powder, if using, and vanilla.

Place one split layer on a plate, cut side down (the bottom, browner side is easier to frost than the cut side). Place wax-paper strips under the edge of the cake so the plate will stay neat.

Using round-tipped steel spatula, spread with a layer of whipped cream filling; top with second cake layer (the baked, brown top facing up). Frost second layer. Top with sliced bananas.

Add third layer (second bottom, browner side up) and add more filling, then top with fourth layer (again, the baked, brown top facing up). Frost sides with remaining whipped cream.

Add whipped cream rosettes piped with pastry tube, if desired. Or add dollops of whipped cream dropped from a teaspoon. Garnish rosette in middle with maraschino cherry.

Remove wax-paper strips. Refrigerate until serving.

Note: Xanthan gum and Instant ClearJel stabilizer are available at the Decorette Shop in Tigard and at the Foster Road location, at some natural foods stores, or in the cooking departments of some craft stores.

Note: Using a combination of real and artificial vanilla gives a better texture.

Note: The Bohemian Bakery apparently used dried, ground cake crumbs—not necessarily banana cake—pressed onto the outside of the frosted layers. You can skip this step, or buy a couple of muffins, toast broken-up pieces in a toaster oven, and process them to crumbs in a food processor.

Note: Commercial cake strips that go around cake pans help cakes bake perfectly level on the top and prevent overbrowning. But strips made from old bed sheets, folded 4 layers thick and thoroughly dampened with cold water, work as well. Folded, they should not rise above the edge of the pan. Wrap them around pans, under the pans' rims, and pin to secure.

WHIPPED CREAM ICING (GELATIN FORMULA)

MAKES ENOUGH TO FILL AND FROST 1 (9-INCH) LAYER CAKE

If you'd rather not use a commercial stabilizer, use this icing that is stabilized with unflavored gelatin.

> 1 packet unflavored gelatin (2 teaspoons)
> ½ cup cold water
> 2 cups heavy whipping cream (preferably not ultrapasteurized)
> 1 teaspoon vanilla extract
> ¼ cup or more powdered sugar

In a small saucepan, dissolve the gelatin in cold water. Heat the mixture slowly to dissolve gelatin completely. Remove from heat to cool slightly. (You don't want to cool completely, or gelatin will set up. If you don't let it cool enough, it will melt your whipped cream.)

In a medium bowl, use an electric mixer to whip cream, adding sugar to taste and vanilla. Slowly add the gelatin mixture and whip until cream becomes stiff. Use to fill and frost cake.

DROP-KICK SHIP-ANYWHERE CAKE

MAKES 24 SERVINGS

The late Foodday writer Andrew Mershon once told his friend Ardie Larsen that no one should mail a cake. A week later, a banana nut cake showed up at his office, looking perfect. But it only took two days to travel from Albany, so Foodday challenged Ardie to send a cake to Dallas, Texas, where Andrew's son would re-label the cake and ship it back to Portland. After a total of eight days of travel, the cake showed up with only a few cosmetic flaws—and still tasted moist and delicious. Ardie said that for mailing, she prefers making the cake in two 7-by-11-inch pans, using all of the batter.

1 cup butter, softened (2 sticks)
2¼ cups granulated sugar
3 eggs, separated
3 cups cake flour
1½ teaspoons baking soda
1½ cups mashed ripe bananas
6 tablespoons buttermilk
1 cup chopped pecans or walnuts
½ cup creme de banana liqueur or brandy (see note)

EASY FANTASY FUDGE FROSTING:
¾ cup butter (1½ sticks)
3 cups granulated sugar
⅔ cup evaporated milk
1 (12-ounce) package semisweet chocolate chips (2 cups)
1 (7-ounce) jar marshmallow creme
1 teaspoon vanilla

To make cake: Preheat oven to 350 degrees. Grease three 9-inch round cake pans and line with wax paper.

In a large bowl, cream butter and sugar until light and fluffy. Add egg yolks and beat well.

In a separate bowl or on a sheet of wax paper, sift cake flour with baking soda.

In a small bowl, mix mashed bananas and buttermilk. To butter mixture, alternately add the dry ingredients and buttermilk mixture, beating well after each addition, beginning and ending with the dry ingredients. Stir in the chopped nuts.

In a clean bowl, beat egg whites until they hold a peak; gently fold them into the batter. Divide batter among cake pans.

Bake about 25 minutes if using 9-inch pans, about 35 minutes if using the 7-by-11-inch pans. Cakes are done if a toothpick inserted in the center of the cake comes out clean. Cool 10 minutes. Sprinkle each layer with creme de banana, using total of ½ cup.

Remove cakes from pans; cool layers completely and frost.

To make frosting: In a heavy 2½- to 3-quart saucepan, mix butter, sugar, and milk; bring to full boil, stirring constantly. Continue boiling 5 minutes over medium heat or until candy thermometer reaches 234 degrees (soft-ball stage), stirring constantly to prevent scorching. Remove from heat.

Gradually stir in chips until melted. Add marshmallow creme and vanilla; mix well.

Thin icing, if necessary, with 1 or 2 tablespoons hot water or coffee. Makes enough frosting for a 7-by-11-inch two-layer cake or one 9-inch round three-layer cake.

Frost cake and allow it to air dry until frosting is completely set. Wrap well in plastic wrap, followed by bubble wrap. Box in packing peanuts. Overnight delivery is best.

Note: The liqueur is essential to keep the cake moist during its travels.

— From Ardie Larsen

DEVIL'S FOOD CUPCAKES WITH CHOCOLATE GANACHE FROSTING AND CENTERS

MAKES 12 CUPCAKES

Bake Space founder Babette Pepaj swears these cupcakes have made grown men cry. After tasting them in our test kitchen, we believe her. The chocolate ganache, which is both the filling and frosting for the cupcakes, needs time to set.

GANACHE:

1½ cups plus 2 tablespoons whipping cream
12 ounces bittersweet chocolate, chopped
   (or one 12-ounce bag semisweet chocolate chips; 2 cups)

CUPCAKES:

⅓ cup good-quality, unsweetened cocoa
   powder, such as Valrhona
1 cup boiling water
1 teaspoon vanilla extract
¾ cup mayonnaise (fat-free works fine)
2 cups sifted cake flour
1 cup granulated sugar
1¼ teaspoons baking soda
½ teaspoon salt

To make ganache: In a medium heavy-bottomed saucepan, bring cream to a simmer. Remove from heat, add chocolate and stir constantly until mixture is smooth. Set aside to cool. Refrigerate, covered, until ready to use.

To make cupcakes: Preheat oven to 375 degrees. Line cupcake tin with paper liners and set aside.

In a medium bowl, whisk together cocoa and boiling water until combined. Set aside until cool (or, for faster cooling, refrigerate). Whisk in vanilla and mayonnaise until mixture is smooth.

In the bowl of an electric mixer set to low speed, combine cake flour, sugar, baking soda, and salt. Add cocoa mixture and increase speed to medium, mixing well. Pour part of the batter into a 2- or 4-cup measuring cup with a spout and fill each cupcake cup one-quarter full. Using a teaspoon, spoon out portions of ganache, shape into a small ball, and place one ball in the center of each partially filled cupcake cup. Use remaining batter to fill all cups three-quarters full.

Bake for 15 to 20 minutes, until cupcakes are set and a toothpick inserted into the cake portion comes out clean.

Cool completely on a baking rack and frost with remaining ganache (you won't use it all). Refrigerate leftovers for another dessert.

Make ahead: You can make the ganache a day ahead of time, or if you're in a rush, chill it in the freezer for about an hour until it sets before proceeding with the recipe.

— From Babette Pepaj, founder, BakeSpace.com

MOCHA CREAM HAZELNUT TORTE

MAKES 6 TO 8 SERVINGS

This torte is one of those dream desserts that looks like it took hours but is actually incredibly easy. And yes, the measure for the flour is correct; the bulk of the cake mixture comes from hazelnuts you grind in a blender. If you use a food processor or an electric mixer instead, the nuts must be finely chopped before they are added to the egg-sugar mixture.

Not to gild the lily, but Eloise Damrosch says this cake is fabulous with sliced strawberries between the layers and on top—in addition to the frosting.

CAKE:

4 eggs
¾ cup granulated sugar
1½ cups raw hazelnuts
2 tablespoons all-purpose flour
2½ teaspoons baking powder

FROSTING:

½ cup granulated sugar
½ cup unsweetened cocoa powder
1 tablespoon instant coffee granules
1½ cups whipping cream
2 teaspoons vanilla extract

To make cake: Preheat oven to 350 degrees. Grease the bottoms and sides of two 8-inch cake pans and fill with two greased rounds of wax paper.

Place the eggs and sugar in a blender and blend at a high speed for 20 seconds. Add the whole nuts and blend thoroughly.

Sift together the flour and baking powder. Add the dry ingredients to the nut mixture and blend until incorporated.

Divide the batter equally between the prepared pans and bake for 30 minutes, or until the sides come away from the pans and the tops are just firm. Do not overbake. The layers will be quite thin.

To make frosting: In a small bowl, combine the sugar, cocoa powder, and coffee granules. In a separate bowl, beat the cream until almost whipped, gradually adding the sugar mixture and vanilla. Spread the cream between the cooled torte layers and on the sides. Keep the torte refrigerated and remove 30 minutes before serving.

Make ahead: This torte can be made and refrigerated a day ahead.

— From Eloise Damrosch and Anne Damrosch

CARROT-ZUCCHINI CHOCOLATE CAKE

MAKES 12 SERVINGS

No one ever guesses that this cake contains vegetables—even three cups' worth. It's so dark and moist that it doesn't need any frosting, just a liberal dusting of powdered sugar. And when you shred the carrots and zucchini in the food processor, it really goes together fast. The bonus is that it uses vegetable oil instead of butter. Health food anyone?

2 cups all-purpose flour
2 cups granulated sugar
½ cup unsweetened cocoa powder
1 teaspoon baking powder
1 teaspoon baking soda
1 teaspoon ground cinnamon
½ teaspoon ground nutmeg
½ teaspoon ground allspice
½ teaspoon salt
1½ cups shredded carrots
1½ cups shredded zucchini
1 cup semisweet chocolate chips (6 ounces)

1 cup vegetable oil
4 eggs
Powdered sugar

Preheat oven to 325 degrees.

In a large bowl, mix flour, sugar, cocoa, baking powder, baking soda, cinnamon, nutmeg, allspice, and salt. Stir in carrots, zucchini, and chocolate chips. In a small bowl, beat oil and eggs; add to dry mixture and stir to moisten well.

Spread batter in an oiled 9-by-13-inch baking pan. (This cake also works in a Bundt pan, but baking time may take longer.) Bake until a toothpick inserted in center comes out clean, 50 to 55 minutes. Cool on a rack.

Just before serving, sprinkle generously with powdered sugar.

Make ahead: Cake can be made, covered, and stored at room temperature for up to two days.

— From Mary Sutton, Spokane, and *Sunset* magazine

CARDAMOM-POACHED APRICOTS WITH YOGURT AND PISTACHIOS

MAKES 4 TO 6 SERVINGS

This Middle Eastern-inspired dessert is a wonderful change of pace and a lighter way to end a meal. Cardamom and apricots have a natural affinity, and after the dried fruit has poached in the spiced syrup, it becomes silky smooth. Leftover apricots can be chopped fine and mixed with granola, and the syrup may be used to flavor hot or cold tea, spritzers, or cocktails.

½ cup granulated sugar
1¼ cups water
3 long strips lemon zest (avoid including any white pith)
1 cinnamon stick
4 green cardamom pods, lightly crushed
Pinch salt
8 ounces dried (sulfured) apricots, quartered
Full- or low-fat plain yogurt (not nonfat)
¼ cup chopped pistachios, to garnish

In a small saucepan, combine sugar, water, lemon zest, cinnamon stick, cardamom, and salt; bring to a simmer over medium heat. Reduce heat to medium-low, add apricots and cook, stirring occasionally, until apricots are very tender and the cooking liquid is syrupy, 25 to 35 minutes. Cool to just warm or room temperature. Serve over yogurt, garnished with pistachios.

Note: Green cardamom pods are available at East Indian markets, Uwajimaya, Penzeys Spices, Barbur World Foods, Williams-Sonoma and in bulk at many stores.

— From Matthew Card

FRESH BERRY GELATO

MAKES ABOUT 1 QUART

Bob Lightman of Mio Gelato uses fresh strawberries to make Gelato di Fragole, but it's hard to think of a berry that wouldn't be fabulous in this recipe. We tried it with boysenberries and couldn't keep our spoons away from it. Be sure to taste the mixture before freezing it; cold mutes flavors, so it should be slightly sweeter than what you expect in the finished gelato.

> 1 pound fresh berries
> 1½ cups granulated sugar, or to taste
> ½ cup cold water
> 1 tablespoon lemon juice (optional)
> ½ cup whipping cream

Rinse and hull berries, if necessary, and drain well. If using strawberries, slice in half. In a food processor, place berries, sugar, water and lemon juice, if desired; process until liquid and smooth. If using berries with large seeds, press mixture through sieve with medium holes to remove seeds.

Whip cream until slightly thickened (it should be about consistency of buttermilk). Add to berry mixture and pulse or stir until thoroughly blended. Freeze in ice cream maker according to manufacturer's directions, until texture is compact but creamy.

Serve immediately, or scoop gelato into lidded container and freeze. For best eating quality, serve within 3 to 4 hours after it's made.

Make ahead: Gelato can be made and frozen for up to 1 month.

— Adapted from Bob Lightman, Mio Gelato

MEYER LEMON FROZEN YOGURT

MAKES ABOUT 1 QUART

If you've been looking for an excuse to buy an ice cream maker, here it is. This frozen yogurt is bright and fragrant, and a lovely combination of creamy and lemony. It's also incredibly easy, since you don't need to make a custard base.

2¼ cups plain low-fat yogurt
¾ cup whipping cream
¾ cup granulated sugar
2 tablespoons light corn syrup
⅓ cup fresh Meyer lemon juice
1 tablespoon grated Meyer lemon zest

In a medium bowl, whisk together yogurt, cream, sugar, corn syrup, and lemon juice and zest. Process in ice cream machine according to manufacturer's directions.

Make ahead: You can mix the ingredients up to a day ahead of time and chill them in the refrigerator, but make the frozen yogurt no more than an hour or so before serving.

— From Michelle Vernier, pastry chef, Paley's Place

THE MAGIC OF MEYER LEMONS

The difference between Meyer lemons and regular is marked. Meyer lemons are believed to be a cross between a lemon and an orange. The skin of a Meyer lemon is darker, smoother, and thinner than that of a regular lemon, and the juice is sweeter and less acidic. While swapping one for the other probably won't ruin most recipes, the difference is likely to be detectable. Meyer lemons are typically available November through May.

EASY CHOCOLATE ICE CREAM

MAKES 1 QUART

When we first saw this recipe, we wondered how a no-churn ice cream could succeed. But it does—and amazingly well. The coffee adds complexity to the flavor, but if you're not a java lover, you can reduce or omit it.

1 teaspoon instant coffee granules or
    espresso powder (see note)
1 tablespoon hot water
4 ounces bittersweet chocolate, chopped fine
½ cup sweetened condensed milk
½ teaspoon vanilla extract
Pinch salt
1¼ cups cold whipping cream

In a large microwave-safe bowl, combine coffee granules and hot water. Let stand until coffee dissolves, about 5 minutes. Add chocolate and sweetened condensed milk; microwave on high, stirring every 10 seconds, until chocolate is melted, about 1 minute. Stir in vanilla extract and salt. Let cool.

In a separate bowl, whip cream with electric mixer on medium-high speed until cream forms soft peaks, about 2 minutes. Whisk a third of whipped cream into chocolate mixture. Fold remaining whipped cream into chocolate mixture until incorporated. Freeze in airtight container until firm, at least 6 hours.

▶

Make ahead: Ice cream can be made and frozen up to two weeks. If you plan to store the ice cream for more than a few days, place plastic wrap directly on its surface before freezing.

— From *Cook's Country* magazine

BITTERSWEET CHOCOLATE FOOL WITH MOCHA AFFOGATO

MAKES 4 TO 6 SERVINGS

A fool is usually made of cooked and puréed fruit that is chilled and folded into whipped cream. But this one goes in another direction entirely, using espresso powder and chocolate for a sophisticated twist.

¼ cup granulated sugar
¼ cup water
2 tablespoons instant espresso powder
2 tablespoons Dutch-process cocoa powder
Salt
1 (3½-ounce) bar good-quality bittersweet or semisweet chocolate, broken into small pieces
2 cups whipping cream (divided)

In a small saucepan, add the sugar and water, bring to a boil, and stir until sugar is dissolved. Remove from the heat and whisk in the espresso powder, cocoa powder, and a pinch of salt until smooth. Set aside.

Put the chocolate and ½ cup of the cream into a double boiler (or a heavy saucepan over very low heat); heat until the chocolate is melted. Whisk until you have a creamy mixture. Stir in a pinch of salt. Remove from the heat but keep warm so the chocolate stays fluid.

In a large bowl, whip the remaining 1½ cups cream until it forms soft peaks. Gradually pour in the chocolate as you continue to whip, until the chocolate is blended in and the cream is fluffy and holds stiff peaks. Don't overwhip; you can fold in any remaining chocolate streaks with a rubber spatula.

Chill the fool about 2 hours to firm up. Spoon into pretty glasses. Stir the espresso mixture to loosen it, adding a few drops of hot water if needed, and pour as much as you like over each serving. (You'll probably have more than you need; it will keep for 1 week in the fridge.)

— From Martha Holmberg

ROSEMARY-ORANGE ICE CREAM

MAKES ABOUT 1 QUART

Herbs love ice cream. And homemade ice cream flavored with fresh herbs is a revelation. Here, the rosemary adds a bright top note that balances the richness of the cream. For a lighter, brighter flavor, omit the cream and use 3 cups milk.

    1 cup whole milk
    2 cups whipping cream
    2 large, gently bruised rosemary sprigs
    Zest of 1 orange, cut into long strips
    5 egg yolks
    ⅔ cup granulated sugar
    1 pinch salt
    ¼ teaspoon orange extract

In a large, heavy saucepan, place milk and cream, rosemary, and orange zest; bring just to a boil over medium-high heat. Or, place the mixture in a microwave-safe container and microwave on high for 3 minutes. Let stand, covered, for 1 hour. Strain out solids, bring infused mixture back to a boil, and turn off heat.

In a medium bowl, whisk together the egg yolks, sugar, and salt until very smooth. Pour about a quarter of the hot infused mixture into the egg mixture, stirring constantly and vigorously. Stir in another quarter of the hot infused mixture. Finally, whisk the egg mixture into the saucepan with the remaining cream.

Cook over medium-low heat, stirring constantly, until it thickens enough to coat the back of a spoon. Do not let the custard boil or the eggs will curdle. As soon as the custard thickens, pour it through a fine sieve set over a bowl. Stir in the orange extract. Cover the bowl with aluminum foil or plastic wrap and refrigerate until well-chilled. Freeze in an ice cream maker according to the manufacturer's instructions.

Make ahead: Custard can be made and refrigerated up to 2 days ahead.

— From *The New Spanish Table*, by Anya von Bremzen (Workman)

BOURBON CARAMEL SAUCE

MAKES ABOUT 2½ CUPS

Use this insanely good sauce to add a personal touch to a store-bought apple pie or ice cream. Or, give it as a hostess gift or Christmas present for neighbors and friends. It's also simple to make—you won't even need a candy thermometer.

2 cups granulated sugar
½ cup water
1 tablespoon corn syrup
6 tablespoons unsalted butter
1 cup whipping cream
½ teaspoon kosher salt, or to taste
½ teaspoon vanilla extract
¼ cup bourbon whiskey

In a deep, heavy-bottomed saucepan, add sugar, water, and corn syrup; stir over medium-high heat and until sugar dissolves. Stop stirring and continue to cook the mixture, swirling the pan to promote even browning, until caramel is nut brown. Remove from heat and stir in the butter, cream, and salt (careful, the caramel will bubble furiously; if it hardens, set the pot back over the heat to rewarm). Stir in the vanilla and bourbon. Serve warm or refrigerate. Rewarm gently (microwave at medium power) before serving.

Make ahead: Sauce can be made and refrigerated a couple of weeks ahead.

— From Danielle Centoni

COOKIES, BARS, AND CANDY

SMOKED SALT, DRIED APRICOT, AND ALMOND CHOCOLATE BARK

MAKES 1 POUND

This sophisticated candy from Portland author Diane Morgan makes an outstanding holiday gift. There are only four ingredients, so make sure your nuts and fruit are fresh, and that you use a good-quality chocolate. The tempering process, which gives the chocolate a glossy finish and the proper snap when broken, isn't complicated, but you'll need to be precise and keep an instant-read thermometer at hand.

½ cup dry-roasted unsalted almonds, coarsely chopped
⅔ cup chopped dried apricots
1 pound bittersweet chocolate (at least 64 percent cacao), finely chopped
1½ to 2 teaspoons coarse smoked salt

Line an 11-by-17-inch baking sheet with parchment paper.

In a medium bowl, combine the almonds and apricots.

Place three-quarters of the chocolate in the top of a double boiler, or in a metal bowl set over (not touching) barely simmering water and stir occasionally until melted. (Be careful that no water drips into the chocolate, or it will seize.) Check the temperature of the chocolate; it should be about 115 degrees (heat briefly if necessary). Place the bowl or the top of the double boiler on a towel. Add remaining chocolate and stir constantly until it is completely melted and smooth, and chocolate drops to just below 84 degrees. At this point, very slowly and carefully heat the chocolate, bringing the temperature back to 88 to 90 degrees. The chocolate is now tempered and ready to spread.

Working quickly and using an offset spatula, spread chocolate in an even layer about ¼ inch thick on the parchment-lined baking sheet. Evenly scatter the apricots and almonds over the chocolate, then gently press them in so they adhere. Immediately sprinkle salt over the top. Set aside in a cool, dry spot to harden, about 1 hour. Break into irregular pieces.

Make ahead: This bark can be enjoyed for up to 1 month when stored in a cool, dry place.

— From *Gifts Cooks Love: Recipes for Giving*, by Sur La Table and Diane Morgan (Andrews McMeel)

POSSE FUDGE

MAKES 6½ POUNDS

In the late '70s, the father-in-law of former Foodday home economist Sharon Maasdam tasted her fudge and told her to get her sister-in-law's recipe. "It's better than yours," he told Sharon. So she did, and has made it every year since.

1 (7-ounce) Hershey milk chocolate bar
2 (4-ounce) German chocolate bars
2 (12-ounce) packages semisweet chocolate chips (4 cups)
1 (16-ounce) package miniature marshmallows
1 (13-ounce) jar marshmallow creme

1 (12-ounce) can evaporated milk (do not
substitute regular milk)
4 cups granulated sugar
½ cup butter (1 stick)
3 cups chopped walnuts (optional)

Butter a 12-by-17-inch pan or two 9-by-13-inch pans.
In a very large bowl (Sharon uses a 12-quart stainless
steel bowl), break up chocolate bars into small pieces.
Add chocolate chips, miniature marshmallows, and
marshmallow creme; set aside.

In a heavy-bottomed 4-quart saucepan, heat
milk, granulated sugar, and butter. Place over medium heat and bring to a boil, stirring occasionally.
Wipe down the sides of the pan with wet paper towels

to be sure there are no sugar crystals. Boil 6 minutes
or to 230 degrees on a candy thermometer, stirring
occasionally.

Pour the hot sugar mixture over the chocolate in
the bowl; stir vigorously until chocolate and marshmallows are melted and the mixture is smooth and
creamy. Add nuts and continue to stir until nuts are
mixed throughout.

Spread fudge in the prepared baking pan(s). Let
cool for several hours at room temperature, then cut
in desired number of squares.

— Adapted from *Chuck Wagon Cook Book,* by
Wallowa County CowBelles (Fundcraft Publishing)

AS CLOSE AS YOU CAN GET TO MRS. FIELDS' CHOCOLATE CHIP COOKIES

MAKES 5 DOZEN LARGE COOKIES

This is the go-to chocolate chip cookie recipe for
Foodday staffers, who made it for years before it
occurred to us to run it in the paper. The recipe
makes a ton, but we don't think you'll have trouble finding takers.

2 cups butter, at room temperature (4 sticks)
2 cups firmly packed dark or light
    brown sugar
1½ cups granulated sugar
2 tablespoons vanilla extract
3 eggs
6 cups all-purpose flour
1½ teaspoons baking soda
1½ teaspoons salt
2 (12-ounce) bags chocolate chips (4 cups)
2 cups chopped walnuts (optional)

HOLD THE GREASE FOR BAKING COOKIES

Do not grease a baking sheet unless stated
in the recipe. Most cookies containing butter or
shortening do not need a greased sheet. If you do
grease it, use a very thin coating of butter or shortening. Do not use vegetable oil, which will burn
and make the pan sticky. Do not grease baking
sheets for making meringue-type cookies, which
will spread if the pan is greased. Instead, use
parchment paper for easy removal.

Preheat oven to 350 degrees.

In a large bowl, cream together butter and sugars.
Beat in vanilla and eggs, mixing well. In a separate
bowl, stir together the flour, baking soda, and salt;

▶

thoroughly mix into butter mixture. Stir in chocolate chips and walnuts, if using.

Line a baking sheet with parchment paper, or use it ungreased. Scoop spoonfuls of dough with a small ice cream scoop or large spoon onto baking sheet.

Bake 8 to 10 minutes. Cookies will not look totally baked. Let cool 5 minutes on baking sheet. Remove cookies to rack. These will be gooey until completely cooled. Repeat with remaining dough.

MY GINGER COOKIES (AKA SCREAMING GINGER COOKIES)

MAKES ABOUT 4 DOZEN (2¼-INCH) COOKIES

Baking authority Alice Medrich says these are her favorite spice cookies, with crunchy edges, a chewy center, and beautifully crackled top. They're also loaded with diced crystallized ginger, so if you want to tone down the heat, omit the fresh ginger and cut down on the crystallized ginger. They'll still be great. You can make an amazing wintry ice cream sandwich by pairing them with vanilla bean ice cream.

2 cups unbleached all-purpose flour
2 teaspoons baking soda
2 teaspoons ground ginger
1½ teaspoons ground cinnamon
½ teaspoon ground allspice
¼ teaspoon salt
½ cup unsalted butter, melted and still warm (1 stick)
¼ cup dark molasses (mild or robust)
½ cup granulated sugar
⅓ cup firmly packed brown sugar or light muscovado sugar
2 tablespoons peeled and finely minced or grated fresh ginger
1 egg
¾ cup diced (¼-inch) crystallized ginger (4 ounces)
About ¾ cup demerara or turbinado sugar or ¼ cup granulated sugar, for rolling

Position racks in the upper and lower thirds of the oven; preheat oven to 350 degrees. In a medium bowl, combine the flour, baking soda, ground ginger, cinnamon, allspice, and salt; mix thoroughly with a whisk or fork.

In a large bowl, combine the warm butter, molasses, granulated sugar, brown sugar, fresh ginger, and egg; mix thoroughly. Add the flour mixture and crystallized ginger, and stir until incorporated. The dough will be soft.

Form the dough into 1-inch balls. (Refrigerate unrolled dough between batches.) Roll the balls in the demerara or turbinado sugar and place them 2 inches apart on lined or ungreased baking sheets. Bake for 10 to 12 minutes, or until the cookies puff up and crack on the surface, then begin to deflate in the oven. Rotate the sheets from top to bottom and from back to front halfway through the baking time to ensure even baking. For chewier cookies, remove them from the oven when at least half or more of the cookies have begun to deflate; for crunchier edges with chewy centers, bake for a minute or so longer.

For lined pans, set the pans or just the liners on racks to cool; for unlined pans, use a metal spatula to transfer the cookies to racks. Cool the cookies completely before storing. May be kept in an airtight container for several days.

Milder variation: Turn down the heat by omitting the fresh ginger and decreasing the crystallized ginger to ½ cup.

— Adapted from *Chewy Gooey Crispy Crunchy Melt-in-Your-Mouth Cookies*, by Alice Medrich (Artisan)

BLACK TRUFFLE CHOCOLATE PECAN COOKIES

MAKES ABOUT 5 DOZEN COOKIES

If you like chocolate with your chocolate, these cookies are for you. Former Foodday test kitchen director Linda Faus says they're "slightly crisp on the outside and pure chocolate and pecan goodness on the inside."

1 pound bittersweet chocolate, chopped
11 tablespoons unsalted butter (1 stick plus 3 tablespoons; see note)
½ cup all-purpose flour
½ teaspoon baking powder
Pinch salt
4 eggs
1½ cups granulated sugar
1½ tablespoons instant espresso powder
1½ tablespoons vanilla extract
1¼ cups coarsely chopped pecans
1 (12-ounce) package semisweet chocolate chips (2 cups)

Preheat oven to 350 degrees. Lightly grease baking sheets or line with parchment paper.

Place the chocolate and butter in the top of a double boiler over simmering water until melted, stirring occasionally; set aside.

In a small bowl, sift together the flour, baking powder, and salt; set aside.

In the bowl of a stand mixer using paddle attachment (or a large mixing bowl using a wooden spoon), beat the eggs, sugar, espresso powder, and vanilla until well-combined. Pour in the chocolate mixture and mix well. Gently fold in the flour mixture, pecans, and chocolate chips.

Drop by heaping tablespoonfuls, 2 inches apart, onto the prepared baking sheet. Bake 12 to 15 minutes or until cookies no longer look wet in the middle. Remove to wire racks to cool.

— From Catherine Buford, Daily Cafe at Rejuvenation, Portland

SIMPLE SESAME COOKIES

MAKES 8 DOZEN COOKIES

Slice-and-bake cookies are brilliant because you can stash a roll of dough in the refrigerator for up to a month—or the freezer for longer—and pull it out whenever a craving for cookies hits. Simple Sesame Cookies were a grand-prize winner in a *Ladies Home Journal* Christmas cookie contest many years ago, and as their name implies, they're very easy to make.

> 2 cups butter, softened (4 sticks)
> 1½ cups granulated sugar
> 3 cups all-purpose flour
> 1 cup sesame seeds (see note)
> 2 cups sweetened shredded coconut
> ½ cup finely chopped blanched almonds

In a large mixing bowl, beat butter with electric mixer. Gradually add sugar and continue beating until light and fluffy. Add flour and mix until just combined. Stir in sesame seeds, coconut, and almonds until well-mixed.

Divide dough into thirds. Place 1 third on a long sheet of wax paper. Shape into a roll 2 inches in diameter. Repeat with remaining dough. Wrap the 3 rolls with wax paper and refrigerate for at least 1 to 2 hours or until firm.

To bake, preheat oven to 300 degrees.

Cut rolls into ¼-inch-thick slices. Place on ungreased baking sheets and bake 15 to 20 minutes, or until edges begin to turn brown. Remove to wire racks to cool.

Note: Sesame seeds are available in bulk at some supermarkets and at natural foods stores.

Make ahead: If wrapped well, the rolls of dough can be refrigerated for up to a month, or frozen for several months.

—From *Ladies Home Journal*

CASHEW SHORTBREAD

MAKES 4 DOZEN SMALL COOKIES

We love buttery shortbread. But adding finely chopped cashews gives an ever richer, deeper flavor as the nuts toast while the cookies bake.

> 1 cup unsalted butter, softened (2 sticks)
> ½ cup firmly packed light brown sugar
> 3 tablespoons granulated sugar
> 1 cup finely chopped raw cashews
> 2 cups unbleached all-purpose flour
> ½ teaspoon salt
> ½ teaspoon baking powder

Position rack in center of oven. Preheat oven to 350 degrees.

In a large mixing bowl, place butter, brown sugar, and granulated sugar. Beat at high speed with an electric mixer for about 3 minutes. Stir in cashews. Sift flour, salt, and baking powder directly into the bowl. Use your hands to mix the dough as quickly and efficiently as possible, until it holds together. Form it into a rough ball.

➤➤

Lightly flour a clean, dry work surface. Add ball of dough and roll it out until it is approximately ¼ inch thick. Cut into simple shapes and place them on an ungreased baking sheet.

Bake for 7 to 10 minutes, or until lightly browned on the bottom. Allow to cool for a few minutes on baking sheet before transferring to a rack. Reroll dough scraps and continue cutting and baking cookies until all dough is used.

Make ahead: Shortbread can be made, wrapped airtight, and frozen for several months.

— From *Enchanted Broccoli Forest*, by Mollie Katzen (Ten Speed Press)

PECAN TASSIES

MAKES ABOUT 4 DOZEN TARTS

Pecan Tassies—which are like a tiny wedge of pecan pie—are usually the first thing to disappear on a holiday cookie plate. This recipe is a classic version that came to us more than 20 years ago from the Junior League of Palo Alto, California.

1½ cups butter, softened (3 sticks; divided)
6 ounces cream cheese, softened (two 3-ounce packages)
2 cups all-purpose flour
Salt
1 cup granulated sugar
1 egg, slightly beaten
1½ cups chopped pecans
1 cup chopped dates
1 tablespoon vanilla
Pecan halves, to garnish (optional)
Powdered sugar, to garnish (optional)

Preheat oven to 350 degrees.

In a large bowl, combine 1 cup butter, cream cheese, flour, and ¼ teaspoon salt. Mix until well-blended.

Divide the dough into 4 equal parts, refrigerate for 30 minutes (not essential, but it does make the dough easier to work with), then separate each part into 12 balls, all the same size.

Place the balls into 4 ungreased, miniature muffin tins. Using your thumb and forefinger, or the back of a teaspoon, press each ball into its cup, working the dough evenly up the sides to the rim.

In a large bowl, cream the remaining ½ cup butter with the sugar and ¼ teaspoon salt. Add the egg, pecans, dates, and vanilla, mixing well.

Divide filling among the unbaked shells, filling each completely. Dot each with pecan half, if desired. Bake until golden brown, about 30 to 40 minutes.

Cool on racks before removing the tarts from their tins. Just before serving, sprinkle with powdered sugar, if desired.

Make ahead: The tarts can be baked and stored in an airtight container up to several days before serving, or they can be frozen.

— Adapted from *Private Collection: Recipes From the Junior League of Palo Alto* by Bonnie Stewart Mickelson (Junior League of Palo Alto)

Some recipes call for sifting flour with other ingredients (such as baking powder and salt), which is done to incorporate them more evenly. Otherwise, sifting is not necessary, because all flour is sifted several times in the milling process. To obtain the most accurate measurement, spoon the flour into a standard dry measuring cup and level it off with a metal spatula or flat table knife. Don't dip the measuring cup into the canister of flour, and never shake or tap the cup to level it.

CANDIED GINGER AND WALNUT BISCOTTI

MAKES ABOUT 3½ DOZEN BISCOTTI

Ken Hoyt, Portland designer, writer, and TV host, has developed a number of biscotti recipes, but this is the one his friends clamor for. The crunchy twice-baked cookies are low in fat and sugar, yet bursting with gingery flavor. Enjoy them with steaming latte, cool sorbet, or as the Italians do, with a glass of wine. The recipe can be doubled.

1 cup granulated sugar
½ cup vegetable oil
2 tablespoons ground ginger ¾ cup coarsely chopped crystallized ginger
1 cup coarsely chopped walnuts
4 egg whites
2½ cups all-purpose flour
1 heaping tablespoon baking powder

In a mixing bowl, combine the sugar with the oil. Blend in the ground ginger, crystallized ginger, and nuts until combined. Stir in the egg whites.

Sift the flour and baking powder into the egg-white mixture and stir until thoroughly blended. Cover and chill for 2 to 3 hours.

Preheat oven to 375 degrees. Grease and flour a baking sheet and set aside.

To shape the dough, lightly flour hands. (If hands become sticky, wash and reflour.) Divide the dough in half. Place on the baking sheet and form into 2 logs approximately ½ inch thick, 2 inches wide, and 12 inches long. Be sure to leave at least 2 inches spacing between the logs. Bake in the middle of the oven until golden brown, 18 to 20 minutes. Leave oven on.

Place the baking sheet on a rack and let the logs cool on the baking sheet for 10 minutes. Remove the logs to a cutting board and use a serrated knife to cut ½-inch-thick slices. Lay the slices flat on the baking sheet and return to the oven for 10 minutes, turning slices over once. Remove from the oven, cool and store in a tightly covered container.

— From Ken Hoyt

NORDY BARS

MAKES ABOUT 40 (1-INCH) SQUARES

Some recipes really get around. And that includes these rich and gooey bars made with butterscotch, chocolate chips, and marshmallows. Nordstrom used to make them for its in-store cafes, and the recipe has run in various publications, sometimes as "Yankee" bars.

>   ½ cup unsalted butter (1 stick)
>   1 (11-ounce) package butterscotch chips
>   ¾ cup firmly packed brown sugar
>   2 eggs
>   1 tablespoon vanilla extract
>   1¾ cups all-purpose flour
>   2 teaspoons baking powder
>   ½ teaspoon kosher salt
>   1 (12-ounce) package chocolate chips (2 cups)
>   2 cups miniature marshmallows
>   1 cup chopped pecans

Preheat oven to 350 degrees. Grease a 9-by-13-inch pan.

In a double boiler over medium-high heat, melt butter, butterscotch chips and brown sugar, stirring until chips are melted. Remove pan from heat and transfer to a large bowl. Use a handheld or stand mixer, blend mixture until it has cooled to 85 or 90 degrees. Add eggs and vanilla, and mix until smooth.

In a separate bowl, sift together flour, baking powder, and salt. Add flour mixture to butter mixture, and mix thoroughly, scraping down sides of bowl once. Stir in chocolate chips, marshmallows, and pecans, mixing until incorporated.

Using gloved hands or an oiled spatula, spread into prepared pan and bake 15 minutes. Rotate pan and cook until golden brown, about 10 more minutes. Remove from oven, cool, and cut in squares or bars.

— From Nordstrom

HOW LOW CAN YOU GO?

According to Borden, the maker of Eagle Brand condensed milk, lower-fat or nonfat sweetened condensed milk should not be substituted for regular in most recipes. (When the lower-fat version was introduced, the manufacturer recommended using it for any recipe, but the results were not satisfactory.) Desserts and pies made with the lower-fat products may be too soft or tend to weep.

RED FOX BROWNIES

MAKES 16 BROWNIES

McMinnville's Red Fox Bakery makes a classic fudgy brownie that's dense, rich, and chocolaty. But for those of you who like to live dangerously, our test kitchen developed the three accompanying variations: salted caramel; port-drenched cherries and crunchy cocoa nibs; ancho chile powder, cinnamon, and spicy pecans. Note that the basic recipe makes a lot of batter, which results in deep brownies with crispy sides.

>   12 ounces bittersweet chocolate, coarsely
>   chopped
>   1½ cups (3 sticks) unsalted butter, cut
>   into tablespoons
>   6 eggs
>   1 tablespoon vanilla extract
>   3⅔ cups superfine sugar (1 pound, 9 ounces;
>   see note)
>   Pinch kosher salt
>   4⅓ cups cake flour (1 pound)

Preheat oven to 350 degrees. Grease a 9-by-13-inch baking dish with a butter wrapper or nonstick cooking spray; line with parchment paper or foil leaving 2 inches extra on the long ends to use as handles for removing uncut brownies from pan.

In the top of a double boiler, melt chocolate and butter together over simmering water. Whisk to combine and set aside.

In the bowl of a stand mixer, add eggs, vanilla, sugar, and salt. Using the whisk attachment, whip on high for 5 minutes or until the batter is thick and holds a ribbon when the beaters are lifted from the bowl. Remove bowl from the stand; gently sift the flour over the top of the egg mixture. Using a rubber spatula, fold in the flour gently, taking care to get any pockets of white flour.

Fold the chocolate mixture into the batter quickly, being sure to get all the way to the bottom of the bowl.

Pour batter into prepared pan and bake until the top has a thin, flaky layer, the sides begin to pull away from the pan, and it is slightly domed, about 50 to 60 minutes. A knife inserted in the center will come away with just a crumb or two.

Cool and refrigerate until set before attempting to cut. Best served at room temperature.

Note: Superfine sugar dissolves more easily than regular granulated sugar. C&H Baker's Sugar is one brand. To make superfine sugar, place regular granulated sugar in a food processor or blender and blend for 15 seconds.

— From Laurie Furch, Red Fox Bakery, McMinnville

VARIATIONS

CARAMEL SWIRL BROWNIES WITH SEA SALT

> 1 (11-ounce) jar thick caramel sauce (the sauce should be thick enough that it doesn't pour out of the jar)
> 1½ teaspoons flaky sea salt (we used Maldon brand)

Pour half the brownie batter into the prepared pan. Drop half of the caramel sauce over the batter in dollops. Swirl into the batter. Sprinkle with ½ teaspoon sea salt. Pour the remaining batter over the caramel and spoon the remaining caramel sauce in dollops over the top. Swirl caramel into the batter and sprinkle the remaining teaspoon sea salt over the top. Bake as directed.

CHERRY-PORT BROWNIES WITH COCOA NIBS

> 2½ cups dried tart cherries (about 1 pound)
> 1 cup port wine
> 1 cup cocoa nibs (see note)

In a small saucepan, combine the cherries and port. Bring to a boil, reduce heat, and simmer for 2 to 3 minutes. Remove from heat and let cool. While the cherries are cooling, prepare the brownie batter. Fold the cooled cherries and the cocoa nibs into the batter; spread in the prepared pan. Bake as directed.

Note: Cocoa nibs are bits of roasted cocoa beans. You can find them at specialty grocery stores such as New Seasons and Zupan's.

SPICY CHILE PECAN BROWNIES

> 4 teaspoons ground cinnamon
> 1 tablespoon ancho chile powder (or other pure chile powder—not a chili blend)
> 1 teaspoon cayenne pepper, or to taste
> 2 cups coarsely chopped spiced pecans (see note)

Make brownie batter as directed but stir the cinnamon, ancho chile powder, and cayenne pepper into the flour before folding the flour into the eggs and sugar. Fold the spiced pecans into the completed batter and pour into the prepared pan. Bake as directed.

Note: To make spiced pecans, see recipe for Cran-Apple Spinach Salad with Spiced Pecans, page 26, or use store-bought. You can also substitute candied walnuts or plain toasted pecans.

— Linda Faus

CRANBERRY STREUSEL BARS

MAKES 24 (1-BY-1¾-INCH) BARS

Oregon's cranberry industry may not be as big as some states', but growers here say our berries are larger and redder because we have a longer growing season. These bars showcase the berries' bright, tart flavor in between layers of tender streusel made with nubby oats and walnuts. The fruit and grains might even qualify these bars as breakfast.

Fresh cranberries will keep, refrigerated, for at least two weeks. For longer storage, freeze them in the plastic bag they came in; they'll stay good for up to a year.

CRANBERRY FILLING:

> 1 (12-ounce) bag fresh or frozen cranberries (3½ cups)
> ¾ cup water
> 1 cup granulated sugar
> Pinch salt
> ¼ teaspoon ground mace

BARS:

> 1 cup firmly packed brown sugar
> 1¾ cups all-purpose flour
> ½ teaspoon baking soda
> ½ teaspoon salt
> ½ teaspoon ground cinnamon
> ¾ cup unsalted butter, room temperature (1½ sticks)
> 1½ cups old-fashioned (not instant) oatmeal, uncooked
> ½ cup chopped walnuts (optional)

To make filling: In a medium saucepan, combine the cranberries (no need to thaw berries if they're frozen), the water, and sugar. Bring to a boil over high heat, then reduce to a simmer. Cook, stirring occasionally, until the mixture thickens and the cranberries pop, about 5 minutes. Remove from heat and stir in the salt and mace; set aside to cool. (Mixture will thicken as it cools). Makes 3 cups.

▶

To make bars: Preheat oven to 375 degrees. Grease a 7-by-11-inch pan and set aside.

In a large bowl, combine the brown sugar, flour, baking soda, salt, and cinnamon. Add the butter and, using your fingers, work together until no small lumps remain. Stir in the oatmeal.

Press and flatten half of the mixture in the prepared pan to form a crust. Bake for 10 minutes. Remove the crust from the oven and, while warm, spread the crust with all of the cranberry filling. Add the nuts, if using, to the remaining oatmeal mixture; sprinkle this streusel evenly over filling. Return to the oven and bake 25 minutes, until streusel topping is lightly browned. Cool pan on rack and cut into bars.

Make ahead: Bars can be made and stored in a covered container for up to a week or wrapped well and frozen for up to a month.

— From Sara Bir

BROWN SUGAR BLUES

If you're out of brown sugar, don't despair. For each cup of firmly packed light brown sugar, use 1½ tablespoons molasses plus 1 cup granulated sugar. For 1 cup of firmly packed dark brown sugar, use ¼ cup molasses and 1 cup granulated sugar. Mix the molasses into the sugar with a fork until evenly distributed.

WALNUT-PECAN SQUARES

MAKES 18 (3-INCH) SQUARES

These are Foodday's version of a popular cookie sold at Elephants Delicatessen. They are very rich, so you might prefer to cut them into bite-size (1-inch) pieces instead of the 3-inch squares sold at the deli.

CRUST:

½ cup granulated sugar
½ cup plus 6 tablespoons unsalted butter, at room temperature (1¾ sticks)
1 egg
3 cups unbleached all-purpose flour
1 teaspoon salt
½ teaspoon baking powder

FILLING:

1¼ cups unsalted butter (2½ sticks)
1½ cups firmly packed brown sugar
¼ cup plus 1 tablespoon granulated sugar
⅓ cup honey
⅓ cup light corn syrup

2 cups toasted and lightly broken pecans (8 ounces; see note)
2 cups toasted and lightly broken walnuts (8 ounces; see note)
¼ cup whipping cream
½ teaspoon salt
½ teaspoon vanilla extract

Preheat oven to 350 degrees. Grease a 10-by-15-inch baking pan and line with parchment paper, allowing a 1-inch overhang on the long ends to use as handles for removing the uncut treat from pan.

To make crust: In the bowl of a mixer, cream sugar and butter until light and fluffy. Add the egg and beat until well-combined.

In a small bowl, stir together the flour, salt, and baking powder. Add the flour mixture to the butter mixture; mix until dough comes together. Pat the dough evenly into the prepared pan, building up the edges slightly. Bake for 17 to 20 minutes or until crust begins to brown and set. Remove from oven and cool.

To make filling: Reduce oven to 300 degrees. Place a large baking sheet on the bottom oven rack to catch drips. In a medium saucepan, combine butter, brown sugar, granulated sugar, honey, and corn syrup; bring to a boil over medium-high heat. Boil for exactly 2½ minutes. Remove from heat; stir in pecans, walnuts, cream, salt, and vanilla. Pour filling into cooled crust and spread evenly.

Bake on center oven rack over the sheet pan for 35 to 40 minutes, or until the filling is bubbling in the center. Cool overnight. Cut into squares and serve.

Note: To toast nuts, spread on baking sheet, and bake in 350-degree oven for 5 to 8 minutes or until they start to brown.

— Adapted by Linda Faus from Georgeanne Brennan

MARGARITA BARS

MAKES ABOUT 40 (1½-INCH) SQUARES

Oregonian staffers scarfed up these tart treats as soon as we put them out for sampling. The reposado tequila gives the bars a complex, rich flavor that contrasts nicely with the brightness of the lime. A topping of sugar, lime zest, and a pinch of salt mimics a margarita's salted rim.

CRUST:

2 cups all-purpose flour
¾ cup granulated sugar
1¼ teaspoons kosher salt
1 cup cold unsalted butter, cut into small
    pieces (2 sticks)

FILLING:

½ cup all-purpose flour
1 cup granulated sugar
½ teaspoon kosher salt
4 eggs, plus 2 egg yolks
1 cup key lime juice (bottled is fine)
¼ cup plus 2 tablespoons reposado tequila

TOPPING:

½ cup granulated sugar (or a mix of
    granulated and coarse white
    decorating sugar)

2 teaspoons packed grated lime zest
1 teaspoon kosher salt

To make crust: Preheat oven to 350 degrees. Grease a 9-by-13-inch glass baking dish. Place a sheet of parchment in the bottom of the dish, allowing a 1-inch overhang on the long ends to use as handles for removing the uncut treat from dish.

In a food processor, place flour, sugar, and salt; pulse to combine. Add the butter and process until the mixture looks pale yellow and crumbly. Transfer the mixture to the dish and spread evenly. With the back of a small, dry measuring cup, press the mixture firmly and evenly into the bottom of the dish. Freeze for 15 minutes. Bake crust until lightly golden, about 30 minutes. Prepare filling while crust bakes.

To make filling: In a medium bowl, mix flour, sugar, and salt. Add eggs and egg yolks; mix to combine. Stir in lime juice and tequila. When crust is golden, pour filling over the hot crust and return to the oven. Bake 30 minutes, or until set (filling won't jiggle and may have begun to crack). Remove from oven and place on a wire rack to cool. Refrigerate several hours or overnight before cutting.

To make topping: In a small bowl, mix together sugar, lime zest, and salt until zest is evenly distributed. Just before serving, sprinkle mixture evenly over uncut dessert until lightly coated (you may not use all of it). Run a knife around the edge of the pan before lifting the dessert out using the ends of the parchment. Trim off edges of dessert, cut into 1½-inch squares and serve.

— From Danielle Centoni

IN THE KITCHEN WITH OREGON CHEFS

There's no doubt about it: Chefs have made a major contribution to Oregon's reputation for great food. And Oregonians have responded with enthusiasm. We love to eat out—whether it's a special-occasion meal at a high-end restaurant or a late-night snack at a food cart. While *The Oregonian Cookbook* showcases many recipes from professionals all over the state, we tried to compile a modest list of influential chefs from the past two decades for one special chapter. Our list is by no means complete, as there are just too many talented chefs for us to include them all. But the twenty recipes here represent a wonderful cross-section—some easy and a few challenging. All are delicious.

Andy Ricker has been passionate about Thai food ever since he began backpacking around Southeast Asia in 1987. And while he has cooked at such notable restaurants as Christopher Israel's lamented Zefiro's, it was Pok Pok, Ricker's Thai grill restaurant, that catapulted him to fame and earned him many awards, including *The Oregonian*'s Restaurant of the Year in 2007. He also owns The Whiskey Soda Lounge across the street from Pok Pok. Ricker has successfully exported his famous chicken wings to a storefront in New York City and plans to open another restaurant in Brooklyn in 2012.

GRILLED SWEET CORN ON THE COB WITH SALTY COCONUT CREAM

MAKES 12 SERVINGS

This makes enough Salty Coconut Cream for 12 ears of corn, but you don't have to grill that many ears at once because the prepared cream can be refrigerated for up to two weeks.

> 2 cups UHT coconut cream (see note)
> 1 pandanus leaf, scrunched and bruised (see note)
> 1½ tablespoons granulated sugar
> Kosher salt
> 12 ears fresh corn, shucked (leave the stem on as a handle)
> Lime wedges

In a medium pot, combine the coconut cream, pandanus leaf, sugar and 1½ teaspoons salt. Bring to a boil over high heat, reduce heat and simmer, covered, for about 10 minutes to reduce slightly. Remove from heat and cool. Refrigerate until ready to use.

When ready to cook the corn, prepare an ice water bath in a large bowl. Bring a large pot of water to a boil, add 1 tablespoon salt per quart of water and add the corn. Return the water to a boil, and blanch the ears for 3 minutes. Remove the corn and immediately transfer to the ice bath. You may need to blanch the corn in batches.

Prepare the grill to medium-high (see note). Lightly brush each ear of blanched corn with the cream mixture and grill until golden brown all over, about 3 minutes per side. Remove from grill, and brush again with the cream mixture. Serve immediately with lime wedges.

Note: UHT (Ultra High Temperature) coconut cream is shelf-stable coconut cream that is sold in boxes. Pok Pok uses Aroy-D brand, which is sold at some Asian markets. Canned Savoy brand coconut cream is a good substitute. Do not substitute coconut milk or cream of coconut (which is sweet).

▶▶

Note: Pandanus leaf is a long thin leaf that looks like the leaf of the day lily. It can be found fresh or frozen in Asian markets as pandan leaf or panda leaf.

Note: To check grill temperature, count the seconds you can hold your hand, palm side down, 2 to 3 inches above the rack, until it feels uncomfortable: 3 seconds for medium-high.

— From Andy Ricker, chef/owner, Pok Pok

French-born **Pascal Sauton** received a classic French culinary education and worked in a number of starred restaurants in France before landing in the United States in 1985. He opened the much-admired Carafe in August 2003, and during his time there the restaurant was twice chosen Best French Restaurant by *Portland Monthly*, among other honors. After selling Carafe in 2011, Sauton and his daughter, Prunelle, created Milwaukie Kitchen & Wine, a specialty deli, market, wine shop, gourmet coffee shop, and studio for cooking classes and events.

SALMON RILLETTES AND TOASTED BAGUETTE

MAKES 4 SERVINGS

Rillettes, a sort of pâté, are often served as a spread. But Sauton prefers to create canapes, which are a study in contrasting textures and flavors: crunchy toasted baguette; lacy, clean frisée; soft butter and poached salmon; grassy refreshing herbs; and crisp, peppery radish. Sauton likes to pair this dish with Chablis, a chardonnay from the coolest, northernmost region of Burgundy.

SALMON:

2 cups water

1 cup dry white wine

2 sprigs thyme

1 bay leaf

1 small onion, diced

1 small carrot, diced

1 stalk celery, diced

1 tablespoon sea salt

8 ounces fresh wild salmon fillet, sliced into 8 pieces

▶

RILLETTES:

¼ cup unsalted butter, at room temperature

1 teaspoon Dijon mustard

1 teaspoon chopped fresh tarragon

1 teaspoon chopped fresh chives

1 teaspoon chopped fresh parsley

1 teaspoon lemon juice

¼ teaspoon Piment d'Espelette (ground Basque chile pepper; see note) or ground pasilla chile

Sea salt

8 (1-inch-thick) slices baguette, cut on the bias

1 cup torn frisée or arugula

1 teaspoon lemon juice, or to taste

1 tablespoon olive oil, or to taste

Salt and freshly ground black pepper

1 radish, sliced paper-thin

To make salmon: In a saucepan, place water, wine, thyme, bay leaf, onion, carrot, celery, and salt; bring to a boil, reduce heat and simmer for 10 minutes. Place the salmon in the bouillon, and poach about 3 to 5 minutes or until flesh is cooked through. Remove the salmon with a slotted spoon and refrigerate. Discard bouillon (or save it and make a soup or stock from it later).

To make rillettes: Whip the butter with a whisk, hand beater, or blender until light and fluffy. Add the mustard, herbs, and lemon juice; whip thoroughly. Season with Piment d'Espelette and salt.

With your fingers, flake the salmon into small pieces. Add to the whipped butter and fold in with a spatula.

When ready to serve, grill or toast baguette slices. In a medium bowl, toss greens with lemon juice, olive oil, salt, and pepper. On each plate, pile greens on 2 slices of baguette. Spoon salmon rillette on top. Garnish with radish slices.

Note: Piment d'Espelette is a ground Basque chile pepper that is not too spicy and has a lot of fruitiness that works well with fish. It's available by special order at Pastaworks. Ground pasilla chile is sold in the Latino foods section of supermarkets, such as Fred Meyer, as well as at Latino groceries. If you can't find either of these ingredients, a dash or two of Tabasco sauce should do the trick.

— From Pascal Sauton, chef/owner, Milwaukie Kitchen & Wine

Christopher Israel is truly one of the architects of Portland's emergence as a major food destination. He and former business partner Bruce Carey opened the now lamented Zefiro—a restaurant that sealed their culinary reputations—in 1991. They would also create Saucebox and 23 Hoyt. In 1999, Israel took a sabbatical from cooking to spend six years as associate art director for *Vanity Fair* magazine in New York City. He later returned to Portland and in December 2009 opened Grüner, where he serves "Alpine cuisine."

LIPTAUER

MAKES ABOUT 2 CUPS

Liptauer is a mildly spicy cheese spread that is part of the cuisines of Slovakia, Hungary, Austria, Serbia, and northern Italy (Trieste). Serve the spread with crisp radishes, leafy green celery sticks, and country-style bread or pretzels for the perfect party snack.

1 cup cottage cheese, drained for 15 minutes in a fine-mesh sieve
1 cup cream cheese, room temperature (Israel prefers Gina Marie brand; see note)
1 tablespoon finely minced shallots
2 teaspoons paprika, or more to your liking
2 teaspoons caraway seeds
2 tablespoons minced fresh chives
2 tablespoons finely chopped fresh parsley
Sea salt and freshly ground black pepper

In a medium bowl, add cottage cheese, cream cheese, shallots, paprika, caraway seeds, chives, parsley, and salt and pepper to taste; mix well. Refrigerate for at least 1 hour so flavors develop.

Note: Gina Marie cream cheese has a light, fluffy texture and fresh creamy taste. Find it at Sheridan Fruit Co., New Seasons, Food Front Northwest, and Food Front Southwest.

Make ahead: You can make this recipe a day or two ahead if you wait to add the minced shallots until 1 hour before serving.

— From Christopher Israel, chef/owner, Grüner

Before settling in Oregon, Eric Bechard cooked for several years in Palm Springs, California. After a stint at the Heathman Restaurant in 2003, he became the chef at Alberta Street Oyster Bar, where he was named *The Oregonian*'s Rising Star in 2006. In 2009 he and his partner, Emily Howard, opened Thistle, which was named *The Oregonian*'s Restaurant of the Year in 2011—the first restaurant outside Portland to earn this distinction.

DUCK LIVER PARFAIT

MAKES 8 TO 10 APPETIZER SERVINGS

This silken spread is ideally served with toast and tart pickles, such as a cornichons.

1½ teaspoons extra-virgin olive oil or lard, if you have it

1 pound fresh duck livers (pork, rabbit, or any other fowl works great as well), membrane and other sinew cut away and discarded

¼ cup chopped shallots

4 tablespoons sherry (fino or amontillado preferred; divided)

½ cup unsalted butter (1 stick), at room temperature

1 tablespoon heavy whipping cream

1 pinch freshly grated nutmeg

Salt

¼ teaspoon freshly ground black pepper

⅛ teaspoon unflavored gelatin

In a large sauté pan, heat the olive oil or lard over high heat. When hot, add the livers, and brown them, turning frequently, until carmelized to medium rare—about 4 minutes. Spoon the cooked livers into a blender and return pan to high heat; add the chopped shallots and cook until caramelized, stirring frequently—be careful not to let them burn. Add 1 tablespoon sherry and stir, letting the alcohol cook off completely, another 2 minutes. Scrape shallots into the blender. Add the butter, cream, nutmeg, salt to taste, and pepper; blend into a smooth paste.

Spoon the mixture into four 4-ounce mason jars or ramekins, smooth the tops, and cool.

In a small saucepan, sprinkle the gelatin over the remaining 3 tablespoons sherry and let stand for 5 minutes to soften. Bring to a simmer over medium-high heat, stirring to fully dissolve the gelatin. Cook for 30 seconds. Divide the sherry mixture over the liver and chill.

Serve at room temperature with toast and pickles for a dinner party, or pack into a larger jar or crock, and serve with pickles on a buffet table.

Make ahead: The parfait can be made and refrigerated 4 to 7 days ahead, depending on the freshness of the livers.

— From Eric Bechard, chef/co-owner, Thistle

Anthony Cafiero moved to Portland in 2000 to attend college, and paid his way through school working at Veritable Quandary, In Good Taste, and Paley's Place. By 2004, Cafiero was working for Cathy Whims at Nostrana, then joined Adam Berger at his restaurant, Ten 01. When that venture closed, Berger asked him to become the chef at Tabla Mediterranean Bistro, where he and his cooks conjure up an exciting mixture of modern and traditional Italian and Spanish dishes.

GARLIC ALMOND SOUP (AJO BLANCO)

MAKES 4 TO 6 SERVINGS

Ajo Blanco is a traditional cold soup from southern Spain. It's a refreshing way to balance a meal that includes spicy food.

1½ quarts water
2 cups whole blanched almonds (see note)
3 cloves garlic, peeled (divided)
2 cups whole milk, plus more as needed
1 tablespoon sherry vinegar
½ cup extra-virgin olive oil
1 tablespoon granulated sugar
1 to 2 tablespoons kosher salt
Garnishes: extra-virgin olive oil, paprika, and sliced green grapes

Fill a large stockpot with water, almonds and 1 clove garlic. Bring to boil on medium-high heat and cook for 1 hour.

With a ladle, transfer almonds to a blender, and then add 2 cups of the water from the pot. Add the milk, remaining 2 cloves garlic and the vinegar; blend on high for 4 minutes. If the purée becomes difficult to blend, add a bit more milk and reserved cooking liquid. The resulting purée should have a thick, soupy consistency. With the blender running, slowly stream in the olive oil, then add the sugar and salt.

Pass soup through a fine-mesh strainer into a bowl, using a ladle to push as much of the soup through as possible. Refrigerate for 60 minutes. After chilling, if the soup is too thick, thin it as needed with more milk. Adjust salt to taste as needed.

Serve in bowls and garnish with a drizzle of olive oil, a dusting of paprika, and sliced green grapes.

Note: Find whole blanched almonds at Barbur World Foods (see Resources chapter), or substitute 2 cups slivered almonds.

Make ahead: Soup can be made and refrigerated up to 2 days in advance. Thin as needed with milk.

— From Anthony Cafiero, chef de cuisine,
Tabla Mediterranean Bistro

Chef Jason Stoller Smith began his apprenticeship in Oregon kitchens at the age of sixteen, becoming executive chef of a seafood café in Olympia, Washington, before joining the staff of the National Historic Timberline Lodge on beautiful Mount Hood. Within a year, he was executive sous chef. Four years later, Smith became a partner in the Dundee Bistro, overseeing the kitchen and wine programs. In 2010, he returned to Timberline Lodge as executive chef upon the retirement of Leif Eric Benson. Smith is the recipient of numerous culinary awards and citations and has cooked for President Barack Obama and the First Lady.

TIMBERLINE ALE AND CHEESE SOUP

MAKES 6 SERVINGS

Smith's creamy soup features two of Oregon's favorite ingredients: Tillamook cheddar and microbrewed beer. The flavors of both are beautifully balanced in this easy and delicious soup.

¼ cup butter
2 cups julienne-cut yellow onions
¼ cup all-purpose flour
2 cups low-sodium chicken broth
1 cup mild Northwest microbrew, such as Mt. Hood Brewing Co.'s, Highland Meadow Blonde Ale
2 cups heavy whipping cream
2 cups shredded Tillamook sharp cheddar cheese
Garnishs: croutons, crisp bacon or chopped chives

Melt the butter in a soup pot over medium heat, add the onions, and cook just until translucent (do not let them brown). Add the flour and cook, stirring, for 4 to 5 minutes. Be careful to not let it burn. Add the chicken broth and beer, and cook another 10 to 15 minutes. Reduce the heat to a simmer. Add the cream and cheese, and immediately stir so that the cheese does not settle on the bottom of the pot and burn. Season soup with salt and pepper. Serve hot garnished with croutons, bacon, or chives.

— From Jason Stoller Smith, executive chef, Timberline Lodge

After working with the influential Bradley Ogden at the Lark Creek Inn in Larkspur, California, Scott Dolich did stints with Portland masters David Machado, Cory Schreiber, and Greg Higgins, which led to a spot as executive chef at Tapeo. He opened the popular Park Kitchen in the Pearl District in 2003.

CHILLED CUCUMBER AND ALMOND SOUP WITH MARINATED SALMON

MAKES 6 TO 8 SERVINGS

Dolich has demonstrated this soup in local farmers markets when fresh cucumbers are in season. All the ingredients are readily available and the soup requires less than 15 minutes of hands-on work.

SOUP:

7 medium cucumbers, unpeeled, sliced
    about ½ inch thick (about 2 quarts)
¼ Walla Walla sweet onion, sliced
    ¼ inch thick
2 cloves garlic, chopped
1 cup blanched whole almonds, toasted
    (see note)
¼ bunch fresh parsley, stemmed and
    chopped
Juice and grated zest of 3 limes
1 cup extra-virgin olive oil
Salt

SALMON:

8 ounces wild king salmon (preferably
    belly portion)
2 tablespoons finely diced red onion
½ bunch chives, thinly sliced
⅓ cup extra-virgin olive oil
6 drops lime juice, or to taste
Salt and freshly ground black pepper

To make soup: In a large bowl, combine cucumbers, onion, garlic, almonds, parsley, lime juice, and zest. Allow to macerate for 1 hour.

In a blender, process mixture in small batches using olive oil to emulsify. Adjust seasoning as you go with salt. Pass mixture through fine mesh sieve. If thoroughly blended, very little should not pass through. Chill the soup completely.

To make salmon: Finely dice the salmon and combine with onion, chives, oil, and lime juice.

Season to taste with salt and pepper, and add additional lime juice, if needed.

Divide soup among chilled bowls and garnish on top with the salmon.

Note: To toast nuts, spread on baking sheet and bake in 350-degree oven for 5 to 8 minutes or until they start to brown.

— From Scott Dolich, chef/owner, Park Kitchen

Lisa Schroeder has worked in four-star restaurants in New York and France and teaches classes regularly. She's also appeared on *Good Morning America* and the Today show, among many others. At Mother's Bistro, she focuses on comforting, homestyle fare.

SALMON CHOWDER

MAKES 3 QUARTS; 6 (2-CUP) SERVINGS

"If there's one thing Oregonians cherish, it's Pacific Northwest salmon," says Schroeder. For this chowder she says, "If wild salmon is not readily available or prohibitively expensive, you can substitute farm-raised salmon and get an equally tasty soup."

1 pound salmon fillet, skin and bones
    removed
8 ounces bacon, finely diced (about 1 cup)
12 tablespoons unsalted butter (1½ sticks;
    divided)
2 cups finely diced yellow onions
1 cup peeled and finely diced carrot
1 cup finely diced celery

1 cup all-purpose flour
8 cups fish stock (2 quarts)
½ cup dry white wine
1 tablespoon chopped fresh thyme or
    2 teaspoons dried thyme
1 bay leaf
2 cups finely diced red potatoes
1 cup heavy whipping cream
1 tablespoon finely chopped fresh dill
    (about ¼ bunch)
3 teaspoons salt
1 teaspoon freshly ground black pepper

Cut the salmon into 1-inch cubes. Make sure there are no bones. Place in the refrigerator until ready to use.

Heat a heavy, medium (6- to 8-quart) stockpot

over medium-high heat. When hot, add the bacon and cook until beginning to brown in spots. Lower heat to medium and cook, stirring, until the fat has rendered, about 10 minutes.

Add 2 tablespoons butter, onions, carrots, and celery and sauté until very soft, at least 20 minutes. Remove the bacon and vegetables from the stockpot and set aside.

Reduce heat to medium. Add remaining 10 tablespoons butter to the pot and melt. Stir in the flour with a wooden spoon to make a blond roux: cook, stirring occasionally, for about 5 minutes until the mixture looks like fine, wet sand.

Slowly add the fish stock, a little at a time, whisking constantly and letting the roux absorb the liquid after each addition. (Take your time here. The best defense against lumps is steady whisking and slow pouring. Add the stock in stages, letting the roux absorb each addition before whisking in more.) Bring mixture to a boil, reduce heat and simmer for 10 minutes.

Return the vegetables and bacon to the pot. Add the wine, thyme, bay leaves, and potatoes. Bring to a boil, reduce the heat and simmer until the potatoes are soft, about 20 minutes. Add the salmon and cook just until opaque, about 10 minutes.

Remove the pot from the heat and stir in the cream and dill. Taste and adjust seasoning with salt and pepper as needed. Ladle into bowls and serve hot.

— From Lisa Schroeder, executive chef/owner, Mother's Bistro & Bar

Before deciding to become a chef, Jenn Louis had already received a degree from Pitzer College and worked in the woods of North Carolina, in the Florida Keys and Everglades, cooking meals for base camp staff of Outward Bound, the nonprofit outdoors program for youth. Jenn Louis has also cooked at a number of fine Portland restaurants, including Wildwood. She launched her catering company, Culinary Artistry, before opening Lincoln in 2008, followed by The Sunshine Tavern in 2011. The following year, Louis was named a *Food & Wine* Magazine's Best New Chef.

LACINATO KALE SALAD WITH GRAPEFRUIT

MAKES 2 SERVINGS

For this salad, Louis uses tender lacinato kale, also called cavalo nero, dinosaur, or black kale. The grapefruit sections, lemon juice, and zest add bright notes to the richness of the fromage blanc and pine nuts.

DRESSING:

2 tablespoons lemon juice
2 tablespoons grated lemon zest
3 tablespoons extra-virgin olive oil

SALAD:

1 grapefruit
3 cups ribbons (⅓ inch wide) lacinato kale (stemmed)
2 tablespoons pine nuts, lightly toasted (see note)
1 tablespoon thinly sliced shallot
Kosher salt and freshly ground black pepper
2 tablespoons fromage blanc (see note)

To make dressing: In a dressing bottle or small bowl, combine lemon juice, lemon zest and oil.

To make salad: Use a knife to slice the peel and any white pith off the grapefruit. Working over a bowl, slice on either side of the membranes to release the segments; set aside.

In a large bowl, combine kale, pine nuts, and shallot. Season salad with salt and pepper. Pick fromage blanc into small pieces and toss with salad. Add dressing and toss well. Place salad on serving plate(s); arrange grapefruit segments on top.

Note: To toast pine nuts, place in a small skillet and place over medium heat, shaking frequently, until golden brown.

Note: Fromage blanc is a fresh and very soft cream cheese. Find it at well-stocked cheese counters or cheese shops.

— From Jenn Louis, chef/owner, Lincoln restaurant and Sunshine Tavern

Cathy Whims was part of the team that founded Genoa, and she spent nearly 20 years there serving authentic Italian cooking, eventually becoming co-owner. She honed her skills with Marcella and Victor Hazan, and Madeleine Kamman, and also in the kitchens of notable restaurants in Italy's Piedmont region. It's no wonder then that after opening Nostrana in 2005 with her partner David West, the restaurant quickly earned *The Oregonian*'s Best Restaurant of the Year. She has been a James Beard Award finalist for Best Chef: Northwest for four consecutive years. In December 2011, Whims and her partners opened Oven & Shaker, a pizzeria/saloon in Portland's Pearl District.

NOSTRANA SALAD

MAKES 6 TO 8 SERVINGS

This popular salad has been on Nostrana's menu since the restaurant opened. The radicchio is soaked in ice water to sweeten and crisp it, and Whims reports that people who don't like radicchio say they love this salad.

2 large heads radicchio (see note)

DRESSING:
2 cloves garlic
Salt
3 tablespoons red wine vinegar
2 tablespoons white wine
2 tablespoons mayonnaise
4 oil-packed anchovy fillets, finely chopped
2 egg yolks (see note)
1 cup extra-virgin olive oil
Freshly ground black pepper

CROUTONS:
3 cups cubed (¾-inch) focaccia or other
    open-textured, herb-flavored artisan bread
¼ cup unsalted butter

1 tablespoon (total) chopped fresh sage and
    rosemary
½ cup grated Parmigiano-Reggiano cheese

Tear the radicchio into 1½-inch pieces and soak in water with a little ice for 2 hours.

To make dressing: In a mortar and pestle grind garlic with a pinch of salt; add to a blender or food processor along with vinegar, white wine, mayonnaise, anchovies, and egg yolks. Begin processing, then drizzle in the olive oil until the dressing is completely emulsified. Season with salt and pepper to taste.

To make croutons: Preheat oven to 375 degrees. Bake the bread cubes on a large baking sheet until toasted all over, about 10 to 15 minutes. Meanwhile, in a skillet, melt the butter with the fresh herbs until fragrant. Add the toasted bread cubes, toss well, and let cool.

▶

To assemble, drain the radicchio, spin well in a salad spinner and place in a large salad bowl. Toss with enough dressing to coat well, add croutons, then shower generously with the Parmigiano-Reggiano and serve.

Note: Buy a round variety of radicchio, such as Verona or Chioggia, not the spear-shaped Treviso variety.

Note: Be sure to use clean, uncracked eggs. Because raw eggs carry a risk of salmonella, this recipe is not recommended for people in a high-risk group for contracting food poisoning, including the elderly, the very young, the chronically ill, pregnant women, or anyone with a weakened immune system.

— From Cathy Whims, chef/owner, Nostrana

Cory Schreiber, who along with Christopher Israel and Greg Higgins, led Portland's emergence as a major culinary center in the 1990s. He is the founding chef of Wildwood, which is still a standard-bearer of excellence in the city's Northwest dining scene. Schreiber, a native Oregonian, started his career at age eleven working in his family's Portland restaurant, Dan & Louis Oyster Bar, and later gained experience at top kitchens on the East and West coasts. In 1998, he won the James Beard Award for Best Chef: Northwest. He has written two cookbooks and worked with the Oregon Department of Agriculture's Farm-to-School program, whose goal is serving healthy meals in school cafeterias. He is currently culinary artist-in-residence for the International Culinary School at The Art Institute of Portland.

AYERS CREEK FARM ZEFINO BEANS WITH CHANTERELLES AND QUINOA

MAKES 4 TO 6 FIRST-COURSE SERVINGS

Schreiber's recipe calls for zefino beans, a small, thin-skinned heirloom variety grown by Ayers Creek Farms in Gaston. The dried beans are sold during the winter season of the Hillsdale Farmers Market, but you can substitute dried baby borlotti and flageolet for this savory vegetarian dish.

BEANS:

2 cups dried zefino, baby borlotti or
     flageolet beans
1 large shallot, peeled and the two lobes
     pulled apart
4 cloves garlic, peeled
½ bay leaf
4 sprigs thyme
2 teaspoons kosher salt
Freshly cracked black pepper

MUSHROOMS AND QUINOA:

6 cups water
½ teaspoon kosher salt

½ cup white or red quinoa
2 tablespoons extra-virgin olive oil (divided)
Freshly cracked black pepper
8 ounces fresh chanterelles or cultivated
     mushrooms (such as cremini or
     portobello), cleaned and thinly sliced
4 to 5 leaves kale (preferably lacinato variety),
     stemmed and coarsely chopped
Juice of half a lemon

To make beans: Soak the beans overnight in 6 cups water, at room temperature.

The next day, drain the soaked beans. Place beans into a nonreactive pot. Cover with 3 inches of water. Add the shallot, garlic, bay leaf half, thyme, salt, and peppercorns. (The salt measurement may seem a bit much, but the beans will absorb the salt and make the broth more flavorful.) Place the pot over high heat, and bring the beans to a simmer; reduce heat to maintain a simmer, and cook 25 minutes or just until tender, skimming any debris or foam that rises to the top. Turn off heat, remove the thyme sprigs and bay leaf (leave in the shallot and garlic), and let beans cool in the cooking liquid. They will continue to cook while cooling. You should have 4 cups cooked beans. (The yield can vary depending on the variety of bean you use; if you have more than 4 cups, save the extra for other dishes, or freeze.)

After beans have cooled, scoop ½ cup of them and 1 cup of the cooking liquid into a food processor, and pulse until smooth and creamy. If necessary, add more liquid to achieve a soupy consistency; set this purée aside.

To make mushrooms and quinoa: In a medium-sized saucepan over high heat, bring the 6 cups water and ½ teaspoon salt to a boil. Add the quinoa. When the water returns to a boil, reduce the heat to low, cover, and simmer for 9 minutes, drain immediately. Let the quinoa cool at room temperature. Place quinoa into a bowl, add ½ tablespoon olive oil and some cracked black pepper, and let stand until needed.

Drain the whole beans, reserving ¾ cup of the cooking liquid. In a medium sauté pan, heat the remaining 1½ tablespoons olive oil over medium-high heat. Add the mushrooms, reduce heat to medium, and cook the mushrooms for 3 minutes, stirring occasionally. Add the chopped kale, the drained beans, the bean purée, and the ¾ cup reserved cooking liquid. Stir or toss until ingredients are warm and kale is wilted. Season to taste with additional salt and pepper.

Spoon the bean mixture onto plates; spoon a little quinoa on top. Squeeze lemon juice over each serving.

> — From Cory Schreiber, culinary artist-in-residence, The International Culinary School at The Art Institute of Portland

Vitaly and Kimberly Paley brought impeccable restaurant skills with them when they moved to Portland and opened Paley's Place in 1995, with Vitaly as executive chef and Kimberly as general manager. They chose Portland for the outstanding quality of local ingredients, and the restaurant continues to win awards (James Beard Award for Best Chef: Northwest in 2005) and accolades from publications such as the *New York Times*, *Gourmet*, *Bon Appétit* and *Sunset*. Paley's Place is always one of the first-choice restaurants for Portlanders and visitors.

PAPPARDELLE WITH FAVA BEANS AND MINT

MAKES 4 TO 6 FIRST-CORSE SERVINGS

Serve this delicious dish in early spring when fava beans are just coming to market.

1 pound fresh pasta dough, at room temperature (see note), or 10 to 11 ounces dried pappardelle

All-purpose flour, for dusting

¼ cup extra-virgin olive oil, plus more for drizzling

4 cloves garlic, finely minced

Large pinch of crushed red pepper flakes

2 pounds fresh fava bean pods, shelled, blanched and peeled (see note)

¼ cup grated parmesan cheese, plus more for garnish

½ cup loosely packed fresh mint leaves

Kosher salt

2 tablespoons slivered preserved lemon peel (see note)

If using fresh pasta, flour a baking sheet and have ready. Cut each pasta sheet crosswise into thirds, then fold each third in half. Cut each folded half lengthwise into ½- to 1-inch-wide strips. Place the strips on the prepared baking sheet, lightly sprinkle with more flour, and cover with a clean kitchen towel.

In a large skillet, heat the olive oil over medium heat. Add the garlic and red pepper flakes and cook for 30 seconds (do not let garlic burn). Add the fava beans and cook, stirring gently, until warmed through, about 1 minute. Remove from the heat and keep warm.

Meanwhile, bring a large pot of well-salted water to a boil. Cook the fresh pasta just until tender to the bite, about 2 minutes. If using dried pasta, cook a few minutes longer, just until tender to the bite. Drain, saving ½ cup of the cooking water. Add the pasta to the fava bean mixture in the skillet and pour in the reserved ½ cup pasta cooking water. Place the skillet with the fava bean mixture over medium heat until heated through. Stir in the ¼ cup parmesan and mint leaves. Taste and season with salt as needed.

To serve, divide the pasta and sauce among warm bowls, and garnish with more parmesan and the preserved lemon.

Note: Find sheets of fresh egg pasta at Pastaworks (see Resources chapter).

Note: While you shell the fava beans, bring a pot of salted water to a boil. Add the shelled beans and cook 30 seconds to 1 minute. Drain and rinse under cold running water. Use your thumbnail to nick the outer skin of each fava and then squeeze out the bean.

Note: Find preserved lemons at Barbur World Foods (see Resources chapter) or at stores that carry a wide selection of gourmet foods.

— Adapted from *The Paley's Place Cookbook: Recipes and Stories from the Pacific Northwest* by Vitaly Paley and Kimberly Paley with Robert Reynolds (Ten Speed Press)

David Machado is one of Portland's most visible chefs. He earned his reputation at the downtown restaurants Pazzo and Southpark, then began his own restaurant empire in Southeast Portland with Vindalho and Lauro Kitchen, the latter having a nine-year run. His newest restaurant, Nel Centro, is located downtown in the cool and hip Hotel Modera.

GRILLED SHRIMP WITH FAVA BEAN SALAD AND SALSA GENOVESE

MAKES 6 SERVINGS

This shrimp dish showcases big Mediterranean flavors that are strongly associated with Machado's cooking. You can substitute 2 cups store-bought shelled and peeled favas, but the results won't be quite as good.

SHRIMP:

18 large shrimp, peeled and deveined
½ cup extra-virgin olive oil
1 teaspoon crushed red pepper flakes
1 teaspoon grated lemon zest
1 tablespoon lemon juice
1 teaspoon minced garlic
1 tablespoon minced fresh Italian (flat-leaf) parsley
¼ cup white wine
Salt and freshly ground black pepper

FAVA BEAN SALAD:

2½ to 3 pounds fresh fava bean pods, shelled, blanched and peeled (2 cups shelled; see note)

1 bulb fresh fennel, sliced crosswise very thinly
¼ head frisée, torn into bite-size pieces
1 tablespoon lemon juice
3 tablespoons extra-virgin olive oil
Salt and freshly ground black pepper
1 ounce pecorino Romano cheese, thinly shaved

SALSA GENOVESE:

2 tablespoons red wine vinegar
1 cup chopped fresh Italian (flat-leaf) parsley
¼ cup torn fresh basil leaves
3 cloves garlic, roughly chopped
1 teaspoon sea salt
½ tablespoon freshly ground black pepper
2 tablespoons pine nuts, lightly toasted (see note)
3 tablespoons capers, rinsed
2 hard-cooked eggs, peeled
6 picholine green olives, pitted
1 tablespoon lemon juice

½ cup extra-virgin olive oil

1 cup cubed country bread (remove crusts before cutting), cubes lightly moistened with water

Extra-virgin olive oil, for serving

To make shrimp: In a large bowl, combine shrimp, oil, red pepper flakes, lemon zest, lemon juice, garlic parsley, and wine; let marinade for 1 hour. Season to taste with salt and pepper.

Preheat a grill to medium-high (see note) or a grill pan to medium-high and cook shrimp 2 minutes on each side; set aside.

To make salad: In a mixing bowl, toss fava beans, fennel, and frisée. Add lemon juice and olive oil; season to taste with salt and pepper and toss.

To make salsa: In a food processor, combine vinegar, parsley, basil, garlic, salt, pepper, pine nuts, capers, eggs, olives, lemon juice, and oil; mix until incorporated. While the machine is running, drop bread 2 to 3 pieces at a time into the feeder tube. Add a little more olive oil as needed to achieve a consistency like pesto. Makes about 2 cups.

Divide the salad among six serving plates and top with shaved cheese. Place a large spoonful of salsa on the side of each plate, and place grilled shrimp on top of salsa. Drizzle with a little olive oil.

Note: To check grill temperature, count the seconds you can hold your hand, palm side down, 2 to 3 inches above the rack, until it feels uncomfortable: 3 seconds for medium-high.

Note: While you shell the fava beans, bring a pot of salted water to a boil. Add the shelled beans and cook 30 seconds to 1 minute. Drain and rinse under cold running water. Use your thumbnail to nick the outer skin of each fava and then squeeze out the bean.

Note: To toast pine nuts, place in a small skillet and place over medium heat, shaking frequently, until golden brown.

Make ahead: The salsa can be made and refrigerated up to a day or two ahead.

— From David Machado, chef/owner, Nel Centro

Greg Higgins was a pioneer in the transformation of Portland's restaurant scene and has continued to be a pillar in the city's food community. He was the founding executive chef at The Heathman Restaurant, where, in addition to cooking, he oversaw the baking of breads and the curing of meats. His commitment to serving local, seasonal foods, and his relationships with the suppliers of fish, vegetables, meat, and other products, helped develop the standard of sustainability that has been widely adopted. Among his many honors is the 2002 James Beard Award Best Chef: Northwest.

GRILLED ALBACORE WITH FLAME-ROASTED CHILE RAITA

MAKES 4 SERVINGS

For this recipe, Higgins balances smoky grilled albacore tuna with a tangy and spicy raita made with yogurt, roasted hot and sweet chiles, cucumber, and cumin. Pair this dish with an Oregon pinot noir and crusty ciabatta bread.

2 cups plain full-fat yogurt
1 lemon
2 cups roasted and julienned fresh chiles
   (see note)
1 tablespoon minced garlic
2 tablespoons cumin seeds, toasted (see note)
2 tablespoons honey
1 cup peeled and diced (¼-inch) cucumber
Salt and freshly ground black pepper
4 (6-ounce) medallions of fresh albacore
¼ cup extra-virgin olive oil
Chopped fresh cilantro, to garnish

Drain the yogurt overnight in a strainer lined with two layers of cheesecloth. Discard the liquid whey and set aside the thickened yogurt.

Remove the zest from the lemon in strips and finely mince; add zest to a medium bowl. Squeeze the lemon juice and add to the bowl, along with the julienned chiles, garlic, cumin seeds, honey, and cucumber. Mix well with enough of the drained yogurt to form a thick sauce. Adjust the seasoning to taste with salt and pepper. Cover raita and refrigerate for several hours to allow the flavors to develop fully.

Preheat the charcoal grill to medium-high (see note). Season the albacore medallions with salt and pepper, and brush liberally with olive oil. Grill the medallions 2 to 3 minutes per side, or until medium-rare inside. Garnish with fresh cilantro and a generous portion of the raita.

Note: Try to select a mix of chiles, some sweet and some medium to hot. Fooddday tested the recipe with three each of fresh poblano, jalapeño, Anaheim, and yellow chiles (which look like yellow jalapeños). Roast the chiles on a very hot grill or under a gas broiler, turning them frequently to evenly char on all sides. Place in a bag or covered bowl for 10 to 15 minutes, then peel the charred skin, remove the stems and seeds and cut in a ⅛-inch julienne.

Note: To toast seeds, add to a small skillet, and heat over medium heat just until they start to turn brown and smell fragrant.

Note: To check grill temperature, count the seconds you can hold your hand, palm side down, 2 to 3 inches above the rack, until it feels uncomfortable: 3 seconds for medium-high.

Make ahead: Raita should be made several hours ahead to allow flavors to develop.

— From Greg Higgins, chef/owner, Higgins Restaurant & Bar

Portland's Bunk Sandwiches was a hit the minute **Tommy Habetz** and **Nick Wood**—two former New York cooks with experience in the kitchens of Mario Batali and Bobby Flay—opened in 2008. Their over-stuffed sandwiches have even had Food Network stars Guy Fieri and Chris Cosentino crowing.

OREGON ALBACORE TUNA MELT WITH MUSTARD, PICKLES, BALSAMIC, AND SHARP CHEDDAR

MAKES 4 SERVINGS

Habetz's tuna melt, made with local albacore and Tillamook cheddar, is the ultimate Oregon sandwich. Although he makes them in a panini press, we had great results using a griddle and cast-iron skillet.

2 (6-ounce) cans albacore tuna, drained
¼ cup finely diced red onion
¼ cup extra-virgin olive oil
1 tablespoon balsamic vinegar
1 tablespoon minced fresh basil
½ teaspoon crushed red pepper flakes
Salt and freshly ground black pepper
4 soft ciabatta rolls or Kaiser rolls, split
Dijon mustard
Mayonnaise
8 (¼-inch-thick) slices Swiss or cheddar cheese (6 ounces)
16 (⅛-inch-thick) lengthwise slices kosher dill pickle
2 tablespoons unsalted butter, softened

In a medium bowl, mix the tuna, onion, olive oil, vinegar, basil, and red pepper flakes. Season to taste with salt and pepper.

Heat a panini press or a griddle and cast-iron skillet (see note).

Spread the cut sides of the rolls with mustard and mayonnaise; top each roll half with a slice of cheese. Spread the tuna salad on the bottoms and cover with the pickles. Close the sandwiches and spread the outsides of the rolls with the butter.

Add the sandwiches to the press or griddle and cook over moderate heat until the cheese is melted, about 6 minutes. Cut the sandwiches in half and serve.

Note: If you don't have a panini press, heat a griddle and a cast-iron skillet at the same time. Place sandwiches on the griddle, top with heated skillet, and weight the skillet with another pan. Turn sandwiches if the bottoms start to get too brown.

— From Tommy Habetz, chef/co-owner, Bunk Sandwiches

For more than ten years, **Kenny Giambalvo** was partner and executive chef at Blue Hour—a fixture of the city's upscale Pearl District. He has cooked in such esteemed New York kitchens as La Côte Basque, La Reserve, Gotham Bar and Grill, and Remi (he was also Remi's Los Angeles outpost). Giambalvo, who has lived in Portland since 2000, recently opened Morso, a Euro-style café.

BRAISED-BEEF SANDWICH WITH PROVOLONE AND ONION JAM

MAKES ABOUT 8 SERVINGS

These flavorful sandwiches are perfect for a TV night with friends. Prepare the onion jam and braise the beef the day before you plan to serve (the beef virtually cooks by itself).

BRAISED BEEF:

1 (3- to 4-pound) beef chuck roast, tied with
    kitchen twine (see note)
Kosher salt and freshly ground black pepper
1 tablespoon vegetable oil
1 medium yellow onion, cut in small dice
2 carrots, cut in small dice
2 stalks celery, cut in small dice
2 cups vegetable broth
1 (750-milliliter) bottle red wine
6 sprigs thyme, tied together with kitchen
    twine

ONION JAM:

1 tablespoon vegetable oil
2 large yellow onions (about 1 pound), thinly
    sliced

Kosher salt and freshly ground black pepper
1 cup red wine vinegar
1 cup balsamic vinegar
1 cup vegetable broth

MUSTARD AIOLI:

2 cloves garlic
¼ cup lemon juice
1 teaspoon Dijon mustard
1 teaspoon coarse-grain mustard
1 egg yolk (see note)
1 cup extra-virgin olive oil
Kosher salt and freshly ground black pepper

SANDWICHES:

16 slices provolone cheese
8 portions of baguette or good Italian rolls

To make beef: Preheat oven to 250 degrees.

Season the beef well on all sides with salt and pepper. In a heavy-bottomed oven-safe 6-quart pot, heat oil over medium-high heat until oil is almost

341

smoking. Sear the beef on all sides, about 4 minutes on each side.

Remove the beef to a platter. Lower the heat to medium and add the vegetables. Cook, stirring, for about 5 minutes, or until the vegetables begin to turn slightly brown.

Return beef to the pot, along with the vegetable broth. Add enough wine to almost cover the roast and bring the liquid to a very light simmer. Add the bundle of thyme and adjust the seasoning with about 1 tablespoon salt and 2 teaspoons pepper.

Cover the pot tightly, place in the oven and cook for about 5 hours, or until a skewer slides into the meat without any resistance.

Allow the beef to cool in the broth, and then transfer into a sealed container that will hold the meat and refrigerate overnight. (This will firm up the meat and make it easier to slice into portions.)

The next day, remove and discard the fat that has solidified on the surface. Transfer the broth to a pot and return beef to refrigerator. Place pot over high heat and cook until liquid is reduced to a quarter of its original volume. Reserve the sauce to moisten the beef when reheating.

To make jam: In a heavy-bottomed 3-quart saucepan, heat oil over medium-low heat. Add the onions and cook slowly, stirring occasionally, until almost tender, about 15 minutes. Season with salt and freshly ground black pepper.

Add red wine vinegar, balsamic vinegar, and broth; bring to a light simmer and continue to cook, stirring occasionally, until the liquid has almost completely evaporated and the onions are thick and jammy, about 1 hour.

Remove the pot from the heat, cool and transfer jam to a container with a tight lid. Refrigerate until needed.

To make aioli: In a food processor, place the garlic, lemon juice, mustards, and egg yolk. While the motor is running, slowly add the olive oil and blend until aioli is thick and smooth. Taste and adjust the seasoning with salt and pepper. Transfer the aioli to an airtight container and refrigerated until needed.

To make sandwiches: Preheat oven to 400 degrees.

Thinly slice cold beef and shingle the slices on a rimmed baking sheet so they overlap slightly. Drizzle meat with the reserved reduced broth. Arrange provolone in overlapping slices to cover the beef. Place baking sheet in the oven and heat until the cheese has melted.

Slice open the baguette pieces or rolls. Spread the top halves of each roll with the aioli, and the bottom halves with a spoonful of the onion jam.

Carefully lift the beef and cheese from the tray using a spatula, and arrange it over the jam on the bottom halves of the rolls. Cover with the top halves and serve immediately.

Note: Ask your butcher to truss the beef chuck so that is has an even shape.

Note: This recipe uses uncooked egg, which carries the risk of salmonella. Use a pasteurized egg, or else avoid serving this dish to people in a high-risk group for contracting food poisoning, including the elderly, the very young, the chronically ill, pregnant women, or others with a weakened immune system.

Make ahead: Beef, jam, and aioli can be made and refrigerated separately up to three or four days ahead, and sandwiches assembled before serving.

— From Kenny Giambalvo, Morso

Martha and **Joe Esparza** have been serving up their popular Tex-Mex food to hordes of Portland fans since 1990. Joe Esparza learned to cook by watching his mother and by working in restaurants starting in his early teen years in Dallas, Texas.

POLLO CON MUSHROOMS

MAKES 4 SERVINGS

This is a simple but robust chicken dish. Chef Esparza has provided a spicy variation for those who want a little more heat. Serve with rice, a salad with sliced avocado, and a glass of cold beer.

1 tablespoon olive oil
¼ cup butter
½ cup chopped onion
3 cloves garlic, peeled and minced
4 (6-ounce) boneless, skinless chicken breast halves
Salt and freshly ground black pepper
1½ cups sliced mushrooms, such as button, cremini, or other favorite variety
1 cup diced tomatoes (fresh or canned)
1 cup chicken broth

In a 12-inch skillet, heat the olive oil and butter over medium heat. Add the onion and garlic and sauté until softened, about 3 to 4 minutes. Add the chicken and season with salt and pepper. Cook on both sides, about 5 minutes each. Add the mushrooms, tomatoes, and broth; cover and simmer for another 10 minutes.

Spicy variation: Add 1 tablespoon canned chipotle chiles in adobo sauce or an equivalent amount of canned chopped green chiles of your choice. Add them at the same time with the mushrooms and tomatoes.

— Adapted from Joe Esparza, chef/co-owner, Esparza's Tex Mex Cafe, Portland

Before age thirty, Gabriel Rucker already had an overstuffed marketbasket of culinary awards: *The Oregonian*'s Rising Star in 2007; *Food & Wine* Magazine's Best New Chef in 2007; *The Oregonian*'s Restaurant of the Year in 2008; and the James Beard Rising Star Chef of the Year in 2011. After two years at Paley's Place, and a stint as sous chef at Gotham Building Tavern, he opened Le Pigeon in 2006 and quickly began appearing on everyone's radar. His second restaurant, Little Bird Bistro, opened in 2010. For a chef who has never set foot in France, the Napa Valley-born Rucker has been happily reinventing French bistro fare with astonishing flair.

PAN-SEARED PORK CHOPS WITH THYME AND BACON CRUMBS

MAKES 4 SERVINGS

These succulent pork chops will dazzle for their flavor and ridiculously easy preparation.

> 4 teaspoons bacon fat (or butter)
> ¾ cup fresh breadcrumbs
> Salt and freshly ground black pepper
> 4 center-cut bone-in pork chops, cut 1 to 1¼
>   inches thick (see note)
> 1 tablespoon olive oil
> 2 tablespoons unsalted butter
> 8 thyme sprigs
> Lemon juice

In a small skillet, heat bacon fat over medium heat until melted. Add breadcrumbs and cook, stirring frequently, until golden brown, 5 to 7 minutes. Season with salt and pepper and set aside.

Pat chops dry with paper towels and season liberally with salt. In a large skillet, heat oil over medium-high until shimmering. Space pork chops evenly in pan; add butter and scatter thyme sprigs in pan. Cook until well-browned, about 6 minutes. Flip and cook until second side is lightly brown and meat has attained desired internal temperature, 3 to 5 minutes for medium (140 degrees). Transfer pork to serving platter, drizzle with butter from pan, and allow to sit for at least 5 minutes before serving. Just before serving, spritz chops with lemon juice and top with reserved breadcrumbs.

Note: Try to avoid pork that has been "enhanced" with a salt solution; this kind of meat can exude a good deal of liquid into the pan and alter the flavor.

— From Gabriel Rucker, chef/owner, Le Pigeon,
     Little Bird Bistro

Philippe Boulot's culinary résumé is studded with legendary names. He cooked with renowned chefs Joel Robuchon at Jamin and Alain Senderens at L'Archestrate in Paris during the height of their fame, and also at Inn on the Park in London, The Clift in San Francisco, and the Mark Hotel in New York City. Boulot arrived in Portland to take over the restaurant at the Heathman Hotel, and won the 2001 James Beard Best Chef: Northwest award, as well as many other prestigious honors. While serving as culinary director at the Heathman, he also worked as executive chef at the Multnomah Athletic Club. Just as this book was going to press, Boulot left the Heathman to focus on the athletic club's three restaurants.

THE HEATHMAN'S SMOKED SALMON HASH

MAKES 4 SERVINGS

This popular mainstay of the breakfast menu at the Heathman has been featured in *Sunset* magazine as well as *Best American Recipes 1999*. It uses hot-smoked salmon, which has a firmer texture than cold-smoked salmon such as lox.

 2 pounds russet potatoes
 1 pound hot-smoked salmon (not lox)
 1 small red onion, minced
 1 tablespoon prepared horseradish
 1 tablespoon coarse-grain mustard
 ¼ cup drained capers
 ¼ cup sour cream, plus more to garnish
    (optional)
 Salt and freshly ground black pepper
 2 tablespoons butter
 2 tablespoons vegetable oil
 Whipping cream (optional)

Place the potatoes in a large pan and cover with water. Bring to a boil and cook until tender. Cool completely, peel and cut into ½-inch cubes.

In a medium bowl, shred the smoked salmon. Add the onion, horseradish, mustard, capers, and ¼ cup sour cream. Toss to combine and add salt and pepper to taste; set aside.

In a large, heavy sauté pan, melt the butter and add the oil. Add the cubed potatoes and sauté until golden brown and crisp. Add the salmon mixture; toss to combine and heat through. Add additional salt and pepper, if desired.

Divide among 4 plates and garnish with a little sour cream that has been thinned with cream, if using. Serve immediately.

— From Philippe Boulot, former culinary director,
   The Heathman Restaurant & Bar; executive chef,
   the Multnomah Athletic Club

Allen Routt and his wife, Jessica Bagley-Routt, had plenty of experience behind them when they opened The Painted Lady in Newberg in 2005. Allen interned with Bradley Ogden at One Market in San Francisco, and has cooked in the kitchens of Patrick O'Connell's Inn at Little Washington, Jean-Louis Palladin's Jean-Louis, and Mark Millitello's South Beach. Oregon-raised Jessica interned at Higgins and met Allen while she was working at South Beach. The two of them headed for Napa Valley, California, where she was sous chef at Brix in Yountville. At The Painted Lady, Allen mans the kitchens, while Jessica serves as general manager and assists in menu development.

COCONUT PANNA COTTA

MAKES 8 SERVINGS

This tropical panna cotta is a silky variation of this classic Italian pudding.

2 packets unflavored gelatin (4 teaspoons)
½ cup cool water
1½ cups half-and-half
½ cup plus 2 tablespoons granulated sugar
3 cups coconut milk
1 teaspoon coconut extract
Sliced mango or chunks of pineapple
Shredded coconut, toasted, to garnish
    (see note)

Stir the gelatin into the water and let stand to soften for 5 to 10 minutes.

Place half-and-half and sugar in a pot and bring to a boil. Remove from heat, add gelatin, and stir until gelatin is completely dissolved, about 5 minutes. Add coconut milk and extract and mix well. Pour into 8 glass bowls or martini glasses. Refrigerate for at least 4 hours. Serve chilled and top with your favorite tropical fruit and toasted coconut.

Note: To toast coconut, heat in a dry skillet, stirring frequently, over medium heat until it starts to brown. Be careful not to let it burn.

Make ahead: Panna cotta can be made, covered and refrigerated up to a day ahead.

— Allen Routt, chef/co-owner Painted Lady

Naomi Pomeroy is a native Oregonian and one of the most admired regional chefs in America. Her restaurant, Beast, where diners eat at communal tables, serves a six-course prix fixe menu (and four-course brunch menu) that changes weekly. Among the many accolades she and the restaurant have received are *The Oregonian*'s Restaurant of the Year in 2008 (sharing top honors with Le Pigeon), and Portland Monthly's Chef of the Year in 2008. *Bon Appétit* named Pomeroy one of the country's top female chefs, while *Food & Wine* recognized her as one of the 10 Best New Chefs in America in 2009. In 2010, Pomeroy was also a finalist for the James Beard Award as Best Chef: Northwest.

CHOCOLATE TRUFFLE CAKE

MAKES 14 TO 16 SERVINGS

Pomeroy's spectacular truffle cake impressed the judges during the Top Chef Masters: Restaurant Wars episode in 2011. However, in the interest of space, we've chosen not to include the balsamic-and-truffle caramel sauce or the toasted meringue topping. With just a dollop of sweetened whipped cream and seasonal berries, we think the cake is ideal for a holiday or special occasion dinner.

CAKE:

1 cup water

¾ cup granulated sugar

9 tablespoons unsalted butter, diced (1 stick plus 1 tablespoon)

18 ounces bittersweet or semisweet chocolate (not unsweetened), chopped

1 teaspoon plus a pinch of truffle salt or regular salt

6 eggs

GANACHE:

1 cup heavy whipping cream

8 ounces bittersweet or semisweet (not unsweetened) chocolate, chopped

Lightly sweetened whipped cream

To make cake: Preheat oven to 350 degrees. Butter a 10-inch-diameter springform pan. Line bottom of pan with a round of parchment paper; butter parchment. Wrap bottom and sides in 3 layers of heavy-duty aluminum foil.

Combine 1 cup water and the sugar in small saucepan. Bring to boil over medium heat, stirring until sugar dissolves. Simmer 5 minutes. Remove from heat.

In a large saucepan, melt butter over low heat. Add chocolate and whisk until smooth. Whisk sugar syrup into chocolate; cool slightly. Add eggs to chocolate mixture and whisk until well-blended. Pour batter into prepared pan. Place cake pan in large roasting pan. Add enough hot water to roasting pan to come halfway up sides of cake pan.

Bake cake until center no longer moves when pan is gently shaken, about 50 minutes. Remove from water bath; transfer to rack. Cool completely in pan.

To make ganache: In small saucepan, bring whipping cream to a simmer over medium heat. Remove from heat, add chocolate and whisk until smooth. Pour over top of cake still in pan. Gently shake pan to distribute ganache evenly over top of cake. Refrigerate cake in pan until ganache is set, about 2 hours.

Run knife around pan sides to loosen cake; release sides. Cut cake into wedges and serve with whipped cream.

Make ahead: The cake can be made, covered and refrigerated up to 2 days ahead.

— From Naomi Pomeroy, chef/owner, Beast

REMEMBERING JAMES BEARD

18

James Beard was Portland's hometown boy who made it big in the world of food and was among the first to champion American cooking. He also taught us that ordinary folks could learn to cook the finest foods, that cooking is a skill to be valued.

Beard began life in 1903 in a big way — reportedly weighing 14 pounds. At the time of his birth, his 42-year-old English-born mother, Elizabeth Beard, was almost estranged from Beard's father, John. Elizabeth ran Portland's Curtis Hotel, a residential hotel and boarding house that once stood on Morrison at Southwest 12th Avenue.

With the help of the family's Chinese cook, Jue Let, Elizabeth served spectacular meals at the hotel and developed a reputation for having food as fine as any in San Francisco. She was an accomplished entertainer and some of her son's fondest memories were of the family's lavish Christmas parties, which could have as many 40 guests. From Christmas Eve through the next day the various offerings included wassail, oyster stew, suckling pig, porterhouse steaks and fried potatoes, rare roast beef and Yorkshire pudding, plum pudding, fruitcake, mince pies and espresso.

"Never did a family have such a jumble of traditions, and it was a joy from beginning to end," Beard wrote. Although Elizabeth Beard bought much of her food from the local growers who sold from their horse-drawn wagons, she also kept a small garden and put up her own preserves. There were forays for mushroom hunting and blackberry picking, and during family visits to Gearhart, Beard reveled in salmon, Dungeness crab and razor clams.

All of this early exposure to good food honed Beard's "taste memory," something that he felt, like perfect pitch, was an ability you were or weren't born with. His great love of food also padded his girth. At 6-foot-3, Beard's weight fluctuated between 240 and 300 pounds.

After leaving Reed College, Beard moved to New York City and had a brief fling in theater and opera. Always in demand for his abilities as a cook and caterer, food was what paid the bills, and so he devoted the rest of his professional life to food, mainly writing about it, beginning when there were few popular sources, such as the many magazines and cookbooks of today. He wrote 22 books on food (many still in print), as well as a syndicated column that ran in *The Oregonian* for more than 10 years. In the '50s, '60s and '70s, Beard became one of the most famous culinary celebrities in America. Along with Julia Child and Craig Claiborne (the long-time food editor and restaurant critic of *The New York Times*), he is considered one of the essential influences on America's post-WW II fascination with food culture in the modern era.

Beard died in 1985, at 81. His legacy lives on through The James Beard Foundation, which among other culinary activities bestows annual awards to the best restaurants all over the country, the finest cookbooks and the most outstanding journalists covering food culture. Today there is no permanent marker in the state noting Beard's life here. However, the Historic Portland Public Market Foundation is working to build a daily, year-round indoor-outdoor marketplace in his name. The foundation's vision for the James Beard Public Market includes more than 100 permanent vendors, a restaurant, a teaching kitchen and meeting space. Negotiations are underway for a site at the west end of the Morrison Bridge.

This chapter includes several of Beard's recipes, some that ran in the pages of *The Oregonian*. These recipes were originally published in Beard's very personal and chatty style, without ingredient lists. But times change, and we think ingredient lists are important for ease and accuracy, so we have adapted the recipes to include them. Beard also judged a readers' recipe contest that ran in the mid-'70s in *The Oregonian*. We have shared some of the winning recipes from those contests.

CRAB LOUIS

MAKES 4 SERVINGS

According to Beard, Crab Louis is a Pacific Coast creation. Helen Evans Brown, author of many cookbooks, including *The West Coast Cook Book*, and the authority on West Coast cooking from the 1950s and '60s, claimed it was served at Solari's in San Francisco as early as 1914. Beard also thought it was served at the Bohemian Restaurant in Portland around the same time. In any event, Beard preferred the Crab Louis served at the Bohemian. You can find this dish in oyster bars in San Francisco, and it's on the menu locally at Jake's Seafood. It's a classic that ought to show up on more menus around town. Note that the dressing is excellent on cold, cooked lobster, shrimp, or scallops. Or, turn the dish into a great dip by folding the cream mixture into the crab meat and serving on a large platter with veggies or crusty bread.

DRESSING:

1 cup mayonnaise
2 tablespoons minced onion or shallot
¼ cup prepared chili sauce
1 tablespoon chopped fresh parsley
1 tablespoon chopped fresh dill
Pinch cayenne pepper
½ teaspoon Dijon mustard
Juice of 1 lemon
¼ cup heavy whipping cream

SALAD:

4 cups finely shredded lettuce (iceberg is classic, but you can substitute small spring lettuces, cups of butter lettuce, finely shredded romaine or red leaf lettuce)
4 to 5 vine-ripened tomatoes, quartered lengthwise
4 hard-cooked eggs, peeled, and quartered lengthwise
1 pound cooked Dungeness crabmeat

To make dressing: In a medium bowl, thoroughly mix the mayonnaise, onion, chili sauce, parsley, dill, cayenne, mustard and lemon juice. In a separate bowl, whip the cream until it holds medium-stiff peaks. Fold the cream into the mayonnaise mixture until it is well-mixed. Chill up to 2 hours.

To make salad: In four large, shallow bowls, make a bed of lettuce. Heap the crabmeat in the center of each bowl, and garnish with the quartered tomatoes and eggs. Pour the dressing over all, or pass at the table.

— Adapted from *James Beard's New Fish Cookery* (Little, Brown)

TABBOULEH

MAKES 4 TO 6 SERVINGS

James Beard was introduced to tabbouleh, the popular Middle Eastern salad of bulgur wheat, parsley, and tomatoes, in 1974 on a trip to London. These days, every salad bar serves its own version, but nearly forty years ago, it was considered exotic. Beard considered the salad "an ideal buffet dish to accompany cold roast chicken or turkey, because it doesn't wilt like a green salad." We also think it pairs well with pork or shellfish. Note that unlike more traditional recipes, this tabbouleh has a higher proportion of bulgur than parsley.

2 cups fine bulgur or cracked wheat (widely available in bulk bin sections)
1 cup finely chopped scallions
1 cup finely chopped fresh Italian (flat-leaf) parsley
¾ cup finely chopped tomato
Grated zest of 1 lemon
⅓ cup freshly squeezed lemon juice (about 2½ lemons)
⅓ cup plus 1 tablespoon extra-virgin olive oil
2 teaspoons balsamic vinegar
1¼ teaspoons salt

Freshly ground black pepper
¾ cup finely chopped fresh mint
Garnishes: cucumber slices and pitted kalamata olives

In a medium bowl, soak the bulgur in cold water to cover for about 20 minutes. Drain in a clean dish towel over a colander, then gather the towel together and squeeze as much moisture as you can from the drained bulgur; spread on another clean dish towel to dry for about 20 minutes.

Place the bulgur in a large bowl and add the scallions, parsley, and tomato. In a separate bowl combine the lemon zest, lemon juice, olive oil, and vinegar. Pour dressing over the salad, add the salt and season to taste with pepper; toss gently to thoroughly combine. Chill the salad for at least 1 hour and up to 4 hours. Sprinkle the salad with mint and toss lightly. Taste for seasoning; the lemon taste should be prominent.

Pile the tabbouleh on a platter and garnish with cucumber slices and olives.

— From "Beard on Food," *The Oregonian*, November 7, 1974

OREGON-STYLE BAKED SALMON

MAKES 6 SERVINGS

We adapted Beard's original recipe to remove the green bell peppers, and brightened the flavor by adding fresh dill, capers, and balsamic vinegar. The meatiness of the pancetta gives the fish great flavor, so don't omit it.

4 tablespoons extra-virgin olive oil (divided)
2 tablespoons balsamic vinegar (divided)

Sea salt and freshly cracked black pepper
1 lemon, thinly sliced (divided)
2 tablespoons capers (divided)
4 to 5 sprigs fresh dill (divided)
2 to 3 cloves garlic, finely minced
1 whole salmon (about 4 pounds), cleaned
1½ to 2 cups cherry tomatoes (divided)
1 large onion, thinly sliced (divided)
3 to 4 slices pancetta

Preheat oven to 450 degrees.

In a large roasting pan add 2 tablespoons olive oil, 1 tablespoon vinegar, and sprinkle with a generous pinch of salt and pepper. Lay half of the lemon slices over the mixture in the pan and scatter with 1 tablespoon capers. Add 2 or 3 dill sprigs.

In a small bowl, combine the remaining 2 tablespoons olive oil, and season another generous pinch of salt and pepper. Add the remaining tablespoon vinegar and the garlic. Rub mixture over the outside and inside of fish and lay in the roasting pan.

Stuff cavity of fish with the remaining lemon slices and dill sprigs. Add ½ cup cherry tomatoes, the remaining tablespoon capers, and a quarter of the thinly sliced onion.

Surround the salmon with the remaining tomatoes and sliced onions. Cover the salmon with the pancetta. Bake for 25 to 30 minutes, basting fish with the juices half way through. Cook just until salmon is barely opaque at its thickest part.

— Adapted from *James Beard's New Fish Cookery* (Little, Brown)

LOIN OF PORK WITH PRUNES

MAKES 6 SERVINGS

In James Beard's *American Cookery*, Beard states that this is a great Swedish and Danish favorite (the French also have a version), and that it's also frequently found in the Midwest. The pork is tender, juicy, and flavorful and makes a festive recipe for a holiday table. Serve it with a side of mashed potatoes or creamy polenta.

12 cups water
1½ cups firmly packed brown sugar
Kosher salt
1 (4- to 5-pound) pork loin (cut from the center)
8 dried pitted prunes
½ cup marsala wine
½ cup chicken broth
2 to 3 cloves garlic, minced
1 tablespoon Dijon mustard
3 to 4 tablespoons extra-virgin olive oil
1 tablespoon balsamic vinegar
Freshly ground black pepper
1 tablespoon chopped fresh thyme
1½ teaspoons honey

In a large pot combine water, brown sugar, and ½ cup salt. Stir well until sugar and salt are dissolved. Add pork and refrigerate for 1 to 2 hours.

In a small saucepan add the prunes, marsala, broth, and a pinch of salt. Bring mixture to a boil and cook for about 1 minute, just to plump up the prunes. Strain and reserve liquid for basting.

In a medium bowl, combine garlic, mustard, oil, vinegar, salt and pepper to taste, thyme, and honey; set marinade aside.

Preheat oven to 350 degrees.

Remove pork from brine and pat dry. Cut a deep slit in the pork extending from the tip through the thickest part of the meat muscle. Rub the entire loin with the marinade. Stuff the prunes inside the loin. Tie roast with butcher string and place on roasting rack. Place pan in the oven and roast pork, basting occasionally with reserved marsala mixture and pan juices, until meat reaches an internal temperature of 140 degrees, about 24 minutes per pound. Season with salt to taste, transfer to a hot platter, tent with foil, and allow to rest for 15 minutes.

Meanwhile, place the roasting pan over a burner and cook over medium heat for 1 to 2 minutes, until drippings and basting liquid have reduced and thickened into a sauce.

Carve roast and serve with sauce alongside.

— Adapted from *James Beard's American Cookery* (Little, Brown)

DIONE LUCAS' FLOURLESS CHOCOLATE ROLL

MAKES 8 TO 10 SERVINGS

James Beard loved this elegant and simple cake, made famous by Dione Lucas at her Cordon Bleu Cooking School. Lucas was the first female graduate of Le Cordon Bleu and the first woman to host a cooking show on television. The recipe has been taught at many culinary schools and Beard published it in several of his cookbooks. This scrumptious chocolate roll is pretty easy to prepare and makes an impressive coda to a festive dinner party.

6 eggs, separated
½ cup granulated sugar
6 ounces semisweet or bittersweet chocolate, preferably 70 percent cacao
3 tablespoons strong brewed coffee
1 tablespoon vanilla extract
¼ teaspoon salt
¼ teaspoon cream of tarter
Raspberry preserves (optional)
1 cup heavy whipping cream (see note)
1 teaspoon vanilla extract or 1 to 2 tablespoons cognac, sherry, or kirsch
2 tablespoons powdered sugar
Unsweetened cocoa powder
Fresh raspberries, to garnish (optional)
Grated or shaved semisweet or bittersweet chocolate, to garnish

Preheat oven to 350 degrees.

Butter an 11-by-17-inch jellyroll pan and line it with wax paper. Butter the paper.

In a large bowl, beat the egg yolks until light and lemon-colored. Gradually beat in the granulated sugar.

In the top of a double boiler, add the chocolate and coffee and heat over barely simmering water until chocolate is melted. Let the mixture cool slightly, then beat it into the egg-sugar mixture. Stir in the vanilla and salt, and set aside.

In a clean bowl, beat the egg whites with a mixer until frothy. Add the cream of tarter, and beat the egg whites until they are stiff enough to form soft peaks when you remove the beater. Do not overbeat them to the point of dryness. Add half of the beaten egg whites to the chocolate mixture, and fold until most of the whites disappear. Add the other half and gently fold, while turning the bowl, until no white streaks appear in the chocolate mixture.

Carefully pour the chocolate mixture into the prepared jellyroll pan and with a spatula, gently spread it evenly across the pan. Bake for 15 minutes. The cake is done when a toothpick inserted in the middle of the pan comes out clean. The cake will already be pulling away a little from the insides of the pan.

While the cake is baking, put a medium bowl with clean beaters into the freezer.

Remove the cake from the oven, place on a counter and cover with a slightly damp, clean kitchen towel and let stand for 10 minutes. Meanwhile, arrange two 14-inch lengths of wax paper on a worktable, side by side, and slightly overlapping. Sprinkle the powdered sugar and unsweetened cocoa powder over the wax paper. Run a small spatula or paring knife around the edges of the cake and with one free hand supporting the cake, gently invert it onto the prepared wax paper—it should turn out easily. Carefully unpeel the paper clinging to the bottom of the cake. The cake should be room temperature before proceeding with the next step.

If you desire, spread a thin layer of raspberry preserves over the cooled cake.

Pour the cream into the chilled bowl; beat on high speed for a minute or so. Add the vanilla, or liquor of choice, and sugar; continue to beat until cream holds firm, but soft peaks—do not overbeat. Spread the cream mixture over the surface of the cake, but do not spread to the edges. Lift the edge of the long side of the wax paper closest to you and gently roll the cake away from you. Don't worry if the cake cracks a bit on top. Place the cake, seam-side-down on a large platter.

Slice diagonally and serve with a few raspberries on the side.

Note: For an extra touch of richness you can substitute half of the whipping cream with mascarpone cheese.

— Adapted from *James Beard's American Cookery* (Little, Brown)

THE COACH HOUSE BREAD-AND-BUTTER PUDDING

MAKES 6 TO 8 SERVINGS

The Coach House was a landmark fine dining establishment of New York's Greenwich Village for forty-four years. Nobody was more passionate about its eclectic mix of American and European haute cuisine than James Beard. He dined there often and was a very close friend of Leon Leonides, the restaurant's exacting owner, and his wife, Aphrodite. At the peak of its popularity, The Coach House's interpretation of such signature dishes as osso buco, black bean soup, and this outstanding bread pudding (which Beard declared as "one of the best custards of all time, as far as I am concerned") earned four stars from Craig Claiborne, then food editor and restaurant critic of the *New York Times*. The Coach House served this elegant pudding with a purée of fresh raspberries, but we think it would also be fantastic with rhubarb compote on the side.

12 thin slices French or como bread
½ cup unsalted butter, room temperature
5 eggs
4 egg yolks
1 cup granulated sugar
½ teaspoon salt
2½ cups heavy whipping cream
2½ cups half-and-half
¼ teaspoon freshly grated nutmeg
¼ to ½ teaspoon ground cardamom
1 teaspoon vanilla extract
Powdered sugar

Preheat oven to 375 degrees. Butter a 2-quart baking dish.

Butter each slice of bread on one side. Arrange the slices of bread, butter side up, in the prepared pan.

In a large bowl, beat the eggs, egg yolks, sugar, and salt until thoroughly blended. In a heavy medium saucepan, heat the cream and half-and-half over medium heat. Add a ladleful of the hot liquid into the egg mixture, stirring constantly with a whisk until well-blended. Add another ladleful and whisk until combined. Gradually add this "tempered" mixture into the rest of the hot cream mixture, stirring until well-combined. Sir in the nutmeg, cardamom, and vanilla.

Strain the custard mixture over the bread, pressing lightly on top of the bread so it soaks up some of the liquid. Set the dish in a roasting pan large enough to hold it, and add hot water to a depth of about 1 inch. Carefully place the pan into the oven and bake 45 minutes, or until a knife inserted in the center of the pudding comes out clean. Sprinkle the pudding generously with powdered sugar and glaze it under the broiler until browned on top, but not scorched. Let stand for 20 minutes, then serve warm.

— Adapted from *James Beard's American Cookery* (Little, Brown)

SCOTTISH SHORTBREAD

MAKES 32 LITTLE PIECES

Although Beard preferred to mix his shortbread dough with his hands, which he believed gives you a better feel for the texture of the fully mixed dough, we had fine results using an electric mixer. The dough can be cut into individual pieces before baking, or pressed into cake pans and cut after baking. These are excellent with a bowl of vanilla bean ice cream and fresh berries.

2¾ cups all-purpose flour
¼ cup fine cornmeal
¼ teaspoon salt
1 cup unsalted butter, room temperature (2 sticks)
½ cup plus 2 tablespoons granulated sugar
1 teaspoon vanilla extract
Grated zest of 2 lemons or oranges
1 egg yolk, room temperature

Preheat oven to 350 degrees.

In a medium bowl, sift flour, cornmeal, and salt; set aside.

In a large bowl, using an electric mixer, cream the butter until it is fluffy, about 1 minute. Add the sugar, vanilla, and lemon zest; mix for another minute. Add the yolk and mix just until combined.

Add flour mixture to butter mixture and mix on low speed until the dough comes together. Transfer to a lightly floured surface and knead dough several times to ensure ingredients are well-mixed.

To make cookies: Divide mixture into 4 parts; roll each into a square or a circle, about ½ inch thick. Prick with a fork. Cut each circle into 8 triangles or each square into 8 smaller squares. Place the pieces on a lightly buttered and floured baking sheet. Bake for 15 minutes, then reduce heat to 300 degrees and bake for 30 minutes longer, until the shortbread is a delicate light brown.

To bake in cake pans: Butter two 8- or 9-inch cake pans and line with parchment. Divide the dough into two equal portions and gently press into the pans until the layer is flat and even. Score into 16 wedges and prick with fork. Chill 20 to 30 minutes. Bake for 25 to 30 minutes at 350 degrees, or until edges are lightly golden brown. Cool and cut into wedges.

— Adapted from *James Beard's Simple Foods*
(Macmillan Publishing)

RHUBARB PIE

MAKES 1 (9-INCH) PIE

Double-crust pastry for one 9-inch pie
    (see recipe on page 286)
5 cups sliced (½-inch) rhubarb
1½ cups granulated sugar
¼ cup all-purpose flour or 2 tablespoons
    quick-cooking tapioca
¼ teaspoon salt
1 teaspoon grated orange or tangerine zest
1 tablespoon butter

Preheat oven to 450 degrees. Line a 9-inch pie pan with bottom crust.

In a large bowl, mix rhubarb with sugar, flour or tapioca, salt, and grated zest. Turn into the pie shell and dot fruit with the butter. Trim the edges of the pastry, moisten them, top with second pastry crust, and crimp top and bottom edges together. Cut slits in the top for the steam to escape. Bake for 15 minutes; then reduce the heat to 350 degrees and bake about 25 to 30 minutes longer. Serve warm or cold.

— Adapted from *The James Beard Cookbook*, by
James Beard and Isabel E. Callvert (Marlowe & Co.)

BEARD'S PLAN FOR A SPLENDID PARTY

MAKES 4 TO 6 SERVINGS

James Beard was always ahead of his time. Long before the current glut of books on barbecuing, Beard was an authority on the subject, having co-written *The Complete Book of Outdoor Cookery* way back in 1941. He would go on to write several more books on the subject. As we prepared this special chapter devoted to Beard, we fell upon a column he wrote in July 1973 that could have been written today:

"What with meat costs soaring sky-high, it seems to me that this is the year to learn a different pattern of outdoor cooking and eating. By planning your menus intelligently, and supplementing treats from the grill with treats from the kitchen," he urged readers, "you can have wonderfully good meals without having to buy a lot of meat. By serving less meat, a menu can actually be more festive and much more interesting."

Here are Beard's suggestions for a spread of easy hors d'oeuvres, followed by ideas for satisfying the meat eaters at your party.

➤➤

VEGETABLES À LA GRECQUE:

2 cups water

½ cup extra-virgin olive oil

½ cup wine vinegar (red or white)

2 tablespoons freshly squeezed lemon juice

2 teaspoons salt

2 teaspoons chopped fresh thyme or
   1 teaspoon dried

1 bay leaf

2 or 3 cloves garlic, peeled, and lightly
   crushed

Freshly cracked black pepper

10 fresh basil leaves, torn

¼ bunch fresh parsley, chopped

12 baby zucchini (or 6 medium-small zucchini,
   halved crosswise)

1 (9- to 10-ounce) package frozen baby
   artichoke hearts

To make vegetables: In a 3-quart saucepan, add water, oil, vinegar, lemon juice, salt, thyme, bay leaf, garlic, pepper, basil, parsley, zucchini, and artichoke hearts. Cover and bring to a boil; reduce heat to a simmer and cook until the vegetables are crisply tender, not mushy. Remove the cooked vegetables to an attractive serving dish, but retain the cooking liquid in the pot.

Under high heat, cook the sauce for a few minutes, reducing it enough to thicken. Then pour enough of the hot sauce over the vegetables to cook them a bit more, using only enough of the sauce to keep the vegetables wet without drowning them. Serve at room temperature.

Variation: Beard suggests you can substitute any of the following vegetables in the same "à la Grecque" preparation:

1 pound whole string beans, stemmed

1 pound small firm mushrooms (such as
   cremini or white)

3 dozen tiny white onions

1½ pounds small red or Yukon Gold potatoes

1 small head of cauliflower, cut into florets

1 pound of medium-thick asparagus, bottom
   of the stalk removed and peeled

Additional offerings:

Round out your hors d'oeuvre selection with any of the following:

- A plate of ripe, sliced summer tomatoes, lightly dressed with extra-virgin olive oil, red wine vinegar, and sprinkled with a generous amount of fresh basil leaves, chopped chives, or finely sliced scallions.
- An English cucumber, sliced thin (do not peel) and sprinkled with salt. Toss in a mixture of half mayonnaise, half sour cream, mixed with some red wine vinegar and fresh dill or chives.
- Thinly sliced prosciutto and Italian salami
- Polish sausage, heated in red wine, sliced, and served hot
- Fresh cooked shrimp or crabmeat, served with lemon or mayonnaise
- Marinated anchovies (boquerones), herring pieces, canned sardines
- Halved hard-cooked eggs or deviled eggs, sprinkled with chopped fresh parsley
- Potato salad, coleslaw, or tabbouleh (see Beard's recipe on page 354)
- An assortment of olives and various pickles (cornichons, dill chips, bread-and-butter pickles, etc.)

For the rest of the meal, serve small grilled meat patties in grinder buns; or thinly sliced hanger or flank steak; or a ham slice, grilled and basted with mustard and honey; or grilled salmon. Accompany with lots of crusty bread and sweet butter, and serve with wine, beer, or the beverage of your choice. Finish the meal with a nice bowl of summer fruit: peaches, apricots, nectarines, cherries, strawberries, or any other berry, or melons.

— Adapted from "Beard on Food," *The Oregonian*,
   July 26, 1973

In 1975, '76 and '77, we held The Oregonian–James Beard Recipe Contest, which collectively brought in thousands of entries from readers. Those were narrowed down to a manageable few for Beard and cohorts to test. The contest rules specified original recipes that shunned convenience foods, and Beard declared the contest winners. The following are a few that went on to became favorites with Fooday readers.

HERB CHEESE BREAD

MAKES 1 LOAF, 10 TO 12 SERVINGS

¼ cup warm water (105 to 115 degrees)
1 (¼-ounce) packet active dry yeast
¾ cup hot water
1½ tablespoons vegetable shortening
1½ tablespoons granulated sugar
1 teaspoon salt
¼ cup nonfat powdered milk
1 tablespoon Dijon mustard
½ teaspoon dried rosemary
½ teaspoon dried oregano
3 cups all-purpose flour (divided)
2 cups shredded and loosely packed sharp
    cheddar cheese (8 ounces)

In a cup, dissolve yeast in warm water; set aside.

In a mixing bowl, stir together the hot water, shortening, sugar, salt, and powdered milk; stir in mustard. Crush rosemary and oregano between fingers, then add to bowl. Add 1 cup flour, then yeast mixture; beat well. Add cheese and remaining 2 cups flour. Turn onto floured board; knead until smooth and elastic, about 5 to 8 minutes.

Put into a greased bowl, turn to grease top. Cover and let stand in a warm place until doubled, about 1 hour. Punch down and shape into a loaf. Put in a greased 9-by-5-inch loaf pan and let rise until doubled.

Preheat oven to 375 degrees and bake loaf for 35 to 40 minutes.

— From Lila H. Collman, Warrenton; Grand Prize, 1976

SWEET ONION BAKE

MAKES 8 SERVINGS

7½ cups chopped Walla Walla sweet onions
¼ cup butter
½ cup uncooked rice
5 cups boiling salted water
¾ cup shredded Swiss cheese
⅔ cup half-and-half

Preheat oven to 300 degrees.

In a large heavy-bottomed pot, sauté onions in butter over medium heat until tender. Cook rice in water for 5 minutes; drain and mix with onions. Add cheese and half-and-half. Bake, covered, for 1 hour.

— From Mrs. Robert P. Suman, Lake Oswego;
Second Grand Prize, 1976

GERMAN STUFFED CABBAGE ROLLS

MAKES 16 GENEROUS SERVINGS

1 large head cabbage
1 cup minced onion
1 clove garlic, minced (1 teaspoon)
1 pound ground pork
3 pounds ground beef
8 ounces ham, cut into small pieces
2 tablespoons salt
1 tablespoon paprika
1 teaspoon freshly ground black pepper
½ cup uncooked white rice, rinsed well
    and drained
2 eggs
1 (22-ounce) can sauerkraut
½ cup firmly packed brown sugar
2½ cups tomato juice
1 cup sour cream (½ pint; optional)

Core cabbage and place in enough boiling water in pan to cover. With fork in one hand and knife in the other, cut off leaves as they become wilted. Drain. (Alternate method: cover washed, cored cabbage head with wax paper and place on paper plate in microwave oven for about 6 minutes; remove and allow to cool.) Trim thick center vein of each cabbage leaf.

In a large bowl, mix onion, garlic, pork, beef, ham, salt, paprika, pepper, rice, and eggs. Place a heaping tablespoon of filling on each cabbage leaf and roll up, folding in the ends to make compact rolls.

Place in a large Dutch oven, close together, making several layers if necessary. Leftover filling can be shaped into balls and placed over the rolls before the next step. Arrange sauerkraut on top, then sprinkle with brown sugar. Add tomato juice, plus enough water to make the pot about two-thirds full. Bring to a boil, reduce heat to a simmer, cover, and cook 1 hour.

Serve in soup bowls, garnished with a dollop of sour cream, if desired.

— From Josephine Swank, Milwaukie; 1977

SOUR CREAM SWISS STEAK

MAKES 6 SERVINGS

2 pounds round steak
All-purpose flour
1 teaspoon salt
¼ teaspoon freshly ground black pepper
¼ teaspoon paprika
¼ teaspoon dry mustard
¼ cup vegetable oil
3 tablespoons butter
1 clove garlic, pressed
½ cup chopped onion
¾ cup water
3 tablespoons soy sauce
3 tablespoons firmly packed brown sugar
¾ cup sour cream

Preheat oven to 300 degrees. Cut meat into 6 serving-size pieces. With a mallet, pound as much flour into each piece as it will hold. Dust with salt, pepper, paprika, and mustard.

In a Dutch oven, heat oil and butter over medium-high heat. Sear steaks on one side, then turn. Add garlic, onion, water, soy sauce, brown sugar, and sour cream. Cover pan and bake 1 hour or until meat is tender.

— Esther Richman, Clackamas; Runner-up, 1977

CRAB AND MUSHROOM SANDWICHES

MAKES 6 SERVINGS

3 strips bacon, cut crosswise into
½-inch slices

4 ounces mushrooms, sliced (about 1¼ cups)

¼ cup chopped onion

1 cup cooked crabmeat or bay shrimp (about 5 ounces)

1 cup shredded Swiss cheese (4 ounces)

⅓ cup grated parmesan cheese (1 ounce)

½ cup mayonnaise

Butter

6 English muffins or thick French bread

Dash cayenne pepper

Dash paprika

Preheat oven to 400 degrees. In a medium skillet or saucepan, cook bacon over medium heat until crisp; remove and drain. Sauté mushrooms and onions in bacon drippings until mushrooms begin to turn brown; cool. In a large bowl, stir together the crab, Swiss cheese, parmesan cheese, and mayonnaise. Combine with bacon, mushrooms, and onions.

Spread mixture on sliced, buttered muffin or bread. Sprinkle with cayenne and paprika. Place sandwiches on baking sheet and bake 15 minutes.

—Marilyn Manchester, Portland; Grand Prize, 1977

SALLY'S SALAD

MAKES 6 SERVINGS

GRANNA'S SALAD DRESSING:

¼ cup granulated sugar

2 teaspoons dry mustard

2 teaspoons salt

1 teaspoon paprika

½ teaspoon freshly ground black pepper

1 teaspoon curry powder

2 cloves garlic, minced (2 teaspoons)

1 medium onion, grated

1½ tablespoons Worcestershire sauce

1 (15-ounce) can tomato sauce

1½ cups olive oil

Vinegar

SALAD:

Equal amounts of fresh spinach and
red leaf lettuce

½ cucumber, peeled and thinly sliced

2 small boiling onions, thinly sliced

1 handful cherry tomatoes or 3 small
tomatoes, cut into wedges

½ cup raw cashews

½ to 1 cup fresh mushrooms, thinly sliced

To make dressing: In a quart jar, mix sugar, mustard, salt, paprika, pepper, curry powder, garlic, onion, Worcestershire sauce, and tomato sauce. Slowly add oil and enough vinegar to fill jar. Screw lid on tightly and shake to blend well.

To make salad: Put greens in large salad bowl. Add cucumber, onions, tomatoes, cashews, and mushrooms; toss together lightly. Serve with Granna's Salad Dressing.

— From Sally Head, Tidewater; First Place, Salads and Dressings, 1975

19

RESOURCES

Portland's shopping options continue to grow, and it can be tough to keep up. But the following markets and shops have demonstrated exceptional selection, and/or commendable quality or value.

SPICES

Penzeys Spices: With more than 250 products, this is spice central. Many of the herbs, seeds, spices, and seasoning blends are available in smaller packages, which helps reduce waste.

- 11322 S.E. 82nd Ave., Portland (503-653-7779)
- Beaverton Town Square, 11787 S.W. Beaverton–Hillsdale Highway, Beaverton (503-643-7430)
- 120 N.W. 10th Ave., Portland (503-227-6777); penzeys.com

The Meadow: Featuring a staggering number of artisan salts and chocolates, plus select gourmet items and fresh-cut flowers. Store regularly hosts tastings, dinner parties and other events.

3731 N. Mississippi Ave., Portland (503-288-4633 or 1-888-388-4633); atthemeadow.com.

The Spice & Tea Exchange: This Florida-based franchise offers fresh bulk spices in all the varieties you'd expect (including a half-dozen paprikas), along with more exotic selections such as powdered mesquite (for barbecue sauce) and espresso sanding sugar, perfect for adding a caffeine-laced punch to butter cookies. And then there's the olive oil blends, dried mushrooms, unique varieties of rice, and extensive array of teas.

536 S.W. Broadway, Portland (503-208-2886); spiceandtea.com

Stone Cottage: Dried herbs, spices, teas and chiles are always best when you buy them fresh, and this delightful store allows you to buy just the amount you need. You'll also find oils, bee pollen and honey, herbal remedies, seaweed and sprouting seeds, plus products for bath and body, and garden, including a small selection of plant starts.

3844 S.E. Gladstone, Portland (503-719-6658); herbsspicesteas.com

GENERAL

City Market: European-style market that is home to a Pastaworks, Newman's Fish Market (503-227-2700; newmansfish.com), and Chop Butchery & Charcuterie (503-221-3012; chopbutchery.com). The fresh produce is excellent, as are the gourmet staples. Wine and beer selection is top-notch but not extensive. Parking can sometimes be a challenge.

735 N.W. 21st Ave., Portland (503-221-3007)

Eastmoreland Market & Kitchen: Local, organic produce, and all meat comes from local farms and is hand-butchered on the premises. Plus many specialty foods from Spain and Italy, such as San Marzano tomatoes and Spanish tuna. Exceptional sandwiches, plus ready-made dinners and catering.

3616 S.E. Knapp, Portland (503-771-1186); eastmorelandmarket.com

Elephants Delicatessen: Smart hosts don't try to make everything for a dinner party. Here's where you can pick up some a prepared dish or two from a huge selection of excellent hot or cold takeout. There are several tables for eating in, as well as a small, eclectic selection of gourmet products, tools, and decor.

115 N.W. 22nd Ave., Portland (503-299-6304); elephantsdeli.com

Martinotti's Cafe and Deli: European gourmet foods with an emphasis on Italian products, including porcini mushrooms, San Marzano tomatoes, and arborio rice. Deli meats and cheeses. Serious wine collection represents not only Italy, but France, Germany, Portugal, Spain, Oregon, and beyond.

404 S.W. 10th Ave., Portland (503-224-9028); martinottis.ypguides.net

Pastaworks: Excellent cheese selection plus housemade charcuterie and regionally raised meats. Well-curated selection of oils, vinegars, olives, pasta, and other gourmet foods. Specializing in Italian and Spanish wines, as well as hard-to-find wines from Oregon and points south. Three locations:

- 3735 S.E. Hawthorne Blvd., Portland (503-232-1010)
- Inside City Market; 735 N.W. 21st Ave., Portland (503-221-3002)
- 4212 N. Mississippi Ave., Portland (503-445-1303); pastaworks.com

Sheridan Fruit Co.: A Portland institution since 1916. The retail side of the business has many of the less common fruits and vegetables, and a good meat counter filled with an amazing range of fresh sausages—including some made with duck and elk. Plus cheeses; a large bulk-bin section filled with specialty flours, pasta, nuts, and dried fruits; a deli and grill; and beer and wine.

409 S.E. Martin Luther King Jr. Blvd., Portland (503-236-2114); sheridanfruit.com

Woodsman Tavern Market: Located next door to The Woodsman Tavern, this market carries meat from local producers; cheese from Steve Jones' Cheese Bar; charcuterie from Chop and Fino in Fondo; bread from Little T American Bakery; a well-curated selection of beer and wine; and pastry from Woodsman Tavern pastry chef Nancy Benson. The Market also serves lunch-to-go Monday through Friday.

4537 S.E. Division St., Portland (971-373-8267); woodsmantavern.com

CHEESE AND CHARCUTERIE

Cheese Bar: Exquisite selection of imported and domestic cheeses alongside a splendid wine bar. Owner Steve Jones is behind the counter and readily offers samples and expert advice. Looking for a respite from the rain? The bar invites with an intriguing menu of small plates and cheese/charcuterie, plus a rotating selection of wines and more than 50 beers.

  6031 S.E. Belmont St., Portland (503-222-6014); cheese-bar.com

Foster & Dobbs: Another excellent cheese shop with knowledgeable staff and more than 100 cheeses. Generous selection of handcrafted charcuterie, antipasti, bread, condiments, and other pantry items. Order cheese and meat trays for entertaining. Craft beers and a wine selection focused on small Northwest producers.

  2518 N.E. 15th Ave., Portland (503-284-1157); fosteranddobbs.com

Olympic Provisions: Olympic had the first USDA-approved salumeria in Oregon. Its artisanal charcuterie and salumi—including saucisson, finocchiona, terrines and three kinds of chorizo—are exceptional. Plus, wines and a small selection of cheese. You can take items home, or eat in from the sandwich menu, featuring combinations you won't find anywhere else, such as smoked beef tongue and pickled beets, or house-made porchetta with aioli and balsamic onions.

- 1632 N.W. Thurman St., Portland (503-894-8136)
- 107 S.E. Washington St., Portland (503-954-3663)

  olympicprovisions.com

SEAFOOD

ABC Seafood Market: This small market feels like you've stepped right into China, with its numerous tanks of live crab, lobster, clams, and more. And why would you buy cooked Dungeness elsewhere if you could get it live for a comparable price? Limited produce, but a nice selection of Asian sauces, condiments, dried foods, plus frozen duck and chicken.

  6509 S.E. Powell Blvd., Portland (503-771-5802)

Newman's Fish Market: See City Market in General category.

Mio Seafood Market: This market is affiliated the Portland-based chain of franchise Mio Sushi restaurants. While the selection here is not as extensive as at Uwajimaya or some other stories, the quality is very good. There's a limited deli menu of fish-and-chips and other items, plus a small but nice array of Asian staples and products for preparing your own sushi.

  1703 N.W. 16th Ave., Portland (503-972-1140); miosushi.com

Powell Street Fish Market: This is a retail outlet for Pacific Seafood, a processor and distributor. The selection of fresh fish can vary, but there's always a wide selection of frozen items. Be aware that the market is not open weekends.

3380 S.E. Powell Blvd., Portland (503-233-4891)

Flying Fish Company: This is little more than a shack, but what a shack. The selection is small, but the quality is excellent and everything is sustainably sourced. You'll also find some harder-to-find items, such as black cod, halibut cheeks and dry-pack scallops. Plus, grass-fed beef, local pork and eggs, elk, goat, venison and more. If you're looking for something specific, it's best to call ahead and check on availability.

2310 S.E. Hawthorne Blvd., Portland (503-260-6552); flyingfishcompany.com

Uwajimaya: See Asian category.

MEAT

Edelweiss Sausage Co. and Delicatessen: If you love sausage and cured meats, you will swoon when you visit Edelweiss. Meats are all produced on the premises, and on a busy Saturday you'll hear shoppers speaking German. In addition to cheese and meats, there are lots of imported delicacies such as chocolate, licorice, dried spaetzle, herring, fresh European breads, German and Austrian wines, and hundreds of beers.

3119 S.E. 12th St., Portland (503-238-4411); edelweissdeli.com.

Gartner's Country Meat Market: While the Gartner's location isn't as central as some other markets, it makes up for it with its vast selection—everything from smoked turkeys and hams, to fresh meats cut to order, to marinated flat-iron and tri-tip steaks, and lunchmeats, and smoked sausages. On a busy day (word gets around when you've been in business for fifty-two years), you'll have to take a number, but the line moves quickly. They'll also custom cut an animal for you, as well as process game.

7450 N.E. Killingsworth St., Portland (503-252-7801); gartnersmeats.com

Original Bavarian Sausage Co.: If you love German sausages, this is the place to go on Portland's west side. Varieties include weisswurst, bratwurst, beerwurst, Polish sausage, farmers sausage, plus hams, smoked meats, and meat spreads. Wide selection of German and European beers; limited wines; pastries from the affiliated Neumann's German Bakery at 10528 N.E. Sandy Blvd. In nice weather, you can enjoy your deli lunch on the deck outside.

8705 S.W. Locust St., Tigard; (503-892-5152); originalbavariansausage.com

Otto's Sausage Kitchen: Since 1929, an excellent source for sausages, hams, dry salami, corned beef, pastrami, liverwurst, mettewurst, weiners, house-smoked salmon, and much more. Nice selection of mustards and hot sauces, plus some wine and limited cheese. Or forget about cooking and get something from the deli counter.

4138 S.E. Woodstock Blvd., Portland (503-771-6714); ottossausage.com

Phil's Uptown Meat Market: The gleaming butcher case is stocked with things like mammoth porterhouse steaks, Kobe-style hot dogs, roasting chickens, and ahi tuna. Prices can be high, but so is the quality. The bento cart is renowned, plus an extensive deli menu that includes housemade barbecue, and an eye-opening wine collection downstairs.

17 N.W. 23rd Place, Portland (503-224-9541)

Laurelhurst Market Butcher Shop: A smaller but nicely stocked market that offers hormone- and antibiotic-free pork and beef, air-chilled chicken and Moulard duck breasts. Everything is made in house, including a generous assortment of hand-stuffed sausages and pâtés, cured meats like pancetta and guanciale, and smoked items, such as the hard-to-find Cajun specialty tasso ham. The shop is also a source for rendered duck fat and leaf lard. And we love that it's open until 8 p.m., so you can stop in after enjoying a meal at the adjoining restaurant.

3155 E. Burnside St., Portland (503-206-3099); laurelhurstmarket.com

ASIAN

An Dong: Everything for Vietnamese and Southeast Asian cooking, with terrific prices. Smaller than H Mart, Fubonn, and Uwajimaya, but in many ways more satisfying and authentic. Fresh meats include Carlton Farms pork, in cuts you won't see in a Western market. Wonderful array of sauces, condiments, oils, and vinegar, as well as inexpensive housewares and everything you need for a New Year's celebration.

5441 S.E. Powell Blvd., Portland (503-774-6527)

H Mart: A must field trip for any Asian food junkie. A massive supermarket that includes a mind-boggling variety of fresh and frozen meats and seafood. On one visit we found meaty fresh salmon backs for $1.99 a pound. Plus extensive produce, noodle bar, several kinds of kimchi in bulk, bakery counter, and housewares.

13600 S.W. Pacific Highway, Tigard (503-620-6120); hmart.com

Fubonn: Another giant Asian mart, but less Westernized than Uwajimaya, and less expensive. Extensive produce and Asian staples. Seafood counter offers many fresh fish sold whole; plus dried and frozen seafood, offal, deli counter, and more. The market is inside a shopping center that includes Asian restaurants, bakery, bookstore, jewelers, and tea house, which makes Fubonn a fun expedition.

2850 S.E. 82nd Ave., Suite 80, Portland (503-517-8899); fubonn.com

Uwajimaya: Arguably the best seafood counter in the city, with varieties you're unlikely to find anywhere else. Plus live crab, oysters, clams, and tilapia. Top-notch produce, though less extensive than Fubonn or H Mart. Broad range of Asian groceries includes Indian, Filipino, Malaysian, Portuguese, and Hawaiian staples. Large selection of Asian baked goods; hot takeout counter; big Japanese housewares section. Adjacent Japanese restaurant.

10500 S.W. Beaverton–Hillsdale Highway, Beaverton (503-643-4512); uwajimaya.com

HISPANIC FOODS

Yesenia's Market: All the staples you'll need, from canned pickled jalapeños to mole to fresh tortillas and Mexican pastries. Specialty fresh meats and Mexican cheeses, plenty of dried chiles, herbs, and spices, and the fresh fruits and vegetables you won't find at Western supermarkets.

6611 S.E. Powell Blvd., Portland (503-774-4124)

Yesenia's Market: Different owners as the Southeast Powell location, but similar size, selection, and prices.

1075 S.E. Baseline St., Hillsboro (503-681-9299)

Supermercados Mexico: This store, the biggest of the local Hispanic markets, will put a smile on your face, with its bright and colorful decor, Mexican music—and a fresh meat counter that seems to go on forever, including housemade chorizo, marinated meats, roasted meats, and ceviche. On-site bakery and taqueria; excellent selection of fresh produce.

970 S.E. Oak St., Hillsboro (503-352-5525)

Tortilleria y Tienda de Leon: Freshly made tortillas and a decent selection of staples. The big draw seems to be the takeout menu of tinga, chiles rellenos, carnitas, etc.

16223 N.E. Glisan St., Gresham (503-255-4356)

Mercado Don Pancho: One of the smaller Mexican markets, but with a more central location than many others. The adjacent taqueria does a brisk business.

2000 N.E. Alberta St., Portland (503-282-1892)

WinCo Foods: This chain isn't Hispanic, but you will find a wide selection of Mexican pantry staples as well as many kinds of produce used in Mexican cooking. Terrific prices; be prepared to bag your own groceries.

See website for locations; wincofoods.com

Food 4 Less: Food 4 Less stores are independently owned discount supermarkets that, in addition to stocking mainstream products, also cater to Hispanic and Russian shoppers (depending on location). There's nothing fancy here, but you'll find extensive dried chiles, dried beans, rice, and more. Like WinCo, you'll need to bag your own groceries, but the savings are significant.

7979 S.E. Powell Blvd., Portland (503-774-4665); portlandfood4less.com

MEDITERRANEAN

Barbur World Foods: One-stop shopping for Middle Eastern and Mediterranean foods. Very good meat counter features Carlton Farms pork and Painted Hills beef, plus the best selection of ready-to-cook meat kebabs in the city. Deli counter has many traditional foods like falafel, shawarma, and baba ghanouj; housemade hummus is outstanding, as is the pita bread, baked while you wait, in an open-hearth oven. Good prices on legumes, grains, and dried fruits.

9845 S.W. Barbur Blvd., Portland (503-244-0670); barburworldfoods.com

BAKERIES

Baker & Spice: Julie Richardson, a graduate of the Culinary Institute of America and a classically trained baker, first earned a following with the hand pies she sold at the Portland Farmers Market. Now she sells a range of pastries, cakes, breads, and savory items from this busy store in the Hillsdale neighborhood. The bakery uses top-quality ingredients, such as Callebaut chocolate and seasonal produce, and bakes everything in small batches.

6330 S.W. Capitol Highway, Portland (503-244-7573); bakerandspicebakery.com

Beaverton Bakery: Beaverton Bakery, much like Helen Bernhard Bakery, isn't one of newer or trendy bakeries in town, but since opening in 1925 it has earned an excellent reputation for its cakes (the fresh banana cake is terrific), cinnamon bread, loaf cakes, cookies, and cupcakes. If you're looking for a crusty baguette, go elsewhere. But for traditional baked goods, you can't go wrong.

- 12375 S.W. Broadway, Beaverton (503-646-7136)
- 16857 S.W. 65th Ave., Lake Oswego (503-639-8900)
  beavertonbakery.com

Ken's Artisan Bakery & Cafe: Ken Forkish was among the early artisan bakers in Portland. He has since earned national recognition and continues to make some of the best bread in the city, selling to many local restaurants. The baguette here is all about texture, with its substantial crust and contrasting crumb. The country blonde is one of his most delicate breads, in contrast to the earthy and chewy walnut bread, just made to be enjoyed with a slice of smear of gorgonzola and slices of juicy pear.

- 338 N.W. 21st Ave., Portland (503-248-2202)
- 304 S.E. 28th Ave., Portland (503-517-9951)
  kensartisan.com

Grand Central: A Northwest chain with six Portland locations and booths at two farmers markets. This is a place for rustic, toothsome treats, not for frilly, delicate pastries. We adore their jammers, moist coffeecake, and just about anything made with the bakery's puff pastry, which seems to shatter if you even look at it sideways. The ready-to-thaw-and-bake pie dough is outstanding, and a huge timesaver.

See website for addresses; grandcentralbakery.com

Helen Bernhard Bakery: What started as a hobby for Helen Bernhard in 1924 has become a Portland institution. In addition to birthday and wedding cakes, even "Barbie cakes," the shop sells more a vast array of traditional treats, including luscious danishes and coffeecakes, doughnuts and cookies, cream puffs and eclairs, more than a dozen kinds of pies, and much more.

1717 N.E. Broadway St. (503-287-1251); helenbernhardbakery.com

La Provence Bakery and Bistro/Petite Provence: Traditional breads, brioche, croissants, palmiers, and many fancy French pastries. Full breakfast and lunch menu.

- 15964 S.W. Boones Ferry Road, Lake Oswego (503-635-4533)
- 1824 N.E. Alberta St., Portland (503-284-6564)
- 4834 S.E. Division St., Portland (503-233-1121)
- 408 E. 2nd St., The Dalles (541-506-0037)
  provence-portland.com

Little T American Baker: It may be enough to know that owner/baker Tim Healea was on the U.S. team that competed at the Coupe du Monde de la Boulangerie in Paris, and earned the silver medal in the competition for best bakers in the world. And prior to opening Little T, Healea was the longtime head baker at Pearl Bakery. But the proof of his skill is in the pain au chocolat, the flaky croissants, and the chewy baguettes. In addition to Healea's inspired baked goods, there's a breakfast and lunch menu, too.

2600 S.E. Division St., Portland (503-238-3458); littletbaker.com

Pearl Bakery: We lay awake at night thinking about Pearl's baguettes, with their moist, open crumb, softly nutty aroma, and thin but crisp crust. After fifteen years, this is still one of the best artisan bakeries in the city. In addition to stellar breads, there's a wide variety of sweet and savory items, including French pastries, soda bread, assorted macarons, cookies, layer cakes, and "homestyle" cakes, such as carrot cake or apricot-lemon-pistachio cake.

102 N.W. Ninth Ave., Portland (503-827-0910); pearlbakery.com

St. Honoré Boulangerie: Mon dieu—so many delicious choices. But choose you must, because there's frequently a line of hungry customers waiting behind you. St. Honoré offers handcrafted French breads and pastries, along with a menu of sandwiches, quiches, and other savory items. We love that St. Honoré regularly features pastries you're unlikely to see elsewhere, such as the flaky butter cake from Brittany called kouign amann, and canneles. The coffee drinks are excellent. The bakeries also often host musicians, and parties for watching the Tour de France.

- 2335 N.W. Thurman St., Portland (503-445-4342)
- 315 First St., Lake Oswego (503-496-5596)

sainthonorebakery.com

Lovejoy Bakers: Rye with caraway, olive ciabatta, hearty baguettes . . . The bread here is exceptional. But the sandwiches on the breakfast and lunch menus might just steal the show, starting with the Lovejoy Deluxe, made with fried egg, bleu d'Aubergne cheese, bacon, butter, tarragon, and frisée. For those with a sweet tooth, there's a stellar lineup of pastries, cookies, tarts, and more.

939 N.W. 10th Ave. (503-208-3113); lovejoybakers.com

Back to Eden Bakery Boutique: Back to Eden isn't being pretentious when it uses the word "boutique": in addition to the menu of all-vegan cakes, cookies, muffins, scones, pies, sweet breads, Italian sodas, and frozen treats, the store has a delightful selection of arts and crafts from local artists.

2217 N.E. Alberta St., Portland (503-477-5022); backtoedenbakery.com

Dovetail: Another excellent vegan bakery on Alberta Street. The star attraction is Aunt Miriam's Vegan Sticky Buns, which the bakery uses it in what it calls a "Sticky Situation": a sticky bun sliced in half, turned inside out, and filled with housemade Smoky Savory Tempeh. The menu also offers cakes, pies, whoopie pies, scones, cookies, and muffins and in an ever-evolving selection of flavors.

3039 N.E. Alberta St., Portland (503-288-8839); dovetailbakery.blogspot.com

Crave Gluten Free Bake Shop: Kyra Bussanich, Crave's owner and pastry chef, was the first gluten-free baker to appear on Food Network's Cupcake Wars, and since then, demand for her treats has soared. In addition to the huge line of creative cupcakes—don't miss the Lemon Meringue, and Hot Chocolate—Crave also sells a rotating selection of other gluten-free items, including cinnamon rolls, buttery scones, frosted doughnuts, cookies, and custom-order cakes.

460 Fifth St., Lake Oswego (503-212-2979); cravebakeshop.com

Tula Gluten Free Bakery Cafe: This warm and cheery cafe offers a fantastic assortment of both sweet and savory baked goods, which are not only gluten-free but also labeled for other allergens, including soy, corn, nuts, dairy, and eggs. Pop in to pick up something sweet like a scone, muffin, mini pie, or tart (the vegan lemon tart is outstanding), cupcake, or Tula's signature sea-salt chocolate chip cookies. Savories include a stellar focaccia, South African chard and pinto bean hand pies, and vegan olive bread. Or, grab a seat for lunch and enjoy one of Tula's homemade soups, salads, pizzas, or panini, all gluten-free.

4943 N.E. Martin Luther King Jr. Blvd. (503-764-9727); tulabaking.com

BAKING

The Decorette Shop: These two shops are independently owned, but both are dedicated to cake decorating and candy making, offering special pans (in kid-friendly shapes too), cookie cutters, fondant, dye, toppers and decorations, high-end chocolate like Callebaut or Guittard.

- 11945 S.W. Pacific Highway, Ste. 109, Tigard (503-620-5100); decoretteshop.com
- 5338 S.E. Foster Road, Portland (503-774-3760); thedecoretteshop.com

SweetWares: Find all kinds of baking supplies, from pudding molds to copper cookie cutters to elegant cake stands and linens. While you're there, pop into Baker & Spice bakery a few doors down.

6306 S.W. Capitol Highway, Portland (503-546-3737); sweetwares.com

GRAINS, FLOURS, AND BAKING MIXES

Bob's Red Mill Natural Foods: Portlanders are lucky to have this resource so close to home. Many of Bob's Red Mill grains, seeds, beans, flours, and meals are carried in local stores, but to see the full line of whole-grain products, visit the 15,000-square-foot store and visitors' center. And if you get peckish cruising the aisles, there's also a restaurant and bakery on site.

5000 S.E. International Way, Milwaukie (503-607-6455); bobsredmill.com

FARMERS MARKETS

Oregon Farmers Markets Association: Find complete information on the state's markets, including market times, dates and locations.

oregonfarmersmarkets.org

Portland Farmers Market: Includes seven markets, some open during the winter.

503-241-0032; portlandfarmersmarket.org

Beaverton Farmers Market: The single largest, all-agricultural market in Oregon.

503-643-5345; beavertonfarmersmarket.com

Hollywood Farmers Market: A vibrant market featuring more than sixty vendors. Open year-round.

503-709-7403; hollywoodfarmersmarket.org

OTHER SOURCES

Tri-County Farm Fresh Guide: Featuring more than seventy local farm stands and U-picks in Clackamas, Multnomah, and Washington counties. Sign up for handy crop updates that let you know when weather has delayed your favorite fruits and vegetables.

tricountyfarm.org

Local Harvest: Find local CSA subscriptions, farmers markets, and family farms.

831-515-5602; localharvest.org

Oregon Wine Board: Interactive guide to wineries statewide, plus downloadable brochures from individual AVAs, wine events, and more.

oregonwine.org

Willamette Valley Wineries: Excellent listings for most of the valley's wineries, as well as holiday events, where to eat and stay, and a mobile wine tour for smart phones.

willamettewines.com; willamettewinemap.com

ACKNOWLEDGMENTS

My deepest thanks and appreciation go to:

Ross Eberman, Greg Mowery and Dick Owsiany for their vision and wholehearted support every step of the way. I know that it was like herding cats to keep everyone on track. You handled it all with amazing grace. And to Greg, an extra helping of gratitude for your tireless work on the chefs' and James Beard chapters, permissions and for so much helpful feedback.

To Peter Bhatia and JoLene Krawczak, Mike Heiser and Barbara Swanson, who took a leap of faith, and then put their faith in me.

Grant Butler, who on short notice jumped into the role of acting Foodday editor and with the help of Vickie Nesbit did a superb job in my stead. I am blessed to work with people who have so much skill and positive spirit.

Linda Faus and Sharon Maasdam, for their unerring palates, their amazing depth of cooking knowledge and for answering my countless questions. And to Barbara Durbin, who gave me a goldmine of great Foodday recipes and archival material.

Lynne Palombo, for digging up several unexpected treasures in the course of her diligent research — including the 1910 Oregonian cookbook.

Therese Bottomly, for handling pesky legal issues.

Ian Shimkoviak and Alan Hebel, for their beautiful designs and patience. And to Linda Shankweiler, whose design input was invaluable.

Jamie Francis, for the beautiful photographs captured in a marathon shoot. To Mike Zacchino, for his masterful photo editing; Stephanie Yao, for delving deep into the archives; and Tom Boyd, for my own photo. And to Michael Shay and the crew at Polara Studio, and food stylist Carol Cooper Ladd, for the amazing cover shot.

Kir Jensen, for making James Beard's food even better. And to Tricia Brown, Michelle Blair, Laurie Robinson, and Kathy Hinson, for their eagle-eyed proofing.

The three Foodday editors who each taught me so much: Ginger Johnston, who gave a newcomer a chance, Chris Christensen and Martha Holmberg.

The many contributors and staffers whose great work and recipes have made Foodday possible, including Sara Bir, Matthew Card, Danielle Centoni, Joan Cirillo, Katherine Cole, Leslie Cole, Joan Harvey, Ashley Gartland, Ivy Manning, Laura McCandlish, Deena Prichep, Jan Roberts-Dominguez, Laura Russell, Lynne Sampson Curry and Cheri Swoboda.

The many readers who answered our call for their favorite Foodday recipes and lent not only those, but their kind comments and support. Foodday has the most loyal and generous readers anywhere.

The chefs who so graciously took time to give us their own recipes, and who over the years have also shared their expertise. I would like to especially thank Cory Schreiber for his efforts on behalf of this book. His work inside and outside the kitchen is truly inspiring.

Brenda Shaw, Bonnie Kahn and Fran Arrieta-Walden, for talking me down from the ledge. Often.

And finally, to the Miller and Wigginton families, for their abiding love, support and understanding, and for eating my mistakes.

—Katherine Miller

An idea is only as good as the people who can help you realize the goal. I thank Ross Eberman and Dick Owsiany for showing up at my door and allowing me to spew a few ideas.

As a relative newbie to Portland, I found a vibrant and welcoming publishing community who quickly became friends and mentors: Kent Watson, Mike Campbell, Alan and Ruth Centofante, Doug Pfeiffer, and in nearby Seattle, a long-standing colleague from earlier in my career, Jennifer McCord.

My thanks to Ivy Manning and Diane Morgan, two great cookbook writers, who generously introduced me to the Portland culinary scene.

I've got real cooking gods and goddesses to thank. They inspire and encourage me all the time: Susan Wyler, Rux Martin, Rick Rodgers, Carl Raymond, and Dorie Greenspan.

My New York family for allowing me to make a new life on the Left Coast: Laurele, Karole, Joe, Tricia, Pat, Dyanne, and Susan.

And finally to my mentor, confidante, and best friend, Maryann Palumbo.

—Greg Mowery

CREDITS

CHAPTER 1: APPETIZERS

Ham, Gruyère, and Dijon Palmiers
Adapted from *Puff* by Martha Holmberg, reprinted with permission from Chronicle Books (2008)

Coconut-Curry Macadamia Nuts
Adapted from *Martha Stewart's Hors d'Oeuvres Handbook,*reprinted with permission from Clarkson Potter (1999)

Blue Cheese-and-Jam Savories
Adapted from and reprinted with permission from Pere Coleman Magness

Apricot Coins
Adapted from *The All American Cheese and Winebook* by Laura Werlin, reprinted with permission from Stewart, Tabori & Chang (2003)

Mushroom Pâté
Adapted from and reprinted with permission from Abdel Omar, former owner Brasserie Montmartre and current owner of Bistro 153, Beaverton

Smoked Oyster Spread
Adapted from *Mystic Seaport's Seafood Secrets Cookbook,* reprinted with permission from Mystic Seaport Museum (1990)

Hall Street Hot Dungeness Crab Appetizer
Adapted from and reprinted with permission from The Hall Street Grill, Beaverton

Brie with Roasted Garlic and Kalamata Olives
Adapted from and reprinted with permission from Nancy Taylor, Fabulous Food catering, Portland

Tuna Poached in Olive Oil with Olive Tapenade and Garlic Aioli
Adapted from and reprinted with permission from Adam Berger, co-founder, Tabla Mediterranean Bistro

Baguette Slices with Shrimp, Avocado and Goat Cheese
Adapted from *Dungeness Crabs and Blackberry Cobblers* by Janie Hibler, reprinted with permission from Knopf (1991)

Moroccan Chicken Drumettes
Adapted from and reprinted with permission from Elephants Delicatessen, Portland

CHAPTER 2: SALADS

Butter Lettuce Salad with Vinaigrette Royale
Adapted from and reprinted with permission from Café Castagna, Portland

Vietnamese Coleslaw with Shredded Chicken and Peanuts
Adapted from *Bangkok to Bali in 30 Minutes* by Theresa Volpe Laursen and Byron Laursen, reprinted with permission from Harvard Common Press (2003)

Warm Cabbage and Goat Cheese Salad
Adapted from *The New American Cheese* by Laura Werlin, reprinted with permission from Stewart, Tabori and Chang (2000)

Green Bean Salad with Red Onion and Apricot Vinaigrette
Adapted from and reprinted with permission from Caffe Mingo, Portland

Panzanella di Fratelli
Adapted from and reprinted with permission from Fratelli Ristorante, Portland

Roasted Red Pepper and Mozzarella Salad
Adapted from and reprinted with permission from Annie Cuggino, executive chef, Veritable Quandary, Portland

Roasted Beet Salad with Toasted Pecans and Goat Cheese
Adapted from and reprinted with permission from Marie Simmons

CHAPTER 3: SOUPS

Gubanc's Chicken Tortilla Soup
Adapted from and reprinted with permission from Gubanc's Pub, Lake Oswego

West African Chicken-Peanut Soup
Adapted from and reprinted with permission from McMenamins Blue Moon Tavern and Grill, Portland

Santa Fe Chicken and White Bean Soup
Adapted from and reprinted with permission from Gubanc's Pub, Lake Oswego

Mama Leone's Chicken Soup
Adapted from and reprinted with permission from Elephants Delicatessen, Portland

Sea Hag Clam Chowder
Adapted from and reprinted with permission from Grant D. Jerome, owner, Gracie's Sea Hag Restaurant & Lounge, Depoe Bay

Tomato-Orange Soup
Adapted from and reprinted with permission from Elephants Delicatessen, Portland

Very Fresh Cream of Tomato Soup
Adapted from *Too Many Tomatoes, Squash, Beans, and Other Good Things* by Lois M. Landau and Laura G. Myers, reprinted with permission from Harper & Row (1976)

Matzo Balls in a Late Summer Corn-Parsley Broth
Adapted from and reprinted with permission from Jenn Louis chef/owner, Lincoln restaurant and Sunshine Tavern, Portland

Lentil Soup
Adapted from and reprinted with permission from Al-Amir Lebanese Restaurant, Portland

CHAPTER 4: VEGETABLES AND LEGUMES

Sautéed Eggplant (Melanzana Saltata)
Adapted from *Italian Family Cooking Like Mama Used to Make* by Anne Casale, reprinted with permission from Ballantine Books (1984)

Ruth's Chris Creamed Spinach
Adapted from and reprinted with permission from Ruth's Chris Steakhouse, Portland

Creamy Brussels Sprouts Gratin
Adapted from and reprinted with permission from Eva Katz

Asparagus with Mustard-Dill Sauce
Adapted from and reprinted with permission from Victoria Island Farms, Stockton, California

Braised Red Cabbage with Pears
Adapted from *An Edible Christmas* by Irena Chalmers, reprinted with permission from William Morrow (1992)

Roasted Parsnips with Balsamic Vinegar and Rosemary
Adapted from *Vegetables Every Day* by Jack Bishop, reprinted with permission from William Morrow (2001)

Butternut Squash and Yukon Gold Gratin with Gruyère Cheese
Adapted from and reprinted with permission from David Martin, former executive chef, In Good Taste Cooking School, Portland

New Potatoes with Peas and Coriander
Adapted from *Ginger East to West* by Bruce Cost, reprinted with permission from Running Press (1989)

Fred's Honey-Baked Beans
Adapted from *Dungeness Crabs and Blackberry Cobblers* by Janie Hibler, reprinted with permission from Knopf (1991)

CHAPTER 5: PASTA AND NOODLES

Fettuccine with Sage Butter, Bacon, and Artichokes
Adapted from and reprinted with permission from Jerry Traunfeld

Spaghetti with Tuna, Lemon, and Olives
Adapted from *The Mediterranean Kitchen* by Joyce Goldstein, reprinted with permission from William Morrow (1998)

Spaghetti with Curried Seafood Marinara
Adapted from recipe by *Food & Wine* magazine (February 2004), reprinted with permission from *Food & Wine* magazine

Pasta Alla Puttanesca
Adapted from *The Fine Art of Italian Cooking* by Giuliano Bugialli, reprinted with permission from Clarkson Potter (1990)

Skillet Lasagna
Adapted from and reprinted with permission from *The Best 30-Minute Recipes.* For a trial issue, call 800-526-8442. Selected articles and recipes, as well as subscription information, are available online at www.cooksillustrated.com

Acini de Pepe
Adapted from and reprinted with permission from McCormick's Fish House & Bar, Beaverton

Chicken Yakisoba
Adapted from and reprinted with permission from Hallmark Inn, Hillsboro

CHAPTER 6: FISH AND SHELLFISH

Halibut Piccata
Adapted from and reprinted with permission from Fulio's Pastaria & Tuscan Steakhouse, Astoria

Sea Scallops with Peaches in Basil Cream Sauce
Adapted from *The New Ark Cookbook* by Nanci Main and Jimella Lucas, reprinted with permission from Chronicle Books (1990)

Mussels in Cataplana
Adapted from and reprinted with permission by David Machado, chef/owner, Nel Centro and Vindalho, Portland

CHAPTER 7: POULTRY

Maple Roasted Chicken with Winter Vegetables
Adapted from *Sweet Maple* by James M. Lawrence and Rux Martin, reprinted with permission from Diane Publishing (1999)

Forty-Cloves-and-Who's-Counting-Chicken
Adapted from *Everything Tastes Better with Garlic* by Sara Perry, reprinted with permission from Chronicle Books (2004)

Chicken Cacciatora
Adapted from and reprinted with permission from Patrick Mendola, former owner of Tuscany Grill and current owner of Eastmoreland Market & Kitchen, Portland

Reserve Chicken and Dumplings
Adapted from and reprinted with permission from Vintage Room and Restaurant, The Reserve Vineyards and Golf Club, Aloha

Basil Chicken in Coconut-Curry Sauce
Adapted from *Better Homes and Gardens New Cookbook, 12th Edition*, reprinted with permission from Meredith Books/Wiley (2002)

Pok-Pok-Style Vietnamese Fish Sauce Wings
Adapted from *Food & Wine Cocktails 2010* by the Editors of *Food & Wine*, reprinted with permission from *Food & Wine* (2010)

Chez José Lime Chicken Enchiladas
Adapted from and reprinted with permission from Chez José Mexican Cafe, Portland

Auntie Alice's Teochew Braised Duck
Adapted from *A Tiger in the Kitchen* by Cheryl Lu-Lien Tan, reprinted with permission from Voice (2010)

Chez Panisse Turkey Brine
Adapted from and reprinted with permission from Alice Waters, Chez Panisse, Berkeley

CHAPTER 8: MEAT

Sicilian Pork Chops with Pepperoncini
Adapted from and reprinted with permission from Patrick Mendola, former owner of Tuscany Grill and current owner of Eastmoreland Market and Kitchen, Portland

Monte's Ham
Adapted from *Saveur Cooks Authentic American* by the Editors of *Saveur* magazine, reprinted with permission from Chronicle Books (1998)

Mary McCrank's Meatloaf
Adapted from and reprinted with permission from Gerhard Schopp, chef/owner, Mary McCrank's Restaurant, Chehalis, Washington

Easy Oven Roasted Ribs
Adapted from and reprinted with permission from Brett Meisner, SP Provisions, Portland

CHAPTER 9: VEGETARIAN AND VEGAN FARE

Squash Enchiladas with Spicy Peanut Sauce
Adapted from and reprinted with permission from Chez José Mexican Café, Portland

Leek Bread Pudding with Chanterelles
Adapted by Donna Litvin from *Ad Hoc at Home* by Thomas Keller, reprinted with permission from Artisan (2009)

Roasted Red Pepper-Cashew Spread
Adapted from and reprinted with permission from Chelsea, www.flavcorvegan.blogspot.com

Potato and Asparagus Soup
Adapted from *Vegan with a Vengeance* by Isa Chandra Moskowitz, reprinted with permission from DaCapo Press (2005)

Classic Macaroni and "Cheeze"
Adapted from *Quick and Easy Vegan Celebrations* by Alicia C. Simpson, reprinted with permission from The Experiment (2010)

Mushroom Burgers with Barley
Adapted from *Veggie Burgers Every Which Way* by Lucas Volker, reprinted with permission from The Experiment (2010)

Mexican Quinoa with Pepitas and Cilantro
Adapted from *The New Whole Grains Cookbook* by Robin Asbell, reprinted with permission from Chronicle Books (2007)

Acorn Squash with Pecan-Cherry Stuffing
Adapted from *The Urban Vegan* by Dynise Balcavage, reprinted with permission from Three Forks (2009)

CHAPTER 10: QUICK AND EASY

Ginger-Scented Butternut Squash Soup
Adapted from and reprinted with permission from Stephanie Witt Sedgwick, Washington, D.C.

Beaverton Bakery Poppy Seed Cake
Adapted from and reprinted with permission from The Beaverton Bakery, Beaverton

CHAPTER 11: BREAKFAST

Bacon and Egg Bruschetta
Adapted from and reprinted with permission from Ian Duncan, chef, Coppia (formerly Vino Paradiso), Portland

Cherry Scones
Adapted from and reprinted with permission from Carolyn Mistell, president, Delphina's Bakery, Portland

Rich, Hot Orange Rolls
Adapted from *Farm Journal's Homemade Bread* by the Editors of *Farm Journal*, reprinted with permission from Galahad Books (2000)

Oatmeal Pancakes with Walnut Butter
Adapted from and reprinted with permission from Patty Groth, chef/owner, Morning Glory restaurant, Ashland

Apple Puffed Pancake
Adapted from *Cooking for Entertaining* by Marlene Sorosky, reprinted with permission from HP Books/The Penguin Group (1994)

CHAPTER 12: SAUCES, DRESSINGS, AND CONDIMENTS

Sour Cream-Scallion Butter
Adapted from and reprinted with permission from Scott Neuman, chef, ¡Oba!

Honey-Mustard Salad Dressing with Tarragon
Adapted from and reprinted with permission from Anna Perry, chef/owner, Perry's on Fremont, Portland

Ketchup
Adapted from and reprinted with permission from Bruce Fishback, Bread and Ink Café, Portland

Heavenly Sauce
Adapted from *Oregon Hazelnut Country* by Jan Roberts-Dominguez, reprinted with permission from Hazelnut Marketing Board (2010)

Simple Kansas City-Style Sauce
Adapted from *BBQ Makes Everything Better* by Aaron Chronister and Jason Day, reprinted with permission from Scribner (2011)

Chimichurri
Adapted from *Latin Grilling* by Lourdes Castro, reprinted with permission from Ten Speed Press (2011)

Thai Peanut Sauce
Adapted and reprinted with permission from The Hall Street Grill, Beaverton

Advance Planning Turkey Gravy
Adapted and reprinted with permission from *Woman's Day* magazine

Pinot Noir Poached Figs
Adapted from and reprinted with permission by Greg Higgins, owner/chef, Higgins Restaurant & Bar, Portland

Chocolate Hazelnut Butter
Adapted from *Fancy Pantry* by Helen Witty, reprinted with permission from Workman Publishing (1986)

CHAPTER 13: PRESERVES AND PICKLES

Red Pepper Jelly with Verjus
Adapted from and reprinted with permission by Sarah Schaffer, Irving Street Kitchen, Portland

Plum Chutney
Adapted from *The Oregon Sampler* by the Assistance League of Corvallis, reprinted with permission from the Assistance League of Corvallis (1985)

Blueberry Chutney
Adapted from and reprinted with permission by Greg Higgins, owner/chef, Higgins Restaurant & Bar, Portland

Peerless Red Raspberry Preserves
Adapted from *Fancy Pantry* by Helen Witty, reprinted with permission from Workman Publishing (1986)

Strawberry Marmalade
Adapted from *Blue Ribbon Preserves* by Linda J. Amendt, reprinted with permission from HP Books/Putnam Books Group (2001)

Whole Cherry Preserves
Adapted from *The Glass Pantry* by Georgeanne Brennan, reprinted with permission from Chronicle Books (1994)

Liena's Raspberry Liqueur
Adapted from *My Château Kitchen* by Anne Willan, reprinted with permission from Clarkson Potter (2000)

Crispy Pickled Carrots
Adapted from *Discover Cooking with Lavender* by Kathy Gerht, reprinted with permission from Florentia Press (2010)

Golden Pickled Eggs
Adapted from *The Joy of Pickling* by Linda Zeidrich, reprinted with permission from Harvard Common Press (2009)

CHAPTER 14: BREAD

No-Knead Bread
Adapted from and reprinted with permission from Jim Lahey, Sullivan Street Bakery, New York City

Focaccia with Roasted Grapes
Adapted from *No Knead to Knead* by Suzanne Dunaway, reprinted with permission from Hyperion (1999)

Grilled Cilantro-Mint Naan
Adapted from *Wood-Fired Cooking* by Mary Karlin, reprinted with permission from Ten Speed Press (2009)

Buttermilk Rolls
Adapted from and reprinted with permission by Elephants Delicatessen, Portland

Popovers
Adapted from *Barefoot Contessa Parties* by Ina Garten, reprinted with permission from Clarkson Potter (2001)

Quickie Olive Oil Biscuits
Adapted from *Entertaining 1-2-3* by Roxanne Gold, reprinted with permission from Little, Brown (1999)

Heceta Lighthouse Orange Bread
Adapted from *The Lighthouse Breakfast Book 3rd* Edition by Michelle Bursey and Carol Korgan, reprinted with permission from Westwinds Press (2009)

CHAPTER 15: CAKES, PIES, AND OTHER DESSERTS

Cherry Clafouti
Adapted from *Provence, The Beautiful Cookbook* by Richard Olney reprinted with permission from HarperCollins (1999)

Devil's Food Cupcakes with Chocolate Ganache Frosting and Centers
Adapted from and reprinted with permission by Babette Pepaj, Bakespace.com

Fresh Berry Gelato
Adapted from and reprinted with permission from Bob Lightman, Mio Gelato and Morso, Portland

Meyer Lemon Frozen Yogurt
Adapted from and reprinted with permission from Michelle Vernier, pastry chef, Paley's Place, Portland

Easy Chocolate Ice Cream
Adapted and reprinted with permission from Cook's Country June 2009. For a trial issue, call 800-526-8442. Selected articles and recipes, as well as subscription information, are available online at www.cooksillustrated.com

Rosemary Orange Ice Cream
Adapted from *The New Spanish Cookbook* by Anya von Bremzen, reprinted with permission from Workman Publishing (2005)

CHAPTER 16: COOKIES, BARS, AND CANDY

Smoked Salt, Dried Apricot and Almond Chocolate Bark
Adapted from *Gifts Cooks Love* by Sur La Table and Diane Morgan, reprinted with permission from Andrews McMeel (2010)

My Ginger Cookies (aka Screaming Ginger Cookies)
Adapted from *Chewy Gooey Crispy Crunchy Melt-in-Your-Mouth Cookies* by Alice Medrich, reprinted with permission from Artisan (2010)

Cashew Shortbread
Adapted from *The New Enchanted Broccoli Forest* by Mollie Katzen, reprinted with permission from Ten Speed Press (2000)

Pecan Tassies
Adapted from *Private Collection: Recipes From the Junior League of Palo Alto* by Bonnie Stewart Mickelson, reprinted with permission from the Junior League of Palo Alto (1980)

Red Fox Brownies
Adapted from and reprinted with permission from Jason M. Furch, executive chef/owner, Red Fox Bakery, McMinnville

CHAPTER 17: IN THE KITCHEN WITH OREGON CHEFS

Grilled Sweet Corn on the Cob with Salty Coconut Cream
Adapted from and reprinted with permission from Andy Ricker, chef/owner, Pok Pok, Portland

Salmon Rillettes and Toasted Baguette
Adapted from and reprinted with permission from Pascal Sauton, chef/owner, Milwaukie Kitchen and Wine, Milwaukie

Liptauer
Adapted from and reprinted with permission from Christopher Israel, chef/owner, Grüner, Portland

Duck Liver Parfait
Adapted from and reprinted with permission from Eric Bechard, chef/co-owner, Thistle, McMinnville

Garlic Almond Soup (Ajo Blanco)
Adapted from and reprinted with permission from Anthony Cafiero, chef de cuisine, Tabla Mediterranean Bistro, Portland

Timberline Ale and Cheese Soup
Adapted from and reprinted with permission from Jason Stoller Smith, executive chef, Timberline Lodge

Chilled Cucumber and Almond Soup with Marinated Salmon
Adapted from and reprinted with permission from Scott Dolich, chef/owner, Park Kitchen, Portland

Salmon Chowder
Adapted from and reprinted with permission from Lisa Schroeder, executive chef/owner, Mother's Bistro & Bar, Portland

Lacinto Kale Salad with Grapefruit
Adapted from and reprinted with permission from Jenn Louis, chef/owner, Lincoln restaurant and Sunshine Tavern, Portland

Nostrana Salad
Adapted from and reprinted with permission from Cathy Whims, chef/owner, Nostrana, Portland

Ayers Creek Farm Zefino Beans with Chanterelles and Quinoa
Adapted from and reprinted with permission from Cory Schreiber, culinary artist-in-residence, Art Institute of Portland

Pappardelle with Fava Beans and Mint
Adapted from *The Paley's Place Cookbook* by Vitaly Paley and Kimberly Paley with Robert Reynolds, reprinted with permission from Ten Speed Press (2008)
Grilled Shrimp with Fava Bean Salad and Salsa Genovese
Adapted from and reprinted with permission from David Machado, chef/owner, Nel Centro and Vindalho, Portland

Grilled Albacore Tuna with Flame-Roasted Chile Raita
Adapted from and reprinted with permission from Greg Higgins, chef/owner, Higgins Restaurant & Bar, Portland

Oregon Albacore Tuna Melt with Mustard, Pickles, Balsamic, and Sharp Cheddar
Adapted from and reprinted with permission from Tommy Habetz, chef/co-owner, Bunk Sandwiches, Portland

Braised-Beef Sandwich with Provolone and Onion Jam
Adapted from and reprinted with permission from Kenny Giambalvo, executive chef, Morso, Portland

Pollo Con Mushrooms
Adapted from and reprinted with permission from Joe Esparza, chef/co-owner, Esparza's Tex Mex Cafe, Portland

Pan-Seared Pork Chops with Thyme and Bacon Crumbs
Adapted from and reprinted with permission from Gabriel Rucker, chef/owner, Le Pigeon and Little Bird Bistro, Portland

The Heathman's Smoked Salmon Hash
Adapted from and reprinted with permission from Philippe Boulot, former culinary director, The Heathman Restaurant and Bar; executive chef, the Multnomah Athletic Club, Portland

Coconut Panna Cotta
Adapted from and reprinted with permission from Allen Routt, chef/co-owner, Painted Lady, Newberg

Chocolate Truffle Cake
Adapted from and reprinted with permission from Naomi Pomeroy, chef/owner, Beast, Portland

CHAPTER 18: REMEMBERING JAMES BEARD

Oregon-Style Baked Salmon
Adapted from *James Beard's New Fish Cookery*, reprinted with permission from Little, Brown (1972)

PHOTOGRAPHY CREDITS

CHEFS

INDEX